The Return To Reason Essays In Realistic Philosophy

The Return to Reason

Essays in Realistic Philosophy

The Return to Reason

Essays in Realistic Philosophy

Edited by

JOHN WILD

Harvard University

Chicago · HENRY REGNERY COMPANY · *1953*

Manufactured in the United States of America

BZBZDE

PREFACE

THIS volume is the fruit of a co-operative movement known as the Association for Realistic Philosophy, which has now been in existence for five years. The platform of this association is printed in the Appendix (pp. 354–360). Several of the contributors participated in the formulation of this platform. All are familiar with it. Many of us would disagree in interpreting certain statements. But all of us accept the platform in the sense in which it was formulated, as a program for "critical clarification and defense."

Hence, in spite of many individual variations, and even disagreements, the present essays are more than a jumble of independent treatises. They fit into the sort of coherent pattern which is suggested by the platform. They are all expressions of a realistic way of thought. But within this general pattern, there is room for great divergence and growth. Hence each contributor should be held responsible only for what he himself has said, and not for all the views expressed by others. The philosophical evidence is very vast and rich and its basic structure as yet little known. Even what is known must be rediscovered and reformulated by the living mind. Unsolved problems must be attacked with new methods and hypotheses. A timid clinging to accepted principles is as dangerous to philosophy as is an uncritical scorn for what has been discovered in the past. In this volume we have tried to avoid both these extremes by showing how classical doctrines can be critically reformulated and constructively applied to the problems of our modern age.

We inhabit a universe marked by real structures which exist independently of human knowledge and desire. These structures can be known as they really are, at least in part, by the human mind, not only the more restricted patterns revealed by the special sciences, but also more fundamental ontological patterns which require philosophical description and analysis. Finally, norms are not exclusively man-made. There are norms actually founded on nature which are accessible to human cognition.

By neglecting these realistic principles, and by evading those basic philosophical questions from which alone a disciplined clarification and defense of such principles may arise, we believe that influential Anglo-American philosophies have propagated subjectivistic, irrational, and relativistic modes of thought which are empirically unsound and culturally demoralizing. We are confronted with the strange spectacle of academic philosophers devoting their talents and energies to the task of undermining the rationale of the crucially important task of clarification and discovery in which they are supposedly engaged

Positivists have told us that basic metaphysical questions are not only unanswerable but meaningless, and have advised us to retire to linguistic analysis, abandoning the vast but confused fields of ontological evidence which experience presents to us. Naturalists insist that the empirical evidence is exhausted by the quantitative data of the restricted sciences, and that their methods alone are capable of yielding verifiable truth. Pragmatists deny that reason can penetrate to the structure of things as they really are, and attempt to explain it in terms of the subjectivist categories of human action and adjustment Ethicists following these cues, denying that values are grounded in existence, assert that norms are radically separated from all cognizable, natural facts The widely accepted conclusion then follows, that value is not discoverable by empirical observation of any sort, but is rather arbitrarily constructed by human decree.

The net result is a spreading skepticism concerning the capacity of disciplined reason to shed any real light on the things that matter most, and a readiness to accept spurious substitutes. We do not believe that such irrationalism has as yet proved its case The recent flight from philosophy has left a vacuum which must somehow be filled We are not content with suggested substitutes We believe that many of our contemporaries are disillusioned with antiphilosophical philosophies, that the time is ripe for a *return to reason*

Realistic philosophy, of course, is not entirely new. Many of its basic principles were discovered and partially developed with reference to special problems in classical works of ancient and medieval philosophy as well as in later works of the modern period. There is a core of truth in this tradition. But if this truth is to remain alive among us, it must be rediscovered by each generation and developed in special ways to meet its special needs. These essays are an attempt to restate in modern language this core of realistic truth, to defend it against modern objections, and to apply it to modern problems.

Realistic philosophy, as we understand it, is radically empirical in the sense that its basic concepts and principles are derived from observation and analysis of the immediately given data of experience We wish to have nothing to do with a priori theories which cannot be checked by the factual descriptions of qualified observers We recognize that the term "empiricism" has recently been taken over by certain schools of thought with restrictedly subjectivistic views of the immediate data of awareness In contrast to such views, we believe that these data are far richer and more definitely structuralized than is commonly supposed

Such a broadened empiricism is more adequately suggested by the term "phenomenology," although this word also must be freed from those special connotations it has gained from association with the later transcendental idealism of Husserl For us, this term means the disciplined attempt to describe and analyze the immediate data of awareness as they are given We believe that all philosophical theories of interpretation and explanation must be ultimately based upon such descriptions and constantly checked by them This conception of philosophical method is considered in the first two essays

Phenomenology is still in a very imperfect stage and stands in desperate need of further application and development. But some trustworthy results have already emerged. In addition to the measurable, quantitative data of the restricted sciences, there are pervasive, non-quantitative data of a different order, requiring a different method of investigation and a broader philosophic type of explanatory theory Among these are the all-pervasive data of existence and awareness, the objects of ontology and epistemology

According to realism, the world is constituted by a plurality of active, existent entities which are really related to one another, without being absorbed in a monistic absolute. To describe and clarify the relevant evidence, and to offer an intelligible explanation of this evidence, is the task of ontology Realism also defends the thesis that these actual entities can be known by the human mind, at least in part, as they actually are. To describe the complex facts of awareness, and to defend this thesis in the light of the actual evidence, is the task of realistic epistemology.

The tragedy of earlier realistic movements in England and America was their exclusive interest in epistemology and their failure to accept any responsibility for those ontological foundations upon which any sound realistic epistemology must be based. In Part I we have tried to avoid this mistake and to suggest how the empirical evidence points to a realistic ontology and epistemology which provide each other with mutual support In two of the essays this realistic approach is defended against subjectivistic and positivistic attack

Against the widespread theory that norms are radically separated from existence, realism defends the view that there are norms actually grounded in the tendential structure of being In Part II of this volume, certain problems of the normative disciplines are systematically treated from a realistic point of view. In one essay, the basic realistic concept of natural law, now commonly misinterpreted as a purely authoritarian and dogmatic construction, is traced back to its first sources in the thoughts of Plato and Aristotle. In another, the realistic conception of practical reason, so strikingly absent from recent ethical debate, is analyzed and interpreted Another essay considers the implications of realistic anthropology and ethics for the theory of education. Finally, in a last chapter, the present chairman of the United Nations Commission on Human Rights applies the basic principles of realistic philosophy to one of the great world problems of our day.

Philosophy, of course, will never die as long as man exists. Human life cannot be lived without some guiding view of the world and our place within it. But such views, if uncritically embraced, are notoriously unstable and distorted by error It is the task of academic philosophy to provide this essential criticism, to separate the true from the false and, finally, to arrive at disciplined formulations of philosophical theories which agree with evidence accessible to all. This task is most difficult It is easy for those pursuing it to become lost in sterile minutiae, to become fascinated with spurious substitutes for philosophy and, finally, to fall into despair at the seeming hopelessness of achieving verifiable results. When this happens, academic thought is artificially isolated from the thought of the common man, with tragic effects on both. As the one becomes sterile and artificial, the other becomes more bigoted and fantastic. This has happened in the past. We do not wish to see it happen in our own time.

The basic questions· What is man? What is knowledge? What ought we to do? cannot be evaded without serious damage to the whole intellectual enterprise. We believe that these questions can be attacked in a disciplined way, that theories can be checked by complex but describable evidence. We also believe that the history of philosophy, when critically studied, can give us valuable help and support

If these essays arouse in some readers a deeper trust in philosophy as a co-operative discipline, and a more courageous resolution to struggle against the widespread philosophical skepticism and negativism of our day, our highest hopes will have been fulfilled.

TABLE OF CONTENTS

PART I

I

Realism and Phenomenology

HARMON M. CHAPMAN, *New York University*

MY THESIS in the following pages is that the terms "realism" and "phenomenology" signify inseparable aspects of a single discipline Their intrinsic correlation is revealed by the fact that the world must be an "object of awareness" and that human consciousness is primordially "awareness of the world" My aim is to clarify this correlation as residing in the *intentional* nature of consciousness and to show that its understanding leads to a realism that is one with phenomenology, and vice versa

In Section I, I set forth that human consciousness is dually related to the world· (1) *Empirically* it is contained in the world, (2) *Cognitively* it contains the world Although these relations are coeval, their joint understanding faces the difficulty that whereas the empirical relation is accessible to natural inquiry, the cognitive relation is not Empirical knowledge can only presuppose it, reflection alone can clarify it.

In Section II, I discuss at length the nature of reflection and show how it is at once distinct from, and yet tied to, empiricism

In Section III, I exhibit reflectively the intentional nature of awareness and the hylomorphic structure which it shares with the empirical object of awareness.

In Section IV, I show that awareness as a living act of the subject is *internal* to it and *really* relates it to the object, but that it is *external* to the object and relates it only *nominally* to the subject. Intentionally or cognitively, therefore, consciousness contains the real, whereas empirically or existentially the world contains consciousness. The two relations mutually supplement each other and jointly provide the cognitive basis of mind.

I. CONSCIOUSNESS AND REALITY

A. *Man's Awareness of the World* Among the distinguishing features of human life, one of the most striking is the fact that man not only lives in the world but is also aware of so doing This awareness of the world, expressed in his mores, his religion, his science, his philosophy, and so forth, sets man off from the rest of the animal kingdom and gives his life the characteristic stamp of being an adjustment not only to his immediate surroundings but also to the encompassing all, of which these are only a part. Of man alone can it be said that his environment is the universe, the whole of all that is. For, whereas all other creatures are simply contained within it and pass their existence oblivious thereof, aware—if at all—only of what falls within the limited range of their sensibilities, man, on the contrary, possesses a quickening sense of this whole and attains through it to a level of existence immeasurably removed from that of any other known creature

Now as the world itself is no particular thing or event, so our awareness of the world is no passing thought or perception For like the light of day which, though itself unseen, is yet apparent in all the shapes and colors it illumines, the world is revealed to us in the manifold things we experience; as in everything we see, light is evident, so in everything we experience, the world is manifest—manifest as the all-embracing whole and togetherness of existing things. Thus, too, as an awareness of light attends all our seeing, so an awareness of the world attends all our perceivings and binds them together into one whole of experience. For it is only through this abiding awareness of the world that whatsoever we see or hear or touch or otherwise perceive as real is grasped by us as an integral part of a sovereign whole that cannot itself be so beheld, yet is unmistakably evident as the all-encompassing presence.

Our awareness of the world then shares in a way the permanence of the world itself, and this despite the fact that our *explicit* notice of the world is only occasional For on all these occasions we recognize the world instinctively as something familiar and omnipresent, something that does not really pass in and out of our ken like ordinary objects, but as something ubiquitous and taken for granted—much like light, the atmosphere, or the ground under our feet, things of whose presence we seldom take note but are nonetheless continuously aware It is in this *implicit* or background fashion that our awareness of the world abides like an over-all "frame of mind" within which occur all the manifold awarenesses of self and others and of all things generally. This awareness of the world, therefore, is not an incident or passing thought in the stream of consciousness but is the presiding attitude through which this unremitting stream itself acquires unity and wholeness and takes on the cumulative and contextual character of a single consciousness or experience of the world

As the basic frame of mind or "natural attitude" of life itself, our awareness of the world embraces and unifies the vast stream of experience with all its profusion of detail, binding it into one living whole. I say "living" because, although it has the static fixity of a framework, it has also the dynamical quality of an organic structure ever absorbing into itself fresh contents—our daily experiencings and doings—appropriating these in every instant of our lives and adding them to the accumulated store of past experiences (sometimes called our "apperceptive mass") And so it comes to pass that human experience despite its temporal dispersion, its transcience and flux, yet accumulates, through our presiding awareness of the world, into one living whole of experience.

B. *Consciousness as Correlate of the World* By virtue of this presiding awareness of the world, human consciousness enters into a unique kind of correlation with the world itself. The oneness of life and experience becomes in a way a reflection of the oneness of the world As all things are contained in the world, so all individual experiences are contained within our one experience of the world As every object has the sense of being a real thing within one vast community of existing things, so each particular experience—each thought, each feeling, each sensation, each deed—has its own being and sense within one contextual whole of experience This organic unity or contextual wholeness of our lives makes us all, in a way, living images of the universe, *microcosms* or epitomes of the *macrocosm*

But there is more to this correlation than a mere parallelism between cosmos and consciousness. For were it only a parallel correlation, it would be indeed, as Leibniz assumed, a remarkable synchronism between two separate and detached orders of events, an objective order of things and a subjective order of ideas, in a running one-to-one correspondence, divinely ordained as a "pre-established" harmony Consciousness on this assumption would merely reflect the universe in the detached fashion of a mirror and would be but a succession of inner images corresponding to a succession of outer objects. This mirror analogy, however, is quite inadequate in so far as consciousness does something which the mirror cannot possibly do and which Leibniz overlooked It *apprehends;* it *is aware* of things and of the world, and there is no analogue of this awareness factor in the operation of the mirror In other words, we are one and whole not merely because the world is one and whole and we reflect it *in distans* but because we experience it as such *in propinquo.* We are microcosms because in experience we are *aware of* the macrocosm.

This insistence on awareness and the integrity of experience (the two being inseparable) carries with it an equal insistence on the reality of the world and, indeed, on the existence of the world *as we experience it* For if experience be genuine awareness—and this is precisely what is here contended for—then the common-sense world of people and homes, of towns and nations, of stars and atom bombs, is the real world, the world that science deals with, in which it builds its laboratories and conducts its experiments, the world it seeks to inform us of and in dubious measure to control. This familiar sensible world, in short, is the experienced world of reality and existence in which we live and move and have our being.

Awareness thus turns out to be in league with reality and betrays us into the hands of metaphysics. For we must now assert the antecedent and independent existence of the world as a prior condition of our experience or awareness of it (as well as of our existence within it) And we must also assert that the world is even as we experience it to be, namely, a sensible world—although it may be vastly more than our senses reveal, referring, of course, to the supplementary disclosures of the natural and historical sciences. Now the sum of these two assertions amounts to what is usually, and often scornfully, called "naive realism" or "epistemological realism." That this is a naive view I shall concede, but that it is for this reason also false I shall deny For to say that it is naive is no more than to say that it is not yet a full-blown theory It asserts only, as a pretheoretical certainty, that experience is genuine and that it grasps the real. But as to what experience is and what the real is, it does not presume to say. It is, therefore, only an incipient metaphysics, as yet innocent of what it may portend, and is in need of further inquiry in order to be brought to theoretical fruition.

It is such an inquiry that I am here pursuing, and its first disclosure is that experience, being genuine awareness of the world, sets human consciousness in an intimate correlation with the real, which we have signified as that of microcosm and macrocosm. The next disclosure, however, threatens this "realistic" view, for consciousness now appears to become the correlate of the real only to devour it and absorb it into itself

C *Consciousness as Dually Related to the World.* There is nothing in the world, or out of it, that lies essentially out of the reach of awareness. In some fashion or other, consciousness can bring absolutely anything to awareness The field of consciousness, in other words, extends to the limits of the world and beyond—to the unreal, the merely possible, the impossible, the transcendent—in a word, to whatsoever is conceivable, and there is nothing inconceivable save the self-contradictory So vast and illimitable is the horizon of consciousness that the world of reality shrinks to a mere province within it Nothing can even be thought to lie outside it. Having no "outside," consciousness is absolutely all-embracing and must be regarded as containing or including the world.

I would not detract in the least from this "transcendental" aspect of consciousness, as it has been called. It is, as Pascal rightly observed, the "grandeur" of man. If in another respect he is but a fragile "thinking reed," man in this respect is a titan, for such is the power of his mind that he can reach out and encompass the universe.

But if we take this transcendental view seriously, does it not follow that the world is in some deep and hidden sense really inside consciousness and hence not prior to it at all, as naive realism assumes, but posterior to it and dependent on it? The classical reply of idealism to this question is. "Yes. The world as object of consciousness becomes by virtue of this cognitive relation to consciousness a product of consciousness and exists within it either as immanent content (idea) or, more subtly, as 'transcendentally constituted correlate.'"

My reply, however, is much more circumspect. For to hold thus with idealism is clearly to reject out of hand the view of naive realism, that the real is prior to our awareness of it—a view, it will be recalled, which arose from a resolute effort to take awareness seriously and as primitive. I suggest, therefore, that both views have equal warrant and that consciousness must be, as real, *included within* the world and, as transcendental, *inclusive of* the world, and, too, it must be identically the same human consciousness in either case

It might be useful for purposes of emphasis to state this in the form of a paradox: Consciousness contains the world and the world contains consciousness The paradox, however, is quite transparent, for the word "contain" (or "include") is obviously used in different senses. the one being the familiar everyday sense, and the other an obscure cognitive sense obviously requiring clarification.

It is more significant, therefore, to state the problem as arising from the fact that consciousness is related in two different ways to the world One, it is empirically *contained in* the world as psychical correlate of an organism. Two, it is *awareness* (or *experience*) *of* the world as transcendental correlate of the real. Consciousness, in brief, is clearly both psychical (empirical) correlate of a body and transcendental correlate of the real To show how both these relations can obtain simultaneously without in the least interfering with one another or producing a schism in consciousness, or even threatening its unity, may be said to be the major task of this paper.

D *The Two Relations Not Equally Apparent.* The first relation I shall dispatch as rapidly as possible, but with the explicit reminder that its existence is presupposed in all that follows. That I am born into the world, that I here live out my days and in due course expire, is a "fact" I am unable seriously to doubt. Nor can I doubt that in the process of living in the world I am constantly in vital contact with other existing things and form with them a real community of great complexity, which is nothing less, in the last analysis, than the world itself All this, and more, I take for granted when I assume man's empirical relation to the world.

If the first relation is empirically evident, the second relation is empirically obscure; and its obscurity, I shall argue, is inescapable in the natural attitude of empiricism. Thus, for example, in the traditional causal explanation of perception it is generally believed that once an "outer" stimulus has been supplied and an "inner" sensory response evoked, perception ensues as a purely subjective process of "synthesizing" or "interpreting" or "taking" the sensation thus caused. The subjective process thus assumed is quite out of touch with the object of perception, save for the initial causing of the sensation. In other words, perception is allowed *causal*, but not *cognitive*, contact with its object What is actually perceived, therefore, is nothing but the given (caused) sensation, so that in claiming to perceive the outer object, consciousness is overreaching itself, mistaking an inference (or hypothesis or conjecture or projection) for an apprehension Actually beholding only its own sense data, consciousness takes these as indices of outer objects and then erroneously declares that it perceives these latter

There are two theses embedded in this familiar explanation that merit attention The first is that objective observable processes *cause* subjective sensation in us The second is that *perceiving* is one with *having*, that consciousness (at least in the case of perception) apprehends only its own contents (sensations, ideas, and so forth).

1   The first thesis assumes the empirical relation I have just referred to and is so far on solid ground. But it is not on solid ground when it regards the empirical relation between psychical and physical as one of physical causality. For it is not at all clear how a physical stimulus can (physically) cause a psychical response—unless, of course, we abolish the psychical and reduce it by some artifice of definition to the physical This, however, is patently a speculative measure of doubtful advantage. But, in foregoing this advantage, the difficulty remains as to the precise nature of the "stimulus-response" relation. I suggest that we leave this relation unspecified for the time being and simply refrain in what follows from taking it to be one of mere physical causality.

2. The second thesis asserts that perceiving is having, that I behold only my own (inner) sensations and not the (outer) objects that cause them Now it is highly instructive to note that the causal theory of perception invokes this view only in its account of perceptions and invokes the opposite view at two very critical junctures.

In the first place, assuming with the causal explanation that on grasping my sensations I infer in some fashion to the objects causing them, is it not evident that, once having made the inference, the object of my awareness is no longer the sensation but the inferred outer object itself? Whether I am right or wrong in making this inference is not at all the question The point simply is that if I make the inference, I make it, and in making it I direct my attention upon the outer object as something I do not "have." In thus "inferring" to it, I set myself in cognitive relation to it and establish beyond doubt that awareness, in this case at least, is not one with having.

But, it will be demurred, I still do not perceive the (inferred) object. Very well, then, there are two types of awareness one that is merely having, and another that is precisely not having, so that awareness is not to be identified, in every case, with having

But why, I now ask, is perception regarded as a case of having? Do I really perceive only sensations? Are sensations merely passive, inert states of consciousness which I merely have and behold as such? Are they really devoid of all cognitive character?

E. *Sensation as Sensory Awareness.* So far as I am aware, I have never perceived a sensation *as such*, that is, *as a mere state of consciousness.* Even when my perceptions are patently false, as in dreams, illusions, and the like, I perceive not sensations but *sensible things,* illusory or real Try as I will, I cannot do otherwise in sensing than to sense something sensible. Reflection alone informs me that in sensing I always have a sensation, but what I have is a *sensation of something;* and it is always this something of which I am sensuously aware, be it a color, a sound, a flavor, or what not—real or illusory

In other words, sensations I find are never objects of sense perception, but objects for reflection alone And reflection discovers them never as isolated data or "states of consciousness" but always as factors in a cognitive situation from which they cannot possibly be excised, but only abstracted They are basic elements of awareness in what we call "sense perception" of sensible things. They are, in short, originally cognitive in character, and only as such can they subserve awareness. But if this be true, sensation is not a state of consciousness like pain, and "having" is not one with "perceiving" it. For if I "have" a sensation only when I perceive something sensible, then I have something of which I am originally quite unaware, until reflection informs me of its presence.

Pursuing this matter further, I asked why it was that the contrary view could so long obtain I found that it did not prevail in the ancient world except among the atomists, who held to it, not as a result of analysis or inquiry, but purely as a logical consequence of their atomic theory. For if all things are but atoms and the void, then the senses misinform us and must, therefore, be explained away, at least, as genuine modes of cognition. This view was not again widely entertained until Descartes espoused it and for essentially the same reasons For if the world be as science demands, namely, a *res extensa*, then the senses must be thoroughly discounted and superseded. Descartes proceeded accordingly—without clearly realizing it, of course, for his interests lay elsewhere—to deprive sensation of all cogni-

tive character, to subjectivize it as an inert state of consciousness, albeit
objectively caused, and to declare it no more like its object than pain is like
the sword that inflicts a wound

In this hasty indictment, put forth in the name of science, Descartes
pre-empted the verdict of modern philosophy on the nature of sensation and
committed it *ab initio* to a subjective "sensationalism." With the possible
exception of Locke, whose inadvertence Berkeley quickly exposed, the
modern tradition almost to a man has followed Descartes in this opinion,
even to the enigmatic *hyletic data* of Husserl.

This view of sensation gave birth to two offspring: the problems of the
"given" and of "method"—the two doctrinal dispensations of modern
philosophy For if consciousness be thus initially cut off from cognitive contact with the real, it can attain to a knowledge of things, if at all, only by an
adroit and systematic use of its own resources. The first step accordingly is
to take an inventory of what is "given"—the subjective data[1] of consciousness—and then to consider ways and means (the method) of exploiting
these data as bases for an edifice of reliable knowledge—whether for cognitive or pragmatic purposes, or both.

In rejecting this subjectivism I revert to that state of innocence called
naive realism, or common sense, or the natural attitude. Taking here my
stand, I contend again for the veridical character of experience and, in
particular, for the cognitive character of sense perception as the primordial
mode of experience, first in the genealogy of consciousness. Experience is,
I submit, not fabrication, but apprehension—awareness through and
through, complex, to be sure, and infused at its higher levels with inference,
but awareness nonetheless. The given, accordingly, is not some fancied
state of consciousness, but the real itself—heaven and earth and all the furniture thereof, home, family, friends, and so forth The world is given, in
short, and given as the real sensible world of life and science. And if there
is a problem of method—as indeed there is—it is a problem that takes its
origin precisely here in this original if naive grasp of the real, and not in the
preposterous attempt to manufacture knowledge out of ignorance

That precisely this realistic view is *presupposed* by the causal explanation of perception is unmistakably betrayed in the initial assumption of an
objective order of events that results in the stimulation of our sense organs
—themselves objective—and the consequent "causing" of sensations. This
serene confidence in the objective order, unattended, of course, by any
specific mention thereof, constitutes the second denial, above referred to, of
the thesis that perceiving is but having For if it is not by perception that
we originally know of sense organs and their stimulation by outer objects,

[1] For a more detailed account of the problem of the given, see the essay by John
Wild, pp. 36 ff.

then I have no idea at all how this knowledge is obtained. It can hardly be attributed to inference, for the whole theory of perception as inference from the given is based upon this prior assurance of the real as primordially given.

If this be the case, that sensuous awareness is thus quietly presupposed by the causal theory of perception, then the actual state of affairs signified by the term "perception" turns out to be not only as the causal theory of perception *describes* it but also as it *presupposes* it to be—a situation, namely, that is perceptually grasped and as *originally involving awareness*. Were not the real nexus of subject and object thus primordially apprehended as both empirical and perceptual, the causal theory would not even quietly presuppose it. The perceptual situation, then, is originally both empirical and cognitive. The former aspect alone is evident to natural inquiry; the cognitive it can only presuppose. Both aspects, however, are equally evident to reflection, and it is by reflection alone, therefore, that we can survey the perceptual state of affairs in its full actuality. The cognitive relation, in other words, is not an empirical but a "transcendental" connection accessible solely to reflection.

II. Reflection and the Reflective Standpoint

A. *Reflection and Empiricism* The standpoint of reflection now comes to the fore as the pendant and supplement of the empirical or natural attitude. It is not opposed to this latter, for it seeks rather to substantiate it, to vindicate experience as awareness of the real, and to preserve perception as the basic mode of experience. Perception is not an obscure process of intellectual fabrication based upon a prior given, but a cognitive process of apprehending the real. Reflection holds, then, contrary to the prevailing view, that perception is initially in cognitive as well as empirical contact with the real and that the two relations are coeval.

In combating the causal theory of perception, accordingly, reflection was not opposing empiricism as such, but rather saving it from itself. For in missing the cognitive relation, as it must needs do, empiricism destroys perception as awareness and undermines thereby its own foundations. For when cognition is initially wanting, it cannot be subsequently contrived.

Reflection and empiricism thus stand in a symbiotic relation. Empiricism provides reflection with its sole object of study, the world and our awareness thereof, whereas reflection provides empiricism with the self-scrutiny by which alone it can be clarified. For empiricism lacks precisely this reflexive feature; because of the inherent "extraversion" of the natural attitude, empiricism is preoccupied almost exclusively with the objects of awareness to the virtual oblivion of the awareness itself. Later I shall show that all awareness contains a moment of reflection but that this reflexivity is quite recessive and only implicit in the natural attitude. Reflection alone, by virtue of its posterior position, can explore this dimension and thus bring to fullness our naive experience of the real, otherwise condemned to the partiality of self-ignorance.

What we do in reflecting is briefly this Without completely taking leave of the natural attitude, we yet transcend it, stepping back, so to speak, as though upon higher ground so as to survey not only (as formerly) the world but also our experience of it. Thus, whereas in the natural attitude we are concerned with the world simply, in the reflective attitude we are concerned with both world and experience

From the beginning of this essay, and throughout, I have assumed this reflective standpoint. In seeking to show that our awareness of the world is the presiding frame of mind of human experience, I spoke not from this natural attitude itself but from that of reflection, whence alone I could behold the whole empirical position with its sundry methods of inquiry. Reflecting further, I observed that this empirical attitude is concretely that of naive realism or awareness of the world and that it brings human consciousness into transcendental correlation with the real Still reflecting, I then discerned in this correlation the ubiquitous cognitive relation of consciousness to all things and sought to show that it is not an empirical but a transcendental relation accessible to reflection alone.

B *What Reflection Is Not.* So much claptrap has been written about reflection and the reflective attitude that it is imperative here to disavow most, if not all, of it In the first place, on reflecting I do not "suspend" my natural attitude, I do not withdraw from it my living assent or belief, or in any way modify it. My experience continues unchanged in its unremitting course, and the world persists in its presence. What I do is simply to expand the horizon of attention so as to include within it both experience and the world Thus, whereas formerly I was "naively," that is, unreflectively, absorbed with the world alone, now I am explicitly mindful of both world and absorption.

In the second place, when I reflect, I should be aware that I am reflecting. This means that the reflective standpoint possesses a reflexive feature which is wanting in the natural attitude, namely, it includes itself within its own purview. Because of this reflexive feature (whence it is properly denominated "reflective"), there is no need of a third standpoint from which to view the reflective, or a fourth from which to view the third, and so on ad infinitum. There is no such *regressus* of standpoints simply because, once the reflective turn has been taken, all further reflections occur at the same level. Thus, reflecting on my awareness of the world, I may reflect on this reflection, and so on without limit, but at no point do I leave the horizon of reflection. The iterative nature of reflection simply makes explicit the illimitable character of consciousness as transcendental correlate of the all (which includes consciousness itself).

This point is deserving of some emphasis that reflection must become self-conscious in order to be properly reflective. This means that the occasional reflections in which we all indulge as thoughtful human beings are not yet fully reflective in the explicit sense here intended. For as casual, they are carried out under the aegis of the natural attitude, usually in some empirical interest, and tend accordingly to be unaware of themselves as reflective and as distinct from empirical thought Only when attended by the clear awareness of themselves as reflective can they lose their naiveté and attain to the systematic and methodological clarity of philosophic theory. It is not sufficient, therefore, that we should simply reflect on the natural attitude or the nature of empirical knowledge We must also reflect upon the reflective standpoint itself—as, in fact, we did—and, discerning it, distinguish it clearly from the natural attitude. Only with this explicitly in mind can we then proceed to reflect in the luminous awareness that we are indeed reflecting—awareness always aware of itself in all its inquiries

In the third place, to say that transcendental consciousness is the highest form of self-consciousness does not in the least imply that I forsake the world and withdraw into pure contemplation of myself as a windowless monad immured within its stream of consciousness In reflecting, I do not lose sight of the world but retain it unaltered as the inseparable correlate of my (subjective) consciousness. This means incidentally that subjectivity (for reflection) is not the opposite, but the pendant and correlate, of objectivity, that in its very essence it is world-involvement, and that apart from this living involvement, consciousness is but the empty capacity of awareness In fine, nothing is lost to view on assuming the reflective standpoint, rather, everything is gained.

In the fourth and final place, the term "transcendental" is sharply to be distinguished from the term "transcendent." That alone is transcendent which is outside of and beyond the world. Consciousness is neither; it is *in* the world, and only as such is it real It is transcendental only in the sense of being also *awareness of* the world and hence a universal correlate of the real. There is in this statement, therefore, not the slightest suggestion of our being transcendent observers gazing on the world from without Nor is there any hint of a metaphysical dualism such as that of Descartes, who assumed mind and body to be distinct substances Mind and body are for reflection, as for empiricism, the psychical and physical aspects of one substantial human being.

The conclusion of all this is that reflection is neither occult nor mystical, that it is not the "hifalutin" prerogative of an esoteric brotherhood called philosophers—or, more dubiously, professors of philosophy It is not removed from the common understanding of men, like relativity and the quantum theory, which are properly esoteric. Reflection is rather—and must ever be—in intimate rapport with common sense and experience. I have spoken of it, to be sure, as "higher" than empiricism and have called it, forbiddingly, "transcendental" But these terms are misleading if they suggest anything more than a natural widening of the horizon of attention along a dimension of awareness already latent in all cognition—empirical or otherwise.

So understood, reflection stands in unbroken continuity with empiricism, being but a normal expansion of the natural attitude into that wholeness and completeness of outlook which alone reveals consciousness (to itself) as the transcendental correlate of the real.

Were this a complete account of reflection, I should turn at once to the cognitive relation. But unfortunately, reflection is a discipline of singular difficulty, as the history of philosophy will bear witness Not the least among its difficulties is the unrelenting need for diligence in distinguishing between its own proper pronouncements and those arising from the empirical attitude For if reflection is to be a genuine supplement to empiricism, it is bound to make disclosures which appear strange to the natural attitude—and all the more strange because they are latent in the natural attitude itself, and hence not wholly unfamiliar. A tension is therefore sure to arise between philosophy and naive empiricism, which, if it be not carefully understood, must inevitably lead to confusion This is particularly true at the present time when, in the current obsession with "science," reflection seems bent on its own undoing, declaring all to be unscientific, hence disreputable, that is not verifiable by naive empirical methods

In order to avoid this confusion, I shall exhibit reflection still more concretely in a (reflective) analysis of perception My aim will be to throw light on both standpoints so as to formulate more incisively the difference between them Having thus secured my footing, I shall then turn to the cognitive relation which is the ultimate object of my quest.

C. *"Object Simply"* and *"Object Perceived."* First, let me formulate this difference of standpoints as so far revealed In the natural attitude I am preoccupied with empirical "objects simply," unmindful of my awareness of them. In the reflective attitude I am concerned with both factors, with the "objects as experienced" and with my "experience of objects." Whereas in the one case I am aware only of objects simply, in the other I am attentively aware of both objects and awareness.

Now, for reflection, objects and awareness are in inseparable correlation, for the simple reason that whatsoever I contemplate or speak about becomes an object for me only by virtue of my awareness of it. Hence, to be object at all means for reflection to be object of awareness, and to be aware means to be aware of something as object For this reason the object simply of the natural attitude becomes for reflection the object experienced, object perceived, and so forth. Object and awareness thus take on for reflection a mutual reference which binds them inseparably together

It is important to note that the correlation does not involve any change whatever in the object, that identically the same thing may at one time be regarded naively as an object simply and then again reflectively as an object experienced, object perceived, and so forth. The reason for this is that reflection simply makes explicit what is implicit in all awareness. Thus even in the most naive perception of an object simply, there is latent this sense of the object as also a perceived object The change, therefore, is not in the object at all but solely in our apprehension of it, in the attitude in which we regard it. Assuming, then, that perception is genuine awareness of its object, it is precisely the same object whether considered simply or reflectively as perceived.

With this clearly in mind, let us consider an actual instance of simple perception.

D *Perception Is Essentially Expressible* I see on the desk before me an ink bottle Exercising the usual precautions, I satisfy myself that it is not an illusion but a genuine object of experience Although merely seen, it has its full meed of reality, as something both tactual, auditory, and so forth, having its other side—unseen from this angle—its uses, its history, and the rest.

Assuming that I actually see the ink bottle, then in saying "I see the ink bottle," I am simply bringing my perception to articulate utterance in the proper form of empirical knowledge. This utterance may seem at first glance to be something over and above the mere experience itself, something adventitious or nonessential, and yet somehow connected with it. On second glance, however, I see that the declaration is far from an extraneous addition; for what it expresses is precisely the perception itself in so far as it is an apprehension or awareness. Were my perception devoid of apprehension in this articulate sense, I could not, of course, express it as I do. As it is, however, my experience is essentially such as to be articulately expressible and, hence, although actually unexpressed in most cases, can at any moment be declared and thereby brought to this articulate and explicit form. Hence it is that in extreme concentration we often "talk to ourselves." For perception comes to full flower as empirical cognition only in articulate utterance. And only in so far as it actually does this can we speak or think of what we experience.

E. *Expressible Perception Is Conceptual*   Because experience is thus inherently expressible, its highest actuality as empirical awareness lies in the
propositions in which it culminates. But thus to culminate in propositions
means that experience is essentially conceptual as well as sensual As adult,
reflecting human beings we do not find our experience otherwise, although
with this as our (often unconscious) standard we can depict to ourselves
an experience that is not at all conceptual but wholly sensuous Such a preconceptual experience would, however, be quite inarticulate, like that presumably of animals It would consist roughly in a succession of sense perceivings, each confined more or less to the moment of its occurrence, although retainable in the form of an image, so that the field of awareness at
any given time would consist of the things actually perceived plus such
recalled and anticipated things as the imagination should associate therewith, the whole forming a kind of working unity of awareness, sufficient for
making direct responses and developing habits needful for survival but
quite devoid of the integrated wholeness and over-all unity that are solely
the work of conceptual awareness and are precisely the distinguishing features of human experience

A completely preconceptual experience accordingly would not be what
we know human experience to be. It would be rather a protoexperience, an
experience, to be sure, but one exceedingly difficult if not impossible to
describe, because of the inveterate tendency on our part to render it articulate and hence conceptual after the human standard. This protoexperience
as purely sensuous would be hardly, if anything, more than an unutterable
beholding It might take in all that our senses reveal, or even more, because
of more sensitive eyes, ears, nose, and so forth. But it could not possibly
grasp what we apprehend, namely, that "this is black," "this is an ink bottle," "the bottle is on the table," and so on. In fact, we simply cannot say
what it does grasp, for in saying it we would express our own apprehension
and not that of the protoexperience. Thus, although I am confident that my
dog is at least as sensuously aware of things as I am, that he perceives them
in some sense, and indeed the same sensible things that I perceive, yet I am
quite unable to say what he beholds I cannot express it any more than he
can, for it is intrinsically ineffable; it can only call forth such responses as
wagging the tail, licking the chops, or barking in delight or disgust, and
the like.

To say that human experience is conceptual is not to deny that it is also
sensuous It is both sensation and conception, fused into the unity of a
single perceptual awareness Although the precise nature of this union is
yet to be clarified, we can see in advance of this clarification that the experience of the ink bottle is not a mere seeing, not a mere visual beholding,
but something vastly more—a visual conceiving or a conceptual seeing, an

act of great complexity involving the whole context of experience. For no act occurs in isolation like an atom, but always as a single pulse within the living surge of experience, in which alone it has its being and character as an essentially expressible apprehension.

F. *Perception as a Dual Grasp.* Experience or perception, then, as empirical awareness consummates in experiential or "protocol" propositions, in which alone our primordial grasp of the real becomes articulate and explicit The general form of these propositions is exemplified in the statement "I see the ink bottle" Neglecting for the time being the "I see," the reflective part of the statement, and concentrating on the object side, what I grasp then reduces to "This is an ink bottle." Every perceptual apprehension reduces in its object-grasp to this elementary type of proposition. Besides the ink bottle, I may also grasp that "this is a table," and then the more complex object or state of affairs, that "the ink bottle is on the table" Or I may apprehend that "this is a relation," "this is a color," "this color is black," and so forth. In every case my primitive apprehension, as thus articulated, is a twofold grasp. Namely, I apprehend *that* something is (indicated by "this is") and also *what* it is, in this case an "ink bottle"

Occasionally I fail to grasp the *what* and get only the *that*. My grasp is in this case incomplete, verging on the merely sensuous, and I strive instinctively to ascertain the *what*. If I am unsuccessful, as when impeded by darkness, the thing remains an enigmatic "something I know not what." If only partially successful, I may gather only the *what* of its shape, location, size, and so forth, which will enable me later to describe it to others in the effort to find out what it is. Usually, however—and this is the normal case—I gather both the *that* and the *what*, and my apprehension as propositionally articulated takes the general form already noted.

Now the what in every case is grasped as something not restricted in its occurrence to a particular that, but as capable of being shared by other particulars as well. Thus on being told that this is a test tube, nobody is surprised to learn that this and that and yonder are also test tubes—in other words, that many thats can have the same what Even the child on first learning to talk finds it most natural to identify many things as "kitty," all men as "daddy," and so forth The what, then, is always grasped as a general or universal entity inherently capable of being present in a number of particular things, the number being, so far as the what itself is concerned, completely without limit. The basic formula, therefore, for our normal grasp of the real is· "This is a particular instance of a universal (or essence)."

Every empirical object of awareness, every sensible thing, every sensible attribute, part, or property, every empirical relation, in short every existent or reality, is grasped as the instance of an essence. Our original awareness of the real accordingly is never—in its explicit form—a simple, but always a complex and articulated, apprehension, involving at least these two factors. Because of this duality and because, too, of the fact that we actually find many particulars sharing a common essence, our cognitive interest in the real undergoes an important bifurcation. On the one hand we may focus upon things in their particularity and uniqueness as in the historical sciences, or we may on the other hand focus upon things in their generality and essence as in the natural sciences We are quite at liberty to focus on either aspect as we please, for both are always present. They are present, however, not as separate and distinct empirical objects but merely as cognitive aspects of the same empirical things This liberty consists, therefore, not so much in a choice of objects as rather in a choice of ways of considering objects. All natural or empirical knowledge of the real falls accordingly under two types. It is either historical or natural scientific—existential or essential (or "eidetic" as Husserl calls it)

G *The Reflective Turn* What this all signifies as regards the method of reflection is briefly this I have been describing not "objects simply" as in the natural attitude, but "objects as experienced," or more precisely, "as perceptually grasped" in the propositions in which perception culminates Instead of merely perceiving things, I have been also observing them qua perceived in experiential propositions about them In order to observe them thus in propositions, I had first to perceive them, for naive perception and experience are always prior to reflection The reflective turn, therefore, may now be stated as that from *things simply* in *perception* to *things as experienced* in *propositions.*

In taking this philosophic turn, nothing has dropped from view The original object of perception is still present, precisely as I perceived it, only now I take it explicitly as perceived (which includes its simple status) and consider it henceforth as it now stands revealed to reflection in the experiential propositions about it Thus the ink bottle, originally perceived as an object simply, becomes for reflection a real individual composite of particularity and universality, or, to use the classical terms of Aristotle, "matter" and "form."

This reflective complexity of the ink bottle is quite a different thing from its empirical complexity, its contents, shape, color, uses, and so forth For by the phrase "objects simply," I do not mean that the object itself is empirically simple but rather that our grasp of it is simple or naive in the sense that the grasp itself is unheeded in our preoccupation with the object. Hence the object simply may be of any degree of empirical complexity— all the way up to the "world simply," the most complex of all empirical things. But, and this must now be well noted, whatever complications an object simply may empirically be discovered to have—its parts, qualities, properties, and so forth—all these are in turn and without exception empirical objects simply, that is, real individual existences composite of form and matter (for reflection). For only as such are they naively experienceable as empirical objects.

For reflection alone, then, are empirical objects simply revealed as real individuals composite of matter and form. This matter-form or "hylomorphic" view of the real is, accordingly, a purely reflective, and not an empirical, theory; for neither element, form or matter, is itself a hylomorphic individual and hence cannot be an object of experience. But although not themselves *explicitly* perceived as existent or real parts of things, they are nonetheless *implicitly* cograsped in every perception of the real There is accordingly a latent awareness of them in all natural knowledge. But empiricism must ever remain naive and in a state of unclarity with respect to them; for only the reflective turn from perception to proposition can bring them properly to light.

It is precisely this turn that Socrates describes in his famous *vita* in the *Phaedo*. Having sought in vain for the true "causes" or "elements" of things by the methods of natural inquiry, he gave up, he tells us, the naive observation of things (τὰ ὄντα σκοπῶν) and took recourse to propositions (λόγοι), hoping here to behold the truth of things (εἰς τοὺς λόγους καταφυγόντα ἐν ἐκείνοις [*sc.* λόγοις] σκοπεῖν τῶν ὄντων τὴν ἀλήθειαν —*Phaedo*, 99e). That this novel and radical turn is tantamount to abandoning things themselves for their shadows or images (εἴκονα) he explicitly denies, for, he insists, things are no less present and evident in propositions (ἐν τοῖς λόγοις) than they are in perceptions (αἰσθήσεις). Laying down (ὑποθέμενος) the "strongest" propositions— the experiential or protocol propositions, as we have called them—he then discovers the "forms" or "ideas" as the objective *what* or essence (οὐσία) of things, and in this discovery gives the initial impulse to the whole classical doctrine of realism.

Thus in conscious contrast to all empirical method and procedure, Socrates here directs Western philosophy into the path of reflection, away from "physical speculation" to philosophical analysis—from physics to metaphysics The first fruits of the new inquiry were the forms or universals, which Socrates submitted to inductive study. Plato attained to a far more systematic grasp of the forms and their interrelations and discovered in the process the correlative element of matter, a notion, by the way, which now arises for the first time and which, as thus technically conceived, bears but an etymological resemblance to the speculative empirical "matter" of modern materialism Aristotle, probing still deeper, brought the hylomorphic view of realism to a remarkable state of development and showed by his reflective analysis the only way in which the basic concepts of experience and natural knowledge can be clarified as genuine conceptual apprehensions: reality, existence, being, truth, form, formula, matter, substance, change, motion, potentiality, actuality, and so forth. For only in so far as they are genuine apprehensions can they possibly serve as cognitive vehicles in our empirical knowledge of the real—cognition can be subserved only by cognition.

H. *Reflection and Empiricism.* Because reflection is wholly posterior to experience and has no other basis or object than that provided by naive empiricism, all its basic concepts must derive from thence. Without exception they take their rise in experience and pervade[2] all empirical knowledge even to its highest theoretical developments in history and natural science. But in so far as their role is solely to serve as vehicles of knowledge, they must, in subserving this original and very proper interest, remain implicit and unthematic, that is, not explicit cognitions in their own right For what they grasp—assuming that they are cognitions—is not real individuals or real parts thereof (themselves real individuals) but abstract yet objective parts or elements of the real, pervasive factors graspable by conception alone and hence purely conceptual "objects," coexperienced rather than experienced in all perception.

If hylomorphism appears to be unscientific and to populate the world with entities beyond the reach of scientific verification, entities savoring therefore of the occult, this can only result from an assumed conflict between realism and empiricism that simply cannot obtain Being not of the same rank, they cannot possibly enter the same lists as adversaries. Realism has no other access to the real than through naive experience It does not, therefore, presume to discover in the real, realities beyond the reach of natural inquiry. What it discovers is rather what empiricism already grasps implicitly but cannot of itself bring to explicit recognition and clarity, namely, the abstract elements which comprise the structure of the real For to say that they are abstract is to say that they do not exist in themselves as hylomorphic individuals and hence are not observable as such from the natural attitude. They are nonetheless "there" as objective constituents and factors of the real, only not in the sense of real parts empirically separable Hence it is that Aristotle's *Physics* and *Metaphysics* are sorely misunderstood when they are thought to compete with modern physics and natural science as though aiming to displace them For they are not empirical sciences but reflective sciences of the empirical.

Philosophical reflection arises, therefore, because empiricism possesses insights it knows not of In so far as it explains and clarifies these insights,

[2] For a detailed discussion of these "pervasive data" of experience, see *loc. cit*

reflection may with propriety claims to be a legitimate extension of naive empiricism and to merit the appellation "philosophical empiricism" or "radical empiricism " For the same reason it may claim to be a natural extension of "naive realism" and to merit the title "philosophical realism," the choice of titles being solely a matter of taste or propriety The extension in either case, however, is not to be viewed as a projective extrapolation based on the "results" of natural inquiry, but as an intensive and analytic immersion into the (cognitive) sources and vehicles of natural knowledge. Reflection, therefore, although not of the same order as naïve empiricism, is yet continuous with it and founded solidly upon it.

We can then see why it is that although the eidetic sciences are much concerned with forms or essences, there is yet no possible science of universals as such; that although the historical sciences are absorbed with individuals and particularity, there is yet no possible empirical science of existence or particularity as such; that although empirical knowledge is concerned with material and changing things, there is yet no possible empirical science of matter or change as such, and so on There can be no such sciences, simply because the natural attitude is directed primarily upon real individuals and their real parts, themselves real individuals There are, therefore, only empirical sciences of real individuals—eidetic or historical —and only a reflective science (hylomorphism) of their abstract, but objective and pervasive, components.[8]

There are, in the last analysis, but these two genuinely fundamental standpoints for human thought and theory. the natural standpoint of naive empiricism and the reflective standpoint of philosophy I experience the world and then in due course reflect thereon Since every act of consciousness has a reflective turn, naive experience bears in itself the seeds of reflection, so that reflection is no total stranger to the most naive common sense. Every man, whether he realize it or not, is bound to reflect now and then. But his reflection will be naive and casual so long as it remains unselfconscious and under the aegis of the natural attitude Only when in clear self-consciousness he attains to the reflective view of himself as reflecting on his awareness of the world, and takes his awareness seriously, will he find himself in a position to strike off on that distinctive path of inquiry known to the Occident as philosophy. Once embarked on this venture, he will discover that to "know thyself" is to know nothing less than the real.

In the hope that I have sufficiently clarified the reflective standpoint, I shall now turn to the cognitive relation of awareness on which my whole argument obviously turns Beginning with our presiding awareness of the world, I have contended throughout for the cognitive character of human

[8] For further consideration of these all-pervasive data as philosophical, not natural scientific, data, see *loc cit.*

experience as the root of all empirical knowledge. I have argued that experience as our primordial grasp of the real is a complex apprehension culminating in propositions and uniting within itself both perceptual and conceptual awareness, the latter manifesting itself in the basic concepts of natural knowledge These concepts, however, as ancillary to our empirical interests in real individuals, do not function in the natural attitude as proper insights. Only for reflection do they become explicit cognitions and give rise to the hylomorphic view of the real, but only if they are of the general nature of awareness. This all hinges, as I have repeatedly said, on taking awareness seriously and recognizing it from the very beginning as an irreducible and primitive feature of experience. To this all-important matter I now turn.

III THE INTENTIONAL NATURE OF CONSCIOUSNESS[4]

A. *Consciousness as Awareness of Something* Reflecting once again on my experience of the ink bottle, I now take note of the fact that the course of this experience—for experience is ever in process—may lead through varying modes of apprehension. Besides seeing the ink bottle, I may also touch it, later I can recall it and picture it to myself in imagination In imagination, too, I can anticipate its becoming empty and foresee the need of replacing it. I can also think about it, describe it to others, and write at length about it, and so on Now in all these modes of consciousness—seeing, sensing, perceiving, experiencing, imagining, recalling, anticipating, thinking, deliberating, and so forth—I am aware of one and the same ink bottle, and, indeed, I am aware of it *as the same* in each mode of contemplation. Its identity obviously is not in the least affected by the multiplicity of my apprehensions These, accordingly, despite their evident differences, have one object in common and are all of them but several distinct ways in which I can be conscious of one and the same thing They must, therefore, as apprehensions, be distinct not only from one another but also from the object which in this case they share in common.

As modes of awareness, differing among themselves and distinct from their object, they are obviously but so many ways of being *conscious of something* This generic feature is the primary characteristic of all awareness· To be conscious at all means to be conscious of something—*of* something other than the conscious act itself—to have before one's gaze an object as that *of* which one is aware. This object, I repeat, must be something other than the awareness itself and in every case distinguishable from it As awareness, therefore, consciousness always involves the polar duality

[4] For further discussions of intentionality, see Francis Parker's essay, pp. 158 ff , and Henry Veatch, pp 179 ff

of consciousness and object, which we may signify either as "consciousness of object" or as "object of consciousness," the difference being but a matter of emphasis

For this reason there is no such thing as consciousness simply, as there are objects simply, but only consciousness of object, which ceases even to be consciousness if we as much as attempt to remove the object

Now consciousness in all its modes is *awareness of something* Whenever I perceive, I perceive something Whenever I think, I think of something, and so on Some modes of consciousness, to be sure, may be more than mere awareness. When I am angry at somebody, for instance, I am not merely cognizant of him but am also regarding him in a way that is obviously more than merely cognitive, for it clearly involves emotion, evaluation, and so forth Most of the modes of consciousness in our normal daily lives are of this more complicated nature and hence are more than mere awareness But—and this is the important thing—these modes all include awareness as an indispensable basis and hence are never less than awareness. It would therefore be more accurate to say that consciousness in all its modes is at least awareness and that the phrase "consciousness of object" is a minimum formula of consciousness which reveals at once why there can properly be no such thing as consciousness simply, as there can be objects simply, but only consciousness of objects. This in turn suggests that consciousness is not a proper object of the natural attitude, for which all things are objects simply, but a matter for reflection alone For this reason empirical psychology must ever remain, *qua* merely empirical, an enigmatic and superficial account of consciousness.[5] It is with this basic minimum, consciousness as mere cognition, that I am concerned in this essay. The more complex or "higher" modes, based upon the cognitive, I shall leave for a subsequent analysis.

It pertains, then, to the cognitive nature of consciousness that in every act it have an object or that it possess an intrinsic reference to an object which is other than the act itself. Being intrinsic to the act, this "objective reference" is such that no act can properly be described without specifying also what object it is "of " Thus it is not sufficient to say of an act that it is a visual perception of something. I must, in order to identify the act and to distinguish it from others of the same kind, say also what this something is. I must state, for example, not merely that "I see something," but also that "I see the ink bottle," or "I see the pencil," and so forth Otherwise I could not significantly distinguish between two acts of seeing In describing an act, therefore, two things *at least* must be specified One, we must state its *mode*, that is, that it is a perception (visual, auditory, and so forth) or a

⁵ See below, p 27, for a further reason why empirical psychology must fail of its object—consciousness.

recollection or an anticipation or a conception, and so on; and two, we must carefully state its specific objective reference, for this no less than the former *is an essential part of the act and not a part of the object* But what, more precisely, is this objective reference?

B. *Awareness Is Intentionality.* The classical term for this reference is *intentio* or "intentionality" To say that consciousness is awareness of something is exactly the same as saying that consciousness is intentional, or to say that consciousness has necessarily an objective reference is the same as saying that consciousness necessarily has intentionality The word *intentio* means, etymologically, a stretching or reaching toward or at, implying an exertion of will. It is primarily with this sense of will or volition that the word "intention" is commonly used today, as when we say, "His intentions are not clear." As used to signify the cognitive essence of consciousness, however, this aspect of will recedes from prominence, and emphasis is laid instead upon the directedness of our conscious glance upon something as its object This directedness toward a particular object may well spring from an exertion of will, so that cognition is always at bottom voluntary. But, even so, the volition involved is purely cognitive, its "aim" is solely to grasp and bring to awareness the object "intended" Intention, therefore, as cognitive essence, is to be sharply distinguished from intention in the more familiar sense of signifying a deliberative act of will. The latter is "higher" and presupposes the former, as above noted.

C *Intentional Presence or Existence* Intentionality is thus but a technical and venerable term for awareness, and intention but a synonym for objective reference, so that to specify this reference, which the description of every act requires, is also to specify the intention and hence to further our understanding of the cognitive relation In order to get at this intention or objective reference still further and, particularly, to distinguish it from the intended object, let us consider an instance where the two can hardly be confused. I am "thinking" about Shakespeare, reviewing what little I know about him, imagining to myself what he may have looked like, and in other specific ways making him the intended object of my contemplation. Now in thus thinking of him, William Shakespeare himself—and nothing else— is "present" to my mind, directly and unmistakably—not really present, of course, but only *intentionally* or *cognitively* present. And this intentional presence, something of my own doing, consists chiefly in my presumed knowledge of him, in which and through which he stands before me, in a precise sense, as the specifically and concretely intended object of which I am now aware.

In slightly different words, as I think about Shakespeare, I have *thoughts*

of him, and in *thinking these thoughts* of him I am *thinking about him*—
that is, about Shakespeare himself and not about my thinking or my
thoughts of him These latter are objects only for reflection, so that we must
carefully distinguish between the naive awareness of Shakespeare and the
reflective study of this awareness. From the reflective point of view, the
naive awareness is seen to consist in "thinking thoughts about Shakespeare,"
but in such wise that the thinking and the thoughts are themselves quite
unnoticed, because they are not the object intended. They are rather integral parts or vehicles of the intention, the specific instrumentalities by
which the intended object—Shakespeare—is brought to cognitive presence
and invested with a kind of intentional existence or *esse intentionale.* The
intentional existence or presence in this case excludes Shakespeare's real
existence, or *esse reale,* for I intend the bard among other things as de-
ceased. His presence, therefore, involves only his intentional existence,
which results from my thinking about him and which I distinguish, even in
my naiveté, although without fully realizing it, from his real existence, in
so far, at least, as I realize that my awareness of him may be incorrect and,
in any case, inadequate.

This all means that in thinking of Shakespeare I do not have two objects
before my mind's eye, the poet himself and my intentional duplicate or
awareness of him It is the poet alone of whom I am naively aware, and it is
solely reflection that subsequently discovers in the awareness itself the intentional duplicate of him. Thus awareness intends the object naively and
directly, the very object itself, and in its cognitive absorption with the object "constitutes," as part of the intending, an intentional duplicate of the
intended thing. Hence my "thoughts of Shakespeare" *are in an intentional
sense Shakespeare himself,* they are my consciousness "becoming" one with
its object. I thus "become" the object, however, only intentionally, not
really, and I acknowledge this distinction between intentional and real
being when I speak of my "thoughts of Shakespeare," for I thereby imply
that Shakespeare as a thought is a far different thing from Shakespeare the
Elizabethan poet—even though in another respect they are also one and
the same William Shakespeare.

So far, then, I mean by the objective reference this intending an object
through its intentional duplicate. There is, however, still more to be noted

D *Noesis and Noema.* In all awareness, consciousness becomes its object
in the sense of becoming an intentional duplicate of it, whereby the object
itself acquires an intentional existence in addition to its real existence. Now
as a performance of consciousness, there is involved here the inseparable
duality of doing and deed, of intending and intention. The former is the
active or dynamic phase of doing and is appropriately expressed by the

participle The latter is the more static and structural aspect of what is done, namely, the *esse intentionale* of the object, and is expressed by the substantive. Even ordinary usage reflects this duality. Thus, as in *thinking* I have a *thought* of something, so in *sensing* I have a *sensation* of something, in *perceiving* I have a *perception* of something, in *experiencing* an *experience* of something, in *conceiving* a *conception* of something, in *judging* a *judgment* (proposition) about something, and so on In every case of awareness both aspects are present, the one incapable of occurring without the other, and they form in conjunction what I call the concrete individual act of intentionality or, simply, the intentional act of consciousness The individual act is thus the unit of consciousness, much as the cell is the biological unit of life, experience itself playing the role of the organism

This dual structure of the intentional act is but a special case of the general hylomorphic structure of the real, for every act of awareness is a "reality" Offhand it might look as though the process were a kind of making or constituting which produces the duplicate as an end product, detachable from the process and existing fully only when the process is over and done with, as an automobile comes into being at the end of an assembly line. Such, however, is not at all the case; process and duplicate form a unity wholly unlike that of a manufacturing operation and its finished article It is rather like that of a piano sonata and its actual rendition, the actual playing being the material condition of the existence of the sonata in its full actuality, the sonata being in turn the formal condition of the rendering, the "what" that is played. Process and duplicate, intending and intention, are inseparably united as doing and deed, and are thus related as matter and form.

The process "supports" the duplicate in the sense of providing, like matter, existence and particularity In itself a purely temporal occurrence, the process as such merely comes to pass and is swept away in the stream of consciousness, receding ever deeper into the irretrievable past. It can only occur once and never recur, just as a rendering of a sonata is a unique event which can never literally be repeated It can only be succeeded by other (unique) renditions of the same sonata. Husserl calls this dynamical phase of the act its noetic aspect or "noesis," a term which I shall henceforth employ.

The duplicate, on the other hand, as the specific character, or essence, of the act, the "what" of every noetic occurrence, is that aspect in which the act is *describable* as a "perception of the ink bottle," a "recollection of the last eclipse," a "thought about Shakespeare," and so forth. It is also that aspect in which an act is *repeatable* as the "same" experience, the "same" recollection, the "same" thought, and so on, just as the "same" sonata may be repeatedly rendered. Thus whereas the noesis, like the rendition, is in every instance a new and unique occurrence, the duplicate on the contrary may be the "same" in many noeses, as the sontata may be the same in many renditions, or an essence the same for many real objects Husserl calls the intentional duplicate the noematic aspect of the act or its "noema," and this term, too, I shall henceforth employ

An act of individual awareness is, then, the concrete unity of noesis and noema, just as every reality is the concrete unity of matter and form. Like matter and form generally, noesis and noema are abstract parts of acts and hence are discernible by reflection alone They are inaccessible to introspection or naive reflection, because, like all naive modes of awareness, introspection is primarily of real individuals.

It is for this reason that empirical psychology in treating of cognition has hardly advanced beyond an inventory of acts and their associative connections Unable to grasp the cognitive essence of consciousness, hence also the nature of the higher valuative acts, the empirical study of the psyche tends to dwell in the conditions physical, physiological, social, and so forth that "underlie" it, under the mistaken notion that these material substrata stand to the psyche as cause to effect and not as matter to form. Hence it is hardly surprising that consciousness as psychical, thus misconceived, should be "reduced" to the physical and that its empirical study should tend to become a "psychology without a psyche "[6]

Theoretical reflection alone is in a position to correct this systematic error by showing first of all the need of advancing beyond naive empiricism—primary and inviolable as it is—to the wider transcendental standpoint of realism This higher standpoint, it is worth repeating, does not suspend or alter the former in any way, but embraces it and exploits it to the full, attaining through it to insights which it alone can originate but never clarify Among these insights is that of the noema of intentionality, wherein, I think, we can now behold what idealists and empiricists have been trying to get at for generations under the title "idea." For as intentional duplicate it is at once both subjective idea and objective thing (intentionally) and hence an ambivalent entity quite enigmatic to the casual notice

E *Parmenidean Identity in Experience and Truth* The noema, as we have seen, is an abstract or "ideal" part of the intention (not of the intended) and is the form or essence of the act. Being of the nature of form, it can conceivably enter into "formal" coincidence or identity with the form of the intended object, since it, too, is a unity of form and matter Thus (intentional) act and (intended) object may have the same form, and "truth"

[6] See above, p 23 If reflection has thus shown the essential impossibility of a natural science of consciousness, the fact can no longer surprise us that there is no empirical psychology but only a congeries of speculative theories of mind, personality, and so forth

would signify precisely this sameness or identity of form wherein the intentional being of an object coincides or coalesces with its real being—a
situation obviously requiring, besides the intentional presence of the object,
also its real or actual presence. This dual presence defines for us the term
"experience" in its most primitive sense: Experience is that mode of awareness which occurs only in the actual presence of the object and which consummates in the (formal) coincidence of intentional and real existence (or
noematic and objective form). Experience and truth are thus at bottom
correlative terms. The formal coincidence they require is clearly the culminating point of all awareness or intentionality, the final and fulfilling
moment of all cognition. This coincidence, I think, is what Parmenides had
in mind when he asserted the "sameness of thought and being"—τὸ γὰρ αὐτὸ
νοεῖν ἐστίν τε καὶ εἶναι. (Frag. 5, Diels, Fragmente der Vorsokratiker, I, 152).

This Parmenidean coincidence of form is a subject obviously calling for
further and careful study. For it is not clear from my analysis how form can
serve in a dual capacity and inhere in such totally different individuals as a
real object and the awareness of it. It would seem on the face of it that the
matters involved must play a decisive role, one kind of matter conspiring
with the form "tree," for example, to produce a real tree and another kind
of matter conspiring with the "same" form to produce the perception of
the tree, or a thought of it, and so forth. This would require for its clarification a very detailed study of the whole form-matter complex and its hierarchical order—a study of the highest importance but lying outside the
scope of this paper.[7]

F. *Sense Perception and Its Intention.* Of experience, however, something
further must be said, and especially of that primordial phase of experience
called "the sense perception of outer objects." For in this case the object is
intentionally present by virtue of its sensuous appearances or perspectives.
Now whatsoever I see or hear or grasp sensuously must be seen or heard or
sensed from a certain angle, at a given distance, under these or those particular circumstances, conditions of illumination and visibility, alertness
and sensitivity of my sense organs, and so forth. All these factors are real
and empirical, and play a decisive role in all my perceivings, conspiring to
make the total perceptual situation exceedingly complex in every case and
my apprehension of it no less so. Summing these up in the statement that
whatsoever I sensuously behold can only be beheld through *objectively
grounded* perspectives from definite *real* points of view, we may then also
assert as its correlate that the real can manifest itself sensuously only
through appearances.

Experience on its purely sensuous side is thus but a congeries of perspec-

[7] Again see Parker's essay, already cited in Note 4, above.

tives or appearances in ceaseless flux, no one of which is final and definitive so as to embrace all the rest, properly modified, within one over-all and complete view. There is no such absolute sensuous view, all are equally perspectival and relative to a standpoint with its attendant real circumstances

Were perception nothing more than sensuous awareness, it would consist exclusively of these "sense data," combined under the aegis of imagination and memory into momentary unities of apprehension This kind of apprehension, however, being preconceptual, would, as I mentioned above, be inexpressible because lacking in the conceptual apprehensions which alone bring about that articulated grasp characteristic of human experience in its contextual wholeness.

G. *The Role of Conception in Perceiving.* Taking conception as a mode of awareness or intentionality, we can roughly picture its original activity in conjunction with sensation as that of penetrating the apprehensions of sense and attaining through them to a direct grasp of those objective but abstract factors of the real which are the philosophic data pervading all experience. The data of sense are suitable vehicles for conception because they are originally intentional or cognitive in character, genuine appearances of the real and not mere states of consciousness like pain or anger, and so forth Perceiving, therefore, as we know and practice it, is more than merely sensing; it is also using our sense data, not as bases for discursive inference, but as refracting media through which the discerning glance of conception reaches not only *to* the appearing object but also *into* it, as it were, to its pervasive structural elements, through which alone the object can be articulately grasped as a concrete individual and expressed (as thus grasped) in propositional form. All this, of course, on the assumption that conceiving is a kind of awareness, a way of apprehending things—or comprehending them—and not an alleged subjective manipulation of so-called generalities or universals solely "mental" or "logical" in their provenience and non-cognitive in nature.

That in thus penetrating the data of sense, conception also synthesizes these data is evident But the synthesis here involved, unlike the synthesis of Kant, is not a prior condition of perception, an anterior process of constituting both perception and its object, but rather a cognitive synthesis *in* apprehension, that is, a uniting or "comprehending" which is one with the apprehending itself. In other words, perception and experience are not the results or end products of a synthetic process a priori, but are themselves synthetic or comprehensive apprehensions whose structured unity is prescribed solely by the nature of the real, that is, by the intended objects in their togetherness and not by consciousness itself whose (cognitive) nature is to apprehend the real—as it is.

Conception fuses in this wise with sensation to yield perception and experience. Like all awareness, perception involves intentional duplication of its object, determined in this case by the real presence of the object through the sensuous perspectives that reveal it. The object being both really and intentionally present, there may now occur that formal coincidence of real and intentional existence which is the hallmark of (true) perception It is this Parmenidean identity of *esse intentionale* and *esse reale* that gives to experience in all its forms its compelling sense of finality and fulfillment and reveals it (to reflection) as the primordial mode of awareness, than which no more ultimate mode can be conceived; there can be no further grasp than that of the "object itself."

H. *The Tentative Nature of Sense Perception.* This is not to say, however, that sense perception is final and definitive in any absolute fashion; for it clearly is not The real can be sensuously grasped only through its appearances, and although the primary office of appearances is to reveal, they can also conceal For one thing, sensible appearances are very complex functions of the whole perceptual situation—including as it does subject, object, intervening medium, and so forth—so that their penetration is often difficult and misleading Also, they are potentially infinite and hence inexhaustible in number And, finally, they are temporally dispersed throughout the duration of the object, thus making memory indispensable—and memory is not infallible—thus pointing up the fact that every sensory coincidence (or verification) is unavoidably momentary as well as partial, and therefore intrinsically subject to revision, or even cancellation, by subsequent experience.

But although this possibility of error attaches without exception to every individual act of sense perception, it does not attach to experience itself as a living whole. For the contemplated modifications can only be brought about by subsequent acts which are themselves parts of the same experience It is thus not only the fallibility of human perception that is to be asserted but also, and as its condition, the correctibility of perception by further perception. When these are both asserted, as they must be, the integrity of experience is not threatened by the general fallibility of perception, as is so often assumed, it is rather quickened and vitalized by the possibility of self-correction, which alone enables us even to recognize the errors of perception.

In the case of sense perception, therefore, the formal coincidence of intention and object is no static affair like superposing homologous triangles in geometry. It is rather an unremitting process in which each coincidence is but the passing and momentary fruition of intention The process, however, is also cumulative and progressive, which means that the present is ever securely bound to the accomplished past and to the open future, giving these a kind of contemporaneity and thus serving as the vital point where the dynamical whole of experience comes ever to focus as a unity embracing all time.

This is obviously a matter calling for an exhaustive study beyond the limits of my present undertaking. I must therefore restrict myself to the rather casual observation that the momentary coincidence even in its transience is also the ever-present consummating phase of intentional fulfillment—the ever changing and yet abiding "now" phase of experience in which we are in constant living contact with the real Experience thus consummates, as it were, in every present act of perception, and in the succession of acts, it pursues its course as one progressive fulfilling and reinforcing of intentionality or awareness Only in this ongoing fashion, at once sequential and contextual, can the real become manifest as the one world of experience Only thus, too, can experience consolidate and correct itself, all the while remaining our one experience of the real.

Not all perception, however, is an intentional duplication through appearances. This is a characteristic of "outer" sense perception alone. There are no appearances in the case of introspective observation. A feeling or an emotion, for example, has no perspectives We can contemplate it in different relations, to be sure, as we deliberate on its consequences or grounds. But in itself it is utterly incapable of being viewed from a multiplicity of standpoints like an object of sense Similarly, experience itself as an object of reflection is incapable of being viewed now from this side, now from that. It can be more or less deliberately intended, more or less clearly discerned, and so forth But these variations are not in any literal sense perspectives of the object, they are rather attentional phases of clarity, distinctness, and adequacy in our grasp.

IV. REALITY AND THE CONSCIOUS SUBJECT

A *The Subject of Awareness.* The structure of intentionality or awareness is reflectively before us. The act is a real individual, concrete of noesis and noema In the case of truth (originally, true perception) the intention coincides with its object in the Parmenidean sameness of noematic and objective form Correlatively, the intended object has acquired besides its *esse reale* also an *esse intentionale,* the latter being the noema of the act wherein consciousness "becomes" its object Such, in outline, is what is signified by the minimum formula "consciousness of object."

There is, however, a radical incompleteness in this picture of awareness, in so far as it makes no reference to the subject of consciousness, which alone can be aware of anything at all. For consciousness itself is obviously not conscious, or unconscious, of anything Only the conscious self or sub-ject can be aware or intend. The alleged minimum formula accordingly turns out to have been something less than a true minimum, it is a trun-cated version and must be amended to read· "I am conscious of something." Thus I must now take into account the reflective part of the experiential proposition, "I see the ink bottle," which I formerly disregarded in order to focus exclusively on the objective grasp it contained This being the true minimum, no further corrections will be necessary.

It is not always that we thus formulate our experiential grasp of things More often than not we leave off the "I think," "I perceive," and so forth, and content ourselves with a statement of the object alone Thus I am more likely to say "The children are home," "The milk has arrived," and the like. These locutions serve their purpose quite adequately, for our interest (in-tention) in the natural attitude is invariably focused on the object in ques-tion But it is important to see that from the reflective standpoint these are all elliptical expressions and carry with them even in the natural attitude an implied "I think that. ," "I see ," and so on As Kant correctly put it, the "I think" must be able to attend every act of consciousness. And this means that every act, no matter how intensely it may be focused upon the object, is also an incipient (reflective) awareness of the acting subject As I remarked before, there is a reflexive phase in all human awareness—all object-consciousness is also (although only implicitly) self-conscious-ness Theoretical reflection, accordingly, is but a systematic and explicitly self-conscious development of this original naive reflexivity inherent in every act of consciousness

By the subject of consciousness I mean nothing other than myself as I really am—a real, living human being or person, the conscious psycho-physical individual we all know ourselves to be As such, I am *in* the world and conscious *of* the world. It is precisely this "I" who is related intention-ally in every act of consciousness to the object it contemplates. In other words, *intentionality relates not consciousness and object but subject and object—consciousness itself being the intentional or cognitive relation* Consciousness, too, is related to its object, but this relation is solely that of Parmenidean coincidence which is in no wise to be confused with aware-ness or intentionality itself This coincidence of form is only a factor in awareness, its fulfilling or consummating moment Awareness itself is vastly more, namely, consciousness with its noetic-noematic structure as indi-vidual act of an intending subject

B. *Intentionality Relates Subject and Object* Awareness then, or intention-ality, relates not consciousness and object but (conscious) subject and object, and it can be likened to an illuminating beam issuing from a searchlight. Awareness emanates from the ego as its source and focuses by the noesis-noema mechanism upon its object, flooding it with a directed (intentional) beam of apprehension. Although admittedly analogical, there is something appropriate in the image of the ego as a radiating source of awareness (intentionality or cognitive consciousness), illuminating and bringing the real to light. It brings out in any case the directedness or vectorial character of intentionality as issuing from the conscious subject and terminating in the object—even though the object, as in the case of reflection, be the subject itself.

In one respect, however, the analogy may be completely misleading, namely, if it suggests that awareness is a kind of empirical disturbance propagated *from subject to object*, as light and sound are propagated *from object to subject* For unlike these latter, awareness has no velocity and travels through no medium. Not being empirical at all, it traverses space and time in a wholly unique sense which can only be called cognitive or transcendental. Thus to hold with the ancients that sight emanates from the eye, as though reversing the path of light, need not entail any conflict with modern optics or acoustics. For although it involves light, sound, and so forth, as indispensable material bases, sense perception will not "reduce" to these empirical conditions or take its place in their midst. As intentional, it is a "phenomenon" of higher order accessible to reflection alone—but only because it is an integral factor in the real, coeval with its empirical aspects and as such presupposed by all naive empiricism.

The full intentional situation then involves these three elements· (intending) subject, (intentional) consciousness, and (intended) object. Consciousness is the mediating term connecting the other two It attaches to these latter, however, in very different ways. As act of the subject, consciousness is wholly internal and immanent to it, whereas to the object it is just as external and transient. For my acts comprise the intimate concrete detail of my life, I "live" in them But to the object my personal acts are quite indifferent—in so far as they are merely cognitively "of" it. They touch it, so to speak, only from the outside by way of a formal coincidence that is quite incidental to the object itself and hence utterly incapable of altering it, let alone making or constituting it.

Consciousness as awareness or intentional relation, therefore, is internal to the subject but external to the object. Being purely a one-way or vectorial connection, which can obtain in one direction only, namely, from subject to object, it really relates the subject to the object, but because of its irreversibility it only nominally relates the object to the subject Thus, for example, my knowledge of Shakespeare really relates me to him, but it only nominally relates him to me, since my awareness of him can hardly be accounted a factor in his life and doings. In short, then, intentionality (consciousness), because it is internal to the subject, really relates the subject to the object, but because it is external to the object, it only nominally relates the object to the subject.

We tacitly acknowledged this state of affairs when in introducing the expression "object of consciousness," we noted that by the object in this expression we meant exactly the same thing as by the object simply. It is precisely the same object in both cases because the relation to consciousness, which is explicit in the one case and implicit in the other, is purely external to the object and nominal. With consciousness, or rather the conscious subject, the situation is different. Intentionality here is internal and real, so that there is no such thing as consciousness simply, but solely consciousness of object—or "I am conscious of an object"

C. *The Intentional and Existential Domain of Consciousness.* This being the nature of consciousness in its capacity as awareness, we can now see that by the field or domain of consciousness two very different things are to be understood Intentionally, the range of consciousness is without possible limit, there being nothing I cannot become aware of or intend in some way or other. In this respect there is nothing outside or beyond consciousness, it is all-embracing, because everything conceivable is within it absolutely, that is, without possible reference to an outside. Consciousness in this sense is transcendental correlate of the real and "includes" everything —*intentionally.*

Empirically, however, or existentially, consciousness does not include everything. For consciousness really contains its own acts and their components and embraces these in the contextual unity of itself as one life and experience In its empirical existence, therefore, consciousness is the inwardness of a conscious subject and is really contained within the real world. In this respect there is an outside to consciousness, namely, the real exclusive of myself.

I have now described the cognitive relation and answered the question· How can consciousness both contain the real and be contained by it? Intentionally, consciousness contains the real, empirically or existentially, the real contains consciousness. The force of this reply depends entirely upon the success of the reader in framing to himself a clear notion of intentionality as the essence of consciousness and in seeing that it must remain forever unclarified—even though presupposed—by the natural attitude of empiricism

Reflection alone can bring it to light and, in so doing, discover consciousness in its transcendental sense as correlate of the real This discovery, however, in no way abrogates the deliverance of naive empiricism that consciousness is but one of many realities making up the world and that it is, so far, but the psychical correlate—the real inwardness—of an organism. Reflection retains this insight intact and shows how both aspects, although of different levels, are yet supplementary and needs must be combined in any complete view of consciousness as that reality whose nature is to know the real.

For philosophical reflection, therefore, consciousness and reality are indissolubly conjoined in a twofold bond that reflection alone can clarify To know the one is to know the other. If knowing the one be realism and knowing the other phenomenology, then the two disciplines must be inseparable correlates. Husserl, I know, would writhe at this "naively realistic" desecration of phenomenology, for it is indeed a complete rejection of his idealistic theory of transcendental constitution. But if this idealistic theory is, as I think, a speculative venture resulting from his mistaken notion that the cognitive relation is internal at both ends, then in rejecting his idealism we can, by making the needful allowances, retain the bulk of his remarkable analyses. It is with this understanding that I use the term "phenomenology." I use it also out of deference and gratitude, for it is he above all moderns who has taught me to look and see, and indeed in such wise as to see not only with Husserl himself but with others as well, and above all with Aristotle and Thomas. My indebtedness to these three is so unmistakable as to render needless any specific acknowledgments.

II

Phenomenology and Metaphysics

JOHN WILD, *Harvard University*

MODERN "empiricists" have taught us that where there are no distinctive, brute data by which theories can be checked, there can be no distinct, scientific discipline Without brute data there can be only wishful dreams and irresponsible speculation, not science. This is certainly correct

They have also convinced many people, including some philosophers, that there are no distinctively philosophical data, that all given facts belong to the province of some special science If this is true, philosophy must abandon any claim to being a distinct and autonomous discipline If it has any distinctive functions at all, these can be only the purely subordinate tasks of criticizing scientific method and of unifying the reliable results of the different sciences, though, as the positivists argue, it would seem that such tasks can be better performed by scientists actually familiar with the given data. This widely held thesis is, in my opinion, certainly false, as I shall try to show in this paper.

In the first part (Sections I–III) I shall begin by examining five current conceptions of the immediate data of awareness (Section I), each of which fails to recognize certain immediate data and is, therefore, incomplete or reductionist in character Then (Section II) I shall attempt to outline briefly a nonreductionist or realistic account of these immediate data. Finally (Section III) I shall try to show that there are certain pervasive data, quite distinct from those of the special sciences, which require philosophical analysis and explanation. If this account is sound, the place of philosophy as a distinct scientific discipline must be recognized by any consistent empiricist

In the second part of the paper (Sections IV–VI) I shall single out the most pervasive of these data, existence, for special treatment. From the very beginning of realistic philosophy in the West, this datum has been recognized as the peculiar object of the most fundamental of all the philosophical disciplines, metaphysics, or as it is more appropriately called, first philosophy I shall begin (Section IV) with a brief discussion of two first principles which apply in general to being as such. Then (Section V) I shall present a summary of the chief results which have been so far achieved by a realistic analysis of the finite entities which are directly presented in human experience Finally (Section VI) I shall conclude with a condensed statement of that inferential argument to an unobserved primary being to which such an analysis must lead.

Since the time of its first origins in Greece, realism has been a mode of philosophizing which is *radically empirical* in method Such a method must be sharply opposed to any theory of innate ideas and any form of rationalistic apriorism which would conceive the task of scientific understanding along Kantian lines, as one of molding or constructing some form of order out of raw data, and would thus subordinate the given data of experience to other supposedly nonempirical sources of knowledge For the realist, the first canon of sound scientific procedure is the ruthless subordination of all inferential interpretation and theoretical construction to the data as they are given, no matter how extraordinary or unexpected they may be

These data are often confused and partial. Hence inference and constructive interpretation must play a necessary, but *subordinate*, role in the attainment of knowledge The partiality of the data must be completed by rational inference to other entities not immediately given Obscure and murky data must be clarified and explained, but not explained away If the inference is to be sound, it must be based upon data that are immediately given with constraining evidence. If an explanatory hypothesis is to have any real, cognitive value, it must explain precisely what is indubitably given and what can be inferred from *this*, not something else Hence the first task, underlying all further phases of the cognitive enterprise, must be that of describing and analyzing the data which are immediately given to awareness and which cannot be doubted without doubting the cognitive faculties in general and therefore abandoning the whole noetic enterprise

What are these immediately given data: *les données immédiates de la conscience?*

For a realist, as for any radical empiricist, this crucial question must be continually raised, for it concerns the ultimate foundation upon which all genuine knowledge, as opposed to wishful dreams and a priori theories of the world in which we live, must be based Unless we are constantly brought back to the actual brute data by such questions as these, there is a constant danger of confusing them with some brilliant theory of what the data must be If this happens, the noetic enterprise may appear to be making magnificent progress Interesting deductions of extraordinary entities may be made, thus greatly increasing the apparent scope of human knowledge—except that they are not based on any data actually presented Brilliant explanatory theories of vast range may be erected, from which a wealth of conclusions may be deduced—except that what the theory is supposed primarily to explain and clarify does not happen to be the case. I think that it is peculiarly important to raise this question at the present time when the term "empiricism" has become almost a sacred word, universally taken for granted but very seldom carefully examined.

We are literally surrounded by schools of thought each claiming to be thoroughly empirical in its methodology, each claiming to know exactly what experience must be, but each with a view of the data quite opposed to that of all the rest. No one school seems to be as interested in examining the complex data, in order to clarify and justify its claim, as in developing its deductive consequences and applying these to the a priori solution of abstruse problems as well as to the a priori refutation of opposed theories. Surely the first task of any sound empiricist is simply to describe and analyze the brute data, which are usually extremely obscure and complex. The task of such description is arduous and hazardous.

Has this task been seriously undertaken by the "empirical" thinkers of recent times? Or do they rather tend to follow pretty much the a priori procedure of Hume (reputedly an empiricist), who in the very first paragraph of his "empirical" treatise lays down in no uncertain terms exactly what experience necessarily must be (impressions and ideas) with no careful examination of the actual evidence, and then proceeds with ruthless consistency to deduce the many negative consequences which logically follow from this very simple view of the actual data? How often do present-day philosophers seriously compare their usually rather restricted view of what the data *must be* with the actual data *as they are?* How often do they devote themselves to the arduous task of describing a datum, not as it should be, but precisely as it is given, with all the richness, complexity, and obscurity of actual experience? Is it any wonder that artificially simplified and surprisingly restricted views of the actual data are now widely current and extremely influential? This suspicion is verified by recent phenomenological studies, largely of European origin.

In order to illustrate this point, let us examine a few conceptions of the immediate data of experience which are now widely current in this country I do not believe that any of them can be defended in the light of even a rather superficial examination of the amazingly rich and variegated data as they are given.

I. Five Current Conceptions of the Immediate Data of Awareness

By an immediate datum I refer to any empirical item which is thrust upon awareness with constraining evidence Such data can of course be questioned, and must be questioned, by a consistent skeptic, but only at the cost of abandoning the whole noetic enterprise The term, as I use it, excludes two mediate factors (1) inference and (2) constructive interpretation *Immediate* data can only be described as they are given Any addition to data as thus described, any completion purporting to supply what is implicit in the data but not explicitly recognizable by a patient observer, any inference "demanded" by the data, to non-given factors, are ruled out as mediate. Realistic philosophy maintains that the immediate data of experience as thus defined are much wider and richer than is commonly supposed at the present time In order to test this thesis let us briefly examine five restricted views of experience which have exerted a wide influence in modern and recent thought. They are not mutually exclusive Some thinkers hold two or three of them at once But for the sake of clarity, we shall analyze them one by one

A *The Immediate Data as Structureless and Ineffable* The most restricted view of the data that has been defended by contemporary thinkers is that of Professor C I Lewis and the allied view of Professor F. S. C Northrop. According to Professor Lewis, there are indeed immediate data (referred to in the plural). But aside from this minimum degree of structure, they are without form and are, therefore, ineffable As such, of course, they have no cognitive status whatsoever.[1]

"They" must simply be accepted as presented. The *cognitive* task begins with the attempt to *interpret* these data, with practical needs in mind Such interpretation involves the imposition of schemes of classification and interpretation which have no foundation in the data themselves. On this view, the task of "describing" such data is obviously impossible and even absurd. Any description would involve the imposition of concepts arbitrarily chosen for pragmatic reasons.

Professor Northrop's view of the immediate data is very similar, though he would refrain from the plural form For him the immediate datum of experience is a structureless continuum,[2] which is identified with the ineffable object of oriental mysticism [3] As such, of course, it cannot be described Any such description would involve the imposition of postulational categories It can only be gaped at in a mystic trance.

These radically restricted theories of the immediate data seem to me to be radically false for three major reasons. In the first place, I find them both to be empirically false to the immediate data of experience as I find them. It is true that, with Mr. Northrop, I find a certain unity in the data.

[1] C I Lewis, *An Analysis of Knowledge and Valuation* (La Salle, Ill., Open Court, 1946), pp 21 and 25 ff
[2] F. S C. Northrop. *The Logic of the Sciences and the Humanities* (New York, Macmillan, 1947), pp 40 ff , especially pp 48–49
[3] Northrop, *The Meeting of East and West* (New York, Macmillan, 1946), pp 332 ff.

They all share in existence. In this sense they are one. But, with Mr. Lewis, I also find that they constitute a plurality of very different items [4] Many data are marked off from others by radical, specific differences. As soon as I open my eyes in the light, I am presented with a rich expanse of divergent data, marked off by further differences in spatial location and color It is needless to give further examples from other channels of awareness I am immediately presented with a vast array of partly confused but richly structuralized data, full of lacunae and fading off into vague horizons far from the focus of attention. The complex and variegated structure of this vast field may be at first glance very confused and obscure But it is certainly structuralized.

In the second place, it is possible for me to focus on some phase of this vast wealth of structure and to devote myself to the task of describing it just as it is given, with no infusion of constructive interpretation or inference If I have ever tried to do this, I may be aware of the extreme difficulty of this task But I certainly recognize it as possible. The view that I cannot clearly distinguish between an accurate description of what is given and some constructive interpretation of it is clearly false. If this were so, men would never argue together about the actual nature of some event they have both witnessed, and the criticism of testimony by witnesses at a court trial would be absurd

Not only would this be absurd, but the whole conception of empirical verification, which lies at the very heart of scientific procedure would be indefensible How are highly structuralized and intelligible theories to be verified by empirical data that are unstructuralized and ineffable? But the first canon of sound scientific procedure is the supremacy of the brute data, no matter how unexpected or how embarrassing they may be, over any hypothesis or theory, no matter how convenient it may be. Intelligible theories can be compared with the actual data Hence the theory of unstructured data is false.

B. *Essentialism and the Ruling Out of Existence as a Datum.* A second reductionist view of the data is due to a universal tendency of the human mind which received exaggerated emphasis in the philosophy of Descartes and which, through him, has exerted a determining influence on the whole course of post-Cartesian philosophy This tendency is now widely referred to as "essentialism"[5] It may be briefly described in the following manner

The concrete data presented to us in experience are marked off from one another by distinct, structural determinations which are readily abstracted

[4] See Section V of this paper.

[5] For a general description of this tendency and for historical illustrations of it, see Etienne Gilson, *Being and Some Philosophers* (Toronto, Pontifical Institute of Mediaeval Studies, 1949)

from the concrete and clearly grasped by the human mind These essences may be not only mentally separated from their concrete context but also mentally separated from one another and clearly characterized and defined. Regarded abstractly in this way, each is necessarily fixed and changeless Each idea, or essence, is necessarily what it is and cannot be anything else without contradiction. Twoness cannot become threeness They are changeless, nontendential essences Greenness cannot change into yellowness No one has any tendency to another. Each is merely what it is. The clear and distinct ideas of Cartesian methodology are all concerned with such abstract essences.

There are other data, however, just as evidently and just as indubitably thrust upon our noetic faculties, which cannot be grasped by ideas that are distinct and clear One of these is the all-pervasive datum of existence, which permeates every datum in the vast field of experience. This datum cannot be understood in separation from some essence, *that which* exists. Hence we can form no distinct idea of existence as such, alone by itself We apprehend it only as something perfecting or completing or realizing some essence Furthermore, since that which actually exists is always concrete, including within it an unlimited variety of structural determination, we can gain no clear (that is, abstract) conception of it Hence the tendency either to disregard existence altogether or to view it as a mere mode not really distinct from the essence which determines it

In spite of these difficulties in apprehending it, existence is a peculiarly distinctive and indubitable datum of experience As a matter of fact, it pervades all the other more restricted data, for a nonexistent datum is impossible. This has been recognized by the more scrupulous thinkers from the first beginnings of philosophy in the West. Thus in a well-known passage[6] the modern philosopher Kant, in criticizing the ontological argument, pointed out the tremendous difference between one hundred possible dollars and one hundred existent dollars, actually jingling in his pocket. Yet this tremendous difference between being and non-being, the most radical difference there is, does not belong to the order of anything essential that can be clearly and distinctly defined. For the one hundred possible dollars may share in every definable, essential trait possessed by the actual dollars Existence belongs to an order quite distinct from the order of essence.

It is regrettable that Kant, after noting this crucially important, empirical fact, did not pay more attention to it but, in accordance with the idealistic trend of modern thought, let it drop far from the central focus of his attention More recently the modern movement of existentialism, which began with Kierkegaard's violent attack on Hegel's idealistic confusion of

[6] Immanuel Kant, *Critique of Pure Reason,* A599, B627

necessary, universal essences with contingent, individual existence, has rebelled against this trend. But in its radical suppression of essence, and of the intelligibility of being, it has often pushed this reaction to an equally dangerous and one-sided extreme

In spite of this recent rebellion, the essentialist trend of modern philosophy is clearly manifested in many forms of so-called empiricism For Hume and his followers, existence is never sharply focused but is airily dismissed as something automatically attaching to any impression [7] For Husserl and his orthodox followers, the ultimate and most certain data are those determinate essences which are the objects of an *eidetic intuition* [8] Existence is a more dubious matter, associated with common-sense prejudices and questionable attitudes, which must be "bracketed" by the phenomenologist who wishes to grasp the indubitable content of experience [9]

Against all such essentialist reductions, the realistic empiricist must recognize existence as an all-pervasive and constraining datum of awareness. This datum not only pervades every object of awareness in some mode but also pervades the awareness itself. If one is aware of something, then it is at least clear that something exists. No datum is thrust upon us with more inexorable constraint than this. It cannot be consistently questioned without also questioning all immediate data and thus abandoning the whole noetic enterprise. The difficult task of describing it, and distinguishing its various modes and their basic structures, cannot be evaded by any radical empiricist.

C. *Logical Atomism and the Reduction of Relational Structure.* Logical atomism is a peculiar form of essentialism which has been closely associated with the movement of so-called British empiricism It analyzes every continuous datum into separate, discrete essences, each enclosed within itself and incapable of tending toward anything distinct from itself or of exerting any influence on anything else Continuous change is analyzed by the atomist into a series of separate items, each entirely distinct from the rest, and thus reduced to succession Relational structure, like that of causal dependence, is reduced to atomic units, simply lying side by side or succeeding one another in time Relation itself, so far as it is recognized at all, is conceived not as an existential incompleteness, tending to something distinct, but rather as itself an atomistic rope or bond situated "be-

---

[7] David Hume, *A Treatise on Human Nature*, ed. by T. H Green and T H Grose (London and New York, Longmans, Green, 1898), Part II, Section VI, p. 370.

[8] Edmund Husserl, *Ideas General Introduction to Pure Phenomenology*, trans. by W. R Boyce Gibson (New York, Macmillan, 1931), pp 55 ff

[9] *Ibid*, pp 56 and 110 ff.

tween" two other atoms and thus "neutral" to the other atoms it relates [10]

This atomistic reduction of the data of experience has been very thoroughly criticized and shown to be guilty of what we may call the postanalytic fallacy The human mind readily analyzes the rich profusion of concrete experience into atomic color patches, feelings of pain, hardnesses, and so forth, with no remainder, and easily projects this analytic dust back into the original experience, as though it were a mere complex of such atomic fragments But this is to confuse the results of a very partial analysis with what is being analyzed. When examined carefully, the original data show themselves to be characterized by many other phases as well. Certainly in the case of ourselves, and in the case of others with whom we can communicate, we are aware of a constant factor running through our changes and evolutions. Our own being is relational or vectorial in the sense that we directly know ourselves to be reaching out and tending to something not yet fully realized but beyond us [11] We need not elaborate these points.

The radical empiricist will not follow Hume in assuming, before he has carefully examined the evidence, that experience must be exclusively made up of discrete, atomic essences or impressions, merely juxtaposed with one another or merely succeeding one another in time [12] If the immediate evidence so indicates, he will be prepared to give up his atomistic prejudices and to recognize in addition to distinctness and substantial difference the ever-present data of dynamism, continuity, tendency, potency, and the dependence of one thing on another. He will be prepared to recognize these latter data as hard facts, even though he may have difficulty in clearly and exactly defining them and even though he may have an extreme difficulty in reconciling them with prevalent theories of nature. He will do this because, as an empiricist, he will recognize as the first canon of all truly empirical procedure the necessary priority of the brute data as they are directly given, over all explanatory theory and hypothesis, no matter how appealing such theory may be.

D. *Subjectivism and the Reduction of the Outer to the Inner.* The plausible hypothesis that the individual, knowing agent is a separate, material atom, entirely enclosed within itself, has led to the formulation of a theory of the immediate data which is now extraordinarily widespread but which is by no means borne out by a careful study of the data themselves. Accord-

[10] This curious conception of an atomic "relation" lying "between" its terms has been widely propagated, especially among the logicians, by Bertrand Russell See his *Problems of Philosophy* (London, Oxford University Press, Home University Library, 1912), Chap 9, "The World of Universals," pp. 153–54.
[11] See Section V of this paper.
[12] See Hume, *op. cit*, Part I, Section VII, p. 332 *et passim.*

ing to this atom-motivated hypothesis, all the original data of experience must be enclosed within the subjective consciousness (conceived in nonrelational terms) of the individual self The data themselves are regarded nonrelationally as little globules, lying *inside* a larger atom of consciousness. On this theory, all I can know directly are my own private states [13] My physical organism is in no sense directly given but, together with the whole, external world of extended physical entities, has to be inferred on the basis of what is itself purely private and subjective.

This theory of what the data must be is extremely plausible to many minds But it is certainly not verified by an examination of the data which actually are presented. We shall not dwell on the internal difficulties of the theory itself. The chief of these concerns the basis for any such projection, or inference, to what is in no sense whatsoever given. From consistently subjectivist premises it is difficult to see how anything nonsubjective can validly be inferred or even where we should ever get the notion of anything *outside* at all These difficulties have been pointed out many times We shall be content merely to refer to the data themselves, which do not bear out this theory as to what the data must be. So far as the actual data are concerned, there is no priority of the inner over the outer. When I look about me here and now, a great expanse of objects not given as inside me is just as evident as the sphere of my inner states and feelings If anything, the former is more clearly and evidently given than the latter Certainly my own body is as immediately given to me as my awareness [14]

The realist may not be in possession of any a priori theory which will explain this remarkable fact. But as an empiricist he must certainly recognize that inner and outer are correlative phases of the original experience, which certainly involves both, with no priority of the one over the other. The internal is never actually experienced without the external To reduce the latter to the former is a biased distortion of the primordial data. In my original experience, something outside is presented to me with the same indubitable evidence as something inside.

E. *The Theory of Sense Data and the Reduction of Awareness* Concrete experience is always presented to us in a bipolarized structure. One of these poles is a relational awareness or cognitive act within the organism of the knowing agent The other pole is an object of some kind. They can be clearly distinguished in the original data but are never found in separa-

[13] Russell, *Human Knowledge, Its Scope and Limits* (New York, Simon and Schuster, 1948), p 174
[14] For a very definite statement of the prevalent, opposite view, see Russell, *Human Knowledge, Its Scope and Limits, op cit* , pp 195 ff "I should define a 'mental' occurrence as one which can be known without inference," p. 201 Hence I must infer even my body from mental data.

tion. No object is ever given without some awareness. No awareness is ever given which is not the awaieness *of* some object Each is given with equal immediacy as an evident aspect of the concrete, bipolar data

A noteworthy characteristic of this bipolar structure is the predominance of the object over the indeterminate act of awareness Apart from a priori theory, *in* the data, it is never the object which is determined by the faculty but always the noetic faculty which is specified and determined by the object. As a result of this significant fact, it is far easier to find the object than the act, especially at the lower levels of sensory awareness where the domination of faculty by object is more marked than at the higher levels, and where it is far more difficult to focus the acts of sensing and perceiving Furthermore, many of the more usual objects of awareness, like colors and shapes, are easier to grasp by clear and abstract concepts than that obscure, *relational* mode of being which belongs to an *awareness of* something.

For these reasons, there is a strongly marked tendency in recent epistemological theory to evade these peculiar data of intentionality, or to attempt to reduce them to the level of atomistic objects, that can be described and analyzed in more usual ways Several other manifestations of this flight from intentionality are criticized in this present volume [15] We must here refer to one which is widely influential at the present time—the sense-datum theory.

According to this theory, we are never aware of anything independent of our awareness, exactly as it is The immediate data are numerically distinct fiom the real object "out there" The elliptical penny I see is quite different from the round penny that physically exists [16] The sense datum, which is immediately sensed, is neither an independent object nor an act of awareness, but a strange amalgamation of the two. It is not an act of sensing but an act reified into a datum—a sense *datum* Neither is it a normal object or datum It is rather an object merged with and distorted by an act of sensing—a *sense* datum. But in this peculiar amalgamation it is the objective aspect that piedominates. It is a peculiar kind of *datum*, rather than a relational act of awaieness, an act reduced to the level of an atomic datum—a sense-act datum.

These peculiar data are neither wholly internal nor wholly external They certainly do not belong to the physical world. The physicist does not have to take sense data into account But neither do they seem to belong to the psychical processes and acts studied by the psychologist They are neither purely physical nor purely mental, neither internal nor external In

[15] See the essays by Francis Parker, pp 152 ff , and Henry Veatch pp 177 ff , see also R. M. Chisholm, "Intentionality and the Theory of Signs," *Philosophical Studies*, III (June 1952), 56.

[16] See Russell, *Problems of Philosophy, op cit* , Chap. 2, and C D Broad, *Mind and Its Place in Nature* (London, Kegan Paul, 1925), pp 180 ff

its more extreme forms, the theory affirms these data to be *neutral*. According to this view, neither the physical nor the mental is directly observed, but only a relatively small field of subjectively twisted, neutral data, from which mental and physical realities must be inferred by some mysterious process of "animal inference" or deduction which has never been clearly explained.

In its less extreme forms, it is admitted that these twisted data are apprehended[17] in some obscure way, but these acts of awareness are left unanalyzed, and the impression is conveyed that when properly understood, these acts also will turn out to be data of the usual kind, though no doubt very complex. The net upshot of these theories, however they are developed, is a strong tendency to remove the peculiar intentional acts of awareness, which permeate the whole of experience, from any central focus of attention Like Hume, the modern epistemologist never seems to be able to find an intentional act of awareness. Wherever he looks, he finds only an object of some kind. His awareness of the object always slips through his fingers. Nevertheless, the awareness is really there in the immediate data. The reader may perhaps be reminded of this important fact by a few brief criticisms of the sense-datum theory.

In the first place, this theory, in its extreme form, is evidently neglecting certain immediate data which are always present in any human experience of any sort It is absolutely impossible to be aware of any object whatsoever without being aware of it, and this awareness is not idealistically identified with the object. This applies to every mode of awareness, even that of sense As Mr G. E Moore has pointed out,[18] if my seeing of green were identical with the green which I see, I could never see yellow or any other color, for green is not the same as yellow. It is surely evident that the objects may vary, while the mode of awareness remains constant, and also that the same object may be an object of several different channels of awareness, as when I *sense* the green blotter here before me, *imagine* it with my eyes closed, and then *think* about it in conceptual terms

In the second place, the notion of objects which are neutral in the sense of lacking internality as well as externality is unconfirmed by any direct datum of sense. Every object of sense is either inside me or outside me. I feel immediately the pleasure or pain within me. With equal immediacy I feel the wooden surface pressing against my finger. But something neither internal nor external, neither a subjective act nor an objective entity—such a curious, nondescript, *ad hoc* entity—no one has ever directly felt.

Turning now to the less extreme view, which would admit that we must

---

[17] See Russell, *Problems of Philosophy, op. cit*, Chap 1, p. 17 Russell later abandoned this view It is defended by Broad, *op cit*, pp 209 ff

[18] *Philosophical Studies* (New York, Harcourt, Brace, 1922), Chap. 1.

become aware of sense data by other acts of awareness, we find difficulties of a no less formidable kind. If I cannot ever directly become aware of a physical entity as it is in nature, but only of some twisted distortion that is a result of the combined influences of object and sense organ, then why does not this same argument apply to the supposed awareness of sense data? How can I ever become aware of a sense datum as it really is?

If it is asserted that at some point, perhaps when the datum becomes sufficiently internalized, I can actually grasp it as it is by a distinct act of awareness, why then could I not have grasped the original object in this way? Surely the mere physical presence of something *inside* my organism cannot make it more *knowable*, for there are many things within me which are extremely obscure and many about which I know much less than about what is external. On the other hand, if the theory is consistently maintained and it is asserted that I can never become aware of anything as it exactly is, but only of some numerically distinct distortion, then I am certainly caught in an infinite regress which will make it impossible for me to know anything at all

Indeed, this is the fate of anyone who invents fictitious objects. They always tend to multiply themselves. If we are to be honest in following the immediate data, we must use Occam's razor in disposing of these nondescript entities which are supposed to lie between us and the realities we wish to know The immediate data are very rich, they belong to many variegated regions and kinds. The basic kinds are two: (1) a vast field of existent objects including the extended, measurable entities of physical science, and the personal objects of the social sciences, and (2) many different levels of awareness, including sense, imagination, memory, and rational acts of defining, judging, and arguing All the immediate data of experience fall under one or the other of these poles

The reduction of these vast fields of data to a set of neutral entities between both poles, but belonging to neither, is completely unsupported by the data. In particular, the peculiar, intentional acts of awareness, obscure though they may be, must be recognized as immediate data permeating the whole of our experience and given with the same constraint, as the most certain of their objects.

II. Phenomenology as the Basic Descriptive Discipline

If the preceding argument is not wholly mistaken, the immediate data of experience are far richer than is commonly supposed. They cannot be reduced to what are now called sense data. In addition to a vast field of objects, there is a rich manifold of intentional acts of awareness which attend these objects and which are given with equal evidence and immediacy. Experience is not exclusively subjective, or psychical, in character. In addition to the psychic tendencies and acts of awareness, vaguely localized within the body of the knowing agent, a rich manifold of extended objects, both internal and external to this body, are also presented directly with an equally compulsive, noetic constraint In their primordial immediacy, these data are all very vague and confused But no one of them enjoys any marked, noetic privileges over the rest It is no easier to doubt the primary, noetic revelation of something outside me than that of something inside me

It is impossible to reduce experience to a set of isolated impressions or atomic units. Relational structure is also given with equal evidence and certainty The immediate data are full of determinate structure, which is easily abstracted by the mind and grasped as universal essences or possibilities But in the original experience, all these determinate objects are pervaded by another peculiar datum marked by tendency, activity, and causal diffusion, the datum of existence This manifold array is first presented to us in a state of vagueness and confusion. But the data are certainly not totally unstructuralized or ineffable.

To what discipline must we assign the task of describing this basic structure of experience and classifying its many diverse kinds? Since explanatory hypotheses and theories can be verified only by reference to the brute, given data, this task cannot be avoided. Even the most simplified and reductionist view of the nature of experience can be defended and justified only by an attempt to describe the brute data precisely as they are given This task of pure description has always played an important role in the development of realistic thought, but it is only in recent times that it has been recognized as the province of a peculiar, autonomous discipline, now widely referred to as phenomenology The word "phenomenon" is apt to suggest certain very questionable, subjectivist assumptions [19] But since the word is now generally accepted, and since these assumptions may be guarded against, the word may be used as a convenient means of referring to that basic, noetic discipline whose function is to describe the structure of the immediate data of experience, to classify their different kinds, and thus, in brief, to clarify what is vaguely and loosely referred to as experience [20]

All constructive interpretation and inference must be eliminated from strict phenomenological method, which is purely descriptive in character.

[19] These assumptions are certainly involved in the orthodox, Husserlian conception of phenomenology See M Farber, "Experience and Transcendence," *Philosophy and Phenomenological Research*, XII, No 1 (September 1951), 1–23.

[20] For an instructive and interesting exposition of realistic phenomenology, see F. Van Steenberghen, *Epistémologie* (Louvain, Aux Editions de L'Institut Supérieur de Philosophie, 1945).

Yet what is desired is hardly a catalogue of all the discernible items in a given, concrete situation. This would be impossible to achieve, for the data are too rich What is desired is a description of those recurrent structures which, though capable of indefinite variation, are themselves essential to experience and therefore constitutive of any concrete datum whatsoever. The phenomenological clarification, so far as it is achieved, results from the laying bare of such constitutive structures, always present in the concrete data, and the classification of their major manifestations

As we have already indicated, the immediate data of awareness are very rich, much richer than is ordinarily supposed There is a constant danger of oversimplifying the evidence by attempting to reduce peculiar types of data to those which are more readily grasped and assimilated by a certain point of view. There is the ever-present temptation to read into the data certain unobserved conclusions of explanatory theories, to confuse what we think the data must be with the actual, presented data The discipline is still in a relatively youthful and undeveloped condition. Nevertheless, certain limited conclusions concerning the nature of experience are strongly indicated not only by the descriptive studies of classical realistic thought but by the results of modern phenomenological research

Existence is an immediate datum which permeates every phase of concrete experience.[21] It cannot be attributed to constructive interpretation, for this must be based upon something originally given which is interpreted, and *nothing* cannot be given Neither can it be attributed to inference, for all inference must be ultimately based upon an evident datum existing in some way. From the *nonexistent*, nothing can be inferred.

Existence penetrates the whole of concrete experience. But this experience is always presented in a peculiar, bipolar structure—an awareness united with an object of awareness. Each of these poles is given with equal immediacy, and neither one is ever given without the other. The awareness pole is immediately felt to be vaguely localized within a limited volume, commonly referred to as the *body* of the knowing agent The immediate objects of awareness (the objective pole) are not necessarily localized in this way.

These objects fall into three major classes First, there are the external, ever changing, extended objects, distinct from the observer's body, certain measurable aspects of which are the peculiar concern of physical science. Second, there is the body of the observer with its internal states and tendencies, to which he has cognitive access both by internal and external sense. Third, there are other psychophysical agents to whose internal awareness he has access by the processes of communication.

The phenomenology of human communication is still undeveloped, and

[21] See Sections IV and V of this paper for a condensed analysis of this datum.

disciplined studies of the data are lacking But the existence of two distinct types of communication is certainly indicated by the data now available. The lower levels of sensory and imaginal awareness, being deeply tinged with subjectivity, can be only indirectly communicated by sympathetic *Einfuhlung* and inferential interpretation of signs. But the higher levels of awareness, involving universal concepts and judgments, can be *directly* communicated. Without such direct communication of abstract concepts, the shared awareness of science, and intersubjective agreement and disagreement concerning the very same objects, would be impossible.

Awareness is directly given as a peculiar, relational activity of sensing, feeling, remembering, defining, and judging, definitely centered in the psychophysical organism of the agent of awareness.[22] These acts are always intentionally relative to some object I cannot feel without feeling something. I cannot remember without remembering something. I cannot judge without judging something Intentional awareness of this kind occurs in three distinct modes, though in concrete experience no one of them ever occurs without the others.

The most basic level (1) is that of sensory awareness Its internal and external objects are always concrete and individual, and it is dependent upon the physical reception of a physical influence by a physical organ. The objects of memory and imagination (2) are also individual and repeatable, but this mode of awareness is free from dependence upon physical conditions and is subject to internal and voluntary control. This is also true of conceptual awareness (3). But its objects are no longer the confused, individual blurs of sense and imagination

The conceptual power is able to analyze such vague agglomerations into their component aspects and to grasp each of these, not concretely as it is fused with other distinct determinations here and now, but abstractly as it must be whenever or wherever it occurs Then in the judgment it is able to recombine these conceptual components together as they are combined in the existent entities which act on sense. Reason and imagination can also combine these analytic units together in all sorts of arbitrary ways The truth or falsity of such constructive combinations (their agreement or disagreement with concrete existence) can be discovered only with the aid of sense A true theory is one in which sense, imagination, and discursive reason all confirm each other in their different ways of apprehending one and the same given object. The task of arriving at a more exact description, analysis, and explanation of these data of awareness belongs to the disciplines of logic and epistemology [23]

[22] This fact is denied by idealistic philosophy with its doctrine of an "objective" or "absolute" floating awareness

[23] On the distinctive features of realistic or intentional logic, see the essay by Veatch. On realistic epistemology, see Parker's essay.

This, of course, is only a brief summary of certain results of phenomenological investigation, which may be verified by anyone who has the capacity to follow Descartes in bracketing his various prejudices and uncritical assumptions concerning what experience must be, and who will patiently turn to the concrete data themselves The discipline of phenomenology is still in a most imperfect state, and many problems have not even been referred to, owing to limitations of space. But these results have been fairly well established.

The vast, bipolar flux of immediate experience, in addition to the essential, constitutive data we have described, contains many questionable interpretations and inferences to unobserved entities. It may even include constitutive data beyond what we have described But *these* data are always present in any concrete experience of whatever kind Throughout my waking life I am always directly aware of a great field of voluminous extension surrounding my body. I am also directly aware of my own body, with its internal states and tendencies, which is vaguely placed within this field. Finally, I am aware of others with whom I exist and with whom I can communicate Even when I am alone, this awareness is with me, for aloneness is a privative mode of social existence.

This objective pole dominates the whole field of experience and is much more readily focused But there is always an awareness given with the objects. I am always sensing both internal and external objects and at least vaguely discriminating them. I am constantly completing these limited vignettes with the aid of memory and imagination, and making conceptual judgments of various abstract phases of what I am feeling, touching, seeing, and imagining.

None of these data enjoys any special epistemological privileges over the rest. All are given with equal immediacy and certainty Furthermore, the bipolar structure we have just described is constitutive of every experience These constitutive data are given with every more restricted datum of whatever sort When our attention is focused on some *special* object, they may recede to the periphery of awareness. But they are *always* present, and if we make the necessary effort to discover them, they may be found. Even though he may not be aware of them, they are present to the scientist in his laboratory. With divergent specific determinations they are also present to him when he leaves his laboratory and walks home Wherever he is, whatever he is doing, whatever his attention is concentrated on, he is always confronted by a field of extended objects, by internal feelings from his own body, and by others with whom he can communicate. These objects are directly thrust upon an awareness which, throughout the whole period of waking life, is sensing, remembering, imagining, and thinking. They are omnipresent and inescapable.

All the more restricted variations of these primordial data are incomplete until they are fitted into this all-encompassing framework. It cannot be reduced to them. Any explanatory hypothesis which accounts for certain limited data only, when philosophically generalized into an attempt to account for the whole of experience, will lead to some form of a priori reductionism, open to the charge of ignoring certain relevant data, the most certain and inescapable data of all. Philosophy, of course, is the attempt to analyze and explain these all-pervasive data. Is this attempt really hopeless? Is philosophy an empirical or scientific discipline? Can philosophical theories be checked by evidence inaccessible to the specific sciences? Are there peculiar, philosophical data which can be clearly distinguished from the empirical data of the restricted sciences?

Positivistic thinkers have accustomed us to negativistic answers to these crucial questions. But such answers have seldom been backed up by any careful examination of the constitutive structure of experience. Are there philosophic protocols? If not, the positivists are right in refusing to recognize philosophy as a scientific discipline. If so, philosophy is not only possible but is an indispensable necessity. Let us examine the question.

III ARE THERE DISTINCT, PHILOSOPHICAL PROTOCOLS?

Scientific method begins and ends with the observation of brute, sensory data, or protocols, which are irrevocably thrust upon the human observer. They can then be described and analyzed by universal concepts and thus communicated to other observers. The next step is the discovery of similarities in the public data, which may be generalized in the form of empirical laws. On the basis of such laws, unobserved agencies and entities may often be inferred. Finally, explanatory theories of a very general character may be formulated, from which subordinate generalizations may be deduced and individual occurrences actually predicted in the concrete. When some such event, deducible from the theory, is not observed to occur, the theory is false, and has to be abandoned or modified. In so far as all the observable data which can be deduced from the theory are observed to occur under specified conditions, the theory is verified. Such is the general nature of all scientific method. But as we have seen, the world is very rich, and offers us a vast variety of diverse data differing in the most radical ways. Each different type of data demands a different mode of approach.

The observed data and inferred entities of the physical sciences are of a very special and restricted kind. The scientist is not interested in the awareness which always pervades his observations. He abstracts from this. He is not interested in the existence which also pervades the object on which his attention focuses. He abstracts from this He is interested as a scientist only in the extended objects of nature, and only in the quantitative aspects of these So far as certain objects possess awareness which can be communicated, he is not interested Neither is he interested in any qualitative aspects they possess, except in so far as some, such as sound or color, can be correlated with quantitative properties such as wave lengths The objects of his study are the extended entities of nature so far as they can be quantitatively measured.

These abstract objects so far as they can be observed, the position of a scale or a pointer reading, are relatively simple and require no laborious description and analysis to be understood. The important factor here is the necessary completion of these macroscopic data by inferences to microscopic and submicroscopic entities which cannot be directly observed, and the formulation of explanatory theories taking account of such entities, by which all the actual phenomena may be understood and from which new occurrences may be predicted

We may summarize this analysis of scientific method in the following way The data of physical science are restricted and nonpervasive, these data are quantitative and therefore measurable, the data which can be directly observed are very partial and can be completed only by inference to a vast complex of microscopic entities which play a crucially important role in the enactment of observed phenomena, but which cannot themselves be observed; finally, these observable data are relatively simple and can be grasped, at least in essence, with a minimum of arduous description and empirical analysis No scientific data are all-pervasive. Each distinct science is ultimately defined in terms of restricted data of a certain kind

Do the different sciences then exhaust the field? Are the positivists right in asserting that these are all the data, that any datum whatsoever must fall within the province of some specific science? Or are there further data that can be clearly distinguished from these? It is time for us now to face this fundamental question

There are such data How do they differ from those of the specific sciences?

The answer should be clear from the preliminary account of the nature of human experience. In accordance with a linguistic usage that has prevailed up to the present time, we shall refer to these data as *philosophical*. First, we shall point out how they are clearly distinct from scientific data. Then we shall select one of them (existence) for a brief but more exact analysis.

First of all, these philosophical data are *pervasive*. The most basic are all-pervasive By this is meant not merely that these data are loosely associated in some way with all other data This could be said of quantity. What is meant is that these philosophic data are essentially constitutive of experience itself and are, therefore, inescapably present in the apprehension of any datum whatsoever Others, like quantity and change, pervade the data of two or more special sciences. Existence, the object of metaphysics or first philosophy, and awareness, the object of epistemology, are such pervasive data, as we have pointed out. Existence pervades every datum whatsoever of whatever kind. Nothing cannot be a datum.

Awareness pervades experience in another way It does not necessarily constitute its objects But it necessarily belongs to the experience of any object, in some one of its many modes No datum can be given which is not given to some level of awareness. It is present throughout the whole of waking life, to the scientist in his laboratory, also when he is at home No data of the restricted sciences are all-pervasive in these peculiar ways

In the second place, the basic data and most of those less basic are non-quantitative and, therefore, not measurable by any of the techniques of physical measurement [24] This becomes evident if we reflect upon the fact that nonindividual, immaterial objects, like the concepts, judgments, and arguments of the logician, *exist.* They are not nothing, or logic would be impossible But logic is possible and exists as a necessary discipline Hence these objects of logical study also exist, and existence cannot be exclusively restricted to material entities alone.[25]

In the third place, these all-pervasive non-quantitative data of philosophical science are extremely complex and, therefore, difficult to describe and analyze, even in their observable aspects This does not by itself serve to distinguish philosophy from some of the sciences devoted to the study of higher entities But it sharply distinguishes philosophy from the *physical* sciences, where the element of exact description of observable data is far less important.

Taken together, these three characteristics, especially the first, sharply mark off a set of distinct and peculiar data not belonging to the limited fields of any special science The arduous task of analyzing and explaining them, so far as this is possible, must be recognized as essential by any empiricist, for these data are immediately given with constraining evidence. They pervade the objects of more than one restricted science and cannot be reduced to them The most pervasive of these is existence, the object of first philosophy.

[24] This is even true of quantity Such techniques of measurement cannot help us to determine the essential nature of quantity and how it differs from other modes of being like quality Such empirical investigations lie beyond the province of any restricted science and must be allotted to another discipline, usually called *philosophy.*

[25] For a critique of the naturalistic and materialistic reduction of being to material being, see the essay by Oliver Martin, pp 68 ff.

The realist holds that in the course of its history in the West certain negative results have been well established by this discipline Certain reductionist views like idealism, which identifies existence with mental existence, and materialism (or naturalism), which identifies existence with individual, physical existence,[26] have been carefully compared with the data and found wanting The realist believes that both modes of being are presented in experience He also believes that while first philosophy is still in a very imperfect state, certain positive conclusions of genuine importance have also been established It is only in the light of these conclusions that the basic concepts and principles of realistic philosophy can be clearly understood In view of their fundamental importance, we shall devote the remainder of this paper to a summary of them. The exposition must be very brief. But it may perhaps serve as an adequate characterization of those basic metaphysical concepts which must lie at the root of any genuinely realistic philosophy

IV. Two Basic Principles of Realistic Philosophy

The most pervasive of the immediate data of experience is being,[27] which permeates not only every object of whatever type but every level of awareness as well Hence the task of describing, analyzing, and explaining this omnipresent datum is allotted to the central, philosophical discipline of metaphysics, or first philosophy as it is more appropriately called The first phase of this discipline, *general metaphysics,* is the analysis of being in general and those traits which any existent entity must possess as such. Concerning general metaphysics we shall have time to consider very briefly only two basic principles which belong to this field and which are then presupposed by all the more restricted sciences. These are the so-called "law of contradiction" and the so-called "principle of sufficient reason."

The first fact that becomes evident when the datum of being is clearly focused is its peculiar, unrestricted range. Everything that is experienced in any way must exist. But when we examine it carefully, we find nothing which demands that it be restricted to this experience or to that, or indeed to any experience at all Being is unlimited in scope What belongs to being as such will belong to everything whatsoever, whatever and wherever it may be. If we ask ourselves what is then excluded from this unrestricted or transcendental range, only one answer can be given: nothing at all, the

---

[26] A realistic critique of these doctrines will be found in *loc cit*

[27] We are here using *being* as referring to both *that which can exist* (essence) and the *existence* which brings it into act, and thus as excluding only nothing. See Section V below However, since essence *apart from existence* has no being at all, we shall sometimes use *existence* as equivalent to *being.*

nonexistent, the impossible. From this, being is divided by the most radical
of differences, that which is commonly but somewhat inaccurately referred
to as *contradiction* All other differences are less absolute than this, for they
all have something in common But being and nothing lack any common
factor They are *absolutely* opposed. The principle expressing this factual
opposition is the law of contradiction Being is not nothing

Since the scope of being is unrestricted, the scope of this law is also
unrestricted. It applies to any entity. The being of such an entity, whatever
it may be, is radically sundered from its non-being No entity whatsoever
can both be and not be all at once, in the same respect This law is often
referred to as a mere law of diction or of logic, which is indeed partially
true. *If* we are to think of real existence as it is, we must never contradict
ourselves But this necessity is not engrained in the structure of human
thought. If so, we should never contradict ourselves It is engrained in the
very structure of existence Hence if we are to think being as it is, our
thought also must follow this law.

Another significant fact about being is its intelligibility This is stated by
the so-called law of sufficient reason: Being contains its sufficient reasons
within itself Two necessary conditions for the intelligibility of being are
hereby asserted: (1) It can be understood, or "contains reasons", (2)
These reasons are sufficient. In connection with (1) it is important to recognize that by a *reason* is meant any phase of being so far as it is clearly
and rationally understood.

To understand a fact is to know not merely that it is (which we may
attain by sense) but the reasons *why* it is, those phases of being on which
it depends in any way. They can be clearly grasped by rational cognition
alone and are therefore known as reasons. Thus the assertion that being
"contains reasons" is equivalent to "being is intelligible in itself "

It also asserts (2) that there are no other reasons, these being sufficient
How do we know that some phase of being may not turn out to be wholly
opaque to insight and purely irrational? Because by the concept of being
and the law of contradiction, we have actually grasped, though in a confused way, all that is and can be How do we know that, having grasped
all this, some other vital reason may not be missing? Because from all the
reasons there are, only nothing is excluded, and nothing contains no reasons. Since being contains reasons, and contains all the reasons there are,
it is intelligible.

Like the law of contradiction, this principle applies to being as such,
and must hold good whether being is one or many, but in different ways.
If being is one, then it must be self-sufficient, or contain its own sufficient
reason within itself But if not, then the sufficient reason of one being must
be found either in it or in some other entity, since nothing has no sufficient

reason for anything at all. This principle of first philosophy is also presupposed by every scientific discipline, as by the whole intellectual enterprise of man. Otherwise these disciplines would not continue to seek for the reasons and explanations of events not yet understood but would abandon the whole quest for understanding and would wither away and die.

There are other basic facts and principles which may be derived from an analysis of the all-pervasive datum of being as such. But we must be content with this short comment on two such principles and pass on to another topic, the existential analysis of those finite, changing entities, including ourselves, which are directly presented to us in the immediate data of human experience.

V An Existential Analysis of the Finite Changing Entities of Nature

So far we have been concerned with the object of general metaphysics, being as such. The facts we have observed apply to any being whatsoever, whether finite or infinite, changing or immutable, multiple or one. Now we must turn to an existential analysis of the entities which are presented to us in our immediate experience. How do these entities exist? Are they changing or immutable? Do they exist in themselves or in something else distinct from them? Are they one or many? Is their existence atomic and self-enclosed or incomplete and tendential? Is their existence necessary or contingent? These basic questions cannot be answered by any of the sciences restricted to non-pervasive data. They are philosophical questions which can be scientifically answered only by a careful description and analysis of the philosophical data which constitutively pervade the whole field of experience. Let us now turn to these peculiar, existential data and attempt such an analysis.

How do the entities of our experience exist? They are evidently finite, mutable, and multiple. We shall start with the data of mutability, then turn to those of multiplicity, and conclude with a brief discussion of the more basic datum of finitude which underlies both.

A *The Datum of Change.*[28] Unlike existence, the datum of change is not all-pervasive. There is nothing about existence as such which requires that any existent entity must be mutable. Nevertheless, change does pervade the data of human experience. The extended objects of nature are constantly undergoing those modes of physical change which are peculiar to them. I feel many kinds of psychophysical change proceeding within my-

[28] This topic is discussed in further detail in the essay by Jesse De Boer, pp. 92 ff.

self, and through the agencies of human communication I am aware of
those manifold modes of social and cultural change which make up the
complex web of human history From this it is clear that change is too pervasive a datum to fall within the restricted province of any one of the
special sciences Each science studies only a special kind of change from
its own special point of view.

Modern philosophy has not been clearly aware of its own peculiar data
but has been deeply impressed by the positivistic view that every datum
belongs to the special province of some restricted science Hence when
one raises the fundamental question *What is change?* even in philosophical literature, he looks in vain for an intelligible answer. Many philosophers, like Dewey, insist upon the universal occurrence of what they call
process and flux. But they seem almost wholly unaware of the need for a
philosophical analysis and explanation of this peculiar and complex, philosophic datum Instead of analysis, they give us merely synonyms.

Bergson was certainly aware of the unique importance of this ubiquitous datum But he gives us no analysis Instead, he merely points at poign-
ant images—the rocket bursting in the sky and the snowball rolling down
the hill. What is change? What do all changes have in common? What are
its major kinds? Nowhere does Bergson give us any coherent answer to
these basic questions.

Many recent philosophers, following Descartes and the British empiricists, simply assert that change, or event, is an ultimate, irreducible category with no structure at all But this is certainly false. Whatever else it
may be, change is certainly not a simple mode (Descartes) or simple idea
(Locke and Berkeley). That which is simple cannot change, though it
may be annihilated and created All change is from a *terminus a quo*, distinct from the *terminus ad quem* This is enough to show a complexity in
its structure All change is *from* something already existent *to* something
quite distinct, not there at the beginning. All change is discontinuous Is
this all?

Many have thought so, including the Milesian philosophers of ancient
times and Herbert Spencer in the modern era They have defined change
in terms of two opposite principles, love and hate, light and dark, the simple and homogeneous as against the complex and heterogeneous. Is this
enough? It is not enough to describe the actual data of experience, for
these data show that change is not only discontinuous but continuous as
well. Greenness, we know, cannot turn into redness This is impossible. It
is the leaf, having a capacity to be either green or red, which changes from
one to the other This underlies the change.

Hence in the realistic analysis of change, first suggested by Aristotle,
three sources of change are always recognized two opposed structural

principles (such as green and red) to account for the discontinuity, and one potential or dispositional principle (matter) to account for the continuity When this third, dispositional principle is not clearly recognized, change is reduced to the pure discontinuity of succession, first one specific determination and then another opposed determination, annihilation and creation *ex nihilo* On this view, the end of a process would have nothing in common with the beginning, and anything could come out of anything But there is a vast array of empirical evidence against this conclusion You cannot make a silk purse out of a sow's ear nor a poplar tree from an apple seed. Change is continuous as well as discontinuous

What, then, are the major kinds of change? If we stick close to the data, we shall be forced to recognize two types in particular which are so important that we shall single them out for a brief analysis.

B. *Accidental Change and the Distinction of Substance and Accident* At the present time, there are several deep-seated misconceptions of substance and accident. Since this topic is treated more thoroughly elsewhere,[29] we shall confine ourselves here to a brief consideration of these major misunderstandings, which are three in number.

The first is a widespread impression that the distinction of substance from accident is derived primarily from epistemological considerations and must be defended, if it is to be defended at all, on the basis of epistemological evidence. On this view, the accidental properties of a thing are supposed to be directly sensed The realist is held to believe that back of these accidents, underlying them, is a noumenal x, or substance, in which they inhere like separate pins in an underlying pincushion. This conception is far removed from any realistic conception of substance and accident

In the first place, this distinction is concerned not with epistemological facts but with dynamic facts.[30] It is required to explain not the structure of knowledge but the structure of change. As we have just noted, there is a factor of continuity in all types of change. But in certain types, this continuous factor is constituted by a complex, formal pattern (or essence) which persists throughout the process. At the level of inorganic nature, where our entitative knowledge is less exact, we cannot clearly grasp the formal unity of what is changing But in the case of individual plants and animals, we can grasp something of this substantial structure As the roots are extended, the stalk grows, and the buds ripen and fall, the plant endures as a single, corporeal, living entity.

[29] See especially the essay by Manley H Thompson, Jr., pp. 125 ff.
[30] See L de Raeymaeker, *La philosophie de l'être* (Louvain, L'Institut Supérieur de Philosophie, 1947), pp. 199 ff , for an illuminating and accurate account of the realistic theory of substance and accident.

Somewhere between the simplest physical transformations and the processes of life, certain forms of unified structure have gained sufficient domination over limited bits of matter to enable them to persist through the various accidental transformations to which they are subject. Thus I am directly aware of various evolutions and transformations, resulting in the gain or loss of accidental properties, as long as my life endures But I am also aware of the fact that I myself persist through these changes as a corporeal, living, human substance. This is an example of accidental change in which the continuity is provided by a unified, formal structure, partially expressed in the specific definition of the entity.

In the second place, substance and accident cannot be accurately understood as separate entities, merely juxtaposed with, or inhering in, one another as pins in a pincushion. This atomistic conception utterly fails to do justice to the situation Substance is not a *thing*, and accident another *thing*, which happen to be joined. Neither is a thing Each of them is a correlative principle which exists only by virtue of its fusion with the other. The only thing is the concrete entity constituted by this fusion.

Each principle contributes something to the whole entity Thus its identity and individuation are derived from the substantial component, its changing qualities from the accidental component. But it is precisely the *whole, composite entity* which is individuated and qualified, not merely a part. It is entirely wrong to think of the substance as a fixed atom, remaining lifeless and inert as the accidental changes sweep by it. This is a complete perversion of the facts It is the whole entity which changes, and every constitutive phase of the entity is involved in this change, the substance as providing it with continuity and individuality, the accidents as providing it with novelty and discontinuity

Finally, in the third place, it is clear from their correlative structure that neither substance nor accident can be known without the other. It is as impossible to know accidents without substance as to know a father without any children This is a pure figment of atomistic thought But what of human sensation? Surely it is aware of the pure color green, the middle-C sound, which are accidents, but not of that mysterious something I know not what, which John Locke confused with substance.

This last phrase is correct. Sensation knows nothing of *substance* But neither does it know anything of *accident* The color green is the object of a universal concept. It is never sensed What is sensed is a complex flux of quantitative and qualitative characters confused together in an unanalyzed blur. Substance and accident are implicit in this blur But they can be clearly apprehended and distinguished only through a rational analysis of this sensory confusion. Substance is the formal unity which persists throughout the concrete change. The accidents come and go.

C *Substantial Change and the Distinction of Matter and Form* The accidental changes we have so far been considering affect the whole, concrete, changing entity They do not affect the formal essence which maintains the substantial unity of the entity throughout these accidental transformations. There is another more radical type of change, however, which results in the generation or destruction of the entity and which, therefore, does penetrate to the very essence. The death of my cat is not an accidental change, for he does not survive the process. My cat has ceased to be. Nevertheless, the data show that this process is not wholly discontinuous The carcass remains, and while it consists of new substances not in existence before, there is something in them which was once in the cat.

This matter, or capacity to be possessed by different substantial forms, underlies any process of substantial change and supplies it with a minimum continuity. Thus in order to account for the continuity which characterizes even the most radical changes of nature, including the evolution of new species from earlier forms, we must recognize a further composition in the very essence of any natural entity which has come into existence by a process of evolution On the one hand, its essence must consist of a certain formal structure marking off this entity from other species, which disappears when the entity is destroyed. But there must be another essential part which existed before and which will outlast the entity This must be a capacity or potency, able to exist under divergent forms and able to unite both essence and accidents together into a single, material unity.

Here again it is most important to notice how this hylomorphic composition in the essence of any evolutionary entity must be distorted by any atomistic mode of analysis. Matter is not one thing, and form another The essence is no mere addition of quantitative atoms. Matter and form are correlative principles, each of which exists only by virtue of the other It is true that this matter may exist under some other form than that which now possesses it But it cannot exist as an atom by itself alone. Similarly, the form can be found apart from *this* matter, but never apart from matter. Each is a vectorial principle, intrinsically correlative to something distinct from itself, and each contributes something to the whole concrete entity which is thus constituted The matter sustains the entity and gives it an individual position in nature, while the form specifically characterizes the entity as a whole.

Thus in order to account for the pervasive datum of change, we are forced to recognize a fourfold composition in the structure of the simplest conceivable dynamic entity. First (unless it was created *ex nihilo*), this entity must include a matter from which it continuously evolved. It must also include an essential form, marking it off from other *kinds of* entity, which must be in possession of the matter as long as the entity endures, from the moment of its generation to that of its extinction. The matter, when given existence in union with such a form, is a complete substance, which is then capable of undergoing accidental transformations by which further existent properties are gained or lost without the destruction of the entity. These principles are not entities, but vectorial factors by which a concrete natural entity exists Matter cannot exist without form, nor form without matter Substance exists only with accidents, and accidents only in substance.

We must now turn to an even more basic composition which is required by another immediate datum of experience—multiplicity.

D *The Problem of the One and the Many: Essence and Existence* An *order* is a unity in multiplicity The data of change present us with a certain type of order, a temporal multiplicity of determinations united by matter, or by substantial form in the case of accidental change In order to account for these immediate data, we are forced to recognize in any concrete changing entity the distinct, component principles of matter and form, substance and accident. But at any given moment we are also presented with an even more basic *static* order, as we may call it—a multiplicity of diverse entities, all of which share in existence On the one hand, each entity is distinct from, and opposed to, the rest So they are a multiplicity. But on the other hand, they all share in that existence which opposes them all to nothing In this respect they are one How can they be both many and one?

Consider my own being. I am directly aware of myself as radically distinct from all the other entities surrounding me. They are not what I am, and I am not what they are This is an immediate datum of experience, thrust upon me with inexorable constraint I cannot question it without also questioning, if I am consistent, all other data as well, and thus abandoning the whole attempt to know But there is another datum also thrust upon me with equal constraint This is the datum of existence which pervades both self and not-self. The others exist as much as I Existence is shared in common But how is this possible? How can the same entity be both diverse and similar to the very same entities? Unless we are to fall into a radical monism which denies the datum of multiplicity, or into a radical, atomistic pluralism which denies the datum of shared existence, we must find an answer to this problem of the one and the many

There is only one way of solving this problem.[31] That is by inferring another and even more basic composition in the complex structure of a

<hr/>

[31] For a more precise and detailed statement of this answer, see Van Steenberghen, *Ontologie* (Louvain, Aux Editions de L'Institut Supérieur de Philosophie, 1946), pp 57–83

finite entity. This means that an absolutely *simple* Democritean atom, or Humean impression, is impossible Such a simple, atomic entity cannot exist among others even for an instant. A simple, finite entity cannot be both similar to, and distinct from, the very same entities. But the actual entities now existing at this instant are both similar to, and distinct from, the rest Hence they are not simple. Each must include something within it, essence, by which it is wholly divorced from other entities, and something else, existence, by which it is opposed to nothing and in this respect similar to the rest.

Each of these principles is correlative. Neither can be adequately conceived apart from the other Existence is always the existence *of* something (an essence), and essence is always the distinct character *of* something existent When we conceive of an essence not actualized, which we call a possibility, we conceive of it as something that *might be* actualized, and therefore in relation to existence Furthermore, in any actual thing these two principles are fused together in such a way that each determines the entity as a whole. In my concrete totality I am marked off from other entities, and every phase of my being is pervaded by my existence

The essence as such is atomistic and self-enclosed In the second place, it is nontendential and inactive. One essence as such does not tend to other essences, nor can it diffuse anything to another. Each is simply *what it is* Finally, the determinate parts of a concrete essence are more readily grasped by the human mind. Hence, as has been recently noted,[32] there has been a strong tendency in the history of Western thought to emphasize essence at the expense of existence, which is less easily abstracted and fixed by the human mind in clear and distinct definitions by universal concepts. As a result of this tendency, Western thought has been peculiarly prone to philosophies of radical pluralism and logical atomism, which view the world as a set of distinct entities entirely divorced from one another and which have great difficulty in focusing the active, causal phases of being which spring from existence rather than from essence

This essentialist tendency leads to significant distortions and oversimplifications of philosophical doctrine, for existence is more ultimate and more perfect than essence. Essence without existence, though it may be brought before the mind very easily as a logical abstraction, in reality is nothing at all. It is only by virtue of existence that essence emerges from its causes and ceases to be nothing. Though less easily grasped than essence, existence is actually possessed in common by all the data of experience, indeed by anything whatsoever, whether in human experience or not. Furthermore, it is active and diffusive, never atomistic, self-enclosed, and insular, like the essential aspect of finite being. These active, tenden-

[32] See Gilson, *op. cit.*

tial, and causal phases of concrete entities are due to existence rather than to essence. They are expressed in our language by verbs rather than by nouns It is to these existential aspects of finite being that we must now turn

E. *Tendency and Causation* Activity is a special kind of change, namely, that which originates within a finite entity The origination and partial completion of such activity within the entity is *tendency.*

The existence of such tendencies within all the entities we experience is confirmed by a vast wealth of direct evidence. First of all, we constantly feel within ourselves such tendencies as hunger, thirst, curiosity, and so forth Through communication with others, we discover such tendencies in them. In the case of subhuman entities, with which communication is impossible, we find that similar entities act and behave in similar ways. Unless we assume constant, self-originating tendencies, determined by similar, formal structures, we cannot explain the myriad facts revealed by what is called induction

That these tendencies originate within the entity is confirmed by evidence which shows that a given entity will go on behaving in a constant manner even though the surrounding conditions may vary over a wide range Otherwise, the prediction of what a given entity will do in a hitherto unobserved situation would be impossible As long as its structure endures, fire tends to burn, ice to cool, and so on Every natural entity constantly tends to act in ways which are determined by its essential structure. What is the explanation of this constant, tendential factor?

It cannot be explained by reference to essence alone, for as we have seen, essence, like a Humean impression, is always insular, self-enclosed, and exclusive. Tendency is an urge that reaches out beyond essence to more being not yet possessed Hence it is due to existence rather than to essence, for it is by existence that the finite entity is allied to others beyond itself As soon as existence is fused with a determinate, restricted essence, it bubbles over as an active tendency toward further existence. But the specific form of this tendency is determined by the essence Each tends beyond its essence because of its existence.

But the character of this tendency is due to its essence Each divergent kind of thing has correspondingly divergent tendencies. Inorganic things have simpler tendencies, corresponding to their simpler nature Plants have their constant, vegetative tendencies, and individual human beings all possess tendencies to live in human ways determined by their human nature. This basic urge is the root of what is called human obligation, and the realization of these essential tendencies is the standard of human goodness. Any entity is in a sound or healthy state only in so far as it realizes its essential tendencies Good is no mere property or essence, but an *existential category*—the active realization of a given nature [88]

Tendency is, therefore, a necessary result of essence and existence together It must be recognized as a distinct factor in the complex structure of any finite entity There are two distinct types of tendency, the immanent and the transitive Immanent tendencies not only originate but are also completed within the active agent Thus the tendency to knowledge in man is completed within the knowing agent without any change being produced in the environment Such purely immanent tendencies are, however, very rare Most tendencies are transitive in character Such tendencies originate within a given entity, but then pass out of it to effect changes in surrounding entities by which alone the original tendency is realized.

This transitive realization of tendency, which is diffused to other entities, is commonly referred to as *causal efficacy*, or more properly as *efficient causation* Many of these causal influences are directly observed Others are inferred They are expressed in the natural laws or principles of science, which show the dependence of one kind of entity on another. No finite entity can exist by itself, but it is dependent upon other entities in myriad ways

This raises an important question concerning the whole collection of finite entities which constitutes the world of nature. Can it exist alone? Or is it dependent on something extrinsic?

VI The Argument for a First Cause

Can finite entities, having the complex structure described in this paper, account for their own existence? This is the question The uniform answer given by realistic philosophers who have paid any attention to it, from the time of the Greeks down to the present day, has been negative. Many arguments purporting to demonstrate this conclusion have been formulated, some more cogent, and some less so There is, of course, no time within the limits of this essay to do justice to these arguments in any detail. But it may be possible to make a few brief comments on their present status.

In the first place, it must be stated that the best of these arguments are not even known at the present time. Those that are usually discussed today in this country, in elementary textbooks of philosophy and elsewhere, are

---

[88] Hence for a realist there is no radical separation of fact from value. What is *universally* and essentially good for man is determined by his tendential nature, certainly a fact He is in a good condition when this nature is realized, in a bad condition when this is thwarted For the realistic concepts of natural law and natural right, which are implied by this tendential analysis, see the essays by William A Banner, pp 218 ff, and Charles Malik, pp 333 ff

weak and distorted versions made popular by the writings of Kant and Hume. Twisted as they are by the subjectivistic assumptions of modern philosophy, they bear almost no resemblance to the classic arguments of the realistic tradition, which are based upon a realistic conception of the immediate data of experience and upon the distinction between essence and existence, to which an analysis of these immediate data must lead

Recent criticism has shown also that even the classical arguments, as summarized by Aquinas in Question II of the *Summa Theologiae*, are incomplete and weakened by many dubious assumptions [34] The first argument, based on change, may show that it is necessary to infer something beyond the mobile entities of nature But by itself it certainly shows very little concerning the intrinsic character of this primary immobility, even that it is one. The causal principles underlying these arguments are sound. They must be accepted by anyone who accepts the implication of the law of contradiction, that something cannot be explained by nothing. But realistic thought must concern itself with the search for some causal argument that will be free from questionable, nonmetaphysical assumptions and which will reveal something more basic about the nature of the inferred first cause Such an argument has not yet been definitively stated. The least inadequate formulation known to me is that of Van Steenberghen[35] which may be summarized as follows:

Contingent entities which exist require an extrinsic cause (This follows from the meaning of contingency, the law of contradiction, and the principle of sufficient reason. A contingent entity is one whose essence is distinct from its existence and which, therefore, as such, may either be or not be)
The immediate objects of experience are contingent entities which exist (This follows from the analysis of the immediate data of experience which we have just presented.)
Therefore, the immediate objects of experience require an extrinsic cause.

The next essential part of the argument takes a disjunctive form It is required to clarify the nature of this extrinsic cause which is so far indeterminate.

This extrinsic cause is either finite or infinite. (This follows from the law of excluded middle.)
It cannot be finite (If it were finite [essence distinct from existence], not only would it not be in a position to account for the existence of other entities radically distinct from it, but it would not even be able to account for its own existence.)
Therefore, it must be infinite. (Infinite here means non-finite, that is, lacking in all the complex composition which necessarily appertains to finite existence. An infinite being is one whose essence is to exist)

[34] See, among others, Van Steenberghen, *Ontologie, op. cit.*, pp 130–38.
[35] *Op. cit*, pp 111–20

This argument is purely metaphysical in character and involves no dubious assumptions concerning the world of nature It is based exclusively upon an analysis of the composite structure of finite being, as involving an essence distinct from existence. It reveals three characteristics of the inferred being. (1) existence, in fact, an unlimited act of existing, (2) causation, and (3) infinity, or radical distinctness from all that is finite From these traits further attributes may be deduced

Such arguments as this have not been carefully and seriously considered by modern thinkers They certainly call for unbiased examination and criticism At the present time, some argument of this type would certainly be defended by most realistic philosophers.

If the argument of this essay has been sound, there are certain pervasive data which are thrust upon our experience with an immediate and inexorable constraint and which do not fall within the limited province of any of the special sciences One of these is the all-pervasive fact of existence, the object of first philosophy During the last four hundred years this datum has been largely ignored and the discipline of metaphysics scorned and neglected. At the present time in the free universities of the West it is dead No genuine empiricist can view this tragic situation with complacency The mysterious but pervasive data of existence, multiplicity, and change cannot be consistently doubted without abandoning the whole noetic enterprise of man They cry out for description, analysis, and explanation

If philosophy is to endure, this difficult task must be seriously undertaken once again The first step in such a revival of philosophy must be a re-examination of the results of classical realistic thought. Some of these results have been briefly outlined in this paper. If these descriptions and explanatory theories are false, they must be replaced by other descriptions and theories which are less inadequate Unless philosophy is to be abandoned, such a movement of revival and reconstruction must take place A realist may be defined as an empiricist who is prepared to dedicate himself to such a task of revolutionary revival, nothing less than the reconstruction of philosophy itself.

III

An Examination of
Contemporary Naturalism and Materialism

Oliver Martin, *University of Rhode Island*

NATURALISTS and materialists profess to be realistic, and they share with
the present writers the belief in the reality of matter There is also a common negative thesis as to the essential falsity of all forms of modern idealism Just as the old village atheist was often more honest, morally and intellectually, than the Baptist deacon with whom he argued around the
cracker barrel, so the professional materialist may sometimes be nearer
the angels than his opponent Paradoxically, the "bad" materialist of fiction
is sometimes the idealist

Speaking statistically, as a person the naturalist or materialist often tends
to be intellectually hardheaded. He tries to understand the infinite ways in
which people fool themselves Because of his respect for facts, at least of
a kind, he rebels against the sham of those who cannot stomach them Because he knows that man is a material creature, he has little patience with
those who, for their own gain, would like to forget it And because of his
natural antipathy to all forms of cant and hypocrisy, he is often the courageous soul to be found in social struggles fighting the myriad of misplaced
dogmatisms that confuse the eternal with some relatively transitory phenomenon

However, it is not with personal types that we shall be concerned but
rather with materialism and naturalism as philosophical doctrines For it is
impossible to appraise the consistency of a person who is called by the
name of the doctrine he professes unless the doctrine is first understood
Unless the question is begged, it might just be possible that the virtues of
the naturalists and materialists exist in spite of, and not because of, their
theoretical positions Of this, we shall say more later.

At any rate, it is necessary for those who consider themselves truly realistic to come to grips with the position of their only rivals to such a claim.

For this purpose we shall consider critically two volumes *Naturalism and the Human Spirit* consists of a group of fifteen essays by different philosophers on contemporary naturalism [1] *Philosophy for the Future* presents the position of contemporary materialism in a group of twenty-eight essays by twenty-seven authors [2] The two volumes are chosen for three reasons First, if contemporary naturalism and materialism are to be found anywhere, they are to be found here Second, the authors frankly admit their positions. And finally, there is little danger of the critic being accused of selecting his evidence.[3]

A word, first, about the meaning of criticism Criticism may be fatal or non-fatal A philosophical system may be appraised in terms of two criteria coherence and adequacy Coherence implies both formal and material consistency These two criteria are necessary in the sense that if an author does not meet them at all, then he may say anything One opinion is as good as another, which is identical with saying that no opinion has any truth value.

There are two kinds of inadequacy. A system may be inadequate because, while taking account of all of experience, it does not do so very well This is not fatal to the system, for it may be improved without self-destruction. Second, a system may be inadequate because it does not account for all kinds of experience. This kind of inadequacy is fatal because, since its essence is defined in part by what it neglects, its improvement is equivalent to self-destruction. We believe naturalism and materialism to be inadequate in this sense

There are also two kinds of incoherence. A system may be coherent with respect to its central theses but incoherent in the application of them This is not fatal On the other hand, a system may be incoherent in the statement of the very theses that define it. This kind of incoherence is fatal and, we believe, is the kind that characterizes naturalism and materialism

Ideally, one should give an exposition of a position before criticizing it This can be done if the position is not fatally incoherent. But if it is, then how can a coherent presentation be given of that which is fatally incoherent in order that the critic may demonstrate such incoherence? The alternative for the critic is to show that an attempt at exposition must include incompatible theses. We have here the unique case in which exposition is criticism, and conversely That this is the case with respect to the two volumes under consideration we shall proceed to demonstrate

[1] Ed. by Y H Krikorian (New York, Columbia University Press, 1944).

[2] Ed by R W Sellars, V. J McGill, and M. Farber (New York, Macmillan, 1949).

[3] The naturalism we are considering is that which is dominant and most influential in the United States—especially in public education The analysis of this paper would not be relevant to some positions which have been called naturalistic, for instance, the philosophy of Paul Weiss

I. The Critique of Naturalism

The central thesis of naturalism is that which defines it, so that to find the thesis is to ask for the definition of naturalism.

Definition in terms of subject matter. In some essays naturalism is defined in terms of subject matter, object, or kind of reality affirmed as basic and ultimate. It is the position that holds nature to be "the whole of reality" (pp 242–43),[4] "that regards everything that exists or occurs to be conditioned in its existence or occurrence by causal factors within one all-encompassing system of nature . . ." (p. 18), that has "an appreciation of the primacy of matter and the pervasiveness of change . . ." (p 65; see also p. 289).

Definition in terms of method "Positively, naturalism can be defined as the continuity of analysis—as the application of what all the contributors called scientific methods to the critical interpretation and analysis of every field" (p 358). Again, "there is for naturalism no knowledge except that of the type ordinarily called 'scientific' " (p. 289). Or, again, "Naturalism has no essential tenets beyond the principle of continuity of analysis" (p. 185).

In appearance there may seem to be no incompatibility in the two modes of defining naturalism But, on further examination, there is. Either there is a begging of the question in defining naturalism, or one mode of definition must be essential and the other derivative Let us examine these possibilities.

If one asserts that physical, spatiotemporal nature is the only reality, then it might plausibly be maintained that the scientific method is the only method of obtaining knowledge. For the purpose of analysis the implication may be granted in this case However, it would be incumbent upon the naturalist to offer evidence for the categorical truth of the antecedent. Two questions may be asked What is nature? And how do we know that nature is all that there is? Very little is said in answer to the first question Nature is spoken of as "stretches of events" (p 289) In another place, nature is called "quite a mess of miscellaneous stuff" (p 358). Generally, the impression is given that nature is simply what the natural scientist finds it to be (p. 288) To illustrate, Mr. Dennes informs us that since from the standpoint of the scientific method causation is really nothing but a "regular correlation," therefore there is little justification for interpreting it as a metaphysical category (p. 291). If so, then naturalism as a philosophy has little to say about what nature is

It has still less to offer in the way of answering the question of how one

---

[4] These, and the following pages in this section, refer to Kríkorian, *op cit.*

knows that nature is the only reality. Certainly not by the scientific method, for it can only tell us *what* there is if one already knows *that* nature is all that there is To put it in another way, the method used in the natural sciences does not in itself tell one that the nature which is studied exhausts the whole of reality. For that, a philosophical method is necessary. Actually, nature as being the whole of reality is simply posited. No evidence is given for the proposition. Such a procedure may be contrasted with that of, say, the classical realism of the Hebraic-Christian tradition. Though the Christian may believe that God rather than nature is basic reality, he has never been willing merely to affirm his thesis In the history of thought there are volumes attesting to the fact that he has at least tried to give evidence, however unsuccessful his critic may have thought his attempts. Even though one may grant that nature is ultimate and that it implies only the knowledge obtained by the scientific method, it would seem that naturalism is inadequate if, *as a philosophy,* it has little to say about the nature that it affirms as ultimate; and even more so if it offers no evidence whatsoever for the truth of the statement itself.

On the other hand, if the essential basis of naturalism is its statement on methodology, then again two questions may be asked First, what is the scientific method? Second, how do we know that the scientific method is the only method by which knowledge can be obtained? We find it difficult to discover the answer to the first question because there is no essay devoted to an analysis of scientific method. Throughout the book there are a few hints about what the method might be. In one place it is identified with "criticism" (p. 271). Such an identification is too general to be enlightening In another place it is spoken of as "nondialectical" (pp. 201, 375), but this is negative. The scientific method is defined as "continuity of analysis" (p. 185), but this is quite noninformative, as it turns out that continuity of analysis simply refers to the unrestricted use of what is called the scientific method (pp 185, 358).

In other places the scientific method is characterized by the adjective "empirical" (Preface, pp 18, 65, 185) We may grant that the scientific method is empirical if we are thinking of the method of the physical sciences. However, "empirical" is a character common to any method, other than that of pure deduction, and is hardly a unique characteristic of the scientific method. The methods used in ethical theory, aesthetics, history, and physics may all have the common property of being empirical. If the scientific method refers to a common aspect of all these particular methods, then it ceases to be *a* particular method In so far as the scientific method is one method among others, then it is not uniquely empirical

More often than not the scientific method is characterized as "experimental" (pp 3, 4, 242, 376, 382). If any adjective uniquely characterizes

the scientific method, it would be the word "experimental," and we are told
that the reference is to those "techniques found so effective in the natural
sciences" (p. 376) The question is Can a method that is uniquely defined
in terms of the physical sciences do justice to other types of knowledge?
Evidently not Mr. Strong, in writing about historical knowledge, points
out that one "must recognize differences of method and result in historical
work in contrast to the work of physical scientists" And he further states
flatly that "the historian cannot experiment" (p 155).

Our conclusion is that it is not at all clear what the naturalist means by
the scientific method. The objection might be made that since it is well
known what the scientific method is, there is no need to explain it Such an
objection would not be relevant The naturalists are not merely saying that
there is such a method Their thesis is much stronger and is to the effect
that the scientific method is the *only* method by which knowledge may be
obtained With such a strong thesis, there is the responsibility to be clear
as to the nature of the method which defines and delimits the whole realm
of human knowledge

The difficulty may be put briefly as follows If the scientific method refers
to the techniques of the physical sciences, then it can be carefully defined
and can be called experimental In that case, however, it can hardly do
justice to the demands of disciplines other than the physical sciences On
the other hand, if it is defined broadly enough to do justice to all fields of
knowledge, then either it is reduced to some property which all methods
have in common, and hence ceases to be a particular method, or it must be
defined contradictorily or ambiguously.

We find an even greater difficulty when we try to answer the second
question, about how we can know that knowledge obtained by the scientific
method is the only kind of knowledge possible We cannot know it by
deduction from the knowledge that nature is the whole of reality, for that
cannot be known itself by the method, as we have already seen It cannot
be known by the scientific method because, while both necessary and sufficient for describing events, relations, and qualities in nature in a genetic
and functional way, the method hardly gives information about itself.
In other words, the experimental method does not give information about
its own nature and limitations, because only the "real" can limit a method.

An objection might be made that the essence of naturalism is not the
assertion of either nature or the unrestrictedness of the scientific method as
absolute, the one being deducible from the other Rather it is the case that
there is a mutual implicatory relationship between them such that each is
evidence for the other Now one might even grant the mutual relation of
implication between the two theses. It might plausibly be argued that if
only physical nature exists, then only those experimental methods applica-

ble to such nature can give knowledge, or, if the experimental method is the only method by which knowledge can be obtained then only nature can be known to exist. But all of this has nothing to do with the nature of the evidence required for the naturalist position. The naturalist must give evidence for one or the other. But if there is no evidence given for either thesis, it is irrelevant to point out that both imply each other

This inability of the naturalist either to be clear about his thesis or to give any evidence for it leads to strange contradictions To the degree that he is clear about the scientific method, its efficacy must be found to lie chiefly in the physical sciences. But in this case the naturalist would be guilty of an a priori methodological reductionism On the other hand, because he takes pride in his so-called empiricism, he must allow the existence of anything—*even that which it would be impossible to discover by the experimental method* For example, we find Mr. Hook telling us, "as for decreeing what does or can *exist,* there is nothing in scientific method that *forbids* anything to exist" (p 42, italics in original, see also p 270) Mr. Lamprecht even goes so far as to say that "the existence of God in the sense of a person is an open possibility" (p 31). Since such "openness" is impossible, it is readily recognized as such by other naturalists Of such wide-open empiricism, Mr. Costello will have none According to him, "philosophy must be partly reductionist. So even the new naturalism has at least one reductionist or liquidationist thesis There is no 'supernatural' God and immortality are myths" (p 295). This view is also confirmed by Mr Krikorian and Mr. Randall (pp 242, 358). This is, of course, saying that naturalism is reductionist by definition!

The conclusion would seem to be that either the naturalists have no thesis or, if they have one, that it is completely arbitrary and is concerned with the unrestrictedness of something called the scientific method, whatever that may be. It was this irrationalism of naturalism that Professor Murphy referred to when he said that "it seeks to settle by stipulation the very issues that we most need to be reasonable about if we can "[5]

In order to avoid the charge of existential reductionism, and in order to offer a contrast to materialism, naturalists seem to admit such notions as levels of reality and emergent qualities, and while these ideas are more or less implicit, and sometimes explicit, throughout the book (pp. 229, 361, 362), nevertheless there are at least three other positions that are taken First, Miss Lavine believes that to speak of levels of reality or emergent qualities or the growth of the "higher" out of the "lower" is "to speak the language of the seer" (p 183) Continuity and discontinuity are apparently "ideas" limited to methodology rather than existence On the other hand, Mr. Dennes believes that "none of the machinery of doctrines of

[5] *The Journal of Philosophy,* XLII (July 19, 1945), 400–417

levels was ever needed" (p. 285) Finally, on the question at issue, Mr. Edel finds it possible for naturalism to be neutral (p 91).

Regarding the uniqueness of man, there seem to be at least three positions In many places the uniqueness of man is *asserted*, often in indignation at the critics of naturalism who question its adequacy in accounting for the moral and spiritual experiences of men (pp 11, 361, 362, 374, 376). At other times we are told that living beings are physical, chemical systems which "reveal no peculiar entities" (p. 243). Mr. Randall seems to imply that only the supernaturalists can "insist on the unique and distinctive character of man or some portion of his being—his soul or mind . . ." (p 356) And Mr Dewey, as quoted by Miss Lavine, can go so far as to say that "to me human affairs, associative and personal, are projections, continuations, complications, of the nature which exists in the physical and prehuman world" (p 183). Finally, Mr Schneider carries the Dewey principle of the denial of certainty to its ultimate, and perhaps consistent, conclusion when he asks the question "Is the human being designed to function as a rational animal or as a beast of prey? Who can tell with certainty?" The reason given for such humble uncertainty is that "the knowledge of nature in general . . . is experimental, and the evidence is not all in " (p. 128).

Whereas Mr Dewey and others seem to emphasize the fact that hypotheses and truths change (p 12, *passim*), Mr Dennes correctly points out that terms, hypotheses, and truths do not themselves necessarily change because that which they describe changes (p. 274). And Mr. Randall assures us that men cannot even live if they constantly shift from one belief to another (p. 382).

Mr Dewey regrets that antinaturalists who "lack respect for the scientific method" often identify naturalism with a practical or ethical materialism. Presumably Mr. Randall is less squeamish, for he points out that "science in the intellectual sphere and common sense 'American materialism' in the environmental" are "the two major themes in the progress of American naturalism . . ." (pp. 320, 321).

As we have said before, if the central thesis of naturalism cannot be stated without confusion, it is little wonder that such derivative theses as the foregoing are equally confusing and contradictory.

Let us return to the so-called central thesis of naturalism and redouble our efforts to fathom its profundity Let us assume that all the contradictions we have discovered are delusions on our part because, as Mr. Dewey says, such antinaturalism as is implied in our criticism "tends to lower the intellectual standards of antinaturalists, to dull their sense of the importance of evidence . ." (p. 10) Let us try again and do our best to keep our intellectual standards up.

One may simply take one horn and assert that the nerve of the naturalist principle is that the scientific method is not only the only method by which knowledge is obtained but that it must not be restricted in any sense (p 185) Surely if there is any common tenet that all the authors hold, it would seem to be this. As we have seen, we have not only not been told what the method is, but no evidence has been given for this thesis But out of kindess, one might simply try to make the best of it and agree with Mr Dennes when he says that naturalism has no positive doctrine about the world at all (p. 288). It is simply a doctrine of methodology

This is quite an admission to make. But after all, it is at least something that is agreed upon, and since the scientific method by which anything may be known is a very important subject, to know that it is the only method is to know a lot But whether or not there is any evidence for such knowledge, if we are to keep our intellectual standards up, we cannot even safely say that, for in several places we are told that naturalism is really only an attitude or temper of mind (Preface, pp 319, 374) Since even a doctrine of methodology is a philosophical doctrine, if naturalism is really only an attitude, then it can hardly be said to be a philosophical doctrine in *any* sense. Since we have found no consistent statement even concerning methodology, and since we have already been told that naturalism is not a doctrine about existence, it would seem that the only thing in common among the contributors is a common attitude or temper. A method may imply an attitude, but the two can never be identified.

It turns out, then, that the naturalists have no rational thesis at all! What pretends to be one cannot even be stated There are not only no "common agreements" as to "specific ideas" (Preface), there is not even common agreement that there is no common agreement as to any ideas.

Now usually an attitude or temper is directed for or against something. If there is nothing in common that the naturalists are *for*, perhaps we can find what they are *against*. The conclusion that the naturalists have no thesis at all is damaging enough, but if the critic were to add that the only unity to the whole book was the subjective attitude of being against the belief in God, then he might be accused of substituting "emotional rhetoric for analysis and discrimination" (p. 10), as Mr. Dewey accuses the anti-naturalists It is undoubtedly unsporting to shoot fish in a barrel, but as a finishing touch we must point out that Mr. Costello confirms what we had suspected.

After pointing out that philosophy must be partly reductionist and that the new naturalism has at least one liquidationist thesis, namely, that there is no supernatural and that God and immortality are myths, he says: "So the naturalist now looks up to the great white throne, where once sat great Jove himself, and exclaims, 'Thank God, that illusion is gone.' But great illusions are not so easy to banish. We must take care lest our suppressed illusions come back to plague us in altered guise, like grinning fiends from out the Freudian deep " And then Mr Costello adds: "I do not find any great unity, otherwise, among these new naturalists" (pp. 295, 296). *Voilà tout!*

What remains of the presumption of naturalism to be realistic? Nothing. However, it is almost unbelievable the claims that are made for what is nothing much more than a vague attitude against belief in God We are told that naturalism is a "fighter's creed" (p 365), is the "starting point of genuine philosophizing" (p. 376), understands and explains values better than any other position (p 381). Furthermore, we are told that this naturalism is strictly "contemporary" and "post-modern" (p 368), correcting the thoughts of others down through history who, for various reasons, have erred From 300 B C through the first century, there was a "failure of nerve" (p 40). Medievalism is obviously false The problems generated before and after Kant are "unreal and irrelevant", in fact, "the major philosophies of the whole modern age, aside from their incidental insights, have for the present 'post-moderns' become largely historical exhibits" (p. 368). But this strictly new naturalism can proclaim a truth or a good having more power to bring wisdom and knowledge than can any church or party (p. 382) Finally, if one is so noncontemporary or antinaturalistic as not to believe all of this, then the unbelief is perhaps caused, according to Mr Dewey, by the dulling of one's "sense of the importance of evidence" (p 10).

Any further comment would be unmerciful!

II. The Critique of Materialism

In addition to the naturalists who think of themselves as realists, there are also those who propose the term "materialism" to characterize their realism The standpoint of a frank materialism has been given by a number of authors in the book already referred to, *Philosophy for the Future* Since a classical or philosophical realism is definitely rejected, and realism is identified with materialism, it will be worth while to examine the central theses of physical realism.

Materialism asserts the ontological primacy of inorganic matter, the existence of qualitatively distinct levels (for instance, the inorganic and organic), and opposition to idealism "Like naturalism, modern materialism is opposed to any other criterion of human value and policy than human needs and aspirations It combats all forms of authoritarianism in morals and arts, opposes reduction of ethics to mere formalism, and rejects the appeal to any supposed extranatural source of experience With the removal of a supernatural perspective, man must stand consciously on his feet. Let him rise to his full stature and dignity" (pp viii–ix).[6] Materialism "therefore combats agnosticism, skepticism, and all irrational confessions of defeat" (p vii).

The difference between naturalism and materialism is apparently one of vigor of assertion In the *Foreword,* there is a quotation from the volume *Naturalism and the Human Spirit* to the effect that "contemporary naturalism recognizes much more clearly than did the tradition from which it stems that its distinction from other philosophical positions lies in the postulates and procedures which it criticizes and rejects rather than in any positive tenets of its own about the cosmos." In comment, it is said that "this passage will serve clearly to distinguish current naturalism from the frank materialism described above" (p ix)

If materialism is simply positive naturalism, or "naturalism with matter," then what exactly is asserted and what is the nature of the evidence? We are told that the scientific method is the only method by which any kind of knowledge may be obtained, that there are no limits to be set to the method, and that the method will "eventually" cope with all basic human problems *(Foreword).* In other places, however, the nature of ultimate reality seems to be the distinctive thesis Modern materialism, we are told, asserts the following. "The inorganic pattern of matter is prior to living, minded and purposive organisms, which arise gradually and only as a result of a complex evolutionary development" (p vi) According to Mr. Churchman, "dialectics imposes no restrictions on the matter of the world" Further, the materialist "asserts the right to raise a question on any issue, *including the issue of the correct methodological* principles" (pp. 478–79, italics his).

Now there arises the question of whether methodology or ontology is the fundamental thesis The same difficulties would seem to confront the materialist here as were pointed out in connection with naturalism Does methodology limit ontology, or conversely, or neither? What is the scientific method? Sometimes the scientific method seems to refer to the methods of the physical sciences At other times, it is defined as "genetic analysis" (pp. vii, 4, 307, 616), or as the phenomenological method (p 616)— and absolutely contradicted by another author (p. 572) The scientific method is also identified with the "dialectic," a philosophical method that is associated with the doctrine of dialectic materialism (p. 47). An essay on the materialism of measurement is the closest approximation to any statement about what the scientific method may be However, the essay is concerned more with the application of the scientific method than with an analysis of its nature It seems safe to say that the dialectical method that

[6] These, and the following pages in this section, refer to Sellars, *et al., op cit*

is associated historically with Marx's communism is a kind of philosophical, metaphysical, or ontological methodology and can hardly be identified wholly with the experimental techniques of the physical sciences

This unclarity about the nature of method is perhaps responsible for the critic's inability to separate the essential from the derivative theses If reality is wholly and completely material, then the narrower methods of the physical sciences might be said to be wholly adequate. Otherwise, they certainly would not be adequate This is perhaps realized by some of the authors. For example, it is said that "a thought is a private possession and as such it cannot be regarded as a datum of science" (p. 239) Now either a thought is a real existent, or it is not If it is, then not it, but only its expression, can be understood or explained in terms of the scientific method Only if the thought is expressed in an act or a proposition can it become "an enduring object that can be examined and reexamined scientifically" (p 239). Again, the affirmation of the reality of substance as an ultimate metaphysical category is admittedly a kind of assertion that can neither be confirmed nor invalidated by the scientific methods And we have already been informed by Mr. Roy W. Sellars that "consciousness itself cannot be an object of any of the physical sciences" (p 98).

If the scientific method is irrelevant to these kinds of realities, then the materialist cannot hold to the absoluteness of the scientific method He may save his thesis, however, if by the scientific method he does not refer to the techniques of the physical sciences but rather is thinking of a broader philosophical method, namely, the dialectical method. Whether or not such a philosophical method is adequate to deal with philosophical matters is not at present relevant. At least it is a possible candidate as a philosophical method, and since materialism is philosophy and not natural science, there is at least no contradiction involved The contradiction occurs when the term "scientific method" is at one time equated with the methods of the physical sciences and at another time identified as a philosophical method This contradiction is either the cause, or the effect, of a confusion in types of *probanda* It is one thing to give a genetic explanation of material things in their relations It is something quite different to state a thesis about the ultimate nature of things Certainly the absoluteness of the genetic method is not itself genetically explained, nor is such an ontological proposition as the priority of inorganic matter the result of a genetic analysis As we have said, it is not clear whether ontology limits methodology, or conversely.

Two analyses may now be given accordingly as one horn or the other of the contradiction is taken If the scientific method refers to the limited methods of the physical sciences, then it would be restrictive and would limit possible realities to the physical Now although there is no evidence for such a methodological reductionism, nevertheless, one can consistently go on and posit the ontological priority of inorganic matter If the other horn of the contradiction is taken and the scientific method is identified with the dialectical method, which is at least applicable to the metaphysical and ontological level, then there are two possible and favorable consequences. First, on the metaphysical level a method may be self-correcting and, as Mr. Churchman pointed out, should not and does not limit the matter or content of the universe The purpose of a metaphysical method should be that of taking account of all kinds of realities and not that of selecting, neglecting, or denying in an a priori manner Second, in all of those cases where we have seen that the methods of the physical scientists were inapplicable, the philosophical or dialectical method may be efficacious But this way leads to realism if there is a non-Hegelian interpretation of the method.

True realism leaves open the question of methodological and ontological decisions What exists and what is real is a matter to be empirically determined There is no initial a priori limitation on either method or content. What nature is, is something to be discovered, not something to be initially stipulated The method or methods applicable and efficacious will be determined by the nature of the object of inquiry There will be no initial determination of methodology because of some bias as to the nature of what exists or does not exist This is true empiricism Since all determination is negation, to the extent that the philosophical realist discovers *this* exists rather than *that*, then, of course, as any metaphysician must, he will make his denials consistent with his assertions But the openness and thoroughly empirical attitude toward both methodological and ontological content will guarantee, at least in part, that his denials and assertions will be based on evidence And so the materialist, too, must offer evidence either for his methodological absolutism or for the absolutizing of ontological content. He must take his choice, but one or the other he must do Otherwise, both absolutes are merely posited.

Realism implies that there is some objective ground for whatever pretends to be knowledge It is not necessary for our present purpose to clarify the meaning of "objective ground." It is sufficient to point out that truth of any kind cannot wholly be determined subjectively by feeling, wish or willing Now either there are moral and religious truths. or there are not [7] If there are not, then moral nihilism is implied. If there are, and the ground is nature, then certainly the concept of nature must contain more than the notion of matter in motion. To say that matter or energy is highly organized in man is true but not sufficient Both Hitler and St Francis were undoubtedly at least highly organized bits of matter. Both had "norms" and "needs," and both were probably in some sense "cultural complications"

[7] Reference is made to propositions *of* and not *about*.

and "projections" of subhuman nature But their ways of life were quite different Which is better? And why?

The "nature" of the natural scientists is neutral to moral norms. The "nature" of the physicists, chemists, and biologists can be used to enhance or to destroy man Such nature knows only the "conditional ought" If an objective ground is to be found for morality in nature, and if one is to be truly realistic, then it would seem that some more adequate notion of nature is necessary. In classical realism the question has often been supplied by a concept of nature and of natural law that is something more than the partial insights obtained by the limited methodology of the physical sciences To point out that such a notion is dangerous because it leads to theological implications is more autobiography than criticism Perhaps it does But if one is really empirical, one does not reject it arbitrarily

Because of the fact that for the materialist the relation of the ethical and the ontological is that of conjunction rather than implication, he tends toward subjective idealism so far as the "practical" is concerned Whether or not a moral position is called "interest theory," "approbative theory," psychological or affective theory, or something similar is of little importance if subjectivism is not surmounted. The mode of subjectivity is irrelevant It would seem that if one were to be realistic, an ontological materialism would imply a moral materialism (whatever that would be)—and conversely In the *Foreword* we find that this is not the case Ontological, cosmological, and historical materialism are acceptable, but to infer that a practical or moral materialism follows is to indulge in an "emotional transfer" (p x) Just why this is so is never explained.

All of this calls attention once again to the consequence of confusing conjunction with implication, that is to say, that the materialists who insist most on what they call the "unity of theory and practice" tend to refute their own thesis The only alternative to this conclusion would be that there *is* unity of theory and practice, that moral subjectivism is implied by ontological materialism Such subjectivism means that moral norms are arbitrary postulates or guides for action which cannot themselves be substantiated or grounded. The concept of "truth" is applicable not to the standards themselves but only to the relation between the acts and standards. In morals there is only "formal," not "material," truth. But such formalism is at least compatible, if not identical, with moral nihilism.

To prevent misunderstanding, the exact point of the criticism may be put in this way. Moral nihilism is not incompatible with ontological materialism No *ad hominem* argument is intended It does not follow, as some critics of materialism have assumed, that if one is a materialist he must in fact be a moral nihilist As a matter of fact, a materialist may not be However, all of this works the other way, too It is also irrelevant for the materialist to constantly insist that he, too, may have moral norms and standards So he can and does But again, the fact that the materialist has them is a historical or autobiographical fact The question still remains whether he has moral standards because of, or in spite of, his materialism

The begging of this question is rather typical and may be illustrated by a remark by Mr Farber. He says that Scheler's critique of naturalism proceeds "assumptively" because he assumes as real and as unanalyzable in "naturalistic" terms such phenomena as "holy love" (p 616) Just why Scheler is assuming, and not Mr Farber, is not at all clear In the history of thought, it seems safe to say that the interpretation of holy love has been essentially the task of nonmaterialists. Mr. Farber's remark is from the last chapter of a book in which it is said that mind is a kind of material behavior, sociology is a biological discipline (p. 231), culture is the "suprasomatic" (p 375), and human behavior "merely the response of the articulate primate organism to cultural stimuli" (p 374) It would seem to be no accidental oversight that, although space is found for a chapter on psychoanalysis nowhere is there any insight even into the nature of the moral virtues, let alone such notions as holy love It seems reasonable to insist that the burden of proof rests on materialism

The difficulties that are responsible for the central thesis carry over to the derivative theses. For example, there is little clarity on the notion of what "matter" is Mr Roy W. Sellars assures us that matter is not "hard" atoms moving about in absolute empty space. His "tentative conclusion," which seems to be his only conclusion, is "that the word 'matter' should be used for material things, macroscopic and microscopic" (p 86) Mr. Churchman informs us that "the 'matter' of the world is taken to be the class of all problems based on human demands, that can be raised about the world" (p 478). If the nonmaterialist is a bit confused by such a definition of matter, he may turn to a statement of Mr Wilfrid Sellars. "We tend today to mean by 'matter' a set of *things* which in no sense are made up of other *things*, and of which all the properties are of a sort which we should call 'physical,' or, at least, would refuse to call 'mental' or 'vital' " (p 548) The inability to be clear about the philosophical category of matter should not be surprising, as the reader has been forewarned in the *Foreword* that "the materialist holds that philosophers cannot improve upon the descriptive concepts of matter supplied by the working scientist of his time" (p vii).

Is process or substance an ultimate category for materialism? We are told that modern materialism is "evolutionary," "organizational," and that it stresses such new concepts as "field," "configuration," and "process" (p 79) On the other hand, in the one systematic, metaphysical essay of the volume, which is by far the most enlightening essay, Mr Nelson believes that "closely reasoned expositions" based upon the category of process are "astonishingly rare" (p 108) The belief in the efficacy of process as a metaphysical category he would call a matter of "faith," and, although somewhat apologetically, he tries to demonstrate that empirical knowledge is not possible without the category of substance

Is materialism proven by experience or not? Mr. Cornforth says that "materialists—unlike some of the representatives of what is often called philosophical 'realism'—justify their 'thesis of the reality of the physical world' and of the material basis of experience, not by general 'metaphysical' arguments a priori, but by appealing to experience itself" (p 507). And yet the category of substance, according to Mr. Nelson, "can be neither confirmed nor invalidated by experience . . ." (p 122).

Is technology merely a means, or is it a norm in terms of which social evaluations may be made? In one place we are told that "technology is destructive as well as creative " As such it would seem to be a "means," and whether or not it was used in one way or another would partially depend upon ultimate ends The same author, however, can tell us that whatever the fate and future of mankind may be, it will be decided by technology (p 380), and also that cultures can be "measured and evaluated" in terms of technology

Are moral truths determined by the facts of the physical and social environment or not? Or are they determined merely subjectively? It is said that "the social institutions which determine the individual are neither good nor bad but valuing makes them so" (p. 287) The criterion here would seem to be subjective (see also pp. 455 ff) In other places morality would seem to be completely the function of technology or culture. For example, "Social systems, philosophies, and art are functions of an evolving technology", and progress (which is usually considered to be an evaluational term) in cultural development can be measured, and "the measurement can be expressed in mathematical terms" (pp. 379, 380, 429) On the other hand, Mr Edel questions such "absoluteness" and prefers to think of the sociohistorical element as entering only "into the 'relative,' not into the 'truth'" (p. 442) Mr Haldane has yet another preference, basing all morality on the probability of the kind that characterizes pure chance (p. 217). In contrast to all of this, Mr Roy W Sellars speaks of absolute moral principles and points out the difference between their validity on the one hand and the validity of the applications of such principles on the other, apparently limiting the notion of relativity to the latter Mr. Edel informs us that just the opposite is the truth, that the distinction between ideas and principles on the one hand, and applications on the other, is idealistic and a Platonic approach (p 429).

In order to take account of the uniqueness of man, some meaning of free will seems to be implied here and there (pp 103. 227, 324, 325) Just how this is possible when reasoning is called a "cultural complication" and "mentation" is "but a further development of the selective and varied, integrative activity of the brain as attuned to the vectorial alertness of the body," is not all clear (p. 103) Mr White seems to be bothered not at all by such a notion as freedom Mind "is but a form of motion of matter cellularly organized." "Culture is merely the name we give to matter-and-energy in symbolic form " "Breathing a prayer" and "loathing snakes" are all "examples of matter in motion." Since all of this is true, it follows that "human behavior is merely the response of the articulate primate organism to cultural stimuli. Human behavior is determined, therefore, by culture. But culture is not determined by man, by his wishes, will, hopes, fears, etc Man is, of course, prerequisite to culture; he is, so to speak, the catalyst that makes the interactive culture process possible But the culture process is *culturally* determined, not biologically or psychologically" (p 374).

What the author is saying is that matter and energy in symbolic form determine matter and energy in symbolic form It is rather terrifying to know that man is merely the catalyst in this gigantic cosmic tautology. But undoubtedly it can all be explained by "failure of nerve." We recall that Mr Roy W. Sellars says: "I am impressed by man's novelty and uniqueness" (p. 103). For the nonmaterialist, the foregoing tends to confirm Mr. Sellars's impression—however, for reasons which the materialist would perhaps fail to appreciate.

In an examination of materialism it is not enough merely to point out the contradictions Some account ought to be given explaining why the contradictions occur No author or group of authors is wholly consistent. But if incoherence constitutes the very essence of a "system," then some explanation is necessary. In what follows we shall attempt to demonstrate what we believe to be one fatal difficulty of materialism, the substitution of conjunction for implication—an idea we have already mentioned and which we shall now further develop

III. Conjunction or Implication?

Let us consider two propositions that the materialist believes. First, that matter or matter-energy is basic reality, and second, that the dignity of the individual person ought to be respected (p. 70). Now the materialist so believes, or he does not. If he does, it proves nothing one way or another. The fact of his belief is autobiography, not metaphysics, and autobiography is history, not philosophy. As a philosopher, the materialist must hold the two propositions, not merely in conjunction, but in implication That is, he may take his choice, but one proposition must imply the other. Let us suppose that the implication is If matter is basic reality, then the moral dignity of the person ought to be respected

1 *The difficulty* Such an implication would be equivalent to saying that if the dignity of the person is denied, then one cannot consistently be a materialist. It is questionable whether anyone would be fearless enough to uphold such an implication, and it is rather certain that historically few, if any, have tried to do so.

2. *What is fatal.* The real reason why the implication cannot be made is that so far as moral matters are concerned, matter is neutral Inorganic matter, so far as we know, is completely oblivious to problems involving the moral dignity of human beings.

The converse of the implication is no more satisfactory If the moral dignity of the person ought to be respected, then matter is basic reality

1 *The difficulty:* The implication here is that if one is not a materialist, then he cannot consistently uphold the moral dignity of the person Perhaps time should not be wasted on further comment

2. *What is fatal* Such an implication would mean that in some sense or other, value determines reality Whether the implication makes much sense or not, in any case it would be a kind of idealism quite incompatible with materialism.

There is, then, no real implication between the two propositions. They stand to each other in the relation of conjunction The first is posited dogmatically, and the second is a psychological or personal, and hence historical, fact. Nominalism knows nothing but conjunction, and it so infects the materialistic thesis that it prevents even its coherent presentation.

When essences are denied, no *real* implications are possible. Few materialists seem to be aware of this nominalistic difficulty. Mr Nelson and Mr Wilfrid Sellars are, for in the very legitimate concern over "conditionals contrary to fact," after having rejected essences and universals, they substitute the notion of "dispositional properties" According to Mr. Sellars, "the concept of the nature of a thing, in so far as it is a coherent one, can be analyzed in terms of the concept of a dovetailing set of dispositional properties which specify both the states by which it has responded to its historical circumstances, and the states by which it *would* have responded to other circumstances" (p 546).

Can this concept of "nature of a thing" make implication possible? No, and for two reasons.

1 The word "it" is question-begging If "it" is something which has "historical circumstances," but is something more than those circumstances, then the traditional notion of "essence" is presupposed On the other hand, if "it" is not something more, then "it" has no nature For if anything is merely "a dovetailing set of dispositional properties," then, since they

change according to "historical circumstances," the very "nature" of anything changes from moment to moment. But this is to absolutize "change," thereby denying any continuity whereby anything can have a nature.

2 Mr. Sellars admits "that the necessity with which the states of things occur" is "tautological" (Note p 566; also p. 545). If so, then on the one hand we have "nominal" definitions with no *real* necessity, and on the other hand we have real "things" without any nature or necessity, because circumstances change every moment So, far from explaining the possibility of metaphysical implication, Mr Sellars has simply given a positivistic analysis, substituting "logical" for "real" universals. We are left on the one side with a nominalistic view of a realm of "reals" without any *real* "natures," and on the other side with nominal definitions, tautologies, or "logical" universals. No wonder that real implication is reduced to conjunction![8] Is there not a fundamental inconsistency in a nominalistic materialism defending itself in terms of universal concepts identically understood by the minds of others where such "minds" are interpreted in terms of physical brain motions that cannot be identical?

Mr. Farber's sensitivity to Mr. Scheler's criticism illustrates another consequence of the confusion of conjunction with implication. This confusion allows the materialist the privilege of having two theses. the one positive and consistently materialist, the other a thesis which is used only in answer to the critics.[9] Positively, man is interpreted essentially on the biological level. Any higher level has little, if any, causal or explanatory power When the adequacy of all this is questioned, the materialist, taking pride in his professed empiricism, may readily admit everything, from moral absolutes to holy love But of what worth are such ideas if they are used chiefly to ward off criticism?

To relieve the abstractness of such criticism, it may be well to take time to give at least one illustration Mr. Roy W. Sellars states unequivocally that he believes in "the *absolute principle* of the moral dignity of human beings" (p. 72, italics his), and he goes on to say that the basis of this "irreducible" principle "is the natural and inevitable demand of self-conscious personality to receive just social recognition" (p 72) Now let us grant these three propositions. (1) Such a principle is exactly what one would expect from a supernaturalist in the Hebraic-Christian tradition, (2) There is no question but that it is a true autobiographical fact that Mr. Sellars and many other materialists do so believe· and further, (3) The principle is true To the unsophisticated reader the following inferences,

---

[8] It is to be noted that material implication, which is a consequence of nominalism, is equated with a conjunction It is false that p is true *and* q is false. While this may be true, is it sufficient for real implication? Or is it the "howler" of which Moore spoke?
[9] This idea of "two theses," although applied differently, is suggested by Mr. Boas in Krikorian, *op cit*, p 148

then, seem reasonable: (1) A materialist can have just as "good" and "lofty" ideals as anyone else, (2) Accusing the materialist of moral nihilism is without foundation, and can be dismissed as an irrational, emotional reaction.

It may seem like a dangerous act of intellectual judo for us to accept these inferences, but that is exactly what we shall do It just so happens, however, that all this is wholly irrelevant to a legitimate criticism of materialism The relevance is only to certain *ad hominem* attacks on materialists, which they justly dislike

We do not doubt that a person may believe in astrology and also believe that the Dow-Jones averages will rise next week But it can reasonably be denied that the truth of the second belief is grounded in, determined, or implied by the truth of the first Similarly, and to repeat once again, it is not denied that a materialist can also believe in the moral dignity of human beings What is affirmed is that there is no evidence whatsoever that such a belief, or the truth of the belief, implies, or is implied by, materialism Such a belief is either something to be used against opponents, or it is a groundless, though fortunate, preference.

To demonstrate the groundlessness of Mr. Sellars's moral principle, let us consider the nature of the consciousness that makes the "demand." Mr Sellars suggests that a neural event may " 'contain' consciousness as a qualitative dimension of its existential content" (p. 99). He also speaks of consciousness as a "natural isolate and as a privately given *feature* of an event in the brain" (p 99, italics his). Now all this is not only consistent with, but would seem to be necessarily implied by, a materialist position. But this raises a question. If materialism itself is merely a set of laryngeal articulations, brain disturbances, and so forth, determined by physical causes acting on some men, then why should any one *freely* pay any attention to it? Other people have different neural disturbances, and hence it is foolish to talk about truth, freedom, or moral absolutes. On the other hand, if the materialist certainly can distinguish between a physiologically determined disturbance involving the utterance of words to which he will pay no attention whatsoever except as symptoms, and the rational defense of a coherent position (materialism) which is in no sense physically caused but rather freely arrived at—if all this is so, then the materialist has freely arrived at an error, for he cannot account for his own freedom. The logic here is as inexorable as in the refutation of "animal faith" philosophy. Creatures that really have nothing but animal faith do not publish reasoned arguments in books upholding such a thesis

Another question is. Exactly how, except verbally, does Mr. Sellars's account differ from the old materialist's conception of consciousness as an "epiphenomenon"? The reductive materialist did not necessarily deny the *experience* that is called consciousness. It was considered epiphenomenal because it was always an effect of matter, lacked causal efficacy, and hence was not amenable to the techniques of the physical sciences Now in the *Foreword* it is said that, concerning matter, the materialist "accepts what the physicist, chemist, biologist, histologist, etc. say as the best approximation at any given time" (p. vii). Since matter is basic reality, it would seem to follow necessarily that the nature of the private "feature" of the brain, consciousness, could not be known by the methods of the physical sciences. And so Mr Sellars tells us when he says, "in short, consciousness itself cannot be an object of any of the physical sciences" (p. 98) Now just how a "private feature" of the "new brain" of a "gifted mammalian biped" with "sensitive hands," which cannot be known by the scientific method, the only method allowed, can turn upon itself in the reflexive relation which is *self-consciousness* and make the demand of the absolute moral principle of human dignity—just how this is possible is perhaps one of the greatest mysteries ever propounded in human history. And certainly the strength of faith required in the dogma of the efficacy of the methods of the physical sciences puts to shame the weak faith of the average Christian

The authors of this present volume are sufficiently hardheaded to prefer to relegate matters of faith and dogma to the realm of the theological, where they rightfully belong

The difference between naturalism and materialism in the volumes considered is that of whether method or content is emphasized. In so far as both are asserted, there is no essential difference between naturalism and materialism. However, since naturalists make their essential thesis methodological, and in so far as they pretend to disown any "positive doctrine," they are forced in one of two directions One direction is toward positivism, of a psychological or logical type—and close inspection would probably disclose both The other direction is toward a metaphysical naturalism, which is materialism. The materialists as realists correctly perceive this dilemma of the naturalist In so far as the naturalists refuse to go in either direction, as they so refuse in the volume considered, then, as we have pointed out, they literally have no positive thesis at all.

Now materialists at least have a metaphysical thesis, however inadequate it may be It is not a coincidence that contemporary materialism has a Marxist tinge and inherits whatever virtues dialectical materialism may have But more often than not, the "matter" of the materialist has been a "weapon" having a *function* but lacking *content* Perhaps the genius of Marxist materialism lies not in any solution but in its critique of idealism in its various forms—the skepticism of positivism, the formalism of neo-Kantianism, the mentalism of the Hegelians, and the voluntarisms of those from Schopenhauer to James All of which, leaving aside the question of truth value for the moment, often had a sociohistorical function as a mask for the sordid *practical*. The materialists have perhaps always been aware of this to a greater extent than some of their more tender opponents The use of the word "matter" as a weapon is found in Marx's choice, as against Feuerbach's, of the term as implying the most extreme opposition to idealism. It is found in Lenin's *Empirio-Criticism* when he states that matter means that something exists independent of our consciousness

Now any realist may grant all this. Where materialism fails is in its positive aspect. For the notion of the reality of matter, whatever it may be, is something common even to classical realism and is not at all unique to materialism. What defines materialism, and hence is unique to it, is the limitation of realism to the "physical" For this reason the materialist is impaled on the horns of two dilemmas.

Dilemma I. Matter is either a metaphysical category, something more than its meaning for the physical sciences, or it is not If it is, then in order to do justice to nature, and especially the moral and religious experience of man, it must bring back in through the window what it kicked out of the metaphysical door, namely, powers, vital forces, potencies, and so forth, avoiding panpsychism only by returning to the hylomorphism of a truly philosophical realism If it is not, then, ceasing to be a philosophical category at all, it leaves materialism without any positive doctrine Contemporary materialism (for the most part) has accepted the latter alternative. In playing safe and leaving the meaning of matter to whatever the physical sciences determine at any given time, the materialists have little *systematic* metaphysics or ontology to present. What is offered consists chiefly of applications, history, and criticisms. together with natural-science essays on such subjects as the psychology of animals and the bigness of the astronomer's universe, all of which are exceedingly interesting but quite irrelevant to materialism either as evidence or as illustration

Dilemma II Either contemporary materialism admits certain moral and spiritual truths ("moral absolutes" and "holy love"!), or it does not If it does, then because of the confusion of conjunction with implication, which we have already demonstrated, it admits that which cannot be accounted for. *A subjective idealism in the realm of the practical is added conjunctively to a physical realism in the realm of the theoretical.* But this produces that gap and incompatibility between theory and practice for which the materialist criticizes the nonmaterialist and which he takes great pride in assuming that he has avoided (pp 3, 445 ff) It would appear that he is precisely the person who is guilty The "practical" is reduced to "relations of ideas" without any existential ground.

On the other hand, if contemporary materialism does not admit such truths, then physical realism is saved so far as consistency is concerned, and the gap between theory and practice vanishes. But so does human nature vanish. What is left is an a priori reductionism, the kind which did not seem to disturb the consciences of the "cruder" materialists of past centuries but which the contemporary materialist is extremely anxious to avoid, and assumes that he has done so.

The only thing "contemporary" about contemporary materialism is its terminology Its difficulties are the same as those of the materialisms of the last three centuries What is fatal to materialism is the "materialism," and not the adjective that characterizes it. Shifting from "mechanistic" to "organic" or "dialectical" materialism solves only those difficulties associated with an adjective, not those stemming from the noun. It may have been crude to speak of the brain secreting thought as liver does the bile. Is it any better to say that mentation is a private feature of the brain as attuned to the vectorial alertness of the body? It may have been crude to think of the mental and spiritual life of man as epiphenomenal, as froth on waves in a sea of matter. Has reductionism been avoided, and enlightenment been gained, by regarding man as a cultural catalyst—after culture has been defined as matter-energy in symbolic form?

In modern history, a cycle has been completed from metaphysical to methodological to metaphysical materialism A test of the long-run adequacy of a metaphysics is its ability, in terms of its categories, to continually integrate the new knowledge of the various disciplines without at the same time being destroyed Past materialism completely failed this test. The materialist's world of the seventeenth and eighteenth, and even much of the nineteenth, century simply exists no longer. It *was the "matter" of the materialists, not of Aristotle, that natural science destroyed.* And, once again, the trouble was this Either matter is a metaphysical category, or it is not. If it is, then by that very fact it must be broader in meaning than any particular concept of the physical sciences, and one is led away from materialism. In a true realism the basic concept becomes being, not matter alone. Being is a transcendental category, different in that respect from a category such as, say, "animal." But it is not on that account "beyond" experience. Rather it is an all-pervasive empirical datum, and its inclusive scope is precisely that which offers a real protection against a priori reductionism of any kind.

If matter is not a metaphysical category, then, of course, one cannot have a materialistic metaphysics Materialism was obtained by trying to have it both ways, by making a metaphysics out of the reigning concept of matter at any time. Temporary concepts were absolutized; and, as happens in all cases where the "changing" is absolutized, materialism was outmoded.

For a time there was the attempt to save materialism, first, through the linguistic technique of calling it "naturalism"—which was a much more respectable term—with the consequence that the older name was preserved chiefly by the Marxists; second, there was the use of such concepts as "levels" and "emergent qualities," with the simultaneous shift in adjectives from "mechanistic" to "organic" and "dialectical" But even if one were to admit the notion of the emergence of levels as factually true, so far from explaining anything, it stood most in need of being accounted for. Instead of an explanation, we were offered "natural piety" and "animal faith." Now as regards such matters, the older materialism simply denied, and having done so had no responsibility to explain On the other hand, the newer naturalism, in order to be new, found itself forced to admit but helpless to explain

To get out of such a hopeless muddle, there was need for a still newer approach, and at this point in the drama of materialism the methodological naturalism which we have examined came on the stage. The solution to the muddle is to have no solution at all, no philosophical system, literally nothing in common, as Mr. Costello admits, except the firm determination to liquidate belief in God. In addition to this firm negative "attitude," there is a "faith," *not a thesis,* as to the complete efficacy of the techniques of the physical sciences for all purposes *By absolutizing a method, strategy became a substitute for the philosophical quest*

It was only natural that materialists, especially those tinged with the Marxist persuasion, would desire something more positive. Either matter is basic reality, or it is not. If it is, let us not only say so but be honest enough to also call it by the right name, materialism The cycle has been completed, and naturalism once more becomes metaphysical, at least in assertion if not always in reasoning. In doing so, all of the fatal difficulties of the older materialism are inherited. It is just as impossible for materialism now as before, and now as it ever will be, to establish any relation of implication, instead of conjunction, between the theoretical and the practical.

A truly philosophical realism has the responsibility of showing that the relation between the practical and the theoretical, the moral and the ontological, is one of implication and not merely conjunction. A further responsibility, in order to avoid an idealism which would reduce existence to essence, or derive the ontological wholly from the moral, is that of giving independent evidence for the nature of the ontological which, in turn, implies the moral or practical Materialism cannot meet this responsibility because of its restricted realism. It is already halfway there, but the most important half is missing.

IV. Postscript

Since writing this chapter, my attention has been called to a recent statement of John Dewey's· "What is needed is not the carrying over of procedures that have approved themselves in physical science, but *new* methods as adapted to *human* issues and problems, as methods already in scientific use have shown themselves to be in physical subject matter "[10]

Such a statement at the end of a career might be dismissed as one of those intellectual lapses to which all writers are prone. A contradiction could be expected from a philosopher whose views are consistent only when dated But if we are to take Dewey seriously, then his recent statement would constitute a repudiation, in essence, of much in his writings for decades. He is recapturing the wisdom of Aristotle as to methodology and at the same time is suggesting a new reconstruction of his own "reconstruction" in philosophy.

Perhaps too much ought not to be made from one statement, but it does seem reasonable to suggest, in the light of the analysis of this chapter, that it is one more bit of evidence showing the confusion and intellectual disintegration of contemporary naturalism The tragedy is that while Dewey is repudiating (whether he realizes it or not) his past thought, the evils following the latter still remain. What is intellectually disintegrating remains institutionalized in many college departments in the teachings of men who not only have been indoctrinated in a nihilistic naturalism secondhand, even thirdhand, but have also been abstracted from the main stream of the philosophy which they reject without even understanding.

[10] "Philosophy's Future in Our Scientific Age," *Commentary*, VIII, No. 4, 393, as quoted by Marvin Fox in an article in *Philosophy and Phenomenological Research*, XII, No 1 (September 1951), 129. (Italics are Dewey's)

IV

A Critique of Continuity, Infinity, and Allied Concepts in the Natural Philosophy of Bergson and Russell

Jesse De Boer, *University of Kentucky*

That philosophy is not without responsibility in the study of nature, that there is a philosophical discipline which may properly be entitled natural philosophy, is attested by two of the leading philosophers of our time, Henri Bergson and Bertrand Russell Both profess a desire to treat philosophical problems in a scientific manner, and both accept an obligation to prosecute their investigations in full consciousness of the methods and results of the special sciences. The agreement of two such brilliant minds on these basic matters is warrant for looking to them for solid gains in a common development of philosophy

Russell, in *Our Knowledge of the External World*,[1] while aiming to make philosophy scientific (p vii), states that such basic characters of nature as change and continuity are not studied by the special sciences (p 17), that philosophy is the proper science to treat of them and is able to "help us to understand the logical analysis of familiar but complex things" (p 18), such as change and continuity (pp. 17, 141–42), number and infinity (p. 201), that while the special sciences move downward from generalities to more detailed propositions, philosophy is required to achieve the extreme of generality and simplicity (pp. 201–2). Unless philosophical errors with respect to the fundamental concepts employed in understanding nature are avoided, thought will be tempted to embrace such irresponsible and extravagant theories as Bergson's anti-intellectualism or some modern version of the static monism descending from Parmenides To be more specific, without a correct philosophical definition of infinity and continuity we shall not resolve the paradoxes of Zeno and shall not know how to understand motion, which certainly is a basic empirical fact.

For all of Bergson's repeated attacks on the intellect, he is a more con-

[1] 2nd ed , New York, W W. Norton, 1929

sistent and interesting example than Russell of a philosopher who recognizes the priority of philosophical or general concepts to those of the special sciences. He seems to be a perfect imitator of the procedure of Aristotle, who said, when entering upon his own analysis of natural process, that he would first take up change in general or "becoming in its widest sense: for we shall be following the natural order of inquiry if we speak first of common characteristics, and then investigate the characteristics of special cases."[2]

No student of Bergson is unaware, of course, that each of his major works is an attack on some special problem or genus of fact, in the manner of a scientific treatise But the reader will observe that at the critical turning points of each study Bergson draws upon his "intuition" of the reality and character of change, duration, the self, of time or evolution. It is his insights into these broad and general facts that control his findings in the special areas *Time and Free Will*[3] is a study of the unmediated "givens" of consciousness, further, it is intended to prove the reality of human freedom. To achieve his goal he contrasts space with time, the former being for him a field for mechanical determination while the latter is a flux affording no foothold for prevision of what is to be; and then he contends that direct inspection of our own life reveals it as proceeding in time, not space, and there is therefore no ground whatever for applying to ourselves the mechanical categories appropriate to space By one bold stroke of metaphysical intuition Bergson thus tries to escape the confines of the mode of thought that denies freedom by applying to consciousness the concepts of space and mechanism. The structure of *Matter and Memory*[4] and of *Creative Evolution*[5] is similar

His shorter philosophical pieces, collected in *La pensée et le mouvant* (1934) and translated into English under the unsatisfactory title *The Creative Mind*,[6] exhibit this structure most clearly Every philosophy, he says in one of them, starts off from, and develops, a simple basic intuition, "the essence of philosophy is the spirit of simplicity," and "to philosophize is a simple act."[7] The errors of Plato and Aristotle in exalting a reality above change are inevitable in consequence of an initial error about the nature of change So too with Parmenides and Zeno and all their followers, who find paradoxes because of simple initial mistakes. If only we can first grasp change and penetrate its essence, says Bergson, all manner of diffi-

---

[2] *Aristotle's Physics* I, vii 189 b 30–32, ed by W D Ross (Oxford, Clarendon Press, 1936) Quotations from Aristotle will use the Oxford translation

[3] London, Allen and Unwin, New York, Macmillan, 1911.

[4] London, Allen and Unwin, New York, Macmillan, 1911

[5] New York, Henry Holt, 1911.

[6] New York, Philosophical Library, 1946

[7] *Ibid* , p 149 I have altered the translation of the second item.

culties, of paradoxes and contradictions, will be avoided; philosophy will be freed after centuries of stagnation and of swinging between such extremes as mechanism and finalism, and advantages will flow into the resources of practical life

In short, Russell and Bergson agree on the theme of the determinative function of general ideas or of philosophy in relation to the problems and investigations of the special sciences. Yet they diverge to an extreme degree in their exploration of the concepts of natural philosophy Considering their coincidence in approach, this opposition is surprising, more important, it is instructive. It enables the student to focus a few basic issues in the philosophy of nature. to single them out and to identify the recurrent modes of treating them. This paper will present an analytic and critical study of the Bergson-Russell conflict in order to arrive at an approach to certain basic concepts in natural philosophy. I shall try (1) to analyze Bergson's theory of change and continuity, his "solution" of Zeno's paradoxes, and briefly his view of space and time, (2) to analyze and test both Russell's critique of Bergson and his positive theory about the same and allied concepts, (3) to state a criticism of Bergson; and finally (4) to offer a few concluding remarks about the problems that exercised both men

I

Bergson is certain that the problem of change is first in order of importance for a philosophy of nature The manner in which a philosophy treats change determines its entire pattern, placing it on the right or the wrong path. Because Plato and Aristotle trusted the intellect to analyze change, and since intellect represents it as a series of discrete forms plus indeterminate becoming, they reached the extravagance of a static ultimate. With completely vivid consciousness of what he is about, Bergson strives to start with an initial intuition of the reality and character of change which is requisite for avoiding the glaring mistakes of most historical systems.

That change occurs and can be apprehended directly Bergson never doubts Aristotle writes: "We physicists .. must take for granted that the things that exist by nature are, either all or some of them, 'in motion— which is indeed made plain by induction."[8] Bergson speaks more vigorously When we perceive a shooting star, he says, we have an "absolutely indivisible sensation of motion or mobility."[9] Again. "But that there is real motion no one can seriously deny· if there were not, nothing in the universe

[8] *Physics* I, ii 185 a 13–14, *op cit*
[9] *Time and Free Will, op cit* , pp. 111–12

would change; and, above all, there would be no meaning in the consciousness which we have of our own movement."[10]

We may neglect the question of whether Bergson's ascription of indivisibility to a sensation can be justified. (A sensation, like every other process, is temporally extended) But it is important to observe that Bergson immediately couples his assertion of change with a far-reaching doctrine about its degree of reality While Aristotle, who also was sure of change and was equally opposed to Parmenideanism, sought to point out factual errors and logical fallacies in the monism of Parmenides,[11] Bergson adopts, without explaining why he does so, and uses as a fundamental premise, the Parmenidean definition of being whenever he has occasion to speak of substances or things, then he uses this definition to extort, by reaction, full assent to his own claim that flux alone is real, that stability is nonexistent. To admit the existence of change, he says, cannot be reconciled with admission of the factor of form, of qualities or essences or things. Reality cannot include both flux and form. This point is so important for understanding Bergson that it deserves more adequate statement.

Judging from its recurrence in the history of thought and from its role as a constant challenge to philosophers who desire to "save appearances," Parmenides's denial of change must be accounted a model of its kind When Bergson reports from direct inspection that change occurs, it is likely that no more penetrating insight can be adduced whereby to confirm or not confirm the report But such a report does not entirely answer Parmenides, who, if I understand him, would not deny what is reported. He tried to show that change is an item that cannot be squared with what is known of reality by some nonempirical route. As known by reason, the real is perfect actuality Aristotle sought to show that Parmenides had no evidence for ascribing only one meaning to the term "being" and that there is evidence that it is used in several senses, including the potential Whether or not his thesis is correct, Aristotle's method is exactly what the case requires

Though Bergson was no doubt cognizant of such a fascinating contemporaneous Parmenidean as F. H. Bradley, he pursues the striking course of accepting Parmenides's assumption whenever he mentions things, and it is then easy for him to deny that things exist. He reasons as follows. Since change and perfect actuality are incompatible when predicated of the same entity, since change is indubitable, and to be a thing is to be static, there is no thing Change is ultimate, things are nonexistent His conviction that Zeno's puzzles cannot be solved unless things are aban-

---

[10] *Matter and Memory, op. cit.,* pp. 255–56.
[11] *Physics* I, ii, iii, *op. cit.*

doned in favor of ultimate flux is evidence that his step was taken in full consciousness. It is not mere Gallic enthusiasm that moves him to say· "There are changes, but there are underneath the change no things which change. change has no need of a support There are movements, but there is no inert or invariable object which moves· movement does not imply a mobile."[12]

His elaboration of the denial of forms or states deserves a brief analysis. For Bergson, the terms "thing" and "form" or "state" are synonymous.[13] It is disastrous to philosophy to admit the reality of forms. They are merely mental snapshots, instantaneous cuts made by the mind in flux. If they were taken as real, thought would represent a change as composed of them, as a multiplicity of stable entities. This is completely wrong It is the absurdity of reducing mobility to a set of immobilities. Of course, the mind occasionally recognizes the artificiality of analyzing a change into forms; but having begun by conceding their reality, it now falls into the useless expedient of adding to them the vague, characterless factor of becoming in general. Thus change is analyzed as a composite of states plus becoming in general Now two errors become visible, says Bergson (1) The notion of an indefinite, general becoming is a fiction; every actual change is individual and unique. Indeterminate flux represents no one change in distinction from another. (2) The mind cannot rest with indeterminate change It is not representable, it conveys no information about any concrete process Accustomed by this time to dividing flux into static factors, the mind now divides this general becoming, and it vanishes in an accumulating powder of new states, ever closer to one another but as perfectly static as ever. The one successful stroke is to begin with the thesis that states are quite unreal, that the reality is change itself, and that real change is continuous and indivisible [14]

Failing to note the significance of those expressions of his in which, in the midst of denying that forms exist, he describes them as "possible stops along the continuity of a progress,"[15] Bergson goes on to claim that at bottom, forms are themselves changes. Their stability is merely apparent. What we call a state of mind, for instance, is "a perpetual becoming "[16] A sensed hue consists on its objective side in a very rapid oscillation and thus is a change Perception of this hue is likewise a process. The mind, as it

[12] *Creative Mind, op. cit*, p. 173 See also *ibid*, pp. 16–17, 169–72, and his *An Introduction to Metaphysics* (New York and London, Putnam, 1912), p 65
[13] See *Creative Evolution, op cit*, p 312· "from childhood once posited as a *thing*"
[14] See *Ibid*, pp 306–8, 312–13, also his *Introd. to Metaphysics, op cit.*, pp 45–55, *Creative Mind, op. cit.*, pp. 170–72, even his *The Two Sources of Morality and Religion* (New York, Henry Holt, 1935), pp 231–32.
[15] *Creative Evolution, op cit.*, p. 312
[16] *Introd to Metaphysics, op cit*, p. 46

were, strikes an average of the variations within the class of data and within the perceptual process, and erects it into a state or quality Every quality, state, or form, every essence, "results from a solidification performed by our understanding " "What is real is the continual *change of form· form is only a snapshot view of a transition.*"[17]

Bergson does not avoid the problem of explaining the appearance of forms and things within the framework of radical fluxism. Form arises from change by way of diminution, through a function of intelligence Merely to make a simple indivisible movement is to provide that an infinity of successive positions be given at once. The positions or "possible stops" cannot compose the motion, of course, but let us execute the motion, and all the stops we please are given for the intellect. Starting from motion, which is the reality, intelligence converts it, by division, into an assemblage of points or formal factors These it recognizes to be infinite, and it takes them to be equivalent to the motion itself Just so the passengers on two trains rushing in the same direction and at the same velocity on parallel tracks may touch each other across the distance between the trains and suppose that the trains are stationary To generalize, the organism and the items of the environment are cases of flux, a parallelism between the oscillations in each term of the relation misleads the observer into embracing the illusion of stability of form. Recent physical science, says Bergson, by positing foci of action or lines of force as the units of nature in place of the older static particles, has contributed specialized confirmation of this thesis

Bergson's description of the intellect's representation of change helps to clarify the general thesis just now sketched. For him, the intellect is equipped to apprehend only the plan of a process· its termini and the infinite series of static factors (points, positions, states) which can be located on its path Thus reducing motion to immobilities, it functions in the manner of a cinematograph If thought were to give a veridical picture of a concrete motion, for instance that of a regiment marching past, it would cut out figures for each of the soldiers and give to each figure the unique motion corresponding to the unique motion of an individual soldier. But for the sake of economy it takes a series of static snapshots of the marching regiment, to which series the intellect adds a characterless, general becoming Thinking thus reduces motion to a series of states, infinite in number, plus a vague, generalized flux for insertion between the states. This vague becoming is an indifferent background, representing no one concrete motion and susceptible to the arrangement upon it of any series of states whatever What has been lost in this procedure is the essence of change: the

[17] *Creative Evolution, op. cit.,* pp 249, 302

individuality of each concrete process, and its continuity, that is, its indivisibility and mobility.[18]

Bergson's rigorous contrast between space and time is not only an important metaphysical proposal but an application of his contrast between the comparative cognitive power of intellect and intuition Space is the perfect achievement by intellect of its ideal of dividing a continuum into static factors, each separate from the others in location and causal efficacy. It is an empty medium or frame, divisible ad infinitum into *partes extra partes*, simultaneous with each other and causally inert It is ideally suited to mathematics, to numeration and measurement. The science of number, says Bergson, exploits space and depends upon it. In order to count sheep one needs to image them alongside one another, one cannot add items into a sum unless they are compresent, the earlier items waiting while the later are being added to them Hence counting removes succession and time.

Time is the opposite of space. Like change, it is continuous and indivisible. Its parts interpenetrate, it implies succession, of course, but its phases fuse, they are not juxtaposed Duration is "a succession without distinction "[19] It is not subject to mathematics, to numeration or measurement, to proceed as if it is, is to spatialize it. To conceive the strokes of a clock as separate items arranged in an order of earlier and later is to conceive them as simultaneous and mutually external, this is to substitute space for time, to miss the fact that duration is qualitative and heterogeneous, a fusion of phases into an organic unity that grows, like the rolling snowball, into ever-novel powers and qualities

Space is an intellectual invention, an empty set of static points or formal factors; since its parts are homogeneous and external, space is mere repetition, "a present which is always beginning again "[20] But time or duration is intuited in self-knowledge, in the present phase of the self, past phases are present as ingredients in an expanding unity Motion cannot occur in space, for its parts are separate positions. Motion depends on synthesis of positions, and this can occur only in duration, which is consciousness To project an act into space is to solidify it, to assert that, even outside consciousness, the past can coexist with the present. "Duration and motion are mental syntheses," while "outside ourselves we should find only space, and consequently nothing but simultaneities, of which we could not even say that they are objectively successive, since succession can only be thought through comparing the present with the past."[21]

[18] See *Ibid* , pp 299–308, also his *Introd to Metaphysics, op. cit* , pp 46, 50–52, his *Durée et simultanéite* (2nd ed , rev , Paris, Alcan, 1923), p 210.
[19] Bergson, *Time and Free Will, op cit* , pp 100–101.
[20] Bergson, *Matter and Memory, op. cit.,* p 178
[21] Bergson, *Time and Free Will, op cit* , p 120, also p 116, see also his *Durée, op cit* , pp 55, 61–62, 88.

Bergson is convinced that the formidable opposition of Zeno cannot be overcome without giving up the intellectual analysis of change, and that nothing less than his own theory asserting the indivisible continuity and the ultimacy of change, is adequate to defend the reality of change against attack from any quarter. In order to understand his solution of the paradoxes, it is necessary to see how he states them.

All the paradoxes, says Bergson, are due to an illusion,[22] and all embody a confusion.[23] The confusion is between two things: the act of motion, which is continuous, undivided, indivisible,[24] and the path it traverses, which is "homogeneous quantity" and is therefore multiple, discontinuous, divisible, and actually divided into an infinity of parts in juxtaposition If we fall into this confusion, we shall embrace the illusion that a motion can be "applied to" the line it traces in space, that what is true of the path will be true of the motion also.[25] The plausibility of the paradoxes derives from our not noticing the absurdity of affirming coincidence between such disparate entities as space and motion.

The "dichotomy," says Bergson, shows Zeno supposing a body at rest Fixing his attention on the infinite number of points on the path to be traversed, Zeno concludes that the body cannot cross the interval containing the infinity of points The "Achilles" presumes two moving bodies. Zeno looks at the space beneath the motion, notes its divisibility, and proceeds to divide the steps of Achilles arbitrarily, just as space may be divided any way we please. This means that Zeno divides Achilles's steps into increasingly smaller units, in such wise that Achilles is occluded from passing his competitor, and Zeno is justified if motion can be "applied" to a line in space Zeno's "arrow" paradox distinguishes in the time of flight a series of indivisible moments, just as points can be distinguished in space, since no motion can occur in a moment, the arrow is at rest in each position in the flight and is motionless along the whole path and throughout the whole time Last is the "stadium" paradox, which for Bergson rests on the same mistake as the others Zeno concludes that a duration is twice itself, because a moving body, while it crosses a given length of a stationary body, crosses double that length in passing a moving body.

We should expect from Bergson a violent answer to these paradoxes. In his view, the intellect represents change as Zeno does, and Zeno is irrefutable without abandoning the intellectual representation For intellect, space is divisible, and divides into an infinite set of points. If it is correct

---

[22] *Matter and Memory, op cit*, p. 250

[23] *Time and Free Will, op cit*, p 112, his *Creative Mind, op cit.*, p. 170.

[24] *Time and Free Will, op cit*, p 112, his *Creative Evolution, op. cit*, p. 311, his *Creative Mind, op cit*, p 169

[25] Bergson, *Creative Mind, op. cit.*, p. 170, his *Creative Evolution, op. cit.*, p. 310; his *Matter and Memory, op. cit*, p 249

to analyze time and motion similarly, they too fall apart into a powder of moments and positions. Motion cannot be constituted by any summation of these immobile, formal factors. The truth is that while space is really divided, motion and time are not, they are simple, continuous, indivisible What is true of space is not true of them The arrow's flight is "indecomposable",[26] it is an "indivisible whole."[27] True, the arrow passes through positions on its path; but these are only points at which it *might* stop [28] "The arrow never is in any point of its course."[29] The positions, then, do not exist, if they did, the arrow would be at rest Space, indeed, can be composed of points; but to say that a position in motion exists only as something at which the body might stop means only that the body is never there.

This general answer enables Bergson to dispose quickly of the several paradoxes If a motion is not analyzable in the way that its path in space is, the "dichotomy" simply falls to the ground There are no positions in the motion. The "Achilles" is plausible only as long as we permit the steps of Achilles to be reduced progressively in proportion to the divisions made of the path. But this is arbitrary and false. Achilles takes long steps quickly, each indivisible, and in a short time he simply overtakes the slower tortoise. "There is nothing more simple "[30] Again, if we boldly refuse to divide the time of the arrow's flight into moments, if we acknowledge its simplicity and indivisibility, there is no difficulty in the third puzzle. If there were positions in its flight, the arrow would stop, it does not stop, so it never occupies a position. And finally the "stadium." This Bergson does not solve by pointing to the fact of relative motion, nor by denying Zeno's assumption (in this paradox alone) that continua consist of infinitesimal units, which implies unit motions occurring in unit times and traversing unit spaces. Instead, he claims that if we intuit the absolute nature of duration and disregard the spaces traversed by moving bodies, we shall not be surprised that a moving body crosses different lengths of two other bodies, one of them at rest and the other moving We cannot untangle this puzzle if we focus on the spaces, but intuition can seize on a fixed duration as an absolute fact and recognize its compatibility with the facts of relative velocity.

II

Rarely in the history of thought has there occurred a more striking clash of ideas between contemporaneous thinkers than in the case of Bergson

[26] Bergson, *Creative Evolution, op cit.,* p. 309
[27] Bergson, *Matter and Memory, op cit ,* p. 246.
[28] *Ibid ,* p 247
[29] Bergson, *Creative Evolution, op cit.,* p 308
[30] *Ibid ,* p 311

and Russell. With one important exception, their stands on the status of intellect and intuition and on the concepts bearing on the changing order of nature are opposed at nearly every point. While Bergson has not seen fit to engage in controversy with his famous rival, Russell has criticized Bergson and stated his own views on the matters at issue in an essay on Bergson's philosophy[31] and in his important book *Our Knowledge of the External World.*

Russell provides a neat summary of Bergson's contrast between intellect and intuition in terms of the objects they are fitted to grasp and of their comparative power to provide metaphysical insight.[32] This summary we need not follow, nor Russell's pedestrian objection that intuition, being akin to instinct, is less adapted than intellect to achieve adjustment to novel circumstances [33] It is questionable whether the intuition of which Bergson speaks is not a more important function than is indicated by the name he gives it, namely, a function of reason whereby it grasps the essential character of some object. If this is so, Russell's attack on Bergson's intuitionism is an attack on a commonplace significance of the term "intuition"; and it leaves open the issue of whether the "faculty" of metaphysical insight does give genuine information about the essence of time and its priority to matter or space.

Russell, of course, considers Bergson's theory of the nature of time.[34] His accurate statement of what Bergson is saying in his description of duration, as contrasted with space, is so clear that Bergson's central error is made perfectly evident Bergson defines duration as he does because the object he is inspecting is his own existence as an organic and conscious being. Central to consciousness is the function of memory, which enables the past to survive into the present. This fact is the key to time's nature: Time spells fusion of elements; past and present are not separate, as in space, the acme of mathematical concepts, but they interpenetrate and mingle, and therefore mathematics does not apply to time.

Russell makes two convincing objections to this theory. (1) Bergson's definition of time is circular. He defines the past as *"that which acts no longer"* and the present as *"that which is acting"* (italics his). The terms "no longer" and "is" presume the ordinary view of time, for which, to follow Bergson's terminology, the past is that whose action is past, the present is that whose action is now.[35] Further, (2) Bergson's description of time is really a description of the mode of existence enjoyed by a remembering

[31] *A History of Western Philosophy* (New York, Simon and Schuster, 1945), Chap 28.
[32] *Ibid* , pp 793–96, 798, his *Our Knowledge, op. cit.,* pp. 14–16
[33] *Our Knowledge, op cit.,* pp 23–27
[34] Russell, *A History, op. cit.,* pp. 806–9.
[35] *Ibid* , p. 806.

and conscious being To say that duration is a unity in which the past fuses with the present is to describe a present memory of the past, not the past itself. Thus Bergson's entire theory of time rests on "the elementary confusion between the present occurrence of a recollection and the past occurrence which is recollected " He confuses the difference between perception and memory with the difference between present and past Hence his theory of time leaves out time entirely [86]

In other words, Bergson takes the *intentional* or *noetic* inclusion of a past fact in the now of consciousness as being its existential presence in the present. He argues that since two events, though temporally separate, are simultaneously present to consciousness, they are really simultaneous. Russell might have pointed out that Bergson's theory of time constitutes an ironic contradiction of his insistence on the ultimacy of time. Since memory has no fixed limits, and the present, which includes the past existentially, can be expanded indefinitely,[37] and since he gives no reason for excluding the future, time itself may be an all-inclusive *totum simul*.[38]

While these criticisms are justified, we should notice that they do not affect important positive theses of Bergson· that duration exists, that it is metaphysically prior to matter or space, that intuition can grasp the nature of duration. A further criticism is addressed by Russell to Bergson's theory of space An initial flaw is found, and rightly, in Bergson's thesis that the concept of space is the presupposition for all thinking about magnitude, plurality, numbers, and geometry, even every kind of separation or distinctness (as between abstract ideas) and of all logic Russell provides the adequate answer: a plain denial of the thesis, plus an invitation to inspect a few relevant instances

Such intensive magnitudes as more and less pleasant, more and less blue, need not be thought in terms of space, no one need think blackness and whiteness as juxtaposed in space in order to think their difference. Nor is one compelled to represent successive sounds alongside each other in space, and hence as coexistent and static, in order to count them Bergson's basic mistake consists in equating thinking with picturing or imaging, in the case of number, he equates having a clear idea of number with picturing a set of dots or sheep Bergson employs the obvious fact that one cannot image a set of physical items except as extended in a spatial field in order to assert the quite independent view that number cannot be

---

[36] *Ibid*, p 807

[37] Bergson, *Time and Free Will, op cit*, p 194, his *Creative Mind, op cit*, pp 178–80.

[38] This criticism was made by A. O Lovejoy, "The Problem of Time in Recent French Philosophy II–Temporalism and Anti-Intellectualism Bergson," *The Philosophical Review*, XXI (1912), 328.

conceived except by a spatial image. Unless imaging is identical with thinking, this is a *non sequitur* [39]

Russell's next criticism[40] of Bergson's theory of space leads to the heart of Russell's equally debatable view. The aim of Russell is to defend the "mathematical account" of change, which Bergson represents as the absurd theory that a change consists of states or immobilities. Bergson counters the "cinematographic representation" with his violent thesis that change contains no states, that a moving body never is in a position during its motion Russell says: "Mathematics conceives change, even continuous change, as constituted by a series of states;"[41] if this procedure is cinematographic, then a cinematograph, properly understood, "will perfectly represent a continuous motion."[42]

Russell proposes to present and criticize Bergson's position by discussing Zeno's "arrow" paradox. Zeno argues that, because at each instant in the time of flight the arrow is in a position, it is at rest throughout the whole time of flight. With the mathematicians, says Russell, we should hold that motion is continuous, and continuous motion can be represented correctly by a cinematograph with an infinite number of pictures no two of which are next or successive. Philosophers to this day have found it difficult to answer Zeno, for they have failed to justify the natural tendency to understand change as involving both things and change The Eleatics said there are things but no changes. Bergson says there are changes but no things. "The unfortunate man who stands in the middle," says Russell, "and maintains that there is [are?] both the arrow and its flight is assumed by the disputants to deny both; he is therefore pierced, like Saint Sebastian, by the arrow from one side and by its flight from the other."

What makes Zeno's argument so strong is, in Russell's view, an assumption it shares with Bergson (and others), namely, that continuous change involves the presence in the thing of "some internal state of change," that is, "the thing must, at each instant, be intrinsically different from what it would be if it were not changing." Now, says Zeno, at each instant the arrow is just where it is, in a position, and therefore "there can be no such thing as a *state* of motion."[43] Holding that motion implies a state of motion, Zeno concludes that there is no motion This argument, says Russell, while it does not affect the mathematical view of change, does refute, prima facie, a view like that of Bergson Bergson meets it by denying that the arrow is ever in a position. Though this solution does escape Zeno, says Russell,

[39] Russell, *A History, op. cit* , pp 800–803.
[40] *Ibid* , pp 804–6.
[41] *Ibid.*, p. 804.
[42] *Ibid* , p 805
[43] *Ibid.*, p. 805.

and is "heroic," it is not a "possible" way of escape—it is "closed to us."[44] What Russell's reasoning may be at this point we shall discover later. At any rate, Bergson's only argument in favor of his solution is the statement that the mathematical analysis of change composes it of static elements, and that this is absurd This absurdity, says Russell, is merely apparent and is due entirely to the verbal form of Bergson's statement. It disappears as soon as we realize that "motion implies relations " A friendship is composed of friends, not friendships, so too "a motion is made out of what is moving, but not out of motions. It expresses the fact that a thing may be in different places at different times, and that the places may still be different how- ever near together the times may be." Thus Bergson's argument against the mathematical account of change is "a mere play on words."[45]

This final criticism offered by Russell is the point at which his thought raises basic issues in natural philosophy and makes it necessary to inspect and test his own positive views What these issues are we may be helped to see if we first inspect, in order to set aside, a few secondary matters brought forward by Russell in the argument sketched in the preceding paragraph

(1) He makes Zeno's argument in his "arrow" seem stronger than it is by talking as if it is obvious that since a time may be divided at instants, it consists of instants This rests on his endorsement of the "mathematical account" and raises one basic issue. (2) Russell's remark about the failure of philosophers to answer Zeno is weakened by his failure to mention any one besides Bergson and the Eleatics (3) He does not make clear why philosophers have found it difficult to retain both things and change; and while he wants to retain both factors, his views of what a thing is, namely, a construction based on the notion of an infinite set of perceptual perspec- tives, or an element entering [without internal change?] into an infinite set of relations, are dependent on the applicability to the category of substance of the "mathematical account," and once more raise the issue just mentioned I do not propose to examine his conception of a thing, though I may say it is ingenious and artificial and perhaps assumes a notion that is in conflict with itself. And finally, (4) his phrase, "some internal *state* of change," is a perfect contradiction, unless the term "state" evaporates into being able to mean anything at all. A state is a character in virtue of which some entity is definite To have a state is not to change in a certain respect To change is to lose one state and receive another. To hold that things change is to hold that they remain the kind of things they are while ex- changing modes of definiteness, that is, states John is the same boy from the age of twelve to the age of thirteen. Yet is he not intrinsically different

[44] *Our Knowledge, op. cit* , pp 149–50, 194
[45] Russell, *A History, op. cit.*, p 806.

at thirteen from what he was at twelve? What Russell means may not be determinable with certainty, and so this way of stating the question may be dropped. Yet what Russell means by saying that Bergson accepts the view that there is a state of change, and by saying that Zeno proves this view false, seems to connect (I cannot be sure) with Russell's contention that the mathematical analysis of change into states is sound and is not affected by Zeno. Russell wishes us to accept the analysis of change into states, against Bergson's view, he wishes us to believe that one cannot answer Zeno while holding that changing things change intrinsically, he offers an analysis of changing things in terms of things and ever-different relations.

These considerations, taken together, show that Russell flatly opposes Bergson's denial that static or formal factors suffice to constitute process, and that he is ready to defend what he means by the method of analysis. Here is the basic issue between Bergson and Russell The latter asserts that continuous change, and time and space likewise, can be analyzed into simple elements without destroying their continuity. "Mathematics conceives change, even continuous change, as constituted by a series of states."[46] Change is complex, involving a succession of states; it demands analysis. In order to be complete, analysis must go beyond smaller changes to factors that are not changes, namely, static factors; and when this is achieved, motion will be seen to consist of states or positions, time of durationless instants, and space of points [47]

Search for Russell's reason for saying that "by the logical necessities of the case"[48] a continuum must be analyzed into discrete, formal elements is hindered by his presentation of two apparently conflicting statements about what is implied by the divisibility of a continuum. Speaking of "the fact that any distance, however small, can be halved," Russell says: "From this it follows, of course, that there must be an infinite number of points in a line "[49] That is to say, the *divisibility* of a continuum is a fact, and this fact implies the presence of an infinity of formal factors. But Russell is equally insistent on the point that division of a continuum, no matter how often repeated, cannot possibly reach indivisible parts: Bisection of a given distance always leaves standing a finite distance which as such is divisible, and there is no end to terminate the process of bisection [50] The latter statement, besides being plain and correct, was expounded thoroughly by Aristotle.[51]

---

[46] *Ibid.,* p 804
[47] Russell, *Our Knowledge, op. cit ,* p. 164
[48] *Ibid*
[49] *Ibid ,* pp 186–87.
[50] *Ibid ,* p 147.
[51] *Physics* VI, 1, *op cit.*

Now if Russell is in earnest about his second statement, the divisibility of a continuum is not for him the ground of its being composed of simple elements. His statement that divisibility implies composition by formal factors is a deceptive form of saying that there is a distinct "logical" principle which applies to every continuum and gives a result which divisibility cannot produce. This "logical" principle says that every complex fact must be analyzable into simple formal factors. A passage cited above claims that motion, since it involves a succession of states, involves relations, and analysis is not complete until it has achieved terms, related as earlier and later, which are not changes. It is of the utmost importance to see that this rule is not drawn from the fact of divisibility, it is laid down as a dictum and authenticated by being called "logical." Now, no exception need be taken to it as long as the factors reached by analysis are such that they suffice to constitute the complex they are said to compose when related by the relations ascribed to them.

But this condition is precisely what Russell's application of the principle cannot meet The issue between Russell and Bergson on this point is perfectly clear, and Bergson is right. Confining ourselves to time, how can it be composed of instants? As Russell himself says, an instant is durationless, no addition of instants will give us time Two instants, not being continuous and divisible, cannot be distinct from each other unless something distinct from them separates them; and this will be time An infinity of instants (no matter how we define infinity) is no more time than one instant, they are no time at all Instants have no boundaries, if they could be in contact, they would be one instant. They are formal factors involved in time as factors that distinguish one part of time from another, they cannot be distinct one from another unless there is time within which they are limits When Russell says that time involves relations and that it consists of instants related as earlier and later, it is time that makes one instant earlier and another later, his use of "earlier" and "later" makes his analysis of time circular, as does also his statement that "the interval between any two instants . . is always finite "[52] Thus Russell's "logical" ground for his analysis of continua is quite fictitious. This conclusion brings us back to a more ancient conception of continuity and the recognition that a continuum, being composed (in a sense to be discussed later) of parts having the same nature as the whole, is divisible because it is continuous, and is not reducible to formal elements. A space is made of smaller spaces, a time of briefer times, a motion of partial motions, and these parts are so connected that the end of one is the beginning of another.

The fundamental error of Russell can be made more clear by exploring the reason he offers for his definition of continuity. He correctly points

[52] Russell, *Our Knowledge, op. cit*, p. 148.

out an obvious consequence of the real continuity of a motion by saying: "at any given instant the moving body occupies a certain position, and at other instants it occupies other positions, the interval between any two instants and between any two positions is always finite . . however near together we take the two positions and the two instants, there are an in-finite number of positions still nearer together, which are occupied at instants that are also still nearer together."[53] Continuity in the classic sense is what justifies this description. Russell, however, defines continuity as a property, or set of properties, of a *series of terms,* and the terms he is think-ing of are points, instants, and positions. A basic property of a continuous series he calls "compactness," which he defines as meaning that "no two terms are consecutive, but between any two there are others."[54] Obviously, if space is continuous in the sense of the classic definition, the points which can be discriminated in it will be compact. Any finite distance can be di-vided (mathematically) into lesser distances, ad infinitum, at points no two of which are consecutive. But it cannot be divided *into* points! As Russell himself insists, infinitesimals are never reached by dividing

Then why does he hold that a space consists of points? Besides his spurious "logical" argument, I find only the statement that it is necessary to admit infinite numbers. This occurs in the context of a discussion of ways in which it is possible to escape Zeno One way was taken by Parmenides and Zeno, who denied motion, space, and time Another is Bergson's, that of denying the composition of continua by formal factors Now, says Russell, both ways of escape will meet Zeno's arguments, but they are "closed to us" because a third way is open if infinite numbers are admis-sible, and they *must be* admitted since there is the series of "all the frac-tions less than 1, arranged in order of magnitude. . . . And we cannot deny that there *are* fractions."[55] To paraphrase: There are fractions, there is such a series as all the fractions less than 1 ordered by decreasing magni-tude, therefore, there are infinite numbers Hence a continuum is a com-pact series of formal factors, and it is necessary to deny both Zeno's and Bergson's mode of escape from the paradoxes.

The one decisive comment about this argument is that it is a pure *petitio.* "There are fractions," says Russell. Granted, but nothing is really granted unless we know what "are" means Does it mean but one thing? Russell never seems to raise this question at all He simply adopts the thesis that to be means to be actual, to be all there at once. "There are fractions" means for him right off that the infinite set of fractions is given all at once But is it? What is the evidence? The fact on which he bases

[53] *Ibid.*
[54] *Ibid.,* p 144.
[55] *Ibid.,* p. 194.

his assertion that the fractions are given at once is the obvious fact that if we take two fractions within a series we *can* find others between them, and that no limit can be assigned to the number of fractions we *can* write down But we should notice the language of his own analysis. The word "can" carries the nub of the fact appealed to. We are *able* to set down more members of the series of fractions, just as we are able to halve a given finite distance or time or motion. Each of these is divisible. Language is not so distorted that *divisible* must mean *divided*. No valid inference can be made from *ability* to augment the number of items, to the entirely different fact that "all" the items capable of entering a series are there at once. But this is Russell's inference, made without taking note of it or giving reasons for it. What he does with numbers, space, time, and motion is exactly what Bergson does with space· Both accept the Parmenidean principle that being is actual only, and both represent a continuum as composed of the formal factors at which (not *into* which) it can be divided.

The arbitrariness of Russell's reasoning (or lack of it) can be seen more clearly by inspecting his conception of infinite numbers and his readiness to apply it to continua In what follows I do not presume to judge of the propriety or utility for mathematics of the newer definition of an infinite number Russell explains this definition admirably, so that even the "vulgar" mind can understand it and be reconciled (perhaps) with its paradoxical implications I shall not discuss the definition as such, nor its implications, though I may refer the reader who is seeking a sound critique to the late Professor DeWitt H. Parker's *Experience and Substance* [56] All I wish to do is to inquire into the kind of reality that is possessed by such infinite numbers as Russell gives in illustration

He mentions as examples the series of "all the natural numbers" and of "all the fractions" between ½ and o Nowhere does he call attention to a set of empirical objects whose number is infinite in the way in which the series of natural numbers is said to be infinite. Thus he does not assert the physical existence of an actual infinite; he insists, in fact, that it is the numbers that are infinite and that such mathematical entities are not known to be certainly attributable to an actual motion, space, or time. However, the mathematical theory is, he contends, a possible and plausible theory and is adequate to cover empirical fact Now, supposing that the definition of infinite numbers given by Russell is not claimed to correspond with physical fact, I wish to state my judgment that it does not correspond to mental actualization either It is easy enough to conceive a few members of an infinite series and to conceive the rule governing the entrance of any item into membership of the series And, of course, when Russell illus-

[56] Ann Arbor, Mich , University of Michigan Press, 1941.

trates an infinite number, he does nothing more than name a few members and state the rule governing entrance into membership.

Can he do anything more? No one can speak for what someone else can conceive, but I should be surprised if anyone's experience in this matter is different from my own And I am aware, when trying to conceive the intention of such a term as "all the natural numbers," that there are given to my consciousness only a few members of the series plus the rule of construction. The phrase "given all at once" is ambiguous, as Russell uses it, it seems to be a blind for an intellectual act which is a miracle, or something more than a miracle, namely, the impossible Does he mean to profess that he grasps together every member of the series, "all the natural numbers," that each member is mentally actual and present to consciousness? The series, I believe, has not even conceptual actuality. The only remaining actuality it can have we may call "definitional", it exists in the mode of being proper to a rule, it is an *ens definitionis* and nothing more. While this is not to say that the concept is not legitimate or useful for the mathematician, who is not bound to the actual, it is to say that Russell is not justified in using the mathematical definition of infinity as a base for asserting what an existing continuum consists of. What cannot be conceived in such wise as to have even mental actuality, certainly cannot serve as analysis of fact

If Russell's theory of the composition of continua is unjustified, if his appeal to the existence of infinite numbers is question-begging, it is not necessary to inspect his detailed answers to Zeno. For they depend on the two factors in his thought which I have just indicated. Speaking of the "dichotomy" and the "Achilles," he says that the infinite divisibility of space implies that there is an actual infinity of points on a line. This is quite false His own clear-cut statement that division of a continuum can never terminate in indivisible parts, and his other clear-cut statement that in a moment a body can neither move nor rest, render it impossible to understand what shred of reason he may think he has for composing a continuum of formal factors If a body cannot move or rest in an instant, how can it move in more than one? His entire conception of time is circular.

I shall not consider whether Russell states the paradoxes accurately; though it would be easy to retort on his remark that, since Aristotle was not sympathetic to Zeno, Aristotle's account of the paradoxes is not likely to be reliable. Russell is not noticeably sympathetic to Zeno or Aristotle or Bergson His "solution" of the paradoxes suffers from the handicap of starting from the presumption that no genuine solution has been found as yet. If God was not so niggardly as to withhold from mankind until Aristotle the power to think logically, it is not likely that he should wait for Russell to provide a sound theory about continua. As for the newer definition of infinite numbers, it means no more, as applied to a continuous motion, than that between any two positions so far distinguished, we can distinguish others, and this has been perfectly familiar, or available for understanding, since the time of Aristotle At bottom, Russell is more Parmenidean than he confesses, and on his theory there is no continuous motion, space, or time Bergson's response to the Eleatics is certainly superior to Russell's, though it is not perfect, and we should now examine Bergson's stand.

III

In this section I shall examine four of the major topics in Bergson's thought so far as it was surveyed in my first section (1) his attack on intellect; (2) his denial of formal factors, (3) his contrast between space and time, and (4) his treatment of Zeno's paradoxes.

(1) Bergson's attack on the intellect is, I believe, one of the least justifiable components in his thought.

(a) It is rendered suspect at the start by his constant reference to intellect as a disembodied agent that does certain things—"the intellect" is a phrase that occurs repeatedly as the subject of sentences which read as though they refer to the acts of a concrete substance. One is tempted to ask, "Whose intellect?" Surely there is no intellect among readers of Bergson that is not someone's intellect, and what reason has Bergson for confidence in his dogma that every man's intellect indulges in the error of composing changes of states? True, Russell does so, but if he is "the intellect," we can easily name people who are not Bergson's reification of the diversely operative intellects of different men is on a level with Russell's procedure in his sentence: "Mathematics conceives change . . . as constituted by a series of states." Such statements are matter for irony

(b) Bergson's strange argument (in *An Introduction to Metaphysics*) against concepts on the ground that they are relative, external, and stable is seen for what it is when we read that he wishes to replace them by "fluid concepts." Suppose his concepts of duration and motion were to flow, what would remain to be understood in his own entire literary corpus? That the concept and definition of change do not change is no bar to change being what it is, and is a requisite for thought.

(c) Bergson's attack on intellect is a mere *petitio* Intellect errs, he says, because it does not see that flux is ultimate and that forms are nonexistent This is certainly a case of supporting a conclusion which is presented as a certainty by a premise which is extremely disputable We may wonder with what faculty we are to understand Bergson's metaphysical thesis. As to whether intellect can grasp the irreducibility of continua to static factors, I see no reason to deny this power—Russell can show that division of a continuum cannot reach indivisible parts, even if he is not "the intellect." In short, Bergson's attack on intellect depends on a hasty generalization about what it does with change and on his assuming as true his own metaphysical doctrine. For this generalization there is nothing like uniform evidence, and the metaphysical doctrine is itself in question.

(2) Bergson's denial of formal factors is certainly his most serious and crucial doctrine. I shall examine in turn the three stages in which he works it out.

(a) His first step is to assert that change is directly given in experience; the states into which the intellect divides it are not so given I am aware of no cogent argument against the first half of this thesis. There is no evidence equally compulsive with the experience of sensing the rapid motion of a shooting star to unsettle this sensory evidence. Not even Parmenides or Zeno questions the fact of the givenness of change. Russell, while acknowledging that there is a sense in which "we see" a motion and not just successive positions, offers theoretical objections to accepting the significance of the experience of change These objections[57] arise from a description of experience which leans on his assumption that the "mathematical account" of process is correct; and therefore they prejudge the issue, and Bergson's report is unaffected.

The second half of Bergson's thesis is more important. He wants to separate change as given fact from states or forms, and to deny the existence of the latter The reasoning behind his general thesis is as follows: Change occurs in fact, if change is divisible, it divides into states, but states cannot compose a change. As against Russell, Bergson is entirely correct. No set of formal factors, such as "being straight," "being bent," no matter how numerous or how near together, can be the transition between any two of them: The states are never in contact or continuous. States are modes of definiteness, what Whitehead calls "eternal objects", they are the factors between which a thing changes.

But this point only brings us to the critical question: Does use of formal factors in analyzing change reduce it to states? At this point Bergson makes his most serious mistake He says that when we divide a motion at positions we are dividing it *into* positions This is quite arbitrary To recognize the continuity of a motion is to recognize that it is one unbroken motion, which, since it is a transition from one place to another, can be divided (conceptually) *into* halves, the halves into quarters, and so forth. These parts *into* which, *at* positions, the motion can be (conceptually) divided are all partial motions themselves, and since no one ever *actually* divides a motion into more than a finite number of parts, their sum is the

[57] Russell, *Our Knowledge, op. cit*, especially pp 150-52.

whole original motion Hence the intellectual division of a change does not reduce it to states, and it follows that intellectual analysis need not falsify. The change is from one mode of definiteness to another, along a path traced by the changing thing, this path can be divided ad infinitum, and the division is never *into* forms but *at* forms *into* continuous components of the continua involved in change And since the forms and the components they divide are not actual or distinct in the motion, though they are mentally *distinguishable* or *realizable*, they do not break the continuity of the motion.

If our dividing a continuum into continua is not dividing it into discrete forms, there is no remaining reason to accept Bergson's repeated ascription of indivisibility to continua. In fact, the two terms conflict. Space cannot be continuous without being divisible: Russell correctly describes the fact when he says that any finite distance can be (conceived to be) halved, for it is a continuous magnitude Bergson himself formulates the divisibility of change when he says that states are "possible stops," that a change *might* stop before it does, he even calls the stops "potential." The only reason I can discover for his neglect of the significance of "possible stops" is his Parmenidean assumption (shared with Russell) that to be is to be actual, all there completely This is betrayed by his statement that, while there really are no points on the path traced by a moving body, the body does, in tracing its path, lay down an infinity of points which are all given at once.

This analysis of possible stops is equivalent to Russell's analysis of "there are fractions" and is equally false. Then, correctly seeing that the stops are not a motion, Bergson swings over to the extreme of denying the reality of formal factors altogether. In other words, it is as if he argued that if a motion were divisible, it would be actually divided into an infinity of positions, this conclusion being false, the motion is not divisible. But to be *divisible* is not to be *divided*, and what we *can* divide the motion *into* is not stops but partial motions, though we do divide it *at* the stops. Bergson would have stuck closer to the facts if he had explored the significance of his phrases "possible stops" and "potential."

I do not wish at this point to defend the concept of potency, but it is worth noting that Bergson's difficulty with divisibility is removed if we are ready to employ it A continuous motion is one motion, the moving body passes without stopping from the position (a form) it occupied before moving to the position at which its motion terminates in rest If the motion were actually divided, it would no longer be one motion—it would be broken by rest, which is to occupy the same position for a time. This, the one motion does not do, but it *can be* divided *by us* at any number of positions discriminable in its path The positions are points at which the moving body might have stopped but did not, and so are not actual in the motion; we are able to actualize them mentally, however, and thereby to analyze the motion and specify its structure (If the mid-point of one motion were actual, it would be both the finishing point of one motion and the starting point of another, but two motions are not distinct unless there is an interval of rest between them)[58]

Mental actualization of what is potential in a motion does not falsify; it does not divide the motion, but defines it. The intellectual analysis is not artificial, it diagrams the motion precisely The divisions are "mental snapshots," indeed, but these are exactly what is needed to understand the motion, to convert it from a fact which is broadly and vaguely apprehended to one which is precisely determined, made as clear-cut as we can make it. Analysis perfects and refines the broad sensory apprehension, which seizes upon at least the rough features of the terminating forms and the path between them traced by the moving body Since the snapshots are known to be not the parts of motion but the formal factors really potential in it, they do not convert mobility into immobility.

(b) Bergson's second step is worked out in connection with his attack on the cinematographic procedure of intellect I wish to examine his essential thesis before remarking on the cinematograph His purpose is to accuse the intellect of the double error of first dividing a change into states and then trying to redress the damage by stringing the states along a general, undifferentiated becoming. Change is thus represented as states plus becoming in general. To this procedure Bergson makes three objections. (i) Change is indivisible and has no states in it, so that this analysis starts out wrong; (ii) Becoming in general is a useless and misleading concept, for every actual change is specific and unique; (iii) The concept of change in general is not one we can hold on to, for, being vague and indeterminate, it falls apart by new divisions into new states ad infinitum and so dissolves into a powder of formal factors.

Objections (i) and (iii) may be set aside by recalling, as previously argued, that Bergson's denial of the presence of states in change is not convincing and that he proceeds upon a mistaken conception of what our dividing a change does to it. Turning to (ii), is there a contrast between a given specific change, which is precisely this individual process, and an analysis of it by a set of formal factors plus the notion of flux in general? I wish simply to deny the point Bergson tries to make, and to support my denial by inspection of the facts he uses in illustration and by the request that we consider seriously the theoretical effect of denying forms

All of Bergson's profuse illustrations of concrete changes are evidence against his thesis. He asks us to acknowledge that "becoming is infinitely

[58] See *Physics* VIII, viii. 262 a 18–26, 263 a 23 – b 9, *op cit*

varied," and at once describes varying *kinds* of movement, such as qualitative (green to yellow), evolutionary (larva to nymph), and extensive
(eating) [59] His description is entirely unobjectionable and obvious, but
he fails to note that the specifying factors whereby the species and sub-
species of change are determinate and varied are all of them forms It is
the termini of a change, plus its route and the formal elements which we
may discriminate in it, that constitute the specificity of the process. If
we tried to realize the theoretical effect of denying forms, we should not
know how to accept Bergson's stress on the variety of actual changes. The
literal meaning of his assertion that "there is no form, since form is immobile and the reality is movement"[60] is that reality is purely indeterminate, a perfect blank Flux cannot be ultimate, for forms are the factors
to which changes owe their character and distinctness

It is instructive to note that while condemning an analysis of motion
such as is typified by a moving-picture mechanism, Bergson admits that
the cinematographic representation is superior to that of cutting out
jointed figures in imitation of soldiers and placing them in motion; the
latter method, he says, does not do justice to the "suppleness and variety
of life "[61] If it is the case that a motion is definite in virtue of form, then the
cinematograph is a reliable means of representing an actual motion—provided it is itself in motion.

Russell makes the mistake of defending it while conceiving it as stationary: For him, the motion *is* the series of pictures. Bergson's protest to this
is legitimate. Russell's theory is patently false unless his reader provides
the supposition that the pictures *move*, in this case, what Russell leaves
out is reintroduced Bergson's opposed mistake is to suppose that in flux
there are no states—he has motion but no specificity, no termini or path
The mechanism when operating consists of two ingredients. the series of
snapshots, as numerous as we please, which are static cross sections of a
concrete motion, fixing the positions of the object at instants in the time of
motion, not to speak of the termini in which the object persisted for a
time, and also motion or process. The two ingredients are coessential The
snapshots are the counterpart of mental actualizations of potential stops
in a real motion, the turning of the reel returns the snapshots to continuity.
And so, as Bergson himself says, the separate pictures "continue" one
another, and the motion is faithfully reproduced, in both its mobility and
its formal structure Russell talks as if the mechanism is not turning;
Bergson, in retort, talks as if the pictures are of nothing at all

(c) It is clear already that Bergson's third step is sure to go awry If

---

[59] *Creative Evolution, op. cit.,* p. 304.
[60] *Ibid ,* p. 302.
[61] *Ibid ,* p. 305.

forms are coessential with flux in the constitution of concrete specified changes, they cannot be reduced to flux It is simply not the case that a form is a case of flux At one time Bergson was untaught in Latin, later he reads Cicero, the characters which come and go do not change Forms are the structural factors without which change would be blank, I suppose this is what is meant by the ancient term "chaos," or by Plato's Receptacle. The illustrations Bergson offers to show that forms are only derivative appearances rising out of flux are peculiarly unsuited to his purpose The figure of the two trains is replete with formal stabilities the two *trains, parallel* tracks, *equality* of velocity, a definite *kind* of flux, namely, locomotion, and two *observers*. Again, when Bergson says that a supposedly stable quality is really a host of oscillations, he refers us to definite motions, not to formless flux. The self, too, is far from being mere flux. It is a focus of definite and intricate modes of function, exceedingly complex and formally distinct from other kinds of function.

Form and flux are distinct and coingredient factors in the natural order. Flux is not form and does not "cause" it, without form, flux is indeterminate, and indeterminate motion is not an entity we experience Form is not flux; it does not change. Squareness is just what it is and not something else. Nature is filled with entities which change, passing from possession of one form to possession of another, along a path that can be made definite for us as the track between actual stops and by intellectual cross sections which actualize mentally the "possible stops" in the various distinct transitions

(3) Bergson's doctrine of space and time is a metaphysical doctrine which contrasts two types of natural existence and tries to show that one of them is prior to the other It is not a description of the two familiar and *sui generis* features of nature which are ordinarily intended by the two terms. My summary of his theory about space, in Section I, shows that space means for him a kind of existence, extended in both space and time (in the ordinary acceptation of these terms) but composed of events whose past does not modify the present and whose future does not grow into novel powers and qualities All of this is condensed in Bergson's statement that space is mere repetition, "a present which is always beginning again."[62] What Bergson means by time or duration is a mode of existence whose present is enriched and growing toward novelty by virtue of its capacity to save up the past. It is typified by the rolling snowball and is apprehended through self-consciousness. As he explicitly says, duration cannot occur outside of consciousness, it is the kind of existence which we name by the terms "organic" and "historical."

If we take his analyses of space and time as analyses of the entities

[62] *Matter and Memory, op cit.*, p. 178.

ordinarily denoted by these names, it is easy enough to point out several errors in his discussion. Russell has done this, and we need not retrace his argument. I wish to add only the remark that these criticisms, together with some of my observations in earlier parts of this section, enable us to say that Bergson is not justified in making the assertions that space falls apart into points and that time is non-quantitative and non-measurable. Hence his repudiation of the applicability of mathematics to time is needless If Bergson had clearly specified what his doctrine of space and time really is intended to show, his whole metaphysics would have been more intelligible. It is regrettable that he did not so choose his words as to avoid confusing his readers with statements which are really contributions to the age-old controversy between materialists and idealists.

(4) Inspection of Bergson's statement of the pardoxes of Zeno has to be controlled by the sources by which they can be known. The basic sources are Plato's *Parmenides*[63] and Aristotle's *Physics*,[64] and only the latter outlines their structure in sufficient detail to reveal their assumptions and to suggest an adequate solution. I am convinced that recent writers on the paradoxes, and they are neither few nor lacking in ingenuity, add nothing substantial to our understanding of the paradoxes and often are given to supposing that some novel solution is required To Russell's proposals, already examined, I shall not return, though they have interesting parallels to Bergson's.

A crucial question about Bergson's treatment of the paradoxes concerns his thesis that all of them assume the applicability of motion to space, and also his judgment that they are all valid if this assumption is granted. If his analysis is wrong, his judgment that they are valid on the assumption he ascribes to them will fall away I shall try to show that Bergson's analysis holds of not one of the paradoxes

(a) The "dichotomy" concerns space only, arguing simply that since a finite distance can be divided ad infinitum, a moving body, in crossing it, would have to touch an infinite number of points, which it cannot do in a finite time The finite distance is infinite as containing an infinity of points, and these cannot all be gotten through or touched in a time that does not contain an infinity of instants and is consequently as infinite as the space Zeno does *not* argue that because space is composed of an infinity of points, and because motion can be applied to a line, motion must consist of an infinite number of states and cannot occur; he argues instead that a given time, presumed to be finite, is not enough time for the body to touch an infinity of points.

(b) The "Achilles" has the same structure as the "dichotomy," except

[63] 127e – 128e.
[64] VI, ii· 233 a 13–31, VI, ix: 239 b 10 – 240 a 18, VIII, viii: 263 a 4 – b 9, *op. cit.*

for a small detail, and Bergson's interpretation is therefore incorrect.

(c) He fails to notice that the "arrow" employs an assumption peculiar to itself. It is simply not the case that Zeno deduces the divisibility of time and motion into instants and positions from the divisibility of space into points, he *assumes* that *time* is composed of elements such that motion cannot occur in them Time is made of moments, he says, and since at every moment the arrow is in a position, the arrow rests at every moment of its flight, that is, it does not move at all.

(d) The "stadium" rests on assumptions which cannot with certainty be ascribed to any other paradox. Contrary to Bergson's contention, it assumes that there is one time in which a moving body crosses twice as much length of another moving body as it crosses of a stationary body, hence Zeno takes for granted the different relative velocities and does not argue that a time is twice itself because there are two spatial tracks, one twice the other The controlling assumption that gives the stadium its power is this. Both space and time are divisible into infinitesimal parts, least spaces and least times. Without this assumption it cannot be argued that a body cannot cross half a least length of one body while crossing a least length of another With it, the paradox is convincing. There cannot be difference of velocity And I am sure that Zeno was dialectician enough to provide himself with precisely those assumptions that he needed to make his conclusion follow.

An inaccurate statement of the paradoxes could hardly be expected to yield a successful solution. Bergson's solution of each paradox needs scrutiny; and since (a) the dichotomy and (b) the Achilles have the same structure, we may take them together His solution comes to simply this We must admit the infinite divisibility of space into an infinite set of points, but we intuit the indivisibility and continuity of time and motion, if we refuse to analyze motion in a manner parallel to our analysis of space, Zeno's conclusion does not follow Here are several errors, which may be briefly indicated since they have been pointed out before in a wider context (1) The divisibility of space follows from its continuity, which is as easy to intuit as the continuity of time or motion, and it does not mean that space is made of points (ii) Time and motion cannot be both continuous and indivisible They are indeed continuous, but no more so than space; and all three are divisible. (iii) There is no danger that, by applying motion to space, motion will dissolve into a powder of states. (iv) Bergson himself applies motion to space when he points out that "Achilles" divides the steps of Achilles arbitrarily, Achilles does not take progressively smaller steps, says Bergson, but maintains a pace which is inherently distinct from the tortoise's pace. The difference appealed to here can be a difference in nothing but the magnitude of space traversed.

If this appeal does not characterize a motion in terms of space, it does nothing

Zeno's (c) arrow and (d) stadium most likely serve to complete a complex argument. The first two puzzles assume in common that space is infinitely divisible, and use this premise to render motion unintelligible. An objector may be supposed to have suggested that an alternative premise might not lead to the same conclusion So Zeno obliges by postulating that division of time or space, or both, ends in reducing them to indivisible parts or elements. So far there is a common approach; but from this point on, the two paradoxes diverge The arrow *seems* to assume that time divides into instants, that is, into strictly non-temporal components, while the stadium almost certainly assumes that both space and time reduce to indivisible but extended parts. "Seems" is used advisedly Our sources do not make certain whether the components of time are taken by the arrow to be instants or least times, but it is quite clear that the stadium does not make sense without the assumption I have ascribed to it.

Now, in answering (c), the arrow, Bergson erroneously admits that to grant the presence of instants in time and of positions in motion is to compose time and motion of these factors and that, since to be in a position is to be at rest, the arrow does not move. Once more he translates division *at* formal factors as meaning division *into* these factors, and he adopts the entirely unjustified notion that saying a body is in a position at an instant is saying that it is at rest The body cannot rest unless it remains in a position for a time, this time being bounded by instants and divisible at instants, hence continuous motion is not broken by a body's being where it is at any given instant Therefore Bergson's radical solution, namely, his denial that there are instants in time or states in motion, is entirely unnecessary besides being untrue to fact. A simpler solution, pointing out the continuity of space, time, and motion, and their consequent divisibility *at* formal factors *into* continuous parts, is quite adequate

(d) The stadium, too, is not answered successfully by Bergson Since it assumes a similar analysis of both time and space, not of space only, it cannot be answered by accepting this assumption as applied to space while denying its applicability to time or motion. It is easy to show that if time is continuous, space is so, too, and this means that Bergson's solution is unacceptable And finally, it is not possible to pursue his recommendation that we disregard space and look at time by itself in order to intuit the absoluteness of duration. How can intuition of an absolute duration help us understand the diverse and relative ways in which a moving body traverses space (more of a moving body than of a stationary one) when what has to be understood is the tracing of lines, that is, space itself, with its quantity, continuity, and divisibility? All Bergson does, indeed, is to point to a fact of experience. A moving body does cross a greater length of a moving body than it does of a body at rest Zeno was aware of this fact, I am sure To answer him it is necessary to formulate the principle that makes the fact intelligible, while this is not difficult, Bergson does not do it.

IV

I wish to begin this final section by sketching what I consider a successful, but by no means novel, solution of the paradoxes Certain detailed aspects of the first two paradoxes I shall only mention It is easy, for one thing, to ascertain by mathematical analysis the precise point at which Achilles does overtake the tortoise. And secondly, it is easy to restate in semi-mathematical terms Aristotle's general analysis of these puzzles and thereby to make clear a fallacy common to both of them Zeno's argument may be rephrased as follows: Since "there is" (in a sense) a series of terms (for instance, fractions between 1 and 0) such that it never reaches a point toward which it continues to approach, the series is infinite, the point outside it to which it converges is infinitely distant from the first term in the series and cannot be reached The analysis of, and objection to, this argument given by Broad[65] are identical in principle with Aristotle's.

Contrary to the opinion of Bergson, the paradoxes are not all based on a single confusion, yet they are all answerable by a single proposition and by an elaboration of its classic significance Space, time, and motion are each continuous—this one proposition, evident to experience and unimpeachable by reason, is the key to a genuine solution.

(4a) The dichotomy and (4b) the Achilles alike contend that the infinity of points in the space traversed by a moving body prevents its being crossed in a finite time. But the time is just as divisible as the space and hence is infinite in the same way Their infinity is the potential infinity of divisibility—which means that while each is finite, it *can be* divided by us as often as we choose, and always once more than the number of times (always finite) it has been divided already. Since the points and instants discriminated in the time and space of a single motion are not actual, and since we never succeed in mentally actualizing more than a finite number of them, the time and space, and the motion likewise, remain finite quanta in themselves and do not fall apart into an infinite set of formal factors A point is not actual unless there is formal difference between the content of spatial regions Time does not contain an actual instant unless this instant bounds or limits formally different content. And these limit-

[65] C D Broad, "Note on Achilles and the Tortoise," *Mind*, XXII (1913), 319

ing, formal factors, since they are at once the end and the beginning of
the parts of space and time which they limit, do not interrupt the continuity of the continua to which they attach. Time itself is not broken by
the presence of motion on one side of a moment and the presence of rest
on the other It is a continuum in the simple but basic sense. a whole definable (in the mode of resolution, that is, by means of parts which are
not actually distinct) as containing parts which are the same in kind as
the whole, themselves continuous and each continuous with others Thus
the single motion of Achilles is one continuous motion, unbroken by rest
and enduring through the definite bounded interval required to catch and
surpass the tortoise; its continuity is not broken by the mental act of dividing it into partial motions at positions describable precisely by spatial
and temporal co-ordinates, that is, by points and instants, for these formal
factors are not parts of the motion or of its space and time, and their infinity is never more than that of a finite set capable of being added to:
The finite set of formal factors divides the continuum into continua, each
itself finite and further divisible, whose sum is equal in quantity to the
whole undivided continuum. And since the divisibility of the continua involved in motion is not dividedness, Achilles has not to cross an actual
infinity of formal factors He simply crosses a finite space in a finite time,
neither of which contains, except potentially, an infinite set of formal
limits.

The arrow and the stadium are answered in the same way (4c) Certain
details in interpreting the arrow cannot be worked out on the available
evidence. Obviously, it does not bring space into the argument, yet, while
it clearly does argue from the assumption that time is composed of indivisible parts, we cannot decide whether Zeno conceived them to be times
or instants, or how he represented their number In any case, the error in
this paradox is plain· Time does not consist of indivisibles, it is strictly
continuous. And supposing that the moments he speaks of are really
moments, not small times (if they are times, there is no way for him to
draw his conclusion), it is clear (1) that such entities cannot be parts of
time, and (11) that to be in a position at a moment is not to be at rest.
Thus the arrow vanishes (4d) The stadium can be interpreted with comparative certainty· It rests on the assumption that both space and time
consist of least spaces and times, and motion of least motions—these parts
all being indivisible. On this assumption, a least motion crosses a least
space in a least time. This assumption is an error, and once we deny it on
the strength of recognizing the continuity and infinite divisibility of motion, space, and time, the paradox collapses entirely and relative velocity
presents no problem.

I am aware that the above solution of the paradoxes, which follows

Aristotle, is not expounded with the frequency that its pertinence and success justify Where the cause of its neglect is some principle that lends itself to definition and discussion, and not primarily a prejudice against its antiquity or in favor of some novel analysis which borrows prestige from employing the most recent concepts of physics or mathematics, considerations like the following seem to play a decisive role.

First, there is often a failure to focus on the manner in which concepts may surpass or transcend the formal structure actually present in the objects of knowledge There prevails a habit of proceeding as if it is hardly necessary to distinguish mental being from real being, what may be conceived from what exists. This sort of issue is involved, though never satisfactorily discussed, in the thought of both Bergson and Russell about our ability to analyze continua with the help of cross sections

Then there is in modern thought a tradition of opposition to the mention or use of the potential Rationalists like Royce and Bradley agree with Russell in leaping from a rule to the actuality of items subject to the rule It is plain to Russell that "there are fractions" and that they are given and actual "all at once " Bergson follows the same pattern but then recoils from his misguided inference that a continuum consists of formal factors. Empiricists insist that the potential is not sensed or given, and is thus invention or artifice, empiricism, however, rarely has the courage to deny the givenness of change, and it is not easy to see how it accounts for the occurrence of fictitious ideas Philosophy today, facing the incessant contest between rationalists and empiricists in their modern posture, seems stricken with a poverty of alternatives Though I do not propose to provide an adequate discussion of these two serious considerations, which really are allied, a remark or two seems necessary.

(1) Russell is certainly among those who leap directly from what can be conceived to the character of fact. But the propriety of drawing a line is enforced by noting that when he speaks of infinite numbers and asks us to conceive them with him, he never does more than name a few members of a series and state the rule controlling membership. He gives no evidence that he conceives as actual "all" the members of the infinite series, nor does he succeed in inducing the reader to do so. I shall not trouble to argue that the thing simply cannot be done. But if he does so little toward exhibiting the actuality of an infinite set, how can he speak as if "all the fractions" are there at once? And, since he rests his analysis of a continuum on the reality of "all the fractions," we see that the analysis into formal factors is entirely groundless.

What needs to be done is to inspect a continuous motion, an unbroken spatial surface or span of time In each of these, there is no actual division, no actual limit. The table top is a single uninterrupted magnitude, ending only where the table is bounded by air, and extended through both table and air is space itself, a continuous quantum, intrinsically unbroken and devoid of actual divisions. Abstractly or mathematically, we can conceive the table top divided as often as we please, but the limits and parts so achieved are not actual in the table The table might be cut into separate pieces, but it is not; we mentally actualize the points and lines at which the division might occur, but this act, while intellectually significant and based on what might occur in the fact, does not mean that the table is divided. What exists potentially in the fact is lifted into formal realization by analysis, and the analytic results transcend the actual

By way of parenthesis, a denial of the actual division of a magnitude *qua* magnitude is not a denial that a concrete physical thing or motion is, besides being a continuous magnitude, also a unity of finite number of material parts. A continuous process of walking thirty feet includes, say, fifteen actually separate steps, an organic body is a unity (at a given moment) of a finite number of cells, and each cell is a whole of a finite number of chemical elements. As long as each such part is continuous, it is infinitely divisible by mathematical division, but physical division is certain to destroy it by reducing it to simpler elements, to entities of a different order. The possible stages of such physical division are likely to be finite in number, that is, there are ultimate material components of all physical substances, which unite at successively higher strata under progressively more complex forms. What these least material elements may be is a problem for physical science.

(2) The thesis of the next to the last paragraph raises the question of the potential Sir David Ross boggles at the potential and on this account rejects the Aristotelian solution of the paradoxes. A continuum, he holds, must contain an actual infinity of formal factors, for their actual pre-existence is presupposed (*a*) by the mental act of dividing it or of counting formal factors in it, (*b*) by a body's passage along a path to the point of termination, (*c*) by the infinite divisibility of a continuum For, he reasons, an act of dividing or counting can only discover what is there—it does not create its object, again, a body cannot rest at, or pass through, a point that is not there in act, and infinite divisibility implies an actual infinity of points or lines or moments or states Were this not the case, the act of dividing or counting, and a body's motion or coming to rest, must be held to create, to call from nonexistence into existence, such formal factors as points, instants, and so forth. Hence a moving body, in order to traverse a finite distance, must have got to the end of a series that has no end, and motion is incomprehensible Aristotle has answered neither the first nor the second paradox.[66]

[66] *Physics, op. cit.,* pp 53, 69, 74–75.

Ross at least formulates reasons for rejecting the potential, which is something not to be found in Russell or Bergson But his argument is a *petitio*. It proceeds *from the assumption* that what is not actual is entirely nonexistent, that the sole alternative to the actuality of points in a continuous line is their being created *ex nihilo* by the act of dividing or by a body's coming to rest at them. Aristotle asserts that these two alternatives are not exhaustive, all Ross does is to suppose they are and to dismiss the alternative of creation

Thus we are driven to inspect the facts. Where there is no formal distinction between regions or extents, there are no actual forms in a continuous space or time or motion When we count five actual sheep, we are counting items that are actual and distinct, but when we conceive the five sheep as divided neatly into ten half-sheep, we are not conceiving actual lines or divisions but are only mentally actualizing what is potential in the undivided sheep Surely this simple process is a type of what happens in numberless conceptual dealings with continua. As to Ross's view that infinite divisibility implies an actual infinity of forms, enough has been said in the criticism of Russell

At the conclusion of this discussion it is not out of place to recall that Socratic criticism did not serve merely as a purgative To clear one's mind of ingenious speculations about basic concepts in natural philosophy is to gain a greater freedom for a study of fact, it is also to become more ready to appreciate the tradition of classical realism.

(1) The fact of change is certainly obvious enough to count against the rationalist *caveat* of Parmenides. There is no need to embrace a dogma making change unintelligible, to begin at the wrong end of a problem Bergson's radical denial of things can be understood if we recognize at the start that he has committed himself to a Parmenidean thesis on the kind of being things would have if they did exist Russell also starts with Parmenideanism, and the result is his analysis of continua into a plurality of discrete forms His theory of the composition of continua resembles Descartes's hypothesis that at every instant the universe needs to be created anew if it is to endure, the components of motion, for Russell, cannot be continuous with one another This tendency in natural philosophy is a confession that change cannot be understood, and is an appeal, in order "to save appearances," to the principle of the miraculous.

(2) It is better to state principles that do not transmogrify facts out of all recognition. Change is a distinctive mode of being, possessed by substances that change. It is complex: a transition undergone by something, from one formal determination to another Forms are incapable of change, but at least some of the things in which they exist do change. These things contain a principle of indetermination, traditionally known as matter,

which is the bearer of potency. Transition is continuous in the classic sense, as are space and time. These simple observations I do not intend to elaborate, I wish only to claim that they help us understand the familiar aspects of experienced flux and that to declare them distortions of the given or rationally perverse is to speak from a groundless dogma.

(3) And finally, appreciation of the complexity of flux, as being a way of existing found in things and as involving matter and potency, revives the relevance of classic causal analysis and of a realist theory of the categories A natural philosophy which does justice to flux and to causes will be qualified to lead up to metaphysical investigations whose progress is not spoiled by arbitrary speculations or skeptical dogmatism, whose horizons are broad enough to include more than one sector in the panorama of existence, and whose temper is receptive to wisdom regardless of the century when it was attained, whether by Whitehead in our own time or by the most commanding thinkers of the classic or Christian eras. A natural philosophy, serving thus to restore breadth and penetration to metaphysical insight, would also serve the deepest practical needs of our time.

V

On the Distinction between Thing and Property

Manley H. Thompson, Jr., *University of Chicago*

In this paper I shall discuss some of the problems involved in explicating the notions of thing and property In order to limit the scope of the discussion, and by way of introduction, I shall begin by considering these two notions as they are used in the analysis of the intension and extension of terms. Only things and properties will be assumed as entities at the start, and the question of further entities, such as classes, will be considered later.

In speaking of *things* I shall always mean, unless I explicitly indicate otherwise, actually existing things. The words "intension" and "extension" will be used as synonymous with "connotation" and "denotation," respectively, and the usual doctrine which regards terms as having intension and extension will be interpreted, in accordance with the decision not to assume classes, as meaning merely that terms connote properties and denote things. The word "term" will be applied only to what are called categorematic words in traditional logic, that is, words like "man," "animal," "white," "tall," which taken by themselves signify things or properties in contradistinction to words like "some," "and," "every," which do not by themselves signify things or properties. The verb "to signify" is taken as expressing the most general relation between terms and reality and thus as holding wherever to denote, to connote, or another relation to be explained later, holds.

I

It has been said that a thing in the strictest sense (a thing that can be properly called a substance) is that which has independent existence, while a property is that which has existence only in the sense of belonging to, and hence of being dependent on, a thing One great difficulty with this traditional view has been that of explaining the alleged dependence of properties on things, for as soon as we try to state what the thing is, we seem to be unable to do so except by ascribing properties to the thing, and in this sense the thing depends on its properties It has thus been maintained that properties are no less self-subsistent than things, and it becomes difficult to explain how we can talk about a thing as distinct from its properties. While it might be urged that this problem may be avoided by assuming classes, which are actually what we mean by extensions, I do not think such an assumption would really help matters For a class which is said to comprise the extension of a term is unintelligible except as determined by the property which is taken as the term's intension, and this determination will amount to specifying that any object x is a member of that class if, and only if, x possesses that property. The relation of possessing which holds between a thing and its property is thus unavoidable and clearly supposes some sort of distinction between things and properties. The assumption of classes as separate entities does not escape the problem.

In some cases, however, it seems quite easy to render intelligible the distinction between a thing and its property. This is certainly true as long as we can specify the thing independently of its possessing the property in question. For example, if the property is brownness and the thing is specified as a dog, there is no difficulty in distinguishing between the brownness and the dog. It makes perfectly good sense to say that the term "brown" denotes the dog and connotes brownness. But if, on the contrary, we analyze the term "dog" in the same fashion, and still specify the things only as a dog, we are left with the problem of distinguishing between a dog and dogness. Here we can say easily enough that dogness is that set of conditions which must obtain if we are to apply the term "dog," though this, of course, succeeds merely in relating dogness to the term and not the *thing* dog. We might specify simply that the thing is a brown thing and then argue for the intelligibility of the distinction between brown thing and dogness. Such a procedure regards brownness and dogness as properties in exactly the same sense and assumes that except for the degree of specificity desired, either property is equally capable of determining a thing. Yet in many respects the two are clearly not the same kind of entity. Brownness is a simple sensory quality and as such defies analysis, while dogness is obviously complex and is subject to analysis in a variety of ways. Whatever the analysis might be, the notion that dogness somehow or other finally determines a kind of thing rather than a kind of property seems inevitable. Even if one contends that dogness is merely a collection of sensory and other qualities, such a collection would seem to determine the kind of thing signified by "dog" rather than a new kind of property. To be sure, the epistemology and metaphysics usually associated with this position may relegate the notion of a thing to a sort of I-know-not-what which

THE DISTINCTION BETWEEN THING & PROPERTY 127

is said to cause or to underlie the appearance of those qualities which constitute a dog But a thing in this sense is admittedly unsignifiable, and it becomes necessary to reintroduce the notion of a thing as being simply that which *is* a certain collection of qualities [1] With this analysis, then, any difference between a dog and a dogness seems to have been destroyed There is merely the particular collection of qualities, and one may just as well call each occurrence of this collection a dogness as to call it a dog I shall not consider here the epistemological problem of how one is to decide whether such an occurrence constitutes an actual perception of a dog or an illusion. The only point I want to illustrate is that the analysis just mentioned allows for a difference between brownness and dogness as kinds of entities and at the same time permits some sort of intelligible distinction between thing and property, even if the distinction covers only the simplest variety of properties At least the simple, unanalyzable sensory qualities are always properties, while a thing always involves a collection that contains such qualities.

A brown thing must then be a collection of this sort in which one of the qualities is brownness, but when such a thing is specified merely as brown, the specification does not determine the thing, that is, the collection, but only a particular elementary property which the thing possesses. It is thus that "brown" may be said to signify directly, mean, or connote brownness and to signify indirectly, indicate, or denote a brown thing. By analogy one might expect that "dog" can be said just as easily to connote dogness and to denote any collection of properties which contains dogness. But here there is the difficulty that what is treated as a property appears on the analysis given so far to be identical with the collection supposed to comprise the thing To specify a thing as a dog, in other words, determines the thing rather than one of its elementary properties. We might, of course, give the connotation of "dog" by enumerating just those properties which must be in the collection in order for it to comprise a dog, and it would then seem possible to argue that dogness is a subclass of any class of properties constituting an individual dog Yet before we can do this we must have some means of delimiting the wider class, as clearly we do not want to argue that every possible class of sensory and other qualities in which dogness could be included as a subclass constitutes an individual dog. It thus becomes necessary to specify another connotation by enumerating a still larger list of properties the collection of which is to be taken as comprising an individual dog, say Rex. But such a collection is perfectly analogous to the

---

[1] For a defense of a similar position, see Bertrand Russell, *An Inquiry into Meaning and Truth* (New York, W W Norton, 1940), pp 97–98 Russell's view differs from the one mentioned here in that for him "brown" and "dog" are equally things. Our problem now is to see how close we can come to Russell's position and still retain some sort of intelligible distinction between thing and property.

one which we previously identified in each of its occurrences as being indifferently a dogness or a dog, and hence we may just as legitimately refer to every occurrence of this new collection as a Rexness. "Rex," then, would seem to denote these occurrences and to connote Rexness But here, as in the case of "dog," what is treated as a property seems indistinguishable from the collection supposed to comprise the thing, and we must search for a wider class of properties which this time will include Rexness as a subclass This might be accomplished by specifying Rex-barking as a collection of properties which comprises a thing denoted by "Rex" and possesses the property of Rexness. At this point, surely, it should be clear that we have embarked on an infinite regress which may proceed from Rex-barking-joyfully as a thing denoted by Rex-barking to Rex-barking-joyfully-and-wagging-his-tail, and so on, to say nothing of similar regresses for Fido and Rover, should we tire of Rex.

II

In order to cope with such regresses, we may distinguish two different ways of specifying, or otherwise singling out, a thing These two ways are illustrated roughly by the questions "what kind of thing?" and "which thing?" An answer to the first would normally involve terms like "acid," "iron," "vertebrate," "dog," and so forth, although in certain contexts a sufficient answer might be given by terms like "brown," "large," "short," and so on But even with the partial and naive analysis of a thing outlined above, terms of the latter sort, which always specify a thing only with reference to its possessing simple sensory qualities like brownness, did not appear to be capable of determining a kind of thing Admittedly the question calls for a great deal of further analysis, but for the present we will divide the class of terms which may be used to answer the first question into two divisions, without attempting to justify our procedure Terms like "acid" and "vertebrate" will be called K-terms because they appear to signify directly the kind of thing in question, while "brown," "large," and the like will be called D-terms because at least in most contexts they seem to describe the thing in question rather than to signify its kind.[2]

[2] This distinction between K- and D-terms corresponds fairly well to one form of the medieval distinction between absolute and connotative terms I have not used the medieval expressions because of the variety of meanings they have acquired in the history of logic. The distinction as drawn here comes closest to Occam. See Ernest A Moody, *The Logic of William of Ockham* (New York, Sheed and Ward, 1935), pp 54-57

It should be noted that this distinction cannot be made within the framework of contemporary symbolic logic If "man is white" becomes "if man x and then white x" or "man x and white x," depending on whether the variable is universally or particularly quantified, "man" and "white" are both terms of exactly the same sort There is clearly

We shall assume that the question "what kind of thing?" can be answered properly only by specifying K-terms, and if D-terms are used the answer is given only in so far as these terms are employed in such a way that the appropriate K-terms can be inferred from them As for example, a botanist might be able to infer the kind of tree from a sufficient description of it, although certainly in most cases the description itself would also contain some K-terms such as "tree." On the other hand, the question "which thing?" can never be answered without using either proper names or D-terms, and what is most important for our purposes, the satisfactoriness of the answer here depends on a particular context of questioner and answerer. If the experience and memory of the questioner happens to be sufficient, and if he is not inclined to be contentious, a single proper name may suffice for an answer But at the other extreme, the only factors to limit an infinite regress are the ingenuity of the questioner, the good disposition of the answerer, and the physical endurance of both

There would not seem to be this same sort of dependence where the question is strictly "what kind?" The adequacy of the answer in this case does not depend on the extent to which it satisfies a person that he knows which thing someone else is talking about, but rather on the extent to which it truly states what kind of thing something is However, it might appear that since a person obviously cannot judge whether a thing has been truly specified as to kind unless he first knows which thing it is, the question "which thing?" is the fundamental one, and any dependence that applies here will also apply to the other question. In so far as we are unable to consider either question apart from a context of communication, this extension of the dependence is unavoidable Yet clearly the fact that a certain thing is of such and such a kind does not depend on anybody's knowing which thing is meant, and in this respect we may regard the answer to the question "what kind?" as given entirely by the signification of the appropriate K-terms quite apart from any context of communication. We do not even have to assume that these K-terms already exist as words in any language, since the question is strictly what kind of thing something is and the answer is therefore dependent only on the nature of the thing and not on the availability of words.

Now if all this is granted, can the process of specifying a kind of thing proceed indefinitely? Quite emphatically *yes*, if we mean to ask whether we can ever be sure at a particular stage of inquiry that further investigation will not disclose greater degrees of specification and necessitate revi-

no basis for calling the first a K-term and the second a D-term. The value of this departure from contemporary logic may be measured by the extent to which the distinction in question enables us to give an intelligible account of the difference between thing and property. I shall return to this point briefly in the final section of this paper.

sion of our classificatory scheme But just as emphatically *no*, if we mean to
ask whether we can speak intelligibly about specifying a kind of thing
when we insist that this can only be done by literally adding specifications
without end. And this negative reply does not mean merely that for practical reasons one must stop somewhere An infinite series is not specified
by an endless enumeration of terms but by a statement of the appropriate
mathematical formula, and such is the case not because mathematicians
are mortal and unable to effect the enumeration but simply because the
second procedure and not the first leads to a specification of the series
Similarly, outside mathematics the kind of thing something is, is specified
by a formula of K-terms which locates it properly within the appropriate
scheme of classification, and even if at a certain place in the scheme an infinite number of varieties must be allowed, this is to be accomplished by
provisions in the formula and not by an endless enumeration The situation
is entirely different, however, when the question is "which thing?," since the
dependence here on a particular context of questioner and answerer removes all considerations except those of a practical nature.

In the light of these remarks, our previous attempt to distinguish between
thing and property by regarding a thing as a collection of qualities, resulted in confusing the two questions we have since been arguing should
be kept separate When we assumed that a thing had been specified as a
dog, instead of accepting this as the specification of a kind of thing, we
regarded it as the specification of a property called dogness and went on
to ask which thing possesses that property There seemed to be no escape
from an infinite regress, because there was nothing to prevent us from repeating this procedure for every specification of a thing Yet the regress is
harmless if the specification of a thing by K-terms does specify a thing
and not a property. For in this case the endless quest for a thing which
might proceed from Rex to Rex-barking, to Rex-barking-joyfully, and so
forth, is exactly like any regress that arises when a contentious questioner
refuses to be satisfied that he can tell which thing someone is talking about.

Such a regress has nothing to do with what kind of thing something is,
it applies only to the situation where one is trying to indicate to someone
else by means of proper names and D-terms which thing is in question
Yet the two cases here are inevitably confused if the specification of a kind
of thing by K-terms is treated only as specifying a property, since this is
also just what is achieved by each attempt to indicate which thing, and is
precisely what affords the contentious questioner the opportunity of repeating. "Yes, I recognize the property, but tell me which thing possesses
it." The confusion is rendered more difficult to detect by the fact that K-
terms usually occur in the descriptive phrases we employ to indicate which
thing, and even a single K-term may sometimes provide all the indication

desired Thus in some contexts "dog" might serve to indicate or denote which thing by connoting or signifying directly a collection of properties that provides a mark for identifying the thing. But the denotative function here does not depend on whether the thing is actually a dog but only on what sensory and other qualities someone may have associated with "dog" There is thus nothing to prevent a word which normally functions as a K-term from also functioning in certain contexts as a D-term The confusion in our earlier analysis, then, involved treating all terms as D-terms, and hence the regress that is always possible when the question is "which thing?" appeared to be unavoidable in all cases where we tried to specify a thing.

In accordance with this revised account of the matter, a thing can, of course, no longer be regarded as a collection of properties While the specification of dog as a kind of thing will require a collection of K-terms like "chordate," "vertebrate," "mammal," and so forth, this situation must now be considered without assuming a thing-property terminology Instead we may assume a plurality of different kinds of things and say that each kind is properly specified by a certain position within a classificatory scheme. The scheme itself is to be regarded as an arrangement of K-terms which purports to represent true specifications of kinds of things, and the relations of inclusion and exclusion shown in the scheme signify identities and differences in the kinds of things specified rather than the presence or absence of properties Instead of saying, for example, that a kind of thing which is both vertebrate and mammal differs from other vertebrates by possessing the further property of being mammal, we may say simply that this kind is vertebrate and mammal while other kinds are vertebrate and not mammal

An obvious objection to this simple procedure would seem to lie in the fact that, after all, differences among vertebrates depend on what is observed concerning their morphology, mode of reproduction, and so forth, and this should certainly boil down to something like the presence or absence of observable properties If our concern here were with the warrant or evidence for asserting that one kind of vertebrate differs from another, observable properties would be decisive, but this does not mean that it is impossible to distinguish between what is the case and the sort of evidence we require in order to decide what is the case. Thus we assume that K-terms signify what is the case and that their signification can be analyzed in this respect without regard for the empirical inquiries that provide the only means we have for determining what is the case. Hence the simple statement that a kind of thing is vertebrate and mammal is to be viewed here with the assumption that what is the case is signified directly (as opposed to being merely in some degree indicated or denoted), while the statement that a kind of thing possesses the properties of being vertebrate and being mammal is to be taken with reference to the conditions of evidence required for the significations assumed in the first statement.

Observable properties, then, will provide some warrant for asserting that a kind of thing is vertebrate and mammal, and in the context of inquiry "vertebrate" and "mammal" will connote these properties To the extent that the properties provide the evidence required, the terms will also indicate or denote the actual things under investigation If at this point someone asks what these things are and how we can distinguish them from collections of observable properties, we may reply simply that the things are vertebrates that are mammals. Such a reply, with the assumption that K-terms directly signify actual kinds of things, may afford an adequate answer to the question "what kind of thing?," though certainly not to "which thing?" If the reply is understood in this sense, the difference between a thing and a collection of properties should be as clear as the difference between the two questions.

It was remarked earlier, in passing, that in some cases a single proper name might be satisfactory for an answer to "which thing?" In such a context the proper name does not have, as it is frequently analyzed as having, mere denotation without connotation. It is only because the questioner has certain associations connected with the name—only because the name connotes something to him—that he remains satisfied with "Rex" as an answer to "Which dog do you mean?" An analysis, on the contrary, which tries to show that proper names are purely denotative must begin by divorcing them from any context of communication. Thus in our previous analysis, where K-terms were at first treated as D-terms and our search for the specification of a thing led to an infinite regress, instead of regarding K-terms as signifying what is actually the case with respect to kinds of things, we might have tried to stop the regress by assuming that proper names afford direct indications of things. The latter is, in fact, the course often taken when all terms are assumed to have extension and intension in the sense of denoting things and connoting other entities that are properties.

The course initially seems plausible, since one can argue that whether or not an individual dog is Rex or Rover is a fact no less independent of anybody's knowing which thing is meant than is the fact that the thing is a dog and not some other kind of mammal In addition to the questions "what kind?" and "which?," there would thus seem to be simply the question "what thing?," and the latter is to be answered by a proper name that directly signifies the particular thing in question regardless of the kind of thing it is or who knows which thing it is But this seems to be saying merely that for every individual thing there is a particular mode of succession of marks or sounds which might be correlated with it as its proper name. While this is easily shown to be possible even for an infinite number of things, such a correlation does not in itself constitute signification. The specification of a thing achieved by this procedure is entirely illusory and comes to no more than saying that the thing is what it is and may have something else correlated with it.

On the other hand, one may regard the proper name as merely an abbreviation for a descriptive phrase and say that only in this sense does it constitute the signification of an individual thing If the phrase contains a K-term, this way of specifying an individual seems quite intelligible. We may say, for example, "the dog which is large, brown, with a loud bark, and so forth," and claim to have signified but one individual, because in addition to specifying the kind of thing it is, we have also given some of its properties. For it is a fact independent of any context of communication not only that the thing is or is not a dog with respect to its kind but also that it does or does not possess the properties enumerated. The question "what thing?" thus assumes an answer to "what kind?," and precisely because of this assumption there is no difficulty in distinguishing between a thing and its properties Instead of trying to distinguish Rex from his size, color, and so forth, we have only to cope with the distinction between a dog and his size or color. In this way individuation becomes entirely a matter of indicating properties that belong to a thing already specified as being of a certain kind There is, of course, no reason why a description has to contain a K-term, as one may say merely "something which is large, brown, with a loud bark, and so forth." Yet in such a case we must admit that the thing is actually unspecified, although it is often possible to infer from some of the properties (for instance, that of having a loud bark) some specification of the thing. Difficulties arise only when the difference between K- and D-terms is ignored and the analysis of the specification of a thing is assumed to involve nothing but a list of properties.

III

We may now begin to summarize the results of this discussion of extension and intension with respect to things and properties. The distinction between things and properties seems to make sense in a context where terms are assumed to signify directly what is actually the case, as opposed to signifying those observable properties which are taken as indicating what is the case. A scientist in the process of inquiry when asked what he is investigating might well reply, "things of such and such a kind." In giving an answer of this sort, the scientist professes merely to signify his subject matter and makes no reference to the complicated observational procedures which may be necessary in order to determine that subject matter But if the further question were put, "Show me which things you mean," a reference to these observational procedures would, of course, be necessary In such a context, the things literally are collections of observable properties, and it would be nonsense to demand to be shown the things apart from the properties.

The main contention of the present discussion is, then, that an analysis of the denotation and connotation of terms can be made intelligible only with some reference to the previous context where things are distinct from collections of properties The distinction in this case consists simply in the fact that things are signified by K-terms apart from the signification of properties; and this does not conflict with the fact that things can never be observed apart from their properties. A K-term signifies a thing directly because, unlike a proper name, it determines a place within a classificatory scheme and thereby specifies wholly or partly a certain kind of thing The signification thus depends on the assumption of such a scheme which is absent in the case of proper names. But instead of saying that this determination of a place within the scheme depends on the properties which the K-term connotes, I have proposed in the present discussion to regard the determination as depending directly on the kind of thing which the term signifies.

The force of this proposal may be brought out by contrasting the analysis suggested here with that recently given by Professor C I Lewis. Lewis distinguishes between the intension or connotation and what he prefers to call the signification of a term The former involves all the other terms which must be applicable to a thing if the given term is applicable, while the latter involves all the properties which must be in the thing if the given term correctly applies to the thing. Thus, as Lewis illustrates the distinction, "we should say that the term 'man' *signifies* animality, that animality is included in the *signification* of 'man.' And we shall wish to say that 'man' connotes the *term* 'animal', that this term 'animal' is included in the connotation or intension of the term 'man.' "[3]

Now this analysis occasions no difficulty when it is limited to what we referred to above as the context of inquiry. A scientist investigating men need not worry about distinguishing between a man and that collection of properties, including animality, which he must observe before he applies the term "man," nor does he have any need to regard his classificatory scheme as anything more than an interrelation of terms based on the properties they signify Yet if one attempts to distinguish between thing and property within the limits of Lewis's analysis, I can see no way of avoiding infinite regresses like those we have already noticed The necessity for rec-

[3] C. I. Lewis, *An Analysis of Knowledge and Valuation* (La Salle, Ill , Open Court, 1946), p. 43 Italics in original.

ognizing a context where terms are assumed to signify things directly without regard for properties is illustrated succinctly even by Lewis's conception of the signification of a term as properties *in things*. While it is a truism that within the context of inquiry the application of a K-term is governed by the presence or absence of observable properties, it is quite a different matter when one adds that these properties are in things The addition makes no sense at all as prescribing part of a methodological procedure, but it does not seem meaningless when understood as a reference to the subject matter apart from the conditions of inquiry. We can observe only properties, though we claim to be investigating things, and we may try to express the relation between the two by saying that the properties belong to, or are somehow in, the things The intelligibility of such an expression, however, assumes that things can be specified as distinct from properties.

If we apply Lewis's analysis to this problem, we can say only that a K-term signifies certain properties and denotes any individual that possesses those properties A thing is thus unintelligible apart from the collection of properties which justifies the application of a term. On the other hand, if the K-term in one context can be said to signify directly a kind of thing, we may restrict the distinction between things and properties to that context. We might say, for example, that the thing is a dog, while its properties are its size, shape, color, habits, and so forth Then, within the context of inquiry, the criteria for applying the term "dog" can be given entirely with reference to properties without necessitating that the dog is thereby reduced to a collection of properties We may reinforce the point by adding that the properties are in the dog, and while the addition contributes nothing to our rules of inquiry, it serves to emphasize that we are investigating dogs and not properties

The appeal to two different contexts in the analysis of a K-term is not to be taken as necessarily bestowing two different meanings on the term Our basic distinction refers to what we regarded originally as roughly illustrated by the questions "what kind of thing?" and "which thing?" The former assumed an absolute context in which the answer depended only on the nature of the thing in question, while the latter always occurred in a context relative to conditions of communication What we later called the context of inquiry constitutes a special case of the relative context, since the inquirer in fixing the criteria for the application of a given term is, in effect, deciding which things one should mean by that term. In an absolute context, then, we assume that a K-term specifies those things which inquiry seeks to establish as the things one should mean when he uses the term. The term thus signifies directly any of the things of a given kind, and what is specified by the term is such a thing rather than the properties required to justify the application of the term The distinction between thing and property, then, appears in the contrast between K- and D-terms in this absolute context Terms of the latter sort signify directly a property and indirectly or obliquely anything possessing that property. A distinction corresponding to that between connotation and denotation is thus unavoidable in this case, although it presents no problem regarding the difference between thing and property. The term "brown," for example, connotes brownness and denotes brown things; but these things can be specified apart from the brownness as dogs, cats, vertebrates, and so forth by the K-terms which directly signify them.

In the strict sense, then, only D-terms have a signification which involves two kinds of entities and which is therefore to be analyzed into intension and extension K-terms, on the other hand, signify but a single kind of entity and thus have *simple and direct signification* which is neither denotation nor connotation.[4]

These conclusions yield important consequences for the question of ontology—for deciding the kinds of entities we should assume in order to account for the extension and intension of terms When we regard the thing as specified directly by the K-term rather than by the conditions required for the application of the term, there is no need to assume a property like animality, for example, apart from individual animals. The terms "animality" and "animal" have exactly the same signification, both in the context of inquiry as signifying a collection of properties, and in the absolute sense as signifying kinds of individuals This view does not prevent us from accounting for the fact that "Rex is animal" seems like perfectly good usage, while "Rex is animality" appears absurd. One might utter the first sentence in a context where he wished only to describe which thing he meant, and in such a case he would be using "animal" as a D-term, connoting a property belonging to the thing meant. "Animality" would then name this property, and the second sentence above would identify the thing with the property. If we assume that the distinction between thing and property is intelligible, we would, of course, regard this second sentence as manifestly wrong, and this is precisely what is done in ordinary English usage where "animal" and "animality" have different meanings.

---

4 This notion of simple and direct signification bears a resemblance to what is often called the "name-relation." However, while "dog" may be said to signify indifferently individual dogs, this is not to be taken as meaning that "dog," in analogy with a proper name, is either a mere series of marks or sounds to be associated with any individual dog or an abbreviation for a description that applies to any individual dog On the contrary, "dog" is simply a sign which *means* dogs It is thus more than a series of marks or sounds correlated with dogs, and different from a sign that means a something-or-other (an *x*) possessing canine properties The resemblance to the name-relation is only in the direct reference of sign to thing as opposed to the indirect reference of sign to thing by way of a property the thing possesses.

All well and good until we press the question of the distinction between Rex and his properties When we do this we have found no alternative to the recognition of K-terms that specify rather than describe the thing In so far as "animal" is such a term, "Rex is animal" constitutes a specification of kind Only the one entity, the thing in question, is specified, the assumption of the property animality as an additional entity is not only unnecessary but is fatal to our specification For with this assumption we are left merely with a description of an unspecified thing—an x characterized by the possession of animality Of course, within the context of inquiry we may ignore this circumstance and profess merely to be investigating sets of properties (phenomena) without claiming to specify things apart from the observable properties with which we identify them. But then, we must be content to say that an animal *is* a certain collection of properties, and hence for our purposes the word "animality" which names this collection means nothing different from "animal" We cannot say that animality is that property *in things* which is required for the application of "animal" without encountering the difficulties we have already noted.

If, on the other hand, we wish to keep "animal" as a K-term, we must allow it simple and direct signification; but in this case, too, we can find no separate meaning for "animality." It is only in a context where we assume both K- and D-terms with "animal" taken as one of the latter that we can give "animality" a distinct meaning This is exactly the procedure we would normally use for terms like "brown" and "brownness" Since anything that is brown can be specified by K-terms quite apart from the brownness it possesses, no difficulty results from saying that "brown" denotes brown things and connotes brownness. We thus assume entities that are properties and not things only to account for the signification of D-terms Such an assumption with regard to K-terms is impossible from the very nature of these terms and inevitably results in reducing them to D-terms

With this approach we also avoid the assumption of classes as separate and independent entities required to explain an act of specification, although the point may be difficult to grasp in view of the fact that I have continually said K-terms signify directly kinds of things, which would seem to be the same as saying they signify classes of things. But I have assumed the difference that while a class is a collection of things defined by a common property, a kind constitutes a direct specification of a thing without reference to properties. I have regarded the word "kind" as referring to an act of signification which consists in specifying a thing by one or more K-terms. A kind is thus no more an entity in itself apart from the thing specified than a description is an entity apart from the collection of properties by which a thing is described. The fact that there are usually an indefinite number of individuals of the same kind does not affect the specification, which applies indifferently to any of these individuals and would be just as true a specification if only one such individual existed.

Words like "every," "some," and "the" placed before a K-term thus in no way alter the specification effected by the term "The" normally occurs in a context of communication where the thing specified is also assumed to be described sufficiently for someone to single it out from other individuals, although in the context of inquiry where one has failed to discover more than a single instance of the thing specified the addition of D-terms may be unnecessary, as when one speaks simply of the sun or the moon. Words such as "every," on the other hand, which convey strict universality, are used only where a thing is signified by a term which is assumed to apply to it simply because it is correctly specified as being of a certain kind. A plurality of individuals is not required, as one may say "Every sun is hot" without assuming more than one sun The word "some," finally, is used where a term happens to apply to a thing but is neither assumed to do so simply because of the thing's specification nor considered sufficient to enable us to single the thing out from others. While this treatment of "every," "some," and "the" is obviously contrary to the customary analysis of the existential import of propositions, our problem here is only to render intelligible a distinction between an actually existing thing and its properties We are not concerned with extending our analysis so as to cope with terms like "unicorn" or with the question of whether a unicorn should in any sense be regarded as a thing [5]

The radical character of the analysis I am proposing may thus be summed up by saying that the act of specification by kind is a primitive notion and constitutes the only way of specifying a thing. This means, of course, that things in their individuality cannot be specified—they can only be described As we previously remarked, a description normally contains a K-term which specifies the thing, as well as D-terms which denote the thing by signifying some of its properties. The only entities required, then, are individual things and their properties The word "class" does not refer to an entity apart from the things described, any more than "kind" refers to an entity apart from the things specified.[6] While I have used the expression "classificatory scheme" to mean an arrangement of K-terms which accomplishes a specification of things, it would be more appropriate in accordance with my use of "class" to substitute some such expression as

[5] The present analysis would attempt to account for the null class as a special case of a quasi thing The notion of a quasi thing will be introduced below, but a treatment of the null class will be beyond the scope of this discussion

[6] Words like "mankind" and "men" require "man" as a D-term and thus signify the class of individuals possessing humanity. But the class is a quasi thing and not an entity really distinct from things and properties.

"specificatory scheme." What appear to be relations of class inclusion and exclusion exhibited in such a scheme are to be interpreted simply as interrelations among K-terms. The statement "All mammals are vertebrates," for example, means merely that a thing specified as a mammal is also specified as a vertebrate Instead of assuming two entities, mammal and vertebrate, which can be related by inclusion, we assume only the individual things signified by the terms "mammal" and "vertebrate" and regard the inclusion as nothing more than the fact that whatever thing is signified by the first term is also signified by the second, but not vice versa [7]

Such a position may appear at first glance like an extreme form of nominalism, but I think further examination will show that this label is unjustified. The position usually attacked as nominalism is one which treats all terms as D-terms and hence fails to distinguish between specification and description A thing thus has no status apart from the properties which justify the application of a descriptive name, and since the properties by which a given individual may be described are indefinite in number, there seems to be no way of avoiding an arbitrary selection of properties for any specification of a thing. This arbitrariness has generally been taken as the chief objection to nominalism and has often been summed up by saying that nominalism reduces a kind (which has become indistinguishable from a class) to a mere name.

An opposing "realistic" position may then seek to escape from the arbitrariness by regarding a class as somehow a real entity subsisting independently of names It is not necessary here to go into all the difficulties of this sort of realism. We need only remark that the position does not succeed in rendering intelligible a distinction between thing and property For what should be the specification of a thing turns out to be the specification of another entity called a class, so that the thing still remains unintelligible except as that which is said to fall under the class by virtue of its possessing a certain property.

The position I have been arguing, on the contrary, represents an attempt to avoid the arbitrariness of nominalism by distinguishing between the specification and description of a thing While it is arbitrary which of the indefinite number of properties belonging to a thing we select in order to describe the thing, the specification of the thing apart from its properties is not arbitrary. And it is essential to this position that the specification

---

[7] An explanation of the manner in which we may speak of the relations of inclusion exhibited in the specificatory scheme as interrelations among K-terms requires an analysis of a term as an *intention* (not to be confused with *intension*) in the medieval sense of that word Unfortunately, there will not be space in the present account for such an analysis I shall comment briefly at the end of this paper on the sort of problems involved in an analysis of terms.

refer directly to the thing and not to some intermediate entity such as a kind or class.[8]

But the most important point to stress is that specification in the sense here intended becomes hopelessly confused if K-terms in their absolute sense are not carefully distinguished from K-terms in the context of inquiry Any scientific investigation presupposes at the outset some specification of things as a specification of subject matter. Expressing ourselves very crudely, we might say that the physicist claims to be investigating bodies, the botanist, plants; the zoologist, animals, and so on Yet, however crude the expression, something of the sort is involved in the very inception of scientific inquiry. One does not start out investigating just anything whatsoever—inquiry can properly begin only after one has specified in some way, vaguely and naively as it may be, the kind of thing he intends to investigate This original specification, despite its crudeness, is nonetheless absolute in the sense that as the inquiry proceeds, the investigator will continue to regard the observable properties he discovers as in or belonging to the things he initially specified as his subject matter

To be sure, observable properties are involved at the outset, and if we asked the inquirer to show us the kind of thing he proposed to investigate, he could answer us only by indicating observable properties. However, if we then replied, "So the kind of thing you mean *is* such a collection of properties," he would probably tell us (unless he were wedded to a certain philosophy): "No, I have already specified the kind of thing by the K-terms I originally used, but since you asked me to show you the kind of thing, I could do so only with the help of observable properties, though this does not mean that the thing is the collection of properties." At the risk of exhausting the man's patience, we might offer the rejoinder· "What you are trying to say is that the thing is a bare *x*, a mere denotatum, which is such that it possesses the properties you enumerated."

Whatever the effect of this reply on our hypothetical investigator, it represents an attempt on our part to recognize K-terms only in the context of inquiry and at the same time to demand a specification of the thing in a fashion that is possible only with K-terms in their absolute sense. Instead of the rejoinder suggested, we should have accepted the initial specification of the thing by K-terms, and then added: "What you mean is that you have certain empirical criteria for applying the terms you mentioned, and you

---

[8] It is precisely in this sense that the position here advocated should be called realistic A so-called Platonic realism which is traditionally opposed to nominalism is supposed to accept a two-world view—a world of real form or essences, and a world of individuals The former is the world we really know, the latter remains unintelligible A genuine realism in the sense here intended will seek to explain how forms or essences can be regarded as signs directly signifying real individuals.

will doubtless refine these criteria in the course of your inquiry, but this does not prevent you from saying all along that you are investigating the kinds of things specified by your terms and not mere collections of properties which constitute your criteria."

When K-terms are treated in this way, the traditional problems of universality and individuation take on an entirely different character With terms accepted in the absolute sense, as they must be if we are to specify a thing, the individual becomes identical with the most specific, and whatever falls short of this in specificity is universal For example, let us assume that a thing is specified by the following K-terms· "animal," "vertebrate," "mammal," "dog" We have already argued that this arrangement of terms specifies one kind of entity and not four, and we have remarked that the correctness of the specification is unaffected by the actual number of dogs and would be just as correct or incorrect if only one dog existed The first three terms here are universals because they may be placed before other terms instead of "dog" in order to achieve the specification of a thing, but "dog" itself, as the end term in the arrangement, is not universal in this sense From the absolute point of view, "dog" is an individual term in that its signification constitutes the final specification of a thing. The relation of the individual to the universal is thus the relation of a K-term with maximum specificity to the other K-terms which signify the same thing. This is quite different from the relation of a K-term to the individuals it signifies

Traditional formulations of the problem of universals have often located the problem in this second relation and regarded it as one which connects entities like dogness or animality with the individuals possessing these properties We have found the relation expressed in this form to be unintelligible and to involve a confusion of K- and D-terms. The problem of individuation which arises from this point of view is, in effect. the problem of trying to specify a thing uniquely by means of D-terms Specification of this sort turned out on our analysis to be impossible and to yield a description rather than a specification. Instead of assuming a metaphysical principle of individuation, we admitted that any individual possessed an indefinite number of properties and that it was arbitrary which properties one selected in order to describe the thing.[9] The only limit to the arbitrariness was that in a context of communication the description should be sufficient to enable the interpreter to understand which thing was in question.

Yet it would seem that if we thus take "dog" as an individual term, we

---

[9] I certainly do not mean by this to deny that there is no genuine metaphysical problem regarding individuation. I mean merely that the problem cannot be intelligibly formulated as that of specifying an individual uniquely by means of D-terms. What is needed for the problem in this form is not the assumption of a principle of individuation but a reformulation of the issue

have no way of accounting for Rex and Rover as really distinct.[10] The force of this objection depends on the meaning attached to the adverb "really." If "really" means the same as "essentially," then the objection represents a true statement, but it does not provide a difficulty for the position advanced here. We have already noted the impossibility of specifying (as opposed to describing) Rex qua Rex, and we have remarked that the number of individuals of the kind specified, as long as at least one such individual exists, is immaterial to the correctness of the specification. We can thus readily admit that Rex and Rover are essentially the same in so far as they are both given maximum specification by "dog."

However, if "really" in the above objection means "independently of a description that is relative to a context of communication," the difficulty raised amounts to the following. It would seem that we have as yet no warrant for speaking of Rex and Rover as two rather than one, except that for all practical purposes we feel able to distinguish the one from the other by description. But surely the fact that they are individually distinct is just as real as the fact that they are essentially the same in being dog and animal, and in neither case should the reality depend on someone's ability to single out properties. The answer to the objection in this form is that while we said that a description is always composed of an arbitrary selection from an indefinite number of properties, we did not say that the individual reality of the thing described depended on this selection. The problem, in other words, is simply that of indicating sufficiently for the purposes of communication which thing is meant, and this is not the same as the problem of explaining what we mean by "the individual reality of the thing meant."

Since the latter problem is a metaphysical one and lies beyond the present analysis, I shall limit myself here to the following remarks.[11] The distinction between thing and property has been found intelligible only in a context where the thing can be specified apart from its properties. The act of specification by kind has been admitted to be a primitive notion and to constitute the only way of specifying a thing. The problem we now face requires the admission that an individual thing apart from specification by kind or description by properties can only be indicated nondiscursively by direct experiential contact. If a person fails to grasp which thing we mean

[10] In the discussion that follows, "dog" is assumed to be a term of maximum specificity. While terms like "collie" and "spaniel" might, of course, be added as terms of still greater specificity, this does not mean that the difference between the specific and the individual can become one of degree. On the contrary, the difference always remains as sharp as that between the finite and the infinite. Whenever we can say precisely what it is to be the thing we are talking about, we always have a specific, rather than an individual, thing. The latter is infinite in the sense of defying a precise statement of what it is to be this individual rather than another.

[11] These remarks may serve to suggest something of the way in which the present analysis would lead to a reformulation of the metaphysical problem of individuation.

by "Rex" after we have specified Rex as a dog and given the best description we can from what we have observed of Rex's properties, we have no recourse but to give up verbal designation and try to bring that person in direct contact with Rex—let him see the dog, pat him, and hear his bark. We shall be utterly at a loss to make intelligible to this person any distinction between these experiences and the individual unless we employ specification and tell the person he has observed the properties of a dog. If Rover should now appear on the scene and our friend who has already directly observed Rex should nonetheless claim to have difficulty in distinguishing Rex from Rover, we could help only by trying to direct our friend's attention to those observable properties by which we ourselves had distinguished the two dogs.

In other words, since individuals specifically the same cannot be distinguished by our conceptual network of K-terms, we can only appeal to direct experience One either grasps from his immediate experience that Rex and Rover are different, or he fails to distinguish them There is clearly no science with a specificatory scheme that will enable one to grasp conceptually, apart from his immediate experience, a specific difference between two individuals specifically the same. Yet in admitting all this, we do not make individual reality dependent on someone's ability to single out properties Such reality is simply a brute fact which we bump up against in immediate experience, and it is quite independent of the success or failure we may have in describing it to others

The statement that we cannot by scientific analysis draw a specific distinction between Rex and Rover seems, however, to be in a sense false. Suppose, for example, that Rex has distemper and Rover does not. The science of canine pathology then appears to offer a specificatory scheme that will enable us to distinguish specifically between Rex and Rover But I think we are deceived here by our use of proper names In canine pathology we use "distemper" as a K-term to specify a certain pathological condition and not to distinguish one dog from another. The fact that this specification may apply to the dog whose description we have abbreviated by "Rex" and not to the one whose description we have abbreviated by "Rover" is utterly immaterial to the scientific facts we try to express with the help of the specification Hopeless confusion with infinite regresses of the sort we have already noticed results when we take these proper names as somehow directly denoting, without descriptive connotation, certain of the things which we specify as dog and as distemper. It is thus that we are led to search for a bare denotatum—an unspecifiable noumenal x—underlying our specifications.

The position we have advocated avoids this impasse by accepting the specifications themselves as the only way of making things intelligible apart from properties When we specify a certain organic condition pathologically as distemper, we have used a specificatory scheme only to specify this condition, and it is merely by a confusion of language that we might seem to have specified an individual dog and to have distinguished him from another dog If we made the statement "Rex has distemper" in a context where we intended only to distinguish Rex from Rover, we would be using "distemper" as a D-term signifying observable properties, such as a hot nose This is quite different from the use of "distemper" in an absolute context where we can properly speak of specification, and we are thus obliged to conclude that we cannot by scientific analysis draw a specific distinction between Rex and Rover.

If the above remarks throw any light on the problem of drawing a real distinction between two individuals specifically identical, they also raise another problem for our distinction between thing and property We have just assumed that "distemper" could function as a K-term and hence that the pathological condition it specified was a thing. Yet common usage would seem to regard such a condition as a property rather than a thing The example we have chosen here happens to be a particularly complex one, and it will be better to illustrate the problem by a simpler case. When we say that brownness is a dull color, we seem to be using "brownness" as a K-term with "color" and "dull" as genus and differentia. In order to cope with this circumstance, we may introduce the notion of *quasi thing* and apply it to brownness.

On the one hand, brownness is a thing in that "brownness" functions linguistically as a K-term like "dog" or "animal" and seems to yield a genuine specification. But on the other hand, we have regarded "brown" as a D-term and distinguished its signification from that of "brownness," although we did not follow this procedure in the case of "animal" and "animality." It was only in this way that we were able to distinguish between a brown thing and brownness and thus render intelligible some distinction between thing and property Now in view of this earlier analysis of "brown" and "brownness" it cannot be said without qualification that brownness is a thing, but the use of "brownness" as a K-term is still legitimate if we grant that the thing specified is a quasi thing, that is, a property *treated abstractly* as a thing One is always free to consider a particular property, like a certain brownness, in itself abstracted from the thing to which it belongs, and to attempt a specification of the property exactly as though it were a thing

Without this procedure of creating a quasi thing by an act of abstraction, we should be unable with the present analysis to account for much of what is said in science and ordinary language All of mathematics, for example, requires quasi things—or, as we may also call them, abstract entities—for its subject matter. But rather than entities like brownness, which we would ordinarily regard generically as qualitative properties, mathematics requires entities we might call loosely "quantitative and relational properties" In the refinement and development of mathematics it may be desirable to introduce classes as well as relations, but in this case classes are quasi things specified and are not independent entities necessary for any account of specification. The basic and unavoidable assumption of ontology for the present analysis, then, is simply the assumption of things and properties.

This may be expressed as the assumption that the real world—the world we study in science and talk about in ordinary language—consists of things specifiable as to kind and variously describable by the properties they individually possess. Regarding a property abstractly as a quasi thing does not require the assumption of an additional entity in the real world which is neither thing nor property. The difference between quasi thing and property depends on an act of abstraction which we are free to perform, and not on a factor which we must assume to be in the world independently of our thinking and talking about it. The fact that we continually build systems of abstract entities which turn out to have a correspondence with, or an interpretation in, the real world is to be accounted for by the reality of the properties from which we originally formed our quasi things And this reality will always consist in the fact that at least one individual thing possessing the property in question exists

An elucidation of what is meant by "the existence of" a thing and its "possession of" a property is another metaphysical problem beyond the scope of the present paper It should be remarked here, however, that the problem of determining even at the most generic level the precise number of kinds of quasi things or properties is empirical and mathematical rather than metaphysical I mean, in other words, that the problem of whether qualitative, quantitative, relational, spatial, temporal, and other properties and the corresponding quasi things we form from them are all distinct or not is a problem whose resolution depends on what we find in our empirical investigations. Within the sphere of mathematics we have the peculiar problem of whether to make use of classes, which are the most universal of quasi things, since any property whatsoever can be taken as the basis for abstracting to form a class. I spoke, just above, of empirical *and* mathematical because I regard a problem like that of whether mathematics needs both classes and relations, neither of them, or only one of them to the exclusion of the other, as a technical problem of mathematical investigation, though I shall not attempt here to explain how we should distinguish this from empirical investigation

In our previous discussion of individual reality we gave no consideration to one of the most common ways of trying to isolate an individual, namely, by spatial and temporal relations. It would seem that in specifying a certain space-time point we are also in some sense specifying an individual. I have postponed discussion of this matter until the present because I believe a satisfactory explication of the issues requires the notion of quasi thing It seems to me that whenever we specify a space-time point we have formed a quasi thing from the property of spatiotemporal location. I say, for example, "The pencil is now in the plane of the table top so much to the right and above the center" But the only *thing* specified in this case is the sort of abstract entity we call a space-time point, and its uniqueness and individuality are intelligible only within the abstract system of relations formed from the property of being now on the plane of the table top. Clearly, I have not specified the pencil, since it is something that continues more or less as it is through many space-time points, and we would not say that being at any one such point constitutes all that is involved in being this pencil

To be sure, I have given a definite description of the pencil—definite in the sense that I have specified a property that can belong to one, and only one, individual. But such a description does not amount to what has been called in this paper the "specification of a thing." The only difference between this attempt to specify the pencil and our previous example of trying to specify Rex by his distemper lies in the nature of the properties and not in the degree of our success in specifying an individual. One is just as entitled to ask what is the thing at the space-time point in question as to ask what is the thing that has distemper, and in both cases an answer by specification requires the use of K-terms such as "pencil" and "dog"

Also, in a context of communication where the question is "which thing?," the practical determination of a space-time point may be sufficiently difficult to render the description ambiguous It is only within an abstract system of relations that a space-time point, by definition, represents a single occurrence, while distemper is not so restricted But this is a difference between properties or quasi things rather than a difference between things. We must thus conclude that spatial and temporal relations provide no exception to the view already expressed that individuals in their individuality can never be specified, but only described.

IV

I shall now endeavor to sum up briefly the main conclusions of this paper. Our central problem has been that of trying to make intelligible the specification of a thing apart from its properties. Without specification of this sort, a thing as something distinct from its properties seems utterly unintelligible. The thing may remain as that which we bump up against in experience, grasp by mystic intuition, or in some other way comprehend by nonintellectual means But as soon as we try to state in language what the thing is, we end up with an enumeration of properties and seem forced to conclude that the thing is a collection of properties This conclusion proved unsatisfactory since it led to infinite regresses when we tried to distinguish between a mere collection of properties and a collection which constituted a thing

As a way out of the difficulty, we proposed to accept certain terms as terms whose signification constituted the direct specification of a thing These K-terms, as we called them, provided an exception to the traditional doctrine that the signification of a term should always involve an extension and an intension The attempt to apply this traditional doctrine to K-terms resulted in our original problem all over again, since a term with intension and extension always signifies a thing indirectly by way of its properties and hence fails to specify the thing apart from its properties The specification of a thing by a K-term can only be achieved with the aid of a specificatory scheme or network of K-terms, and the result is always a specification of kind, and not of individuality While we can hope to specify precisely what it is for a thing to be a dog, a man, or a pencil, we cannot hope to specify precisely what it is to be Rex, Socrates, or this pencil Instead, we must be content to describe these individuals with what we have called D-terms, and in the case of such terms the traditional doctrine of intension and extension seems perfectly applicable.

One reason for the common confusion of K- and D-terms and the application of the traditional doctrine to all terms seems to lie in the fact that within a context of inquiry it is always necessary to have a criterion for the use of K-terms Since such a criterion must consist in an enumeration of observable properties, it would seem that the signification of a K-term should be analyzed as connoting these properties and denoting the things in which they are present But on the contrary we may save the distinction between K- and D-terms—and hence between things and properties—if we recognize that inquiry, in order to be intelligible, demands an initial specification of subject matter. This specification is given by our K-terms, and the fact that we must have observable properties by which to apply these terms does not alter the fact that the terms afford direct specifications of our subject matter. The various modifications in criteria and the addition of new K-terms that are made in the course of inquiry may be viewed as refinements of the original specifications In order to distinguish between the simple act of specification and the further refinement of criteria, we spoke of an absolute context as opposed to a context of inquiry. The refinements of the original specifications could then be viewed as an attempt in the course of inquiry to give our K-terms the meanings we assumed them to have when we took them in an absolute context as affording a direct specification of subject matter

Finally, in order to account for much of what is said in science and ordinary language, we found it necessary to allow for the specification of properties as well as of things. Since any specification appears linguistically like the specification of a thing, we proposed that whenever the thing specified is really a property and not a thing, we call it a quasi thing. Ontologically, this proposal does not require the assumption of a special kind of real entity which is neither thing nor property. By *real* entity we mean one that is as it is quite independently of our thinking or talking about it But the formation of a quasi thing from a property depends on an act of abstraction which we must perform, and the result is thus an abstract, rather than a real, entity The fact that systems of abstract entities have correspondences with the world of real entities is to be accounted for by the reality of the properties from which the abstract entities were formed.

V

I want to append a few remarks concerning realistic philosophy and some of the important problems that have been crowded out of this paper Readers who are inclined consciously or otherwise to take all statements made in ordinary English and to reformulate them in accordance with the patterns of contemporary symbolic logic have probably not read beyond the point where the distinction between K- and D-terms was introduced For, as pointed out in Note 2, this distinction simply evaporates when an expression like "man is white" becomes "if man x then white x" or "man x and white x," depending on whether the variable is universally or particularly quantified Now the philosophically important point I want to mention here is that this rendering of the subject of the statement by a variable x raises serious problems about the identification of the subject

On the one hand, there seems no reason to stop short of saying that all statements have the same subject, the Real, the Absolute, God, or whatever one chooses to call it, and the values of x indicate modifications (spatio-temporal or otherwise) of this one subject But if this is the case, it follows that we can never really know what we are talking about, since we can never comprehend the Absolute All our knowledge must remain an incomplete description of an infinite subject Those who find this monistic conclusion (and its many paradoxical consequences which we need not go into here) intellectually discomforting are driven, on the other hand, to search for an ultimate pluralism of subjects This quest, for the most part, has resulted in attempts either to reduce things to collections of observable properties or to assume a plurality of things at the outset as ultimate and perfectly intelligible The former alternative has already been touched on at the beginning of this paper The latter seems to me like an attempt to enjoy the advantages of a realistic philosophy without the intellectual expenditure of rendering its basic notions intelligible

Those who accept this second way out are content to say that a thing is that which has properties, even though they can never say what the thing is except by ascribing properties to it Yet a gift of special insight which renders the phrase "that which has properties" more intelligible than John Locke's "I know not what" does not provide a sufficient basis for explaining our knowledge of the real world. As we remarked in Section III of this paper, when all terms are D-terms, the traditional problems of nominalism are unavoidable In order to account for the subject of a scientist's generalization as something more than his own fabrication (Locke's "nominal essence") it seems necessary to assume classes as real entities Professor Quine has formulated this "ontological" problem about real entities as that of deciding the kind of bound variables one is going to admit in his language [12]

With the position advocated in the present discussion, one would regard the values of all such variables as quasi things. Thus, when one speaks of an x such that "man x and white x," the values of the variable may be taken as space-time points or other quasi things These things are no more or less real than other abstract entities which are taken as values of class variables. Differences of type among such entities determine their role in an abstract system, and not their reality. From this point of view, questions about the admission of bound variables of different types in an abstract system are quite distinct from questions about the reality of entities In the first case, the concern may remain one of technical expediency, but in the latter, metaphysical issues about things and quasi things are involved.

By fusing these two sorts of questions, Professor Carnap has come to the conclusion that final issues concerning the reality of entities are matters of practical choice and hence incapable of resolution by theoretical means [13] But this position leaves us with the problem of finding a precise criterion for distinguishing these questions of practical choice from those which do concern our knowledge of reality and call for some sort of theoretical investigation. Quine has recently expressed serious doubts concerning such a criterion and has advocated a pragmatism "more thorough" than Carnap's.[14] In the end, such a position becomes substantially the same as the

[12] W. V. Quine, "Notes on Existence and Necessity," *The Journal of Philosophy*, XL (1943), 118, see also his *Methods of Logic* (New York, Henry Holt, 1950), p 224

[13] Rudolf Carnap, "Empiricism, Semantics, and Ontology," *Revue Internationale de Philosophie*, January 1950, pp 20–40

[14] See Quine's article, "Two Dogmas of Empiricism," *The Philosophical Review*, LX (1951), 20–43.

monism we mentioned above The real subject of all our knowledge is simply the one infinite whole of reality Any attempt on our part to specify a limited subject we can comprehend must be the result of a choice justified only by its convenience. Our knowledge must remain a series of conveniently selected descriptions of an infinite and essentially incomprehensible subject.

The separation of K- from D-terms and of things from quasi things proposed in this paper is thus an attempt to maintain the realistic thesis that we can speak intelligibly about knowledge of a real plurality of specifically different subjects The central point in the defense of this thesis must be that of rendering intelligible the notion of a thing as the subject of knowledge, and not a mere "that which has properties." As implied by the remarks in the preceding paragraph, if the present account of thing and property is to be sustained, the final determination of what is strictly a thing and in no sense a quasi thing or property must be explained as dependent on ultimate categories of reality, and not on someone's decision to perform an act of hypostatic abstraction. If our discussion, then, has succeeded in making a distinction between things and properties intelligible by differentiating terms with simple and direct signification from those which connote properties and denote things, it has also led us to metaphysical presuppositions.

Among the many important philosophic problems connected with these presuppositions, I shall refer in conclusion to only one—but to the one which I think points out most clearly the limitations of the present analysis This is the problem of explaining what constitutes a term. We have assumed all along that a term as a categorematic word was a perfectly intelligible notion While our elucidation of thing and property thus depended on our distinction between K- and D-terms, this dependence turns out, on further analysis, to be entirely relative to the mode of exposition we employed. Actually, thing and property become fundamental when we try to explicate the notion of a term or categorematic word. We say, for example, that because "and" signifies neither thing nor property, while "dog" signifies a thing, the former is a syncategorematic, and the latter a categorematic, word Or again, since "brown" connotes a property and denotes things, while "brownness" signifies a property as though signifying a thing, both these words are called categorematic Obviously, such statements about words suppose the notions of thing, property, and quasi thing. Our attempt to elucidate these notions by appealing to the distinction between K- and D-terms thus appears to have been putting the cart before the horse

But the situation need not be so bad as this might suggest There are no notions more fundamental or universal than the ones in question, and hence any attempt to explicate them can appeal to what is prior only in familiarity. Thus at the start of this paper we assumed that the notion of a categorematic word was more familiar, though certainly not more fundamental, than the notions of thing and property If our attempt at elucidation has been successful, it should now be apparent, when we consider this problem of explaining what constitutes a term, that we have been trying to explicate the very notions we were all along forced to presuppose and use Our plight resembles that of Molière's M Jourdain when he discovered that he had been talking "prose" all his life.

A recognition that the ontological notions of thing and property are ultimately prior to the logical and grammatical notions of word and term is indispensable to realistic philosophy.[15] If the greater familiarity of the latter notions is taken for ultimate priority, rules of language must precede categories of reality, and a pragmatism like that of Carnap's and Quine's discussed above is the result A similar situation obtains for a notion like that of an act of cognition which, despite its familiarity, cannot be elucidated without the ontological notions of thing and property. In this case too, perhaps more than in the former, it is tempting to identify familiarity with ultimate priority and thus to explain a thing as the object of a cognition. But in a realistic philosophy, notions about how we know things are no more prior than are those about how we signify things—both are ultimately posterior to ontological categories Hence our radical assumption that the cognitive act of specification by kind is a primitive notion and constitutes the only way of specifying a thing must not be understood as giving the ultimate explanation of what determines a thing It is rather that our notion of such an act of cognition is primitive because our notion of a thing as that which determines the act is primitive.

[15] For a realistic account of the logical notion of a term, see Henry Veatch's discussion of what he calls a "concept" in his essay, pp 186–190. Veatch's point that a concept is always *of* something makes clear the fundamental priority of the thing as opposed to the intentional and representative character of the concept.

VI

Realistic Epistemology

Francis H. Parker, *Haverford College*

THERE is such a thing as knowledge The assertion of this proposition is necessarily true if there is to be any assertion at all, for its contradictory is self-contradictory If the assertion "There is no knowledge" is true, then it is false, for that assertion itself purports to be an instance of knowledge. Thus the only alternative to the recognition of the existence of knowledge is, as Aristotle said, a return to the vegetative state where no assertions whatever can be made.

Further, the existence of knowledge is prior to the discipline of epistemology.[1] Epistemology depends on knowledge, knowledge does not depend on epistemology No science creates or determines its subject matter; any which did would not be science but fiction Epistemology does not create knowledge any more than biology creates life or anthropology creates man. On the contrary, every science is brought into being by certain vaguely felt phenomena the growing awareness of which is the science itself. Thus there are certain phenomena which give rise to epistemology and which it is the nature of epistemology to describe and explain. But any description and explanation necessarily presupposes a firm recognition of these phenomena and of their genuineness, for it is these phenomena, as the subject matter of epistemology, which necessarily govern and determine all genuine descriptions and explanations.

This fact seems, unfortunately, to have been forgotten in much of contemporary epistemology, for its explanations seem frequently to be determined by the exigencies of predetermined categories rather than by the nature of the subject matter itself Such an epistemology may even end by denying its own data, in which case it commits suicide by destroying its own *raison d'être*. In order to avoid such suicide, the epistemological enterprise must never lose sight of what it has at the start, its own crude data, even if it never gets any further. This point cannot be overemphasized These basic phenomena must be taken seriously by epistemology, for they

[1] This recognition is common to most schools of realism. See, for example, Edwin B. Holt, *et al.*, *The New Realism* (New York, Macmillan, 1912), pp 66–67

are its lifeblood. Thus if a genuine, realistic epistemology, as the disciplined attempt to clarify, describe, and explain the facts of knowledge, is to be possible, there must first be a firm recognition of the reality and character of these data.[2]

What, then, are the crude data of epistemology, and how are they to be described and explained? In an attempt to answer this question, let us turn first to a consideration of the *general* data of epistemology—the most basic features of all awareness—and then to a consideration of certain specific restricted data. First, then, what are the most basic generic traits of all awareness?

I

The most primitive feature of any act of awareness, as it presents itself to our inspection, is the fact that it is always *of something other than itself.* I have an experience *of war,* for example, or a perception *of a house* or a concept *of a triangle.* But as soon as we notice this primordial trait of all awareness of being of something other than itself, we immediately notice that it is not a simple, unanalyzable trait. On the contrary, "being of something" contains within itself two constituent aspects. (1) the *distinctness* of the something from the awareness of it, and (2) the *identity* of the awareness with the something of which it is an awareness. Let us turn to a separate analysis of these two characteristics.

In the first place, since any act of awareness is of something other than itself, it must be *distinct,* and hence at least minimally *diverse,* from that something of which it is an awareness. All awareness presents itself as a revelation of something other than itself. When I experience something, the experience is a part of me, it is mine, yet the *thing which* I experience need not literally be a part of me, and in any case it is always diverse from my experience of it. This much is perhaps so evident that no one would deny it. But there is more.

In addition to the fact that the object of every awareness is different from the awareness of it, there is the additional fact that whenever we are aware of anything, we are aware of it *as being independent* of the precise act of our awareness of it.[3] This does not mean, of course, that we are always aware of an object as independent of *any* and *every* act of awareness or as independent of any *mind,* for obviously many of the things we are aware of are known to be mental in character or to depend upon some mind for

[2] See R. W. Sellars: "The epistemological task is not the replacement of natural realism but its development," in *The Philosophy of Physical Realism* (New York, Macmillan, 1932), p. v.

[3] See R. B Perry, "A Realistic Theory of Independence," in *The New Realism, op. cit.*

their existence and character—such things as fictions and conceptual beings, for example. But it does mean that every bona fide instance of awareness presumes itself aware of something which is independent of *it*—of
that *particular* act of awareness. This presumed independence of the known
is given, at least implicitly, in the diversity of the object which is present in
the crude consciousness which is the core of epistemology's subject matter.
All experience presents itself to our inspection as a revelation into the lives
of things which are wholly undisturbed by that revelation.

Now the question of whether or not the thing which we are aware of as
independent is *in fact* independent evidently involves the question of the
veracity of our awareness, and since truth is not a universal or generic character of all awareness, we must postpone a consideration of the *factual* independence of objects of awareness until we have considered the restricted
datum of truth. But whether or not the object of any awareness is in fact
independent of that awareness, it still remains true that it is given *as being*
independent in both its character and its existence. In short, whether or
not a particular object is factually independent, it is always presumptively
independent When it is one and when merely the other, we shall see later.
But since the presumptive independence of the object presents itself as a
character of all experience, we must consider it now. And since the object's
independence which every experience presumes is precisely the same independence which an object may possibly have or not have in fact, then in
considering the nature of this presumptive independence we may merely
consider the nature of the independence of the object as such, leaving till
later the question of whether or when such independence is a fact. What,
then, do we mean by the independence of what is experienced from the
experience of it?

We mean that the things we experience are in no way *related* to the
experiencer *by the fact that they are experienced.* This last qualification is,
of course, necessary, for the experienced may be, and usually is, related to
the experiencer by one or more relations other than the cognitive relation.
The paper which I see before me, for example, is related to me by a number of real relations such as distance, dissimilarity, and so forth, and with
respect to *these* relational properties, it *depends* upon me as upon another
natural thing But it is not related to me and hence does not depend on me,
in any of its properties, in so far as I am aware of it This is so because the
act of awareness produces in the thing which I see no real change whatsoever which could serve as the foundation of any relation of dependence
That is to say, no act of awareness is *transitive,* no act of awareness passes
over into its object to produce any real property in it whatsoever On the
contrary, every act of awareness produces its change only *immanently,*

within the cognitive faculty The fact that I see this paper, or the fact that I understand the dangers of atomic energy, makes a difference to me, of course I am really changed by such knowledge, and hence I depend on the things I know, at least to the extent that I know them. But this fact of being known makes no real difference whatever to the things which are known *Knowing* them disturbs *them* not in the least

But here two cautions need to be noted. In the first place, though the awareness makes no change and hence founds no relation of dependence in the thing of which I am aware, it is evident that the *physical conditions* of awareness do make such a change Before I can see something, for example, that thing must be illuminated to a certain extent, the medium between that thing and my eyes must be translucent; my eyes must possess the physical properties of reasonably healthy eyes, and so on All these physical factors do indeed make a difference to what I see. What I see will, as we say, "all depend"—all depend on the multitude of conditions and causes of sight. And these physical conditions do change the thing that I see because they act transitively on the thing to produce new properties in it But awareness itself does not consist in these various physical changes, light striking the eye is not the same as seeing, and air vibrations striking the ear is not the same as hearing. And it is these acts of awareness themselves which produce no change in their objects.

In the second place, it must be noted that once knowledge is acquired, it can of course be *used* in *action* to alter objects. After I understand the nature of a molecule of water, for example, I can then apply that knowledge to change that molecule. But such practical application of knowledge is quite distinct from the knowledge which is thus applied [4] And the knowledge itself, just in so far as it is knowledge, makes no difference in the thing known whatsoever and, therefore, produces no real relation of the known to the knower.

Such, then, is the nature of the independence which every awareness presumes its object to have But such independence may be merely presumptive and not factual Whether or when this presumptive independence of the object is also a factual independence, we must consider later during our examination of the specific data of epistemology, and more particularly after our consideration of truth.

But now let us turn to that other distinct aspect of the fundamental character of all awareness as an awareness *of something*· the aspect of *identity* —the identity of knowledge and thing known. Now this feature of cogni-

[4] The failure to recognize this distinction, however, is not uncommon among philosophers today See, for example, Robert S Hartman, "The Epistemology of the *A Priori*," *Philosophy and Phenomenological Research*, VIII, No. 4 (June 1948), 732.

tive identity has evidently not been so obvious or widely recognized as the trait of diversity, but it is nonetheless just as primordial and necessary a feature of awareness All awareness exemplifies this trait We identify ourselves with the hero of a novel. We share another person's thoughts When I know something I know *it;* I have it in mind; and to the extent that I do not, I do not know it. This is not a mere verbalism; it is rather a necessary and evident truth about the nature of knowledge All awareness consists in an identification with something other than itself.

This character of the identity of knowledge and thing known is, like the datum of diversity, an immediate, universal deliverance of consciousness and is, therefore, a necessary trait of all consciousness Nevertheless, this datum of identity has been denied, especially by that epistemological doctrine called variously "representationalism," "epistemological dualism," the "copy theory," and so forth, whose most noteworthy historical exponents are perhaps Descartes and Locke But this copy theory is self-contradictory, and it therefore furnishes an indirect demonstration of the truth of cognitive identity.

According to the copy theory, our ideas are never identical with, but only similar to, their objects But such a view contradicts the very nature of knowledge and therefore contradicts itself First of all, the copy theory cannot, of course, be taken as a report of actual experience, for it would then imply that in every cognitive act we are aware simultaneously of two different (though similar) things, idea and object, which are related by a relation of similarity Such epistemological diplopia, however, is clearly false When I perceive a tree I do not apprehend two things—an image tree and a real tree I perceive only one tree—though in the case of genuine diplopia I may have two *image* trees. In the second place, granting the fact that only one tree is given in our consciousness—the idea tree—we have then no way of knowing, on the basis of the copy theory, that there *is* a second tree—the *real* tree—which is similar to our idea tree In other words, we cannot know that our ideas are similar to something that we can never know This is the impasse of subjectivism—the "egocentric predicament."

Here, however, it might be objected that we can infer the external tree from the internal tree But such an inference is impossible unless, here again, we grasp, identically, what is inferred To infer something from something is to have the mind pass from the premise—the idea—to the conclusion—the real thing—*itself* But if we thus infer the real thing *itself,* we grasp *it,* identically But since such an identity is denied by the copy theory, there can be no inference to the real thing itself The same remark holds true, *mutatis mutandis,* of the view that the copy idea, which is merely similar, represents or signifies the real thing. If it signifies *it,* then we are led by the sign to the thing itself, identically But this is impossible if the sign is only a copy of what it signifies.[5] Thus our conclusion stands: We cannot, on the basis of the copy theory, know even that there is anything to which our idea is similar.

In the second place, if an act of awareness can never grasp, identically, anything other than itself, then we cannot even know the idea copy which is declared to be similar to an unknown real thing, since the idea which is known is certainly distinct from the act by which it is known If it is objected that we can indeed know the idea itself, identically, then there is no necessary reason for not saying that we can also know the real thing itself, identically And if the reply is given that, while we cannot know the idea itself directly, we can know it through another idea which is similar to it, then the same difficulty arises again, and we are in an infinite regress Thus, on the basis of the copy theory, in so far as it is consistent, we would be able to know neither real things nor ideas In short, on the basis of the copy theory, in so far as it is consistent, we would never be able to know anything But such a theory is self-contradictory because, as we have seen above, it asserts that we know at least one thing, namely, that ideas are not identical with, but rather are copies of, things, which is to say, by the implication just noted, that we know that we cannot know. And since it is self-contradictory, its contradictory—that the idea is identical with its object—is necessarily true

So, identity of knowledge and thing known is a necessary feature of knowledge. "The soul is, in some sense, all things," as Aristotle said [6] But in what sense? Surely it is evident that the sense in which knowledge and thing known are identical cannot be a physical or material sense, for no two physical things are ever identical. The photograph is like the subject, but it is not the subject The wax impression is similar to the signet ring, but it is not identical with the ring. But in awareness such an identity actually occurs Hence it cannot be a physical identity Thus if we are to explain the fact of cognitive identity, we must at once recognize that all awareness necessarily involves a mode of being which is not physical or material In brief, all awareness necessarily (by its primitive feature of identity) involves an immaterial mode of being In what sense are knowledge and thing known identical? In an *immaterial, non-physical* sense.

Thus immateriality is the very root of all awareness. It is so because it is necessarily and directly entailed or presupposed by the fact of identity which, in turn, besides being *given* in awareness, is, as we have seen, entailed as a necessary feature in the structure of knowledge, whose existence, finally, cannot consistently be denied. This fact is so crucially important

[5] This criticism does not hold, of course, when the idea is thought of as a formal, rather than as an instrumental, sign, for the nature of a formal sign is precisely identical with its *signatum*.
[6] *De Anima*, 431b, 20–21.

that it bears repeating. Knowledge is necessarily real, in so far as man is man and not merely a vegetable Knowledge necessarily involves an identity with the thing known And identity necessarily involves an immaterial mode of being, since no two material beings can ever be identical. Hence there is a mode of being which is immaterial and which constitutes the necessary core of knowledge.

From this recognition of the necessity of an immaterial mode of being for awareness, there follows an important corollary: Epistemology depends upon, and logically presupposes, metaphysics. Immaterial being is a mode of being and hence must be studied by the study of being as such—metaphysics; and since knowledge depends upon this immaterial mode of being, the study of knowledge—epistemology—depends upon the study of being—metaphysics Put differently, being is prior to cognitive being, so metaphysics is prior to epistemology. The general modern refusal to recognize this priority of metaphysics to epistemology—due at least in part to Kant—has resulted in much confusion in modern epistemology As one example of this, note on the one hand the declarations of epistemological isolationism by American neorealism and critical realism,[7] and on the other hand the fact that they have, as one commentator has said, "been occupied almost wholly with questions which could be better described as metaphysical" since "their central issue is metaphysical."[8]

Thus awareness necessarily involves an immaterial mode of being which is a part of the proper object of metaphysics [9] But to the extent that this immaterial mode of being is the root of awareness, it may and must be examined by epistemology To refer to this mode of being as "immaterial" or "non-physical" is, of course, only to say what it is not—that it is not that physical or material mode of being with which we are first and most frequently confronted and with which we are consequently most familiar. This negative signification is legitimate and important, however, for it is through its contrast with physical being that we come to understand this non-physical mode of being But what, now, is this immaterial mode of being which is involved in all awareness? How can its meaning for epistemology be more narrowly and positively restricted?

Its essential meaning for epistemology has already been given in describing the basic traits of awareness as those of identity and diversity and at least presumptive independence, and its essential meaning as disclosed in these traits may now be summed up in the embracive trait of *intentionality* The intentionality of all awareness is thus simply what we have already re-

---

[7] See W. P Montague's article in *Philosophy*, XII (1937), 143, Also Durant Drake *et al*, *Essays in Critical Realism* (London, Macmillan, 1920), p. vii.
[8] R M Eaton, "What Is the Problem of Knowledge?," *The Journal of Philosophy*, XX (1923), 178, 180
[9] See the essay by John Wild, pp 36 ff , above.

ferred to as its property of being about something other than itself. Thus to say that awareness is intentional is simply to say that it is identical with something diverse from, and at least presumptively independent of, itself. This active relational structure is exhibited, as we have seen, in every instance of awareness. Every sensation, image, concept, proposition, and so forth is *of* or *about* something, it actively tends to, or intends, that of which it is an awareness Though this term "intention" is more commonly applied only to acts of volition or purposiveness, it has, as is well known, been used technically to signify that dynamic relational structure which constitutes any and every phase of psychic life—cognitive and conative [10] Indeed, conative acts are intentional precisely because they contain a cognitively intentional element—because they are "cognitively mediated."[11]

What, then. is this cognitive, intentional, non-physical being? It is primarily and fundamentally that relational existential act ("being" in the participial sense) which consists in being identical with something which is yet different from, and at least presumptively independent of, the cognitive being itself Thus we may say of this cognitive being that its act, in contrast to the act of material being (participial sense), is such that it makes no real change in the object which terminates it and thus founds no new real relation of that object to the act or agent In short, its act is immanent in contrast to the transitive act of physical being. And because its act is immanent, making no new real change in its object, we may say of this mode of being, secondly, that it relates its agent to its object itself, unchanged and identical, rather than to some new entity which arises in the case of the transitive action of physical being

This cognitive being is not merely a relation, for it is the act that results in the relation, "knower of " Yet it is basically relational in structure Perhaps the best we can do is to say that it is a unique, *sui generis*, relational act, terminating immaterially in an at least presumptively independent object, which it in any case leaves unchanged and with which it therefore unites its agent in a relation of immaterial union. That this cognitive being is unique we already implicitly recognize when we think of the fact that it, unlike the physical being with which we contrast it, enables its agent to transcend the spatiotemporal bounds of his physical relatedness and to identify himself with things physically near and far, past and future, and in fact with things not physical at all—in short, to range the whole of reality without physically changing his place.

[10] See Joseph Gredt, *Elementa Philosophiae Aristotelico-Thomisticae* (Friburgi Brisgoviae, Herder, 1909–12), I, 91–93, II, 306–7; and the essay by Harmon Chapman, pp 22 ff

[11] See R. B Perry, *General Theory of Value Its Meaning and Basic Principles Construed in Terms of Interest* (Cambridge, Mass., Harvard University Press, 1950), Chap 12, *passim*

Thus the root of knowledge is immateriality, and hence the radical principle of epistemology is the recognition of the fact that there is a non-physical mode of being uniquely different from physical being in that it is a relational act of identification with something which is still different from, and at least presumptively independent of, the relational act itself. But now let us return to that other generic trait of awareness which has so far seemed less troublesome—the diversity of knowledge and thing known—and especially to the question of its relation to the trait of identity.

The datum of cognitive diversity and the datum of cognitive identity, and the necessity of each for knowledge, have been separately grasped by various schools of epistemology; but they have seldom been jointly affirmed by any one school. Thus the fact of diversity has rightly been stressed by the school of representationalism; but, as we have just seen, the fact of diversity is there so overemphasized that the fact of identity is denied. The fact of identity, on the other hand, has also been rightly stressed by neo-realism and idealism, but here the identity is regarded as so complete that the fact of diversity is denied. Thus, in general, the theories known as epistemological dualism and epistemological monism each contains an important truth, but each denies the truth of the other. And it is here, in the joint assertion of cognitive identity and diversity, that one of the most difficult problems of epistemology lies.

On the face of it, these two traits might indeed seem to be incompatible. If our earlier remarks are correct, both traits must be equally given and necessary. Yet how can they be? How can knowledge be identical with what is different from it? Clearly the two traits can be present only in different senses—only if knowledge and thing known are identical in one sense and different in another. But in what sense are they identical and in what sense different? How can the coexistence and equal necessity of cognitive identity and cognitive diversity be explained?

We have just seen at least one sense in which knowledge and thing known are identical, namely, in a non-physical sense; so it might seem that we need now only conclude that knowledge and thing known are diverse in a physical sense. But this answer, while containing some truth, is unfortunately neither completely meaningful as it stands nor sufficiently specific. It is, as it stands, not completely meaningful because two things cannot meaningfully be called physically diverse when one of them (knowledge) is, as we have seen, not physical And the answer is not sufficiently specific, for any physical thing is composite, including, most basically, its nature or essence and its existence. Consequently, we must carry our answer further, trying to make as precise as possible the sense in which knowledge and thing known are different. Well, then, what can we say about the nature of this cognitive diversity which will not deny it or any of the other fundamental facets of awareness?

We have just mentioned that any physical thing possesses both its physical existence and a certain nature or essence This being so, may we say, then, that the diversity between knowledge and thing known consists in a difference in both essence and existence? This, as we have already seen, is exactly the point of view taken by the representative theory of knowledge, the view, namely, that what is given in awareness is a different existent from (though similar to) what is believed to be known The origin of this view, as we are now in a position to see, lies in the reduction of that immaterial mode of being, whose action is not transitive but immanent, to material being, whose act is transitive and whose effect is therefore something different from its object which is for that act only a *patient* Such a theory may be called "subjectivistic" because its materialized or quasi-materialized cognitive being brings about a physical or quasi-physical alteration which inheres subjectively either in the object known or in the knower or in both (since for every physical action "there is an equal and opposite reaction").

Such subjectivism has had a wide vogue during the last several hundred years Indeed, the landmarks of modern philosophy consist of the recurrent impasses of solipsism and the subsequent tours de force which inevitably flow from the inner contradiction of this theory. Thus there is the Cartesian egocentric predicament and the tour de force of an external world, the occasionalists' Cartesian solipsism and their tour de force of "vision in God," and the Leibnizian windowless monad and the tour de force of pre-established harmony. The same generic type of sequence is repeated at the sensationalist level in the British empiricists. Locke's restriction of objects of knowledge to ideas and his tour de force of "sensitive knowledge" of material substance, Berkeley's *"esse is percipi"* and his tour de force of other minds, and finally Hume's impressions and ideas and his tour de force of custom This subjectivism or materialization of awareness infects knowing at its very heart, so that the attempt of any disciple to cure one of these materialistically diseased epistemologies within the subjectivist framework is itself a tour de force—witness, for example, the neorealists' "panobjectivism," the flinging of Hume's impressions and ideas outward into the "objective" world.[12]

Now the impossibility of this subjectivistic epistemology has already been sufficiently elaborated so that we may perhaps dispense with any

[12] See Perry, *Present Philosophical Tendencies* (New York, Longmans, Green, 1929), p 307. "Modern realism [namely, neorealism] is closer to the monistic realism of 'ideas' suggested by Hume . ."

further treatment of it here. Such a theory which states that the diversity between knowledge and thing known is both an essential and an existential diversity is impossible because it contradicts that other primitive trait of awareness—identity—and thus, as we have seen, contradicts the nature of knowledge

But if we must reject representationalism, may we not say with the critical realists that knowledge and its object are essentially identical but existentially diverse—that the "what" of knowledge is identical with the "what" of the object, but that knowledge and object are two different existents? Evidently we must, for if knowledge and thing known are not different existents, then the knower would literally *be* the thing that he knows, since the *cognitive* existence is admitted to be a phase of his existence. But, as Aristotle said, "The soul . is certainly not the things themselves [which it knows], for it is not the stone which is in the soul, but rather its form [that is, nature or essence]."[13] The only apparent way of avoiding this view is to follow neorealism in its implicit metaphysical position of denying the reality of existence as anything distinct from essence or quiddity But this position is impossible, for any awareness of anything is an awareness of a *being*, of something that in some sense *is* To affirm that this *esse* is not distinct from the essence to which it is attached is to affirm that every conceivable or imaginable thing (essence) exists *necessarily* and thus eternally, which would be to deny all change and contingency. And on the other hand, to affirm the awareness of an essence which has no *esse* or existence of any kind, which in no sense *is*, is to affirm the awareness of *nothing*—which is no awareness. It was one of the great contributions of the critical realists that they firmly reminded us of the fact that "existence, itself, is not an essence."[14] Consequently, the very nature of awareness as being of something other than itself—and of something which *is* and *is other*—would seem to compel us to maintain that knowledge and thing known must be existentially diverse.

But such an answer at once raises one of the most difficult problems of epistemology. If we say, as apparently we must, that knowledge and thing known are existentially diverse, how can we ever *know existence?* If knowledge necessarily consists in an identification with the thing known, as we have seen, and if knowledge and the thing known are existentially diverse, as we have also just seen, is it not, then, literally impossible, by the very nature of the case, that we should ever be able to know the existence of things? Or, to state the contrapositive If we really know existence or existents qua existents, must we not deny that knowledge and thing known are different in existence (existentially diverse)?

13 *De Anima*, 431b, 29-30
14 Durant Drake's article in *The Journal of Philosophy*, XXVIII (1931), 239.

This is the terrible dilemma which critical realism faced and tried, unsuccessfully, to solve. Since the critical realists saw that knowledge necessarily involves an identity of essence between knowledge and thing known, and since they affirmed that knowledge and thing known are always existentially diverse, they had to say that the existence of the thing can never be known, that existents always and necessarily elude cognition. "*Existence itself*, not being an essence, *can not* be given" in awareness, as Professor Drake said.[15] It can only be "posited" on "animal faith," to use Professor Santayana's terms. But this consequence also contradicts the primitive data of awareness, for awareness always reveals itself as of something that in some sense *is*, as we have just seen.

Thus it would seem that we are faced with the following dilemma: Either knowledge and thing known are existentially diverse, in which case we can never know existence or existents, or knowledge and thing known are existentially identical—the very same existent with one and the same nature or essence—in which case the previously established datum of diversity is denied.[16] Now both horns of this dilemma are untenable if our earlier remarks are correct. And since both horns of the dilemma are untenable, we cannot say that knowledge and thing known are, without qualification, either existentially identical or existentially diverse. Is there, then, some way of escaping between the horns? There is.

There is a third alternative which allows us to say that knowledge and thing known are, in *specially qualified senses*, both identical and diverse— and both identical and diverse not only in existence but also in essence. The key to this third alternative lies in a refinement of the analysis upon which the dilemma is based, and in our earlier recognition of the fact that cognition is *relational* and, more particularly, that it is a relational act of *identification* of the mind with something other than itself.

Now in every ordinary or predicamental relation there are four elements: the *subject* of the relation, the *foundation* of the relation, the *relation* itself, and the *terminus* of the relation. Thus if we consider the relation, "Chicago's being north of Louisville," "Chicago" is the subject, its geographical location the foundation, "north of" the relation proper, and "Louisville" in its geographical location the terminus. All four of these elements, just because they are different elements in the structure of the relation, are different from each other, they are not the same.

Now identity is also a relation, and therefore it also exemplifies this four-

15 *Ibid.*, p. 240.

16 There is, of course, the further possibility, noted earlier, of denying existence as anything distinct from essence, so that there is no existence to be either identical or diverse. This is the position, usually implicit and often explicit, of American neorealism. See especially *The New Realism, op. cit.*, p. 368.

fold structure.[17] In the cognitive relation of identity, "my knowledge of my car," the subject of the relation is "I" (in virtue of my mind), the foundation is the cognitive species in my mind—that character *by* which I know —the terminus is the object before my mind ("my car"), and the relation proper is the identity between the cognitive species and what is before my mind ("my car") [18] Since this cognitive relation is peculiar just because it is a relation of identity, the foundation and the terminus are the same. But since it is a relation of identity, they are different in so far as one is the foundation, and the other the terminus, of the relation Thus the thing known, in so far as it is the terminus of the cognitive relation of identity, is different from the other elements in the cognitive relation, and hence it is different from the whole cognitive relation More precisely, if K is the knowledge, S its subject, F its foundation, R its relation proper, and T its terminus; and if O is the object known, then O is, identically, T in K(S,F,R,T), and O is *not* S, F, R, or K.

Thus the thing known is identical, both existentially and essentially, with the knowledge of it in the sense of being the terminus of the latter's relational aspect, and yet the thing known is different, both existentially and essentially, from the knowledge of it in the sense of not being the non-terminal aspects of the knowledge, just as every terminus is distinct from its relation, foundation, and subject Hence knowledge and thing known are, so to speak, *terminally identical* yet *non-terminally* or *relationally diverse.*

Thus the possibility of escaping between the horns of our dilemma, and the possibility of reconciling the crude data of identity and diversity, rests upon the recognition of the fact that knowledge is relational and, more particularly, a relational act of identity, and the dilemma itself rests upon the treatment of knowledge as if it were merely a simplex term or nonrelational entity So long as knowledge is treated nonrelationally, the knowledge and the thing known are both considered as merely terms and thus as belonging to the same mode or type of existence And so long as knowledge and the known are thus taken to belong to the same terminal, nonrelational mode of existence, their evident difference has to mean their mutual exclusive-

[17] It is possible that the cognitive relation may be better described as a so-called "transcendental" relation rather than as an ordinary "predicamental" relation If this is done, the foundation of the relation and the relation proper will be regarded as merged into one element of the relational structure the foundational act of knowing which is the cognitive species together with its reference to the terminus—the object But the choice between these two interpretations will not make any essential difference to the present analysis

[18] In this sentence the expression "what is before my mind" is used to denote the *presumptively* independent object and the expression "my car," the *factually* independent object, according to the terminology employed earlier Whether or not these two actually coincide must be postponed, as mentioned earlier, until the question of truth is considered.

ness, that is, then difference has to be interpreted as a difference between two instances of the same mode, which two instances are, of course, mutually exclusive since they can be distinguished only by their instantiation. But this mutual exclusiveness, so far as it is an exclusiveness of the existence of knowledge and the existence of thing known, has to mean that no noncognitive existence can ever be known by a cognitive existence, that we can never know existents. If we really do know existents, on this unimodal, nonrelational view, cognitive existence and non-cognitive existence have to be conceived either as numerically one or as unreal (neorealism), which means that diversity is denied. And if diversity remains, then cognitive existence and non-cognitive existence, on this nonrelational view, have to be exclusive (numerically two), which means that any knowledge of existents is impossible (critical realism).

But if we drop this nonrelational view and recognize the fact that cognition is relational in mode, and moreover a relational act of identity, then there is no longer any reason for denying that it can terminate in the identical other existent without *being* the very existence of that existent. In brief, cognition is that unique relational act whose terminus is another existent essence which itself, as the terminus of that relation, is not identical with the relation itself, or its foundation or subject.

Thus our earlier way—and the usual way—of stating the alternative answers to this problem, as those of "essential identity" or diversity and "existential identity" or diversity *simpliciter*, prejudices the question and makes it impossible to find a satisfactory answer. Knowledge is in one sense both essentially and existentially diverse from the thing known (so far as its relational aspects are concerned) and in another sense both essentially and existentially identical with the thing known (so far as the terminus of its relational aspect is the very existent essence known) Thus the idea and its object are *relationally* or *non-terminally* or *modally* diverse, and yet *terminally* identical. Or to put it in a less technical form, we can know by one immaterial mode of existence the very thing itself, its essence and its existence.

Here the question might be raised as to how our knowledge of *knowledge* could be relationally or modally diverse from that knowledge which is known, when the knowledge known is itself relational and hence modally the same as the knowledge of it. But such a situation presents no special problem, for the above analysis applies just as well here. It does so because the knowledge known is, identically, the terminus of the relational aspect of the knowledge of it while at the same time *not* the non-terminal aspects of that knowledge. Thus if K' is the knowledge known (itself a relational act of identity), S', F', R', and T' its subject, foundation, relation proper, and terminus, respectively; and if K is the knowledge of that knowledge

(K'), and S, F, R, and T *its* subject, foundation, relation proper, and terminus, respectively, then $K'(S',F',R',T')$ is, identically, T in $K(S F,R,T)$,
and is *not* S, F, R, or K Thus knowledge and knowledge known are both
identical and diverse, but in different respects: They are terminally identical and non-terminally or relationally diverse And therefore we can
know instances of knowledge, as in the case of other existents, without the
knowledge known and the knowledge of it being wholly identical.

Thus awareness presents itself to our inspection as being fundamentally
a relational act of immaterial identification with something other than, and
at least presumptively independent of, itself. Knowledge is identical, in
essence and existence, with its object, because what is known is the terminus of a relation of identity And yet knowledge is different, in essence
and existence, from its object, which remains at least presumptively independent of its being known, because knowledge is an immanent, relational
act which is, as such, different from its terminus upon which it does not
transitively act. In short, awareness presents, as its most basic generic traits,
its identity with, and diversity from, an at least presumptively independent object; and these traits can be explained only by recognizing that
awareness is essentially an immaterial, immanent, relational act terminating in an existent essence.

II

So far, however, we have considered only the *generic* data of epistemology
—those basic traits which pervade all awareness. Now we must turn to a
brief examination of certain *special* data of epistemology—of certain special traits of restricted areas of awareness. These special, restricted traits
are of two basic types: those of *sense* and those of *reason*

Thus we find in our consciousness two main kinds of objects, each with a
peculiar advantage and disadvantage. I find on the one hand, for example,
a visual image of this sheet of paper, and on the other hand a concept of
paper The sensory image of this sheet of paper is characterized by the fact
that it is utterly individuated and unique, absolutely restricted to the here
and now, and consequently unrepeatable and incommunicable. Neither I
nor anyone else ever has had or will have *this* particular sheet of paper in
his consciousness again. Nor, consequently, can I communicate this image
to anyone else, it is utterly private, lonely, and isolated This uniqueness
and incommunicability is the disadvantage of sense, and it is caused by the
fact that the sensory image is necessarily conditioned by a unique *physical
existent* and its physical action on my sense organs—either now, as in the
case of present sensation, or in the past, as in the case of sensory memory.
But this very cause of the disadvantage of sense is at the same time the

cause of its corresponding advantage, namely, the fact that sense apprehends (though uniquely and confusedly) something actually existent, something actually exercising its physical existence on my organs of sense

My rational concept of paper, on the other hand is not at all individual and unique, it is by no means restricted to this particular sheet of paper at this particular time and place. On the contrary, it is indefinitely repeated in all the innumerable sheets of paper that ever have existed or that will or might exist Consequently, my concept of paper is quite communicable and public. This is the advantage of reason—its universality—and it is due to the fact that the concept itself is not directly conditioned by any particular physical existent But this very advantage of reason has also, in turn, its corresponding disadvantage, namely, the fact that the rational concept does not in itself refer to any actual existent but only to a universal possibility, and can therefore be thought of whether or not any such object actually exists. Thus the advantage of sense and the disadvantage of reason is that the former apprehends an actual physical existent whereas the latter, by itself, does not, and the advantage of reason and the disadvantage of sense is that the former apprehends a public, communicable object whereas the latter does not

Such, then, are the two main different types of objects into which we find the contents of our consciousness divided: the conceptual object and the sensory object (whether of immediate sensation, imagination, or sensory memory). But every cognitive act or intention is necessarily specified by, and appropriate to, the object which it intends. Consequently, these two types of object presuppose two types of cognitive act: the acts of sensory cognition and the acts of rational cognition.[19]

Both types of cognition are absolutely indispensable to the acquisition of knowledge. Sense alone apprehends the individual, the absolutely unique existent entity which is actually there physically acting on the perceiving agent. This is the great insight of nominalism and nominalistic "empiricism" Since we live in a world composed of existent individuals which we can know, and since only sense yields an individual existent, the sensory mode of cognition is absolutely indispensable to knowledge But if sensory cognition were our only genuine mode of cognition, as is maintained by nominalistic "empiricism," we would be as lonely and isolated as the objects of sense, and we would have no communicable and stable knowledge at all But since communication is a given fact, and since communication requires a stable, common, universal object to be communicated, there must be another mode of cognition—that of reason. Reason alone grasps the common, the universal, the stable which is the *sine qua non* of commu-

[19] For a more detailed account of sensory and rational cognition, see John Wild, *Introduction to Realistic Philosophy* (New York, Harper, 1948), Chaps. 18 and 19

nicable and scientific knowledge This is the great insight of rationalism. But on the other hand, reason cannot be the only genuine cognitive faculty, as the rationalists maintain, for then we could never know real existent individuals but only essences, possibilities—since the object of reason is universal and common

Thus an understanding of knowledge requires the recognition of the genuineness of both types of cognition—sense and reason Furthermore, it requires that these two types of cognition be understood as interfused in an extremely intimate interrelation. This statement is, of course, denied by that widely current view which radically separates the act and object of reason from the act and object of sense to yield the two divorced categories of the "a priori" and the "a posteriori." According to this view, only sense is revelatory of the nature of reality, and reason is confined to the housekeeping job of filing and arranging the data of sense [20] But this theory is untenable precisely because it makes stable, communicable knowledge of extramental reality impossible On this view the really cognitive part of our experience is incommunicable, and the communicable part is non-cognitive —that is, not revelatory of any extramental reality

The only way to avoid this difficulty is to recognize the fact that the object of reason is materially the same object as that of sense but is a different formal aspect of it. Or, to put it more precisely, sense and reason have the same material object but different formal objects Thus my visual image of this pencil contains in itself in a primitive and confused way a number of objects, for example, pencil, length, wood, and so forth, which reason alone is able to apprehend as such. Thus reason, as well as sense, is revelatory of reality.

The object of sense is thus a confused welter of natures, each of which can be abstractly and specifically considered by reason. This first operation of reason is the act of conceiving, the act of focusing on some one of these formal traits alone, considering it quite apart from all those other traits with which it is confused in the object of sense but from which it may be, so far as its inner nature is concerned, altogether distinct Thus there is nothing about the nature of wood as such that requires that it be in the shape of a pencil or in any other particular shape, so that we may consider the wood quite in abstraction from shape (and other traits).

It is in this way that we apprehend the first object of reason—the stable nature or essence which is grasped in a concept as a universal possibility But such natures or essences alone do not constitute knowledge in the full sense. Knowledge does not consist merely of such elements as pencil or

[20] For a more detailed criticism of the distinction between the a priori and the a posteriori, see Wild and J L Cobitz, "On the Distinction between the Analytic and the Synthetic," *Philosophy and Phenomenological Research*, VIII, No 4 (June 1948), 651 ff.

length; before knowledge in the full sense can arise, these elements must be combined in assertions. Such combination into complete discourse or propositions is the function of the second rational operation of judging [21]

In addition to, and underlying, this combining function of judgment, however, there is a deeper, more important function that it performs. This function is the apprehension of acts of existing. Now it is true, as we have gone to some length to indicate, that existence is also in a sense apprehended by all other, nonpropositional acts of awareness. But by these other acts existence is not apprehended strictly and abstractly as such Thus sense grasps the existent, an individual which exists—this white sheet of paper here and now physically acting on me Conception, on the other hand, grasps an essence or nature as a merely possible existent—such as paper, white, and so forth—and existence in general, the universal possibility of existing But the proposition, finally, intends some essence or essences as existing in some definite mode, some essence in its very act of existing—such as, "The sheet of paper is lying on the table." And since what the proposition intends is an essence as existing (or as not existing). it, and it alone, can properly be called true or false—for truth and falsity pertain to, and are determined by, what is or is not. And such propositions are verified, as we have seen, only by reason acting together with sense, the former supplying clear, analytic insight, the latter, an apprehension of actual existence in the concrete.

This brings us to the problem of truth and falsity, and at the level at which it first arises—the level of the judgment and proposition That there is error in sense perception is, of course, true, but that a judgment is necessary before this error can arise is fairly generally agreed. Thus Professor Montague says that perception can be false only when "the word perception" is used to mean "the appearance together with the . . . judgment that accompanies the appearance."[22] Though such perceptual judgments are probably seldom explicitly formulated, they are nevertheless always implicit in perceptual experience in so far as it can be called veridical or erroneous And since perception is veridical or erroneous only qua judgmental, we may perhaps abstract from the perceptual aspect here and consider only true and false judgments or propositions. Even this more restricted topic, however, cannot, of course, be adequately dealt with in the brief space available here. But nevertheless it may perhaps be possible to sketch a few considerations on this thorniest of problems What, then, can we say concerning the nature of true and false propositions?

True propositions would not seem to pose any special problem, for they

<hr />

[21] For a treatment of the third rational operation of reasoning or demonstrating, which we shall not here consider, see the essay by Henry Veatch, pp. 192 ff.

[22] The Ways of Things (New York, Prentice Hall, 1940), p 270

simply intend an act of existing as it really is by virtue of that unique act of identification discussed earlier Thus in the true affirmative proposition, for example, "Man is an animal," one or more concepts, each intending an essence as a possibility, are logically unified into one complex concept, and this unity (the proposition as a whole and fundamentally the verb in its existential sense) intends one complex essence as existing in some definite mode of existence—actual, real existence, in our example. And in the true negative proposition, "Man is not divine," for example, the constituent concepts, each intending an essence as a possibility, are logically divided, and their division unified as the whole proposition (and fundamentally the verb in its existential sense) intends these essences as existing separately, or as not existing together, in some definite mode of existence.

But what of false propositions? The possibility of falsehood lies in the diversity between the two modes of existence involved in all knowing—the distinct, terminal existence of the thing which is known, and the intentional, relational existence of the knowledge of it. But as we have seen, great danger lies in overstressing this diversity—the danger, namely, of making knowledge of the act of existing impossible, as is the case with critical realism. On the other hand, if we overemphasize the closeness of the two modes of existence, we run into the danger of denying the datum of diversity and thus making falsity impossible Thus if we say that a false proposition, for example, "Men are divine" or "Men are not animals," simply intends an act of existing itself, then we seem to be forced into the following dilemma [23] Either the false proposition intends a real act of existing, or it intends a merely cognitive act of existing If the proposition intends a real existence, then what it intends is, identically, as it intends it, which is to say that the proposition is true Or if the proposition intends a merely cognitive existence, then what it intends is, again, identically as it intends it, which is to say again that the proposition is true In short, if we say that a false proposition simply intends an act of existing, without qualification, then it would seem that falsehood is impossible But on the other hand, if we say that a false proposition has no existential intention at all (that is, no *propositional* intention), then we reduce the proposition to a mere complex concept, which as such merely intends a complex essence in the mode of possibility But this latter alternative makes *both* truth and falsity impossible, since truth and falsity, as we have seen, follow the act of existence, and this alternative, in addition, makes it impossible to distinguish *actual* instances from merely *possible* instances of the essence [24]

Thus if the false proposition simply intends an act of existing, without

[23] See Plato, *Theaetetus*, 187A ff.
[24] This last alternative seems to be the view held by Professors C I Lewis and H M Sheffer See Lewis, *An Analysis of Knowledge and Valuation* (La Salle, Ill., Open Court, 1946), pp 48–49.

qualification, then it must be true for it truly intends what it intends, and yet if it does not intend any existence, then it is not a proposition. But there *are* false propositions (for there are pairs of mutually contradictory propositions one of which must be false), so evidently they must both intend existence in one sense and not intend existence in another sense. But what are these two senses?

In order to discover these two senses, we must return to our earlier analysis of the structure of cognition as a relational act of identification and now introduce into that analysis one further refinement It may be remembered that we saw earlier that every instance of awareness contains as its relational parts a subject (the knower), the foundation of the relation (the cognitive character or species in the mind), the relation proper, and the terminus of the relation (that which is before the mind, that which is known).[25] And we saw at that time that in so far as this is a relation of identity, the terminus is identical with the foundation, and yet that in so far as it is a relation, the terminus qua terminus is different from the foundation qua foundation and also different from the other parts of the relational act and hence different from the relational act as a whole. And we saw further that since this relational act is immanent and immaterial, it consequently makes no new real change in its object or terminus at all and hence leaves its object at least presumptively independent of itself. But now we must introduce a further distinction, a distinction which is the key to the sense in which a false proposition intends existence and the sense in which it does not, and consequently the key to the nature of falsity

This key lies in the recognition that the terminus of an immaterial, immanent, relational act may have two facets or statuses. In the first place, it has its status just qua terminus, and with respect to this status it is, qua terminus, a necessary part of the relational act and hence dependent upon that relational act That is, there cannot be a terminus as such without there being a relation which is thus terminated Now every relational act, since it is relational, has a terminus qua terminus—if it did not, it would not be relational. And hence every intention intends something, namely, the terminus qua terminus. Now a false proposition is an intention, and, moreover, it is the kind of intention which intends an essence in an act of existing. Hence every false proposition intends an act of existing in so far as an act of existing is the terminus of that relational propositional act. So much, then, for the sense in which a false proposition does intend existence

But this is not all. Though an essence in an act of existing is always the terminus of every proposition, true or false, it is never intended *as being a terminus,* that is, it is never intended in its *capacity* as the terminus, but

---

[25] Again, this relation may be interpreted as transcendental rather than as predicamental without affecting the present analysis. (See Note 17)

rather, as we saw earlier, as being *independent* of that intention or relation. This is so because the relational act is an immaterial, immanent act which does not change its object and thus does not intend what it intends as dependent on itself. But while a proposition never intends its terminus merely as being a terminus, yet it may nevertheless be merely that, what the proposition intends may be merely its terminus qua terminus And when this situation occurs, the proposition is false, it is deprived of its full completion because the terminus that it intends not merely qua terminus is in fact merely a terminus. That is, what it intends is merely a terminus, yet it does not intend it merely as such. Hence the sense in which a false proposition does not intend existence is the sense in which the false proposition does not intend its terminating existence as it merely is—as merely a terminal, qua terminal, existence.

Thus every proposition is an intention of a terminus which is an essence in an act of existing, but it does not intend this terminus as a terminus. Since, however, it may *be merely* a terminus, the proposition may be false Thus, for example, my relation "grandfather of" relates to a grandchild, though not to a grandchild merely *as* the terminus of this relation. But since the grandchild is merely that, the relation is "false" (that is, false when formulated as a proposition). Thus the truth of a proposition consists in the coincidence of a merely terminal, judgmental, dependent act of existing with a non-terminal, extrajudgmental, independent act of existing And the falsity of a proposition consists in the failure of the merely terminal, dependent act of existing to coincide with any non-terminal, independent act of existing. Or to express the same point in another way, a true proposition presumes to, and actually does, terminate in an independent, extrajudgmental act of existing, while a false proposition merely presumes to do this, and does not actually succeed in it.

Hence, in conclusion, we may say that truth is the coincidence of the two modes of existence (the terminal and non-terminal, or the dependent and independent), and falsity is the lack of such coincidence. Or in other words, truth consists in the presumptive independence of a propositional object being also a factual independence, and falsity consists in the lack of this. And this independence can be verified, as we have seen, only with the aid of sense which necessarily terminates in some existent object, though one which is only confusedly apprehended.

But this brings us back to the question which was raised above in Section I—the question of whether or not the presumptive independence of the object of awareness is ever also a factual independence We saw there that the object of every awareness is given *as being* independent, in its character and existence, of the awareness of it, but it was also suggested

then that the question of whether or not the object is *in fact* independent
of the awareness is a question of the veracity of the awareness Having now
touched upon the nature of truth and falsity, we are in a position to consider this question of the actual, factual independence of the object

Now if truth consists, as we have suggested, in the coincidence of the
terminal qua terminal existence, which as such is dependent upon the
relational, piopositional act, with an extraterminal, independent existence,
while falsity consists in the lack of such coincidence, then it would seem
to follow that the object of knowledge is in fact independent of the knowledge of it only in cases of true knowledge. Though every object of awareness, whether veridical or nonveridical, is given as being independent of
the awareness of it, only the object of veridical awareness (that is, awareness containing at least implicitly a true proposition) is in fact independent
of the awareness of it And if truth consists basically in the coincidence of
the terminal, dependent existence with an independent existence, then
evidently there can be truth (and falsity) only if we can intend in propositions an independent existence. But can this doctrine of the factual independence of veridical objects be justified? What evidence is there to
support this view?

In the first place, starting from the presumptive independence of, and
diversity from, its act of awareness which every object possesses, we can by
various processes of testing infer the factual independence of certain
objects of cognition Thus by checking one sense by another, we often find
that the object does not vary to our sense of touch, for example, by the fact
that we open or close our eyes, and so forth. And by checking with another
observer, we find that the object does not vary to his observation by the
fact that we observe or do not observe it. And so on. Such tests of invaria-
bility and independence are also tests which we commonly use for the
veracity of our experience—which fact may be taken as additional confirmation of the view that truth consists basically in the factual independence of the piopositional object.

In the second place, the view that things which are *truly* known (that
is, "known," in the usual and honorific sense of that term) are factually
independent of the acts by which they are known may also be established
by a *reductio ad absurdum* of its contradictory. Suppose that every object
of knowledge is dependent upon the act by which it is known. Now if this
is so, it will be so in virtue of some new real property—"being known"—
having been produced in each object by the act of knowing it, for it is
with respect to such a new real property that the object is dependent upon
the act of knowing it as upon its at least partial producer But if this is so,
then in knowing anything (and hence in knowing anything truly) the

knower would not know *it*, but only some new and different entity which his act of knowing had produced Thus to know something is not to know it, which is a contradiction But true knowledge is a fact, for as we saw at the beginning, its contradictory contradicts itself. Thus since true knowledge is a fact, true knowing produces no real change whatsoever, and hence no relation of dependence, in the thing known

This doctrine of independence has been recognized and stressed by many who call themselves realists, but its explanation has not always been successful Neorealism, most notably, recognized the truth of the fact of independence and rightly stressed its fundamental importance for any adequate theory of knowledge Neorealism's attempt to explain the fact by its doctrine of external relations, however, introduced other difficulties which ought, if possible, to be avoided. Although the idealist theory of internal relations, which the theory of external relations was devised to combat and supplant, is indeed inconsistent with the fact of independence and is therefore rightly to be rejected, it nevertheless does not necessarily follow that the theory of external relations is thereby acceptable.

This theory of external relations is partially right and partially wrong It is right in denying, against the idealist theory of internal relations, that what is truly known is in any way really altered by the fact that it is known—the relation "known by" is "external" to (that is, not really a character of) the thing which is known But it is wrong in suggesting that there is any relation at all, internal or external, *from the known to the knower,* and it is wrong in at least implying that the cognitive relation is external to the knower in the same sense that it is external to the thing known—that is, that what is known does not alter the knower.

For these reasons the factual independence of the truly known can be explained better by saying, with Aristotle, that the relation of the knower to the known is *non-mutual* rather than external, that is, that while the relation of knower to known is a real character of the knower—and thus may metaphorically be called "internal" so far as its subject and foundation are concerned[26]—there is no real converse relation of the truly known to the knower at all It is for this reason (and the deeper reason that the act of knowing is immanent rather than transitive) that the known is independent of the knower, qua knower, and his act of knowing. The peculiar relation "known by" (that is, *truly* known by), finally, is not a real attribute of the thing at all, but only a mental relation set up by the mind when, in reflection, it moves back from the terminus of the *real* relation "knower of" to the foundation of that relation in the knower.

---

[26] It should be noted, however, that the idealist view that all relations are "internal" tends, in effect, to destroy the distinction between substance and attribute For a treatment of this distinction, see the essay by Manley H. Thompson, Jr , pp. 125 ff

Thus there are instances in which the presumptive independence of the object of cognition is also a *factual* independence, and these instances, when they occur in propositions or propositionally mediated awareness, are just what we call true knowledge Every proposition, being a relational act, has a terminus which it intends as being not merely terminal in status but rather as independent of the proposition itself. Speaking structurally or analytically, we may say that when the terminal, dependent existence of the object is also a non-terminal, independent existence, then we have truth, and when we fail in this we have falsity. Speaking from the point of view of verification, we may say that if sense gives us a concrete existent object in which or by which the proposition is intuitively manifest, then it is true, if not, it is false and terminates *really* merely in a possibility. Truth can be achieved only by sense and reason working together in intuitive co-operation. And there are instances of such propositional termination in independent existents, we do have truths. The mind, by virtue of its immaterial, immanent, relational acts terminating in independent existents, can know real independent things as they really are in themselves

III

Thus we have treated of the existence of knowledge, the generic features of all awareness, and the special features of sensory and rational cognition. There is such a thing as knowledge, and it possesses certain necessary traits. The most basic of these traits, which are presented as the data of epistemology, is the intentionality of all awareness—that dynamic relational activity of identification of the mind with something other than, and at least presumptively independent of, itself. If any of these traits is denied, knowledge itself is denied, which is a contradiction Hence a responsible, truly realistic epistemology must take these data as it finds them, acknowledge them, and then proceed to the difficult task of describing and explaining them as carefully as possible.

One such attempt, in the briefest outline form, has been presented here. In knowing, our minds are identified in an immaterial, intentional way with something distinct from, and at least presumptively independent of, our knowledge of it. In sense, this thing is apprehended as a confused individual existent, pregnant with natures which only reason can deliver. In conception, the first act of reason, some one of these natures or essences is apprehended in a pure, abstract form, free from all other essences and from actual existence. And in judgment, the second act of reason, this essence apprehended in conception is intended as existing in some mode of existence, where that existence may be either merely terminal and dependent (as in the case of false propositions) or also non-terminal and independent (as in the case of true propositions).

But any individual attempt to give an adequate explanation of the phenomena of knowledge cannot but fall short of its goal Anything approaching a fully satisfactory explanation of these phenomena requires the co-operative efforts of all those who believe that there is a world of real existence independent of human minds and that this real existence can be truly known as it really is.

VII

For a Realistic Logic

Henry Veatch, *Indiana University*

I The Criteria of the Logical

WHAT sort of a logic is appropriate to, or perhaps is demanded by, a realistic philosophy of the sort advocated in this volume?

At first, such a question may seem impertinent and even preposterous For most of us simply are not accustomed to thinking of logic as being the sort of thing that is cut to the pattern of anything so insignificant as a mere philosophy. Much rather would logic seem to be something autonomous and independent· Logic is logic, no matter what may be one's philosophy. Indeed, so far from philosophy's determining the nature and character of logic, it would nowadays seem much rather to be a case of mathematical or symbolic logic's determining the nature and character of philosophy For it is as if logic were simply a fact and philosophy could do little more than make the most of it. For that matter, need one add that many contemporary philosophers actually do seem to do little more than make the most of logic?

Nor would the case seem to be otherwise with what throughout the last few centuries has usually been called Aristotelian logic Thus one hardly needs to be reminded of Kant's celebrated pronouncement concerning this sort of logic, namely, that "since Aristotle it has not required to retrace a single step"; indeed, "to the present day this logic has not been able to advance a single step, and is thus to all appearance a closed and completed body of doctrine."[1] True, Kant continues, although "some of the moderns have thought to enlarge it by introducing *psychological* . . . , *metaphysical* . . . , or *anthropological* chapters . . . , this could only arise from their ignorance of the peculiar nature of logical science " For "the sole concern" of logic being "to give an exhaustive exposition and a strict proof of the formal rules of all thought,"[2] it makes no difference, presum-

---

[1] *Critique of Pure Reason*, trans. by Norman K Smith (London, Macmillan, 1929), Preface to 2nd ed , B viii.
[2] *Ibid*

ably, what one's psychology or metaphysics or anthropology may be;
logic must perforce be always the same and invariant

In other words, on Kant's account, Aristotelian logic is not something
that is in any way adapted or appropriate to a peculiar kind of philosophy.
On the contrary, it is a wholly independent formal science.[3] And such, too,
is the way most logicians today would regard logic, Aristotelian or otherwise. To be sure, we have all doubtless heard of the expression "idealistic
logic," but since it is now the fashion simply to sneer at anything of the
sort, it is not surprising that very few should have stopped to consider that
the very name "idealistic logic" suggests that logic may not be so independent of philosophy after all.

But be that as it may, we propose in this present paper to run directly
counter to the prevailing habits of regarding logic as somehow autonomous
and sufficient unto itself. Instead, we are going to suggest that on the basis
of the realist platform appended to this volume, we can show both what
sort of logic it is that is appropriate to such a realistic philosophy, and also
that such a realistic logic is radically different both from mathematical
logic and from Aristotelian logic as this is ordinarily conceived.[4]

Thus consider the two basic realistic theses.

1. There are beings that are and are what they are independently of
   their being known
2. Human beings are able to acquire some knowledge of such beings as
   they really are in themselves and not merely as they are relatively
   to their being known

Now granting these two theses, the nature and function of logic would
therewith seem determined and defined. For as to its function, logic on
such a basis would be regarded simply as the tool or instrument through
which human beings could acquire precisely this sort of realistic knowl-

---

[3] We do not mean to imply that this interpretation of Aristotelian logic is necessarily
the correct one; all we mean is that it is the current and common one. Indeed, for the
last three centuries or so, the term "Aristotelian logic" has tended to signify a purely
formal logic, these "forms" being considered quite apart from any intentional function
which they might happen to have. Rather than attempt to revise this conception of
Aristotelian logic or to consider whether it is just either to Aristotle or to the Aristotelian
tradition, we propose simply to accept it at its face value For whether genuinely Aristotelian or not, such a logic, we think, is quite ill-adapted to the purposes of a genuinely
realistic philosophy.

[4] It is well known that mathematical logicians do not consider that the new logic is in
any way contradictory to Aristotelian logic. Quite the contrary, it is merely more extensive and comprehensive, with the result that the older logic can be simply taken up into,
and absorbed by, the new. Again (see the preceding note), we do not in this paper wish
to challenge this view of the relation between mathematical logic and so-called Aristotelian logic On the contrary, as the latter has generally come to be conceived and
understood, the mathematical logician is quite correct in supposing that Aristotelian
formal logic represents but an insignificant part of mathematical logic Our point is
rather that a realistic logic must differ radically from both mathematical logic and Aristotelian logic *as so understood*

edge of things as they are really and in themselves And such being the function of logic, the nature of the logical tools and instruments that are requisite for the performance of such a function can also be determined.

Thus for one thing, such logical entities as propositions, argument forms, predicate terms, and so forth would not be ordinary real beings but rather the sorts of things through which such real beings could come to be known. That is to say, one would hardly expect that a proposition, for instance, would exist or would ever be encountered *in rerum natura* in quite the same manner as an electron or a jellyfish. No, propositions just do not have that kind of existence. Instead, they are unmistakably *intellectual* tools and hence are quite incapable of existing apart from psychological processes of cognition or out of the context of human cognitive behavior. In this sense, indeed, they might be said to be mere beings of reason, or *entia rationis*, to use a Scholastic term

At the same time, they are not mere fictions arbitrarily invented or conjured up at will. Instead, they have to be wholly fitted and adapted to their function of disclosing or representing things other than themselves, precisely as these latter are really and in themselves. Consequently, such logical entities may be said to have a foundation in reality in the sense that they cannot be rightly understood save with reference to the real which they are thus designed to represent.

And this brings us to a third feature of these logical instruments of a realistic philosophy. Thus on the one hand, being only beings of reason, these logical entities are not to be confounded with the real beings which they are supposed to represent On the other hand, being wholly ordered to the representation of the real these beings of reason can only be understood with reference to what they are thus fitted to disclose. But now on the basis of these two determinations we can recognize the third feature, and that is that these logical entities must needs have a peculiarly neutral or almost transparent character about them, for only so could they serve to represent or signify what is other than themselves as it is in itself

Or to put the same thing a little differently, we might say that logical entities are peculiar precisely in that they are nothing but "intentions," their whole nature and structure being that of a thing which "tends toward" something else or which is wholly and completely of or about something else. It is in this sense that we say they must have such a character as will render them completely transparent or wholly representative of that which is other than themselves, or, to use the technical term, will render them completely intentional.[5]

Very well, but if such be the criteria of the logical, considered from the

[5] On this notion of intentionality, see Francis Parker's essay, pp. 158 ff., also the essay by Harmon Chapman, pp 22 ff., above.

point of view of philosophical realism, can we produce any examples of such peculiarly logical or intentional entities? We think we can Indeed, we think that those very entities—concepts, propositions, and arguments—which have always been thought to be in some sense or other the proper concern of logic—these very entities, we think, may be shown to be capable of functioning as intentions and to meet, when viewed in a certain way, all the requirements that a realistic philosophy lays down for logical tools and instruments.

Thus we have already intimated how such things as concepts, propositions, and arguments are mere beings of reason rather than real beings. That is to say, such things as syllogisms or universal concepts certainly do not have an existence *in rerum natura* comparable to that of ordinary natural objects Instead, such being or existence as they have would seem inseparable from the context of knowing and of human cognitive operations.

But further, concepts, propositions, and arguments are certainly intentions, in the sense in which we are using that term Thus a concept, for example, is necessarily the concept *of* something, a proposition is perforce *about* something, an argument is always *in demonstration of* something Indeed, if a concept were not thus of something—that is, if in a concept nothing were conceived—one simply would not have a concept Or likewise, a proposition which was not about anything, or which propounded nothing, would not be a proposition.

In this respect, indeed, these peculiarly intentional or logical entities are quite different from ordinary real beings. Thus a tree or a jellyfish or the color yellow or the relation "greater than" are none of them of or about anything else. They are just themselves For instance, what is it that a jellyfish is about anyway? To be sure, the concept of a jellyfish is of or about it, but it itself is not of or about anything else And likewise with the relation "greater than." When one thing is greater than another, one certainly does not consider that such a relation of one thing to another is of or about something else. No, as a real fact in nature, it is wholly nonrepresentative or nonintentional. Of course, it may be represented or be intended—for instance in a concept of it or in a proposition about it—but it itself is not a representation or an intention at all.

Moreover, having this peculiar character of intentionality, it would follow that intentional entities like concepts, propositions, and arguments, considered precisely as intentions, would have a very different nature and structure from the ordinary real (and hence nonintentional) beings which they are designed to represent. Nevertheless, such a contention, however plausible it might seem to be just in itself, has implications which, as we shall see presently, run directly counter to some of the most fundamental presuppositions of modern logic Thus how often are we told, for example, that logical forms and structures must somehow reflect or resemble or be "isomorphic with" the forms and structures of the corresponding real facts? Particularly with respect to relational patterns and structures, it is often urged that the relational structures of things must somehow be mirrored by the relational structures of logic

And yet if logical entities are simply intentions, and if intentionality is a peculiar and distinctive property of logical entities just as such, then it would seem that the nature and character of an intention would have to be very different from that of its intended object In fact, if by way of example we consider the concept "greater than," anyone would readily recognize that it is a concept of a certain relation, and yet he would also recognize just as readily that its own character and structure, just as a concept, is certainly not one of being greater than something else

So also as regards propositions and arguments, we shall seek to maintain that as intentions these logical instruments must be able to represent certain features of reality as they are in reality And yet for the very reason that they are thus representative, we shall also insist that their nature and structure as thus representative must needs be quite different from the nature and structure of what they serve to represent.

Of course, it remains for us to show just what this peculiar structure is that intentional entities have and that nonintentional entities do not have. But this is something we must consider later For the present we merely hope that we have been able to make our main thesis at least in part plausible, namely, that logical entities like concepts, propositions, and arguments are (1) beings of reason rather than real beings and (2) intentional beings rather than nonintentional beings, with the result that their structure as intentions is presumably quite different from the structure of that which is intended in and through them

Nevertheless, there is still a third criterion of the logical which, as we said, would seem to be demanded by a realistic philosophy and which still needs to be exhibited with respect to the three varieties of logical entities, namely, concepts, propositions, and arguments. Now by this third criterion, logical entities, although, as intentions and mere beings of reason, they are quite different from real beings, still as beings whose whole being is designed and adapted for the disclosure and representation of the real, they cannot well be understood without reference to the real which they are thus ordered to intend or represent. In this sense, as we remarked, logical entities are different from mere fictions in that they have a certain foundation in the real

Very well, turning then to these specific logical entities, concepts, propositions, and arguments, we must address ourselves to the question of how they are ordered or adapted to the disclosure of the real And we might do well to begin by considering just why there should be these three different types of entities In other words, each presumably has a different intentional function to perform, so far as disclosing the real is concerned. What, then, is it?

First, with respect to concepts, we may answer briefly that the function of the concept is to disclose or signify the "what" of things That is to say, anything that is or is real in any sense may be presumed to have some sort of determinate nature or character—an "essence," in the very broadest sense of that much abused and misunderstood term. Thus anything whatever, be it a relation, an event, a quality, a size, an activity, a substance, a sense datum, or what not, will be or have a certain "what" or essence, it will be something rather than nothing. Nor can there be any knowledge or understanding of things, save in so far as we get at their "what's" or essences.

But clearly, however indispensable to knowledge may be such concepts through which the "what's" of things may be apprehended, they at the same time are by no means sufficient for knowledge "Tree," "space-time," "equal to," "commander in chief" may be altogether meaningful and important as concepts in knowledge And yet they hardly constitute knowledge just in themselves. And the reason is that essences need to be recognized not just as such but rather as being and as existing. The "what" must be seen to be a "what is" or a "what that is" And this, we suggest, is precisely the function of the proposition—to get at and recognize the being or existence of essences, that is, to disclose either that a certain "what" is or what a certain "that" is. Indeed, this would seem to be the reason that only propositions and not concepts are susceptible of truth or falsity [6]

And finally, since a "what" only comes to be what a thing is, or an essence only comes to exist, through the operation of causes, it would seem that in addition to instruments for getting at the "what" and the "that," a realistic logic also must needs have an instrument for getting at the "why" And this, as we have already suggested, is the function of argument[7] as a logical tool or instrument of knowledge

In other words, considered in the context of realistic philosophy, logical entities like concepts, propositions, and arguments are to be regarded as intentional beings of reason, whose whole being and nature and structure are adapted simply to the intention and disclosure of the real as it is in itself

---

[6] Again, see Parker's essay, pp 168 ff., above
[7] In this brief essay, we are considering only deductive argument, not induction.

II REALISTIC LOGIC AS CONTRASTED WITH A LOGIC OF REAL FORMS

Let this, then, suffice for a very cursory explanation and defense of our first thesis, namely, that there is, or at least can be or should be, such a thing as a realistic logic, and that the hallmark of such a logic must needs be its radical and thorough intentionality. But now let us turn to our second thesis [8] According to it, it must be recognized that the current types of logic with which we are particularly familiar nowadays—namely, mathematical logic and Aristotelian logic as that is ordinarily understood—such types of logic are not in the nature of a realistic or intentional logic at all. Why not? Well, we venture to suggest that the reason is that developments in modern mathematical logic have tended to introduce into logic a type of formalism which is radically and completely nonintentional

Indeed, to bring the issue to a head, let us quote a rather striking passage from Ludwig Wittgenstein: "We make to ourselves pictures of facts. The picture presents the facts in logical space, the existence and non-existence of atomic facts The picture is a model of reality To the objects correspond in the picture the elements of the picture. The elements of the picture stand, in the picture, for the objects. The picture consists in the fact that its elements are combined with one another in a definite way The picture is a fact. That the elements of the picture are combined with one another in a definite way, represents that the things are so combined with one another This connexion of the elements of the picture is called its structure, and the possibility of this structure is called the form of representation of the picture."[9]

Now without in any way pretending to understand the precise esoteric interpretation that a thorough Wittgensteinian would want to place upon this passage, or without pretending that all modern mathematical logicians would agree to the statements of this passage in their every detail, we nevertheless make bold to suggest that such a quotation serves to point up in a peculiarly vivid way what we should like to call the thoroughly noninterpretational direction that nearly all modern logic has taken. Thus on the one hand, so far as "reality"[10] is concerned, what seems to impress so many mathematical logicians about it is its structured, relational character. And on the other hand, so far as logic is concerned, what it would seem to be is primarily a picturing or a mapping of the corresponding real structures.

Immediately, from the point of view of an intentional or realistic logic, a

[8] See above, p 178
[9] *Tractatus Logico-Philosophicus* (London, K Paul, Trench, Trubner, 1922), p. 39.
[10] This word has often been taken in a Pickwickian sense in the context of modern logic.

number of objections suggest themselves. For one thing, even though it be quite true that one could, and even must, *use* logic in order to come to an understanding of the possible structures and types of order and forms of connection that pertain to things in the real world, still it is not *in* logic that one learns about such things. Or better, while a knowledge of such relational patterns and forms of connection may well come about through logic, still such knowledge does not in any way constitute a knowledge of logic. For logic does not concern itself with the study of real forms and relations, rather its concern is solely and exclusively with the purely intentional forms and relations, through which real relations—and for that matter any other real beings—can come to be known. In other words, the first objection that an intentional logician must raise to such a conception of logic is that it involves a serious confusion of real forms and relations with properly logical forms and relations.

And yet a mathematical logician might well make the rejoinder that in the passage quoted, Wittgenstein does seem to ascribe a definite representative function to logic, in so far as it is supposed to "picture" the facts. And in this sense, it might well be asked whether for Wittgenstein, quite as much as for us, logic might not be said to be an affair of intentions. In other words, is not mathematical logic an intentional logic after all?

In reply to this, we might note that by our account a logic can be intentional only in so far as the nature and structure of logical entities is different from the nature and structure of the objects intended. On the other hand, by Wittgenstein's account, it would seem that a logic could be representative or intentional only in so far as logical forms and structures were somehow like or similar to or isomorphic with, the real forms and structures which they were supposed to represent or intend. In fact, as Bertrand Russell has remarked in another connection, "in a logically correct symbolism there will always be a certain fundamental identity of structure between a fact and the symbol for it; and that complexity of the symbol corresponds very closely with the complexity of the fact symbolized by it."[11]

Now from the point of view of a thoroughly realistic logic of the sort we are defending, what precisely is the import of this basic presupposition of so many mathematical logicians, that in order for logical relations and structures to represent real relations, there must be an isomorphism or structural identity between them?

For one thing, such a view of the nature of representation would seem to come very close to the discredited "copy theory" of knowledge, according to which there must always be a correspondence between the thing

[11] *The Philosophy of Logical Atomism* (lectures delivered in 1918 and published in the *Monist*, 1918–19, republished by the Department of Philosophy, Minneapolis, University of Minnesota, no date), p 12 See also Russell's comments on Wittgenstein in his Introduction to the *Tractatus, op cit.*, especially pp. 8–11

known and what is in the mind of the knower. Moreover, quite apart from the usual difficulties of such a theory according to which it would be impossible for one ever actually to tell whether there was in fact such a correspondence between knower and known, there is another difficulty that is somewhat more immediately germane to our present discussion. For if it be maintained that in order for one to know a given complex structure, the complexity of the symbol must correspond to the complexity of the fact symbolized, the presupposition would seem to be that one can know the fact only by first knowing the symbol.[12]

But then the problem of logical intentions has merely been pushed back one step further. For how, and through what intentional instruments, does one know the symbol? If the only possible intentional instruments are symbols which are isomorphic with the thing symbolized, then a regress to infinity would seem inescapable. And rather than accept this consequence, it would seem necessary to recognize that representation may well involve some other principle than that of isomorphism between symbol and symbolized, or between intention and intended.[13]

Of course, what we have just said must not be interpreted as meaning that the likeness or resemblance of one thing to another can never provide a basis for the one's representing or signifying that other. On the contrary, representation through likeness is not only possible but common.[14] Instead, the only point we were trying to make was that isomorphism cannot well be the only, or even the most fundamental, means of representation or intention, for the reason that in order to recognize a thing through its likeness, it is first necessary to recognize the likeness, and this already presupposes intention and cognition.

And in any case, so far as our earlier contention is concerned to the effect that in mathematical logic there would seem to be a confusion of real forms and relations with properly logical or intentional forms, this contention is simply borne out by the view so current among mathematical logicians that logical forms and structures are isomorphic with real forms and structures. For on such a basis the logician would not be concerned with anything peculiarly and exclusively in the nature of beings of reason and intentions. Rather, his undertaking would amount to no less than a

[12] Otherwise, there would be no point in insisting on the likeness of the symbol to the thing symbolized. That is to say, on this view it is only through recognizing the likeness that one comes to recognize that which it is like. Hence one must first come to know the symbol, and only then does one come to know what is symbolized, on the ground that the former is like or similar to the latter.

[13] On the difficulties of a correspondence theory, see Parker's essay, pp 156 ff.

[14] To use more technical language, one might say that while instrumental (in this case, iconic) signs are entirely proper, one cannot expect them to displace or substitute for so-called formal signs. See John Wild's article, "An Introduction to the Phenomenology of Signs," *Philosophy and Phenomenological Research*, VIII, (Dec. 1947), 217 ff.

Leibnizian *speciosa generalis,* having a veritable ontological or metaphysical objective of determining all the possible types of order and forms of connection in general.

Indeed, this same point is even more strikingly borne out when one considers the theories of those mathematical logicians who would simply reject the notion that logical forms and structure must somehow correspond to real forms and structures. Instead, accepting a more Kantian or even idealistic epistemology, they would question the necessity or even the meaningfulness of talking about a real to which the logical is somehow supposed to correspond And in place of such a correspondence theory, they would make logic and/or mathematics actually constitutive of reality as known Or to put the thing a little differently, logic and mathematics on such a view become actually legislative[15] with respect to the phenomenal world of experience In other words, such a world is what it is and presents itself to us as it does because of the ordering constructs or logico-mathematical systems which we use in our efforts to deal with it.

But clearly here, more than ever, supposedly logical forms and relations have ceased to be mere intentions through which the real comes to be known; instead, they are the actual form and relations of the real itself Or better, instead of being intentional structures through which the order of nature comes to be known, these so-called logical structures actually determine the order of nature as it is for us

III. The Intentional Relation of Identity

Nevertheless, our second thesis still lacks much in the way of confirmation. For if we are to be convincing in our insistence that mathematical logic is not an intentional or realistic logic at all, it remains for us to do at least two things In the first place, having declared repeatedly that intentional relations and structures must be other than the real relations and structures which they intend or represent, we must now try to show just what such an intentional or properly logical relation is And in the second place, having shown what such a relation is, we must then try to show how, in their treatment of concepts, propositions, and arguments, the mathematical logicians consistently fail to recognize the intentional structure of such entities, even confounding them with various types of real forms and structures.

Coming, then, directly to the first question. What precisely is the nature of an intentional relation? The answer we should like to suggest, albeit with some diffidence,[16] is that this relation is always a relation of identity.

---

[15] See Professor Lewis's use of this adjective in *Mind and the World-Order* (New York, Scribner, 1929), p 27

[16] This diffidence proceeds from many sources. In the first place, there are various current senses of "identity" with which identity in our sense must not be confused, but

Thus, we have already argued that logical entities, on a realistic basis, are ordered to a disclosure of the "what," the "that," and the "why" of things. And such intentional functions, we think, can only be effected through this peculiar relation of logical identity

For instance, consider concepts. It is through these, as we have said, that one apprehends the "what's" or essences of things But what is a concept? Of course, it is a product of abstraction and is characterized by universality. But what exactly is a universal? Our answer is that it is simply a relation of identity between an abstracted essence and the individuals from which that essence has been abstracted and to which it is applicable [17] Of course, in fact and in reality, no essence ever exists in a state of abstraction from the individuals which have such an essence, nor is it ever related back to them by a relation of identity. But for this very reason, the relation of identity is purely and simply a relation of reason, with no existence *in rerum natura*. In other words, it is the intellect which, in order to acquire a knowledge or understanding of what a thing is, separates the "what" from the thing itself and then reidentifies the former with the latter, thereby recognizing the thing to be what it is It is in this sense, then, that we say that a universal concept is nothing but such an intentional relation of identity

Similarly with a proposition. For as we have seen, it is through a proposition that one comes to recognize what a given thing *is*, or *that* a certain thing is its own "what." But what is this relation of x to y in "x is y," if not a relation of identity? Thus the y, having been abstracted from the x, is actually reidentified with it in the proposition in which x is said to be its own "what"—that is, a certain "that" is said to be what it is.[18]

almost inevitably will be confused For instance, the idealistic logicians speak of identity, apparently thinking of it as connected with the Absolute which absorbs all differences within itself Also, the mathematical logicians speak of identity after the analogy of equality, as if there could be a relation of identity between individuals or classes of individuals But clearly, the intentional identity of which we are speaking is of neither of these two types

But in the second place, even within the context of realism it would seem necessary to distinguish between the purely logical relation of identity, with which we are here concerned, and that real relation of cognitive identity which is basic to any realistic epistemology (see Parker's essay, especially pp. 163 ff.) The latter is a real relation, the former only a relation of reason Also, the latter is the end, the former only the means to the end For instance, the logical relation of identity between subject and predicate is a means or instrument of the real relation of cognitive identity between knower and known.

[17] Incidentally, it might be remarked that both nominalism and extreme realism seem to overlook the relational character of universals. The former sticks simply to the individuals and refuses to recognize that intellectually it is impossible to abstract their essence from them and so relate it back to them. On the other hand, extreme realism fixes upon the abstracted essence but forgets that, as thus abstract, the essence or "what" is wholly and completely in relation to the individuals from which it has been abstracted

[18] As thus described, the relation of predicate to subject in a proposition would seem to be no different from the relation of abstracted essence to individuals in a concept.

Likewise in the syllogism, where one seeks to get at the "why" of x's being y. Thus, in fact and in reality there would certainly have to be some real cause or real reason why x should be, or should be y Hence any sort of knowledge or understanding of *why* x is, or is y, would seem to require some insight into, or recognition of, the *cause* of this fact. Presumably, then, so-called logical argument is nothing but a device or instrument for getting at the causes of things, just as the concept is an instrument for getting at essences and the proposition an instrument for getting at existence.

Nevertheless, in just what sense and on what grounds are we able to maintain that such a syllogistic instrument must be simply a relation of identity? One obvious reason is this. If the task be one of explaining why x is y, it is quite apparent that x cannot be y in virtue of what it is not, instead, it can only be so in virtue of what x is Besides, if what x is thus said to be is not also y, then one can hardly use such a third concept as a medium for explaining why x is y In short, the syllogism with its middle term would appear to involve a relation of triple identity.

And yet such an apparent explanation seems, on a little reflection, to be much more apparent than real. For, one might argue, if the syllogism is supposed to be an instrument for the intention of causes, then it could not possibly involve a relation of identity, since a cause is hardly identical with its effect Clearly, however, such an objection derives all of its force from the very common confusion of the structure of the intended object with the structure of the intending instrument. After all, the mere fact that a cause is not identical with its effect certainly does not mean that the intentional relation by which such a cause comes to be known or recognized cannot be a relation of identity. Quite the contrary, as we have already seen, the relation of subject and predicate in a proposition is one of identity, and yet what is intended by such a relation is certainly not necessarily a relation of identity For example, there is a sense in which the proposition intends the existence of an essence, and yet in fact, no finite essence ever is its existence Or again, in the proposition "Socrates is bald," what is intended is the real presence of a property in a thing (of an accident in a substance), and yet as we shall see later,[19] the intentional relation of predicate to subject, in contrast to the relation intended, is certainly not a relation between a thing and its property but rather a relation of identity.

So also with the syllogism What it intends may be the real cause of a certain fact,[20] and yet its own structure as an intending relation is not one

---

Nor is it to be denied that a concept, by the very fact that it is abstract and universal, is necessarily predicable of the individuals to which it is related by a relation of identity Still, the concept as such is predicable and identifiable, not actually predicated and identified.

[19] See below, pp. 190–192.

[20] It should be apparent that this notion of a syllogism as being an instrument for the

of cause-effect but rather one of triple identity. Thus, for instance, we may say that the reason towels dry our hands is because of their capillary structure In other words, it is because towels *are* of such a structure, and things of such a structure *are* absorbent, that we can say that towels *are* absorbent That is to say, the only way we can understand why x is y is in virtue of something else that x is. Thus a real causal transaction certainly does not involve any real relation of identity, and yet it would seem that it can only be intended by such a relation of identity.

But now let us turn to the mathematical logicians. If we are right in our view of a realistic logic, concepts, propositions, and arguments are nothing but relations of identity, through which we are able to get at the "what," the "that," and the "why" of things Also if we are right, the mathematical logicians, through their confusion of real forms and relations with properly logical or intentional forms, are bound to misconstrue such things as concepts, propositions, and arguments, not recognizing the distinctively intentional nature of such entities But is this in fact the case?

First as to concepts. Do the mathematical logicians recognize these as the means or instruments for apprehending the "what's" of things? Presumably not. Indeed, nothing is more striking about the ordinary textbook in mathematical logic than the total absence of any treatment of such things as concepts.

And yet it might well be urged that what the modern logician calls "propositional functions" are quite adequate to perform all the functions of concepts. Indeed, propositional functions, it might be argued, are really much more adequate than concepts for the very reason that whereas concepts never can represent anything more than mere properties of things,[21] propositional functions are able to represent relations between things. Thus one can have a function with one argument, and that will represent the relation of a thing to its property or a substance to its accident; or one can have a function with two arguments, representing a relation between two things, or a function of three arguments, representing a relation between three things; and so forth.

But here, surely, there is a very patent confusion of real relations with logical relations For must not such a thing as a propositional function be regarded as a sort of schema for various types of real relations? Thus, for instance, let us suppose that John is the brother of Joe. Now quite apart

---

intention of causes presupposes the realistic view of causal transaction (see Wild's essay, pp 64 ff), see also his "A Realistic Defense of Causal Efficacy," *Review of Metaphysics*, II, No 8 (June 1949), 1–14, in contrast to a Humean view of a cause as an atomic event prior in time to its effect

[21] The distinction between "thing" and "property" here may be taken to be synonymous with the distinction between substance and accident. See the essay by Manley H. Thompson, Jr., pp 125 ff

from the conceptual or propositional form through which this relationship is intended, the fact simply is that there is in reality a real relationship of John to Joe. Accordingly, the function f(x, y) would seem to be simply the form of this real relation, not necessarily the form of the intention in and through which this relation is apprehended Or if one wants to say that the function f(x, y) *represents* the form of the relation rather than simply *is* the form of the relation, then it does so after the manner of an iconic sign— that is, by being like the relation or by corresponding to it or by being isomorphic with it.

But a concept is not this sort of thing at all, and functions quite differently. True, a concept can perfectly well be a concept *of* a certain relation— of a many-termed relation, in fact And yet in such a case the structure of the concept just as such will not be the same as the structure of what is thus conceived or intended. For what is conceived will be a many-termed relation; but the relation through which it is conceived will be a relation of identity, that is, a concept which is precisely such a relation of identity between the real relation that is intended and its "what" or essence. Indeed, any relation whatever, be it one between a thing and its property or between two things or between three things—any such relation, or for that matter any being of any kind, relational or otherwise, must necessarily be what it is Nor can it be known, save through a recognition or apprehension of its "what" But such an apprehension comes about in and through a concept which is simply an intentional relation of identity between such a "what" and that which is such a "what."

Accordingly, if one insists on substituting propositional functions for concepts, he is really only deceiving himself, for such a substitution is not a substitution at all Instead, it simply means that one is shifting his attention from the structure of the intending relation to the structure of the relation intended Of course, there is no reason why the structure of real relations should not be considered, and considered in the greatest detail The only point is that such a concern with the structure of real relations as represented iconically in so-called propositional functions has nothing to do with logic For there still remains the question of what that peculiar intending relation is through which the "what" of a given real relation (as schematized in a propositional function)[22] is apprehended.

Turning, then, to propositions, we find on the part of mathematical logicians the same tendency to confuse the relational structure of the real fact that may happen to be intended by a given proposition with the relational

[22] In other words, there is no reason why a concept of a relation or relational complex could not be represented more or less iconically through the symbolic device of the propositional function The point would be that the relation of the concept to what it was a concept of would be a relation of identity, for all that.

structure of the proposition itself. Thus on our view, a proposition is simply an instrument for intending what something is, or better, *that* something is what it is. Accordingly, in a proposition the concept of what the thing is (the predicate) is identified with the thing itself (the subject)—x is y. Indeed, unless the predicate concept were the concept of what the thing is, one could never say of the subject that it *is* so and so, that is, one could never identify the predicate with the subject

Now in opposition to all this, the mathematical logician would no doubt protest that the function of the proposition is not to be confined to intending only the relation between a thing and its property (substance and accident), instead, through propositions we must be able to intend as well all the manifold relations that hold between things. Accordingly, the old subject-predicate form of the proposition is completely inadequate, instead, the proposition must have a relational form corresponding to the form of the relation which it is supposed to represent.

Unhappily, however, such a criticism of the subject-predicate structure of the proposition rests on a serious misconception; and in consequence, the resultant theory of propositional structure falls afoul of the familiar confusion of real structures with logical structures. Thus to begin with, it should be noted that as we have explained it, the logical relation of subject to predicate is not the same as the real relation of substance to accident. Indeed, it could not be the same, because the former is a relation of identity, whereas the latter is not After all, no substance is formally its accident just as such; otherwise, it would not be a substance On the other hand, any and every predicate concept in an affirmative proposition is identified with its subject—x *is* y.

In short, the error of the mathematical logician is to assume that the relation of subject to predicate is isomorphic with the relation of substance to accident; and then, on the basis of this assumption, he points out, quite rightly, that since there are innumerable other relations besides that between substance and accident, the relation of subject to predicate is wholly inadequate However, as we have just pointed out, the relation of subject to predicate is not this kind of a relation at all, indeed, it is not isomorphic with any real relation, being only an intentional relation of identity; and no real relation is ever such a relation of identity

No, the relation of subject to predicate is a relation between a thing[23] and what it is, and through such a relation of identity we come to know that a thing is thus and so (that is, what it is) in fact and in reality. Not only that, but in order to know that anything, no matter what it may be—a

[23] Here we are using "thing" not in the narrower sense of substance (see above, Note 21) but rather in the broadest sense possible, as synonymous with being itself.

relation, a substance, a quantity, an activity—in order to know that a thing *is* thus and so, one has to employ the intentional relation of identity between subject and predicate

Nor will any relational form such as x R y suffice for this purpose. Thus if it is concerning x that one wishes to recognize that it is thus and so, the only propositional form that will serve is the subject-predicate form   x *is* in relation R to y. Or if it is the relation itself that one wishes to say something about, again the subject-predicate relation of identity is the only one that will perform the requisite intentional function "The relation x R Y *is* symmetrical." Or if one's concern be to state something (a "what it is") about the whole relational complex, x R y, once more, the only intentional instrument is that of subject-predicate—"A situation in which a given thing, x, stands in relation R to y, *is* also one which involves a counter relation of y to x."

In other words, the relational propositional forms of the mathematical logicians turn out not to be propositional forms at all. Instead, they are the forms and structures of real relations but not the forms and structures by which such real relations may be intended Indeed, we might even bring out the point this way The relation of subject to predicate—x is y—is necessarily a relation that intends something else. That is to say, any relation of the form "x is y" is intentional It is *about* something else On the other hand, the relation "greater than" is not about anything, it does not intend anything. True, it may be the object of an intention, but it itself is completely nonintentional. Consequently, to try to make propositional structures isomorphic with real structures is simply to shift one's attention away from the peculiarly intentional relations of logic to the wholly nonintentional relations of mathematics and the other sciences.

Moreover, precisely similar considerations would appear to apply in the domain of argument, quite as much as in that of the concept or of the proposition For once more the mathematical logician apparently thinks that in investigating purely nonintentional structures he is somehow dealing with logic. Specifically with respect to argument, the mathematical logician and also many contemporary Aristotelian logicians seem fascinated by the idea of a purely formal argument or *"argument en forme,"* as Leibniz called it [24] Thus take the syllogism, for example. This is held to be an argument that is valid solely by virtue of its form

All M is P
All S is M
All S is P

[24] *Nouveaux essais sur l'entendement humain* (Paris, Flammarion, n. d), Liv. IV, Chap. 17, § 4, p 428

Here, obviously, it makes no difference what the M and S and P symbols stand for or what they mean The argument is nonetheless formally cogent.

Or again, to use an example borrowed from Alfred Tarski, [25] suppose we are dealing with the relation of congruence between line segments, and suppose we adopt as axioms the assertion that every such segment is congruent to itself and also the assertion that two segments congruent to the same segment are congruent to each other From this it can then be proved that if any segment x is congruent to y, and y to z, then x is congruent to z.

But, as Tarski points out, the cogency of this argument is in no wise dependent on the nature and meaning of line segments or even on that of the relation of congruence On the contrary, the proof would be equally valid even if one supposed that one was talking not about line segments particularly but simply about anything whatever; and not about the relation of congruence in particular but about any relation In other words, conclusions must be regarded as following from premises simply in virtue of certain purely formal and completely abstract structures Accordingly, one of the tasks of logic would presumably be to work out various uninterpreted formal systems, which could then be given interpretations and so serve as a pattern of inference for any number of different possible subject matters.

For that matter, even the form of the syllogistic argument given above could be still further formalized and so shown to be structurally or formally the same as the transitivity of the relation of congruence One could then set up the completely general statement: if x R y and y R z, then x R z. And this completely general theorem could be proved on the basis of the two axioms about congruence, provided they also be completely generalized In fact, the principle underlying all relations of this general type—identity in the syllogism, congruence in line segments, and so forth—could be summed up thus. Any relation that is reflexive and that also has the property P[26] will necessarily be a transitive relation.

Accordingly, the syllogism with its relation of triple identity is by no means the only form of inference On the contrary, there are a whole host of other such forms as well. Not only that, but all these alternative forms can be generalized so as to yield a completely uninterpreted pattern of inference that will function equally well whether one is dealing with line segments in a relation of congruence or concepts in a relation of identity or qualities in a relation of similarity or classes in a relation of inclusion or what not.

However, unless we are very much mistaken, this whole notion of *argument en forme* involves a simple confusion of the structure of certain rela-

[25] *Introduction to Logic and to the Methodology of Deductive Sciences* (2nd rev. ed., New York, Oxford University Press, 1946), pp 121 ff.
[26] This is the way Tarski chooses to symbolize that general relational property exemplified in the relation of equality: Things equal to the same are equal to each other.

tions that may be intended by an argument with the intentional structure of that argument itself For, from the realistic point of view argument is simply an intentional instrument for demonstrating *why* something is what it is. Nor can a thing be what it is in virtue of what it is not, rather this can only be in virtue of what it is—that is, in virtue of something else, or some other "what," that it is Accordingly, all demonstration must be through a third or mediating concept.

Thus suppose one wants to demonstrate that a given type of relation is transitive. Presumably this can only be in virtue of some other "what" or "what's" that that relation is, namely, that it is reflexive and that it has the property P. In short, various types of relation have various properties and characteristics, just like other things And if one wants to know why a certain type of relational structure is what it is and has the characteristics which it does have, he will use the ordinary intentional relation of triple identity as his instrument of demonstration And yet, clearly, the structure of the relation that is thus intended must not be confused with the structure of the intending relation.

Nor does the so-called generalization or formalization of proof make any difference in this regard For what is thus formalized or generalized would seem to be the relation that is intended, not the intending relation Indeed, if one is investigating relations, there is no reason why he should not consider them with respect to their most general and universal features. In this sense, one need not confine his investigation, for example, simply to the relation of congruence. Instead, he might consider any relation having certain structural features, such as, say, reflexivity and symmetry But such a generalization or formalization would be a generalization or formalization of the structures intended by an argument, not of the intentional structure of the argument itself.

Of course, as we have seen, since the syllogistic structure of argument is itself a certain kind of structure, one might make that particular structure the object of his intention and might show it to be isomorphic with certain other types of structure And yet the point is that however one may generalize or formalize the relation of triple identity, once he has made it the object of his intention, still when it functions as an intention, such a relation is radically and thoroughly intentional It is simply of or about or discloses something other than itself. In this respect, it is quite different from all other relations, even though these may in certain cases appear to be isomorphic with it.

Thus, for example, the nonintentional relation of congruence is transitive, just as is the intentional relation of identity And yet the important thing is that the transitivity of the relation of congruence does not signify or intend anything else; it is just a fact, but it is not a demonstration of anything else.

On the other hand, the transitivity of the logical relation of identity can serve to demonstrate something about an intended object other than itself. Hence, whereas the transitivity of the relation of congruence may be an object of demonstration, it itself demonstrates nothing. On the other hand, the transitivity of the relation of identity not only may be an object of demonstration but can also itself be demonstrative: Through it we are able to demonstrate the why of things wholly other than the relation of identity; indeed, even to demonstrate why that relation itself is as it is—say, transitive—we have to use it as our demonstrative instrument

In other words, for a realistic logic the instrument of demonstration is not an uninterpreted formal system which can then be given various interpretations On the contrary, such systems would seem to be nothing but exhibits of various types of real or nonintentional relations considered in their widest generality And of course, such relations have their characteristic properties and attributes However, to demonstrate or show why these very general relational patterns and structures are as they are requires the peculiarly demonstrative relation of triple identity Furthermore, in so far as these general patterns or systems come to be interpreted for various possible contents, one can only proceed by showing that a certain specific relational structure is as it is, and has the characteristics which it does have, because it *is* an instance of a certain more general type of structure. Once again, the instrument of demonstration would seem to be simply the relation of triple identity, even though that which thereby comes to be demonstrated may be the characteristics of a wholly different sort of relation.

IV. Logic and the Mathematizing of the Sciences

Let us consider, then, that our second thesis has been sustained and that modern mathematical logic has been shown to involve a systematic confusion of real relations with logical relations and hence not to be a properly realistic or intentional logic at all. Now if this be true, then it would seem possible for us to provide an explanation of two more or less unexplained features that would seem to characterize so many current theories regarding the logic or philosophy of science For one thing, we refer to that feature according to which formal logic is held to be something totally different from, and in a sense only accidentally relevant to, what is sometimes called the logic of discovery or scientific method And for another thing, we have in mind that feature of so many contemporary philosophies of science according to which no science is considered a really advanced and developed science unless it be, so to speak, mathematized—as if the perfect form of a science were presumably a mathematical form.

To take the second feature first, we think that this can be accounted for as being a direct consequence of the confusion in modern logic of real relations with properly logical and intentional relations. For supposing that logic is what so many mathematical logicians seem to think it is, namely, an investigation of all possible types of order, relation, structure, and forms of connection in general, then logic itself will be precisely a mathematics and not a logic (that is, not in our sense of an intentional logic) As a matter of fact, we do not see why mathematics might not be defined as being simply a science of relations, these relations being considered not as actually existing *in rerum natura* but rather as abstracted from all content and all conditions of actual concrete existence. In contrast, logic, on our view, is not a science of relations in this sense at all, rather it is a science only of relations of a very peculiar sort and kind—namely, the purely intentional relations of identity

Very well Supposing, though, that one does turn logic into mathematics, and supposing one disregards any properly logical and intentional forms altogether, then obviously any science which is not fully mathematical in form and structure will not be fully logical in form and structure either, and to this extent it will not be logically precise and rigorous. On this basis, then, sciences other than physics—biology, anthropology, history, economics, philosophy, and so forth—must be put down as being comparatively crude and undeveloped sciences.

Now all this, of course, is not to be taken as implying that from the point of view of what we have chosen to call a realistic or intentional logic mathematics is to be regarded as unimportant and the use of so-called mathematical methods in the sciences to be discouraged Quite the contrary, we should insist that there is nothing wrong with mathematics, our only contention being that it must not be confused with logic Nor could there be any possible objection to introducing mathematics into any and all the various natural sciences—physiology, archaeology, economics, even ethics. After all, relations are to be found everywhere in nature. Hence if one wants to consider particularly the relational aspects of, say, physiological phenomena, it is only appropriate that he should proceed mathematically

No, the point is not to decry mathematics but rather to distinguish logic from it. For the minute one recognizes the intentional character of logic, he will see that logical forms are in no sense isomorphic with the real forms and patterns of relation in mathematics. On the contrary, as we suggested earlier, being purely intentional, logical forms will be purely neutral and transparent: Through them one can intend anything: mathematical relationships, organic functions, natural substances, act and potency—anything For this reason an intentional and realistic logic, unlike a mathematical logic, never prejudges the issue as to the kinds of realities there are in the natural world. Hence, so far from insisting that there can be only one natural science, namely physics, the realistic logician recognizes that there may be, and presumably are, many sciences and many "knowledges"—just as many, in fact, as there are kinds of things to be known.

And now for that other feature of the present intellectual situation that we proposed to comment upon, namely, that whereas formal logic seems to be productive of vast systems and a priori constructions, the so-called logic of discovery or induction or scientific method or what you will seems to be something entirely different and almost unrelated. But again, we think that this curious situation is the direct result of the neglect of an intentional logic and the attempt to replace it by a logic or mathematics of real forms and relations. For after all, concepts and propositions and arguments, as we have described them, are entirely oriented toward the intention of the real world, and of the real world as that is given in experience. Indeed, the intention of the empirically given could only be an intention in terms of the "what," the "that," and the "why."

On the other hand, with a logic that concerns itself with nonintentional forms, the situation would perforce be entirely different. For such forms do not intend anything else. Hence they are not forms through which the given comes to be known for what it is in itself. Instead, these are forms which come to be known purely a priori and without the slightest reference to any given reality which they might supposedly be designed to intend. Not only that, but these mathematical structures and types of order having almost endless properties and ramifications, they can be exhibited a priori in vast and elaborate systems.

Accordingly, the question then becomes one of how these a priori constructions are relevant to what is given in experience. They cannot be relevant in the manner of intentional forms—that is, as intending the given in terms of what it is in itself. Instead, they might perhaps be relevant as somehow corresponding, through some mysterious pre-established harmony,[27] with the order of things as given. Or perhaps they are relevant, not as corresponding to the order of the given, but as somehow imposing an order on the given or actually constituting the order of the given, as if the mind were somehow legislative and determinative of the relational pattern of our experience.

Needless to say, however, all such idealistic tendencies[28] are quite alien

---

[27] This would actually seem to be Einstein's view. See the article by Professor A. Ushenko in *Albert Einstein. Philosopher-Scientist* ("The Library of Living Philosophers," VIII [New York, Tudor, 1949]), 636.

[28] On these, see again Wild's essay, pp. 38 ff.

to any sort of genuine realism in philosophy. Accordingly, it certainly behooves realistic philosophers to take logic seriously and to realize that the development of a genuine realistic or intentional logic is not an accomplished fact but a crying need, since the sort of mathematical logic that is prevalent today would seem to be not so much an instrument of realism as a serious source of confusion and embarrassment.

PART II

VIII

The Nature of Aesthetics

ELISEO VIVAS, *Northwestern University*

THE NATURE OF AESTHETICS[1]

"AESTHETICS" is the name customarily given to the theoretical and systematic exploration of the questions which arise when men reflect on their interest in the beauty of nature and in the products of the fine arts It has traditionally been considered one of the philosophic disciplines, but many of the questions which the aesthetician asks refer to matters of fact which belong to the domain of science or gradually fall into it as the sciences advance. However, aesthetics is not a science or a collection of sciences in the sense in which modern physicists and most American social scientists use the term, because the aesthetician is not merely confronted with a theoretical task but with a practical one, in the Aristotelian sense of these terms. He seeks, through his influence on criticism and education, to guide the development of taste and, more indirectly, to guide the activity of the creative artist. So long as positive science remains a continuous development of what it is today, and so long as the normative or practical aspect of aesthetics is recognized, it will be necessary to distinguish it from the sciences.

Aesthetics presupposes two types of gifts which popular prejudice assumes to be more or less incompatible: on the one hand, some experience with, and a genuine interest in, beauty and in art and, on the other, a need to formulate that experience in theoretical terms, to clarify it and give it order. The questions which the aesthetician asks are suggested to him by men's actual commerce with beauty and art, when they are not, they tend to be factitious or "merely verbal" in the dyslogistic sense, but they generate in the aesthetician's mind subsidiary questions which must be settled if those that first arose are to be disposed of satisfactorily If the aesthetician does not have some actual experience with beauty, he will not be likely to believe those who, like Plato or Tolstoy, have attributed to it strong powers

[1] In a radically altered and abbreviated form, this essay will appear as Part I of the Introduction to a book of *The Problems of Aesthetics* to be published in the near future by Rinehart.

over the soul. But he is not solely interested in answering discrete questions
He obeys the philosopher's impulse to co-ordinate his answers into a systematic whole, which is not only adequate to the facts of beauty but which
is also adequate to all the other data which his diverse experiences thrust
into his purview As he seeks to satisfy the demands of systematic construction, his original questions tend to be restated in a progressively more
technical terminology This is not peculiar to aesthetics, of course, but happens in the development of any inquiry, whether philosophic or scientific,
but it is a tendency that does not make the aesthetician popular with the
artist, the critic, or the public.

There is another reason for the aesthetician's unpopularity. When God
confounded men at Babel, it seems that He put a greater curse on aestheticians than he did on other men—a curse the historian did not record but
which can be inferred from subsequent events. And the upshot is that what
appears at first as an attempt at communication between the aesthetician
and his readers often turns out to be, on scrutiny, pure soliloquy Charity
advises us to assume that these soliloquies are understood by those who
utter them, but this is a hypothesis which we must hold on faith and sometimes in the teeth of the facts.

We cannot therefore altogether blame those who find the aesthetician an
unpleasant companion. The artist is interested in making objects of beauty,
and not in a thorough and systematic grasp of the meaning of his activity.
His habits and interests keep him on the concrete and the particular and
tend to blind him to the large number of unexamined assumptions which
influence his activity The critic is also oriented toward particulars, since he
is concerned with gaining a firmer possession of the object of beauty than
can be gained without the aid of trained powers of discrimination. For the
former, the making of the object is a basic need, like eating or drinking
Such needs do not seem to him to call for an explanation from those who experience them, but for satisfaction. It is natural that the artist resent the
aesthetician, who does not seem to him to lead him directly to the satisfaction of his creative impulse, but routes him off along the unimproved side
roads of philosophy, on an uncomfortable trip which does not seem to get
anywhere That without such tours his own creative activity and our commerce with his product would not be as rewarding as they are could be
demonstrated to him, but he does not have the patience to follow the proof.
The critic is usually a little more tolerant. He has found that the aesthetician is sometimes helpful to him. But his interest in pure speculation soon
flags The pull of actual beauty is one he cannot and does not want to resist.
The flights of the philosopher into a realm of abstractions seem to him as
often to obfuscate as to help him grasp the "splendor of form shining on the
proportionate parts of matter" which radiates from a Maillol or a Renoir.

They do not seem to him always to justify the weariness they produce by improving in a noticeable way his capacity to capture his dream. The critic ends up by confessing that he can take the aesthetician in doses that must be small and far between.

The difficulty which we encounter when we try to justify the discipline of aesthetics increases the closer we look into its domain. For the man who undertakes its investigation needs a discouragingly large assortment of skills and knowledge that very few men are versatile enough to possess. Unlike the physicist or the chemist, if the aesthetician is comprehensive in his interest, as he must be if he is to be systematic, he finds himself confronted by diverse questions which can only be attacked with a very wide range of information He must ask questions about the nature of the talent which the artist possesses, about the structure of the object of beauty, and about the source of its power and its effects on the spectator. To answer even these few questions he requires versatile knowledge: He must be a psychologist, a sociologist, a critic of sorts, who has a working knowledge of what men like Barnes, Tovey, and Brooks discover about actual paintings and musical compositions and poems. Nor is this all, for in so far as beauty affects the life of men, the aesthetician must be acquainted with what Aristotle called the most authoritative art and that which is most truly the master art—the art of the moralist or legislator.

Some thinkers argue that the aesthetician has no need of the art of the moralist. Indeed he has no need of any normative discipline whatsoever; nor are there any to help him even if he needs them or thinks he does All he need do or can do is keep rigorously within the range of, so to speak, purely "descriptive" questions—his business is not to tell us what kind of art men ought to enjoy, but what kinds they in fact enjoy, to find the facts and to discover the determining causes of our preferences and choices is task enough The normative task has no validity, since value judgments when analyzed can in one way or another be reduced to fact. Whatever the differences that divide them, they are united in their belief that those who trace the normative character of such judgments to some sort of value entity taken as a part of the furniture of reality are making false ontological assumptions Reality, they are certain, is value-free. At some future time, no doubt, the historian of ideas will be able to give us the reasons why our contemporaries cling so resolutely to the prejudice that reality is value-free. The realist contends that the reduction of aesthetic facts to mere value-free facts is false, since it fails to do justice to the data to which such judgments refer: to value aspects or characters of aesthetic objects which can be pointed out to those who have the necessary equipment, native and acquired, to perceive them as constituting the distinctive traits of aesthetic objects.

Elsewhere I have stated at some length what I take to be the grounds for holding that values have what I call "ontic status " All that can be done here is to summarize these arguments briefly. These can be divided into the practical and theoretical. The practical grounds have no strong probative force and serve merely to establish the advisability of seriously entertaining the question about the ontic status of value They are all based on the fact that decisions must be made in art, as in moral matters, in regard to conflicting values The museum director has to decide between one picture and another which he wishes to buy or hang, the director of an orchestra or the head of a library faces similar problems, critics must in some sense "justify" their judgments of preference or they can claim no authority This is not the only point at which normative judgments enter our actual commerce with art, but it is the most obvious In view of the fact that the more thoroughly rational analysis can guide our decisions, the less is the resultant waste, it is advisable not to jump too readily at a view that precludes the possibility of conceiving aesthetics as a "practical science" in the Aristotelian sense of this term For although the view that value judgments are beyond rational control is put forth as a purely theoretical account of their nature, it cannot be kept from entering into the practical judgments of men as a persuasive factor leading them to abandon the search for rationality earlier than necessary. The maxim that advises those genuinely interested in science not to block inquiry is a purely practical maxim, but it is wise and deserves respect even though it does not preclude the possibility that inquiry will unexpectedly come up against road blocks which it can neither remove nor go around This is no less true of questions of value. It is not prudent, then, to close our minds to the possibility of objective normative judgments in aesthetics.

But are there any reasons compelling us to believe that values have ontic status? That at the phenomenological level aesthetic values present themselves as objective cannot be doubted by those who examine the data Even R. B. Perry, who is one of the high priests of subjectivism in value theory, cannot altogether deny this claim. He tells us that "there is at least a certain *seeming* evidence in its favor."[2] Lest we misunderstand him, he underlines the word "seeming " But this is all the evidence we require, the evidence of experience. and it is conclusive phenomenologically, since it discloses the fact that the beauty of objects is in the objects and not in us. Whatever factors examination may later reveal to be involved in the discovery of the beauty of an object, these can easily be shown to be the conditions of the discovery or of its presence in the object, and cannot impugn the objectivity which experience discloses The realist maintains that what is true of aesthetic value holds also for other values. And it seems advisable, since the objectivity of aesthetic value hangs or falls with the question of objectivity

[2] *General Theory of Value* (New York, Longmans, Green, 1926), p. 33.

of value in general, to indicate what is involved in the general claim.

When I say that an act is dishonest or that a man is a good man, I am not pointing to traits, features, qualities, or characters that exist in the depth of my subjective self, but to features to be discovered in the object or event to which I point in the real world I may have difficulty in convincing you that what I say is in some sense valid or true or reasonable; indeed I frequently fail to do so after strenuous effort, and you convince me of the contrary. But if the possibility of error condemned knowledge to subjectivism, all knowledge would be subjective Even when we follow the contemporary reductionistic fad, and we define the good or the beautiful in terms of subjective approval plus a request expressing the desire that the approval be accepted generally, it is still meaningful to ask what in the object or event do we approve of. A generous act may be approved of for many reasons, or not approved of at all, and it still remains what it is I may approve of it because it benefits me, or because it is intrinsically desirable, because it is fitting, or because it is useful in some sense to someone; or I may disapprove of it because it is done to a man I hate And yet in any one of these cases, and in others which need not be mentioned, I can still recognize the generosity of the act irrespective of the approval or disapproval of which it is the object in a given context by a given public.

It is not possible to argue that approval springs out of our souls in a perfectly random fashion toward one object now and toward another later. Almost infinite and heterogeneous in kind as seem to be the things men approve of when they approve ethically or aesthetically, the problem always remains· What is it in the objects of ethical or aesthetic approval which calls it forth? We know that what calls forth the approval is not the physical features of the object as such, since a discrimination of these features analytically or in their interrelatedness is not identical with the apprehension of the value of an object. And we also know that the value of an object is not the affective response, however defined, that it elicits, since we can distinguish our response clearly from the value and recognize that there are things to which we respond as we respond to value, but to which we deny value It is the object that we call valuable, and not its physical arrangement or our response to it In what, then, consists its value? But for deep-rooted prejudice, it would seem that the simplest account is to say that what makes an object valuable is the presence of a value in it, and that it is this value, supervening on the physical structure, that is the source of our affective response

The realist, however, is not content to hold that values are phenomenologically objective. He also holds that he does not create them and project them into the objects in which he discovers them. They do not "emerge" in the process of his desiring or of approving an object. They exist or, rather, have a status which is ontic and which makes the act of valuation possible. This is a hypothesis which suggests itself to the axiologist (1) when he critically examines the grounds on which men like Galileo and Hobbes and their followers declared at the beginning of modern philosophy that all but primary qualities were subjective, (2) when, freed from the subjectivistic prejudice by such critical inquiry, he asks himself what stands in the way of asserting the ontic status of value, and finally (3) when he considers what are the advantages for his discipline of asserting this hypothesis Let us comment succinctly on each one of these heads.

1. The reasons given by Galileo for asserting the subjectivity of all but what came soon after to be called primary qualities was that he dogmatically declared the objects of physics to be exhaustive of the reality of the physical world. It was an easy confusion for the student of classical mechanics to fall into, nor could its consequences be felt to be ominous in the seventeenth century, since the laws of physics which Galileo and his immediate successors sought applied without serious translation and adjustment to the things in the physical world in which they lived. But for the twentieth century the confusion becomes fatal, since it is no longer possible for the physicist as physicist to talk about the ordinary wooden table at which he sits. Or more precisely put, the physicist robbed the world from which he abstracted the objects of his inquiry of the reality which unphilosophic man has always in a more or less confused way attributed to it, in order to give that reality to the objects of his inquiry exclusively. Galileo said he could think of body without the qualities we now call secondary and tertiary, but not without those we call primary And this is true, nor is it astonishing since he was a physicist But we ought not to fail to see that his definition was a methodological classification, for us to accept it as valid ontologically is to disregard the fact that his conception of body was determined by his purposes as a physicist.

In defining body as he did, he was going beyond his role as a physicist and was philosophizing uncritically. And his philosophy was a kind of degenerate Platonism, according to which the real is that which is knowable That what he sought to know was restricted to certain limited aspects abstracted from a world which had as much title to be called real as the objects of physics was something he never stopped to consider Be that as it may, to claim that the reality of the physical world is confined to the qualities which the physicist is interested in, whether in the seventeenth century or in our own, is a piece of dogmatic ontologizing for which philosophic proof ought to be offered.

Primary qualities—primary in the sense that they are primary for the physicist—are abstracted by the physicist from the ordinary world in which we live, a world freighted with all sorts of qualities which are as real in that world as those in which the physicist happens to be interested No objection, of course, can be advanced against the abstractions of the physicist. The objection arises when the physicist, or the philosopher who limits his universe to that of the physicist, argues that what the physicist happens to be interested in is the only thing that is real. This is what, in fact, Galileo did when for the physical object he substituted the object of physics and defined it in terms of primary qualities exclusively And this is what physicalism has been doing ever since

2 When the realistic axiologist reaches this point in his speculations, he finds that there can be no reason for denying to the common-sense physical world in which we live the reality which much of modern philosophy has attempted to deny to it. It is this world in which we live, the physical world and not the world of physics, that is for our purposes, if not for those of the physicist, real But as real, it has among its basic discoverable features many which cannot be dealt with cognitively unless we employ the categories of end, purpose, and value, in order to grasp it as it is If the purposes of the physicist are allowed to define the limits of the cognitive activity, these categories are superfluous But they are not superfluous when the inquiry refers to the complex data of practical experience, as encountered by men in the complex world, to which values and ends and purposes are inextricably bound. To accept instead of this complex world of values and ends and purposes the abstraction of the physicist as the really real is to accept an ontological conclusion which the physicist as physicist cannot justify

3 Since the grounds on which the subjectivism of modern philosophy is accepted are not justified, it is not necessary to accept the deep-rooted prejudice of subjectivism

We are now ready to ask ourselves the question: Is there anything to be gained by positing the ontic status of value? The answer is in the affirmative. And the reason is that the hypothesis best accounts for the following data we have to explain the requiredness of value, the nature of obligation, the objective appeal intended in our value judgments, and the grounds on which we correct, when we do, our valuations—these are the central data which the value theorist or axiologist has to explain. These are the data which cannot be accounted for satisfactorily in terms of subjectivism. The claim here made is that the hypothesis of the ontic objectivity of value is capable of explaining it. For axiology, then, the ontic status of value is a hypothesis. It is the business of a complete metaphysics to analyze being and show that values are part of its structure. This task, it goes without saying, cannot be tackled here

It is possible, then, to argue that there are grounds on which to rear a normative discipline of aesthetics. But the aesthetician has another foe to contend with: the man who, pointing to the heterogeneity of the problems

of aesthetics, would abandon the traditional view of the discipline. This
man argues that to conceive of aesthetics as a single discipline is to dump
a great number of heterogeneous problems in the lap of one man who, since
he undertakes to be a Jack-of-all-trades, cannot be a master of any one of
them. The best such a man can do is to build a pseudo system, since he does
not employ a single method consistently throughout its construction and
since he builds with scraps of secondhand facts which are seldom able to
stand rigorous investigation Would it not be better to follow the advice of
the "analytic philosophers" and leave the various problems to the sciences
that can deal with them competently instead of launching forth on speculations about questions which someday will be susceptible of strict scientific
solution? Were such a plan to be followed, there would still be enough work
for the philosopher to keep him busy, since he would still have the task, in
the phrase of a well-known practitioner of philosophical analysis, of "sharp-
ening the tools" which are employed by those who talk about art.

Let us examine the wisdom of this advice. Note, first, that those who give
it assume, in the words of one of them, that aesthetics "is not in a thriving
condition at the moment." Dewey's *Art as Experience,* for instance, is, we
are told, "full of profound and stimulating suggestions" but is, nevertheless,
"a hodgepodge of conflicting methods and undisciplined speculations"
Since this condition ought to be remedied, and since the method of philosophical analysis has not been applied to aesthetics, and other methods
have, it would seem fair to apply it [3]

Whether aesthetics is thriving at present or not, the recommendation of
the analytic philosopher deserves a hearing, since it is the duty of those interested in the discipline to be constantly on the lookout for ways of improving it. But when we ask the analytic philosophers to define for us their
method, we discover that they have not yet been able to make up their
minds about what precisely it is that they advocate. Does the analytic philosopher want the aesthetician to confine himself exclusively to the linguistic aspects of his problems, leaving matters of fact to the sciences, or does he
advise that the aesthetician analyze linguistic expressions taken in relation
to the subject matter to which they refer?

The former seems to be what a man like Gilbert Ryle has in mind when
he defines the function of philosophy as the restatement of expressions
which are transmutations of syntax, controlled by desire to exhibit the forms
of the facts.[4] On Ryle's view, aesthetics would become a discipline whose

[3] Arnold Isenberg, *Analytical Philosophy and the Study of Art* (privately mimeographed and distributed by the author, 1950), p 9
[4] "Systematically Misleading Expressions," in *Essays on Logic and Language,* ed by
Anthony Flew (Oxford, Oxford University Press, 1951), p. 36.

referential language is clarified without reference to the facts themselves. To say what one has to say so clearly that it is not open to more interpretations than those specified by the speaker is the all-controlling desideratum. But the stubbornly realistic mind is not easily able to see how the analytic philosopher can analyze referential language in abstraction from the facts to which it refers.

All language is referential; and if it is not, it is mere prattle.[5] For this reason, to clarify language is to institute an inquiry into the relation between linguistic expressions and the various things to which they point We cannot know that discourse is confused unless we know the facts to which the discourse refers. To know that I am using a term ambiguously—to take the simplest form of confusion into which I can fall—I must know the two or more distinct referends to which the term points, and when mere verbal analysis can remedy my confusion, it is because analysis can take for granted that I know that the referends of my term are distinct. In fields of inquiry in which the facts may be taken for granted as perfectly known, if there be any such, it may be possible to clarify language without instituting an inquiry into the facts themselves But this is hardly the case in aesthetics, where our confusion is not merely a confusion of language but of facts, which are complex, illusive, and poorly known. The clarity which the analyst calls for in aesthetics must remain specious, since at best it can only be linguistic clarity about confused data.

This is best shown by specific reference to a concrete piece of linguistic analysis, and for this reason I shall examine below an essay by O K. Bowsma. The examination will prove that the truly difficult but important problems of aesthetics do not end but begin when the language of aesthetics is subject to a preliminary clarification But even this preliminary clarification is never merely a linguistic clarification of language, but a clarification of language through reference to the facts such as they are taken to be at the time the analysis takes place. But whether a certain modicum of clarity can be gained by mere analysis of language, the aesthetician—as distinct from the "verbosopher," as Douglas Morgan so felicitously calls him—is interested in considerably more than mere linguistic clarity. What he is

[5] This is no less true of mathematics than it is of physics and of the language of practical living Mathematics refers to intelligible objects and relations, nonexistential, substantial, which are directly intuited by the mind These objects are initially abstracted from experience, but once abstracted, their source is disregarded and the mathematician plays with them freely, building implicative systems which have as much or as little to do with the empirical world from which they were first abstracted as the rooks, knights, bishops, kings, queens, and pawns and their movements have to do with the actual warfare which may have first suggested them to the inventor of chess. The language of mathematics, however, is referential, since it is in the objects for which the symbols stand and not in the symbols that the mathematician is essentially interested This is not to deny, however, that some notational systems may be better than others.

interested in is to explore the facts and to interrelate them into a theory which enables him to guide criticism and improve taste. Some of the facts in which the aesthetician is interested are almost wholly unknown, and some not well enough known. No doubt as the science will advance, some of them will be better known. But such as the facts are, or are taken to be, they can be roughly tested and interrelated into a systematic formulation which in its rough way controls the activity of the teacher, the critic, and, in an indirect way, even that of the artist.

Aestheticians would like as far as possible to work with well-certified facts. But they have the task not merely of "explaining" them—in any reasonable sense that the theoretical scientist may wish to assign to the word—but of using them. Their aim is not merely to gain a theoretical grasp of the phenomena of art and beauty but to gain a grasp which would serve as the basis for its evaluation as a mode of human experience. Their explorations are recorded in language which is as vague as the facts are elusive and fluid and difficult to certify. But since it is the facts and their relations that the aesthetician is after, the ideal of the analytic philosopher does not seem attractive to him, for he would rather risk confusion in order to talk about his subject matter than talk clearly about nothing. The problem, then, for the aesthetician is not whether he can talk clearly but to what extent and by what means he can manage to talk as clearly as he can about his more or less confused, and not yet fully explored, subject matter.

A clarification which is not clarification of subject matter reminds one of the men of whom Socrates speaks in the *Phaedrus*. They know how to apply drugs and give a vomit and a purge, and knowing this they claim to be physicians, but they do not know to whom to give their medicines and when and how much. They expect the patient who consults them to be able to do these things for himself. Phaedrus, with Socrates's approval, calls these pure analytic philosophers of human health madmen or pedants. He should have added that they are thoroughly irresponsible as well—but perhaps that would have been redundant.

There are philosophers, however, who call themselves analysts, and who seem to be recognized as such, who are interested in the elucidation of subject matter. For these men aesthetics is a substantive discipline, and some of them maintain that in order to achieve their ends they need to devise real definitions with which to organize their data. Can we have any objection to their program? In principle, none whatever so far as I can see. The possibility, of course, that the results of empirical inquiry will be rejected in part or as a whole always remains open, but if some of the alleged results are rejected, it is by the application of the same method or of an improved version of the method by which they were initially obtained. There remains, however, a question of the exact claims made by these analytic philosophers, since it does not seem easy for the outsider to distinguish them from ordinary aestheticians whose orientation is empirical.[6]

Recently there appeared in the same collection of analytic papers two essays which illustrate the two conceptions of philosophical analysis which we have distinguished.[7] In one of them, Charles Stevenson, analyzing the problem of "Interpretation and Evaluation in Aesthetics," makes the point that the aesthetic judgment refers both to matters of objective fact, in so far as it points to discriminable traits in an object, and to a subjective factor or component which is beyond the reach of rational suasion. Whether this theory will prove more acceptable than other accounts of the same subject matter put forth by nonanalytic philosophers remains to be seen. It has been vigorously challenged by Hungerland,[8] and its view of the moral judgment has called forth, as is well known, an enormous amount of adverse criticism. In any case, the theory deserves as careful consideration in aesthetics as it is receiving in moral philosophy. But its acceptance or rejection will not depend on the rigor of its linguistic analysis alone. It will depend also on the facts—on whether our valuations do indeed express in part an attitudinal component which can properly be conceived as in fact beyond reach of all rational suasion. This is not given here as an adequate statement of the question which Stevenson's claim poses, but as a stenographic illustration of the fact that his theory refers not merely to questions of language but to questions of fact—in this case, questions of psychology as well as questions of logic.

In the same volume O. K. Bowsma undertakes to examine "the expression theory of art." It is quite clear from the very first paragraph of his essay that Bowsma intends to analyze the problem on an exclusively linguistic plane. Bowsma claims to discover an ambiguity in the word "expression," and to expose confusions in the use of the word "emotion." This is possible only because Bowsma refers to the facts—namely, the fact that art both expresses (in one sense of the word) and arouses emotion, and that the emotion expressed is not the same as the emotion aroused. Without reference to these facts no verbal clarification could be achieved. It should be added that at least one reader of the essay has failed to see what contribution, what clarification is made by the writer which had not already been achieved by other aestheticians.

Yet assuming that Bowsma does clarify our use of the words "emotion" and "expression," the problem of expression in art still goes abegging, for it

[6] Or, if you prefer, "scientific" in the loose and uncontrolled sense in which some aestheticians use the term today. But the use of the term "scientific" in that loose and uncontrolled sense is itself a most unscientific use of it.

[7] *Philosophical Analysis*, ed. by Max Black (Ithaca, N. Y., Cornell University Press, 1950), pp. 341–83 and 75–101 respectively.

[8] In a review in *The Journal of Aesthetics and Art Criticism*, IX (1951), 334–37.

is not a purely linguistic problem but a substantive one It is not a question
of ambiguities in the use of the word "expression" and confusions in the
word "emotion." It is a question of a theory that can be made to stand up
under examination which will explain how, on a given meaning of the polysemic word "expression," the fact of expression actually takes place. It is
also a question of the facts and of their interrelation, to which the polysemic
word "emotion" refers. We know pretty clearly what is meant by various
kinds of people when they say that art expresses emotion The literature on
this subject is abundant. What we lack are satisfactory hypotheses about
how art arouses emotion, what it actually arouses when it is said to arouse
emotion, and how it expresses it, when it does not arouse it, or whether it
also expresses it when it arouses it, and, if it does both arouse and express
emotion at the same time, how does it accomplish it, and so forth. These are
not questions of language exclusively, but of language and of fact.[9]

In his recently published book, Morris Weitz announces that he intends
to consider certain problems of aesthetics in the analytic manner.[10] But
Weitz, like Stevenson, deals with subject matter throughout, as well as with
questions of a purely linguistic nature. Like Stevenson, Weitz is an empiricist in Munro's sense, and if there is any difference between him and other
empiricists like Prall, Pepper, Dewey, Ducasse, Munro, Alexander, and a
host of others, it can only be found in the degree of alleged concern for the
rigorous use of language Whether it is the case or not that Weitz is more
rigorous than his predecessors is not at issue here All that is being pointed
out is that between his approach and that of Bowsma there is an abyss of
difference If analysis means the sort of thing that Stevenson and Weitz do,
no one can have any quarrel with its practice; all that one would have to
query are the claims that are made for it, since neither in method nor in

----

[9] The literature on this subject is too abundant to give anything more than a small
sample of the diversity of its approach and of the way in which its problems are attacked by the various writers The problem is treated in Albert Chandler, *Beauty and
Human Nature* (New York, Century Psychology Series Appleton-Century-Crofts,
1934), R G Collingwood, *The Principles of Art* (Oxford, Oxford University Press,
1938), C J Ducasse, *The Philosophy of Art* (New York, L MacVeagh, The Dial Press,
1929), W Kohler, *Gestalt Psychology* (New York, Black and Gold Library, Liveright,
1929), S K. Langer, *Philosophy in a New Key* (Cambridge, Mass , Harvard University
Press, 1942), S C Pepper, *Aesthetic Quality, A Contextual Theory of Beauty* (New
York, Scribner, 1938) and his more recent *The Principles of Art Appreciation* (New
York, Harcourt, Brace, 1949), M G Rigg, "The Expressions of Meanings and Emotions
in Music," *Philosophic Essays in Honor of Edgar Arthur Singer, Jr.* (Philadelphia, Uni-
versity of Pennsylvania Press, London, H Milford, Oxford University Press, 1942); M.
Schoen, *The Effects of Music* (London, K Paul, Trench, Trubner, New York, Harcourt,
Brace, 1927), E Vivas, "A Note on the Emotion in Mr Dewey's Theory of Art," *The
Philosophical Review*, September 1938, his "A Natural History of the Aesthetic Transaction," *Naturalism and the Human Spirit*, ed by Y H. Krikorian (New York, Columbia
University Press, 1944); and his "The Objective Correlative of T. S Eliot," *Critiques
and Essays in Criticism, 1920–1948*, ed by R. W. Stallman (New York, Ronald Press,
1949)
[10] *Philosophy of the Arts* (Cambridge, Mass., Harvard University Press, 1950).

attitude is it different in kind from what aestheticians, particularly empiricists, have tried to do with the problems which confront them If it means
the sort of thing Bowsma does, it has not yet begun to demonstrate that it is
worth doing or even that it can be done at all.

I am not certain which of the two interpretations is given by Isenberg to
the term "analysis " In any case, his conception of the analytic task raises an
issue of great moment which it is necessary to investigate He tells us:

The best thing that philosophy can do for the art studies is to bring clarity to
those issues with which modern criticism is rife—which have arisen "naturally,"
as it were, out of recent aesthetic preoccupations For this reason [Isenberg has
decided to] avoid those ancient and well trodden grounds of the aesthetician—
The Aesthetic Object, The Nature of the Aesthetic Experience, The Nature of the
Creative Act—important as these topics are and large as is the amount of work
which remains to be done on them [11]

Since Isenberg is careful to tell us that the analytic philosopher is not
merely interested in a heap of unrelated definitions but that he seeks a
theory or system of the subject, the following criticism seems pertinent
That the aesthetician is after a system, in the sense that he cannot be satisfied with a heap of unrelated definitions and hypotheses, is, of course, to be
taken for granted What the mind seeks in science and in philosophy is systematic clarity, and it is not possible to have clarity which is not systematic
But we are not told how we can succeed in rearing a system of the subject
when we start by turning our backs on those well-trodden grounds of the
aesthetician, the aesthetic object, the nature of the aesthetic experience, and
the nature of the creative act For well trodden as these grounds are, and
yet difficult as it is to tread through them, they control whatever answers
we give to any other question we pose in the field of aesthetics It would
seem, therefore, that the result of following Isenberg's advice would be further to encourage the divisive atomization of knowledge from the devastating consequences of which we are already suffering intensely, both in the
field of knowledge and in the field of social relations It can be shown that
the solution of one problem in the field of aesthetics not merely illuminates
but determines materially the solution of the others. If this is the case, following Isenberg's analysis would merely increase the evils which he seeks
to remedy

But even if these considerations are not admissible, there is an assumption back of the analytic philosopher's advocacy of his method that requires
investigation. His conception of the function of inquiry is purely "theoretical," in the Aristotelian sense of this term. But long before it was given its
name by Baumgarten, aesthetics undertook not merely to obtain pure

[11] Op cit, p 2.

theoretical knowledge of the phenomena of art and beauty but practical
knowledge which could be used in guiding the creation of beauty and in
controlling its enjoyment. Aesthetics has always done this practical work
more or less successfully since its birth (as far as our records permit us to
discern) with Plato's discussions of several of its problems. The depth and
extent of its practical influence on Western art can be easily demonstrated,
here it is only necessary to mention the name of Aristotle to indicate how
intimate (even if often unconscious and unacknowledged) has been the
relation of theory to the practice of the artist and to the way in which his
work is accepted and used by the public. Nor is the relation a happy accident. The guidance of practice by theory is demanded by as genuine and as
imperative a human need as that which leads to the development of theoretical knowledge In spite of this, the two needs—the need for pure theory
and the need for enlightened practice—cannot easily be harmonized, and
under actual cultural conditions one frequently gains the primacy over the
other

In our day, in certain academic quarters, the theoretical tends to assume
what has been happily called "the autocracy of a dominant interest." Our
socially institutionalized schizophrenia is a potent factor in the separation
at the intellectual level of theory and practice. But even when the theoretical interest does not tend to become autocratic, the aesthetician's product usually exhibits the tensions which are the mark of his failure to balance
nicely the disparate and conflicting interests of his discipline. And yet, although the difficulties are great and although our day is not likely to listen
to anyone who recommends a prudent balance of the practical and the theoretical, it is nevertheless true that it is not wise to imperil the practical role
of aesthetics.

It is not possible or legitimate to interdict anyone who wishes to dedicate
himself to the activity to which the linguistic analyst would confine the
efforts of the aesthetician. But whatever any one man or group of men
choose to do, the practical task must be undertaken Traditionally, the discipline of aesthetics has been made up of a more or less stable compound
in which empirical inquiry, axiological speculation, and linguistic analysis
have been more or less successfully applied to the complex subject matter
of beauty, the arts, and their effects on human beings. In spite of the multiplicity of disparate problems which it has been necessary to consider, there
was good reason for keeping them together, since only in this way could a
modicum of rationality be brought to bear on criticism and education.

It is not superfluous at this point to remember that the claims of the
analytic philosopher about the superiority of his method are grounded on
pure faith, since they are not justified by the agreement which philosophical

analysis has already achieved either in aesthetics or in other fields. The philosophical analyst retorts that although the amount of disagreement may be as great as ever, the plane of disagreement is higher in the dimension of technicality, intensity, and circumspection [12] But of course the same thing exactly can be rightfully claimed for philosophizing at any period— even for that which was carried on before philosophical analysts conceived the notion of separating questions of fact from those of language The denial of this assertion is made by those who assume that, with the exception of a few philosophers like Hume and of a few pages from some philosophers like Plato, the history of Western philosophy until 1859 or some such date is nothing more than a smelly unguent of confusion and logomachy concocted by crypto-medicine men who have called themselves metaphysicians It bespeaks little knowledge of the history of aesthetics to ignore the fact that the clarification of the language of aesthetics is something that aestheticians have always worked on

It is true that the clarification achieved by one aesthetician one day is often of little use to someone else the next, while scientific advance is cumulative But the reason for this, in part at least, inheres in the nature of the discipline and seems, therefore, to constitute one of the conditions to which we must submit if we are to remain faithful to its practical function The reason is that the subject matter of aesthetics is not self-identical throughout its history like that of the physical sciences, but is in a constant state of flux, the very laws of whose change seem, so far, to have eluded the grasp of the philosopher of history. The nature which the physicist of one culture investigates is the identical nature investigated by his colleague across the border, and the nature whose laws Galileo sought is the same nature that Faraday and later Bohr and Urey pried into. But whether art is one and the same under any climate and at any time and in what sense it is one and the same—this is itself an empirical question that does not admit of a purely analytic answer.

There are complex factors of diffusion and autonomy governing the development of art in culture which militate against analytic generalization. That there must be something in common between the art of Altamira, that of ancient China, African art, and ours we may assert on analytic grounds. But what there is in common among different arts are generic traits, and the aesthetician who tries to maintain his practical orientation is not happy to go too far away from his concrete data Obviously we cannot claim in an unqualified sense that art is self-identical throughout its history, for radical changes in form, style, and expressed or imitated matter are not difficult to perceive. Again its function has varied, or has been taken to vary, from cul-

[12] *Ibid.*, p 7

ture to culture, in a way which so far has proved to be unpredictable It is this fact that George Boas emphasizes, and the fact is incontrovertible [13]

And yet it is also a fact that such objects as the paintings of Altamira, those of ancient China, and those of modern Paris and New York, widely different structurally and functionally as they may happen to be, nevertheless in some sense belong to one class The sense in which they may be said to belong to one class is one which the aesthetician needs to discover, and when he does so he takes the first step toward a systematic approach to his subject. The upshot of these considerations is that the aesthetician who studies to remain empirical must be ready to shift his language and even his concrete techniques of investigation as his concrete subject matter changes. Nor should he be surprised if his predecessors and even his contemporaries envisage their problems in different terms and from different points of view.

The domain of aesthetics is, then, the heterogeneous conglomeration of theoretical and practical questions which arise from a thinker's interest in beauty and art. It can be shown that these can be defined exhaustively in advance of any effort to answer them; but what it is desirable to emphasize here is that the student, confronted with so many diverse problems, ought not to expect to solve them in the same successful way in which the mathematician or the physicist solves his problems. His aim is not that of the positive scientist, and the demands of the unity of the method of science ride roughshod over this essential difference The aesthetician values clarity, but to the best of his ability he must try to keep his eyes on all the facts and on his complex and not easily harmonized ends.

If his results lack the quality of those achieved by the positive scientist, he can console himself by remembering what Aristotle pointed out— namely, that there are some subjects that "admit of much variety and fluctuation of opinion," and in them "we must be content .. to indicate the truth roughly and in outline," since we are "speaking about things which are only for the most part true and with premises of the same kind to reach conclusions that are no better " Aristotle goes on to say that the conclusions should be accepted in the spirit in which they are offered, "for it is the mark of an educated man to look for precision in each class of things just so far as the nature of the subject admits, it is evidently equally foolish to accept probable reasoning from a mathematician and to demand from a rhetorician scientific proofs."

The fact that the discipline of aesthetics admits of much fluctuation of opinion does not make its cultivation impossible nor does it diminish the importance of the questions it poses. That importance is fundamentally practical, and the man interested in the clarification of his commerce with art and

[13] *Wingless Pegasus A Handbook of Art Criticism* (Baltimore, Johns Hopkins Press, 1950)

in the guidance that rational activity can give it cannot wait till the sciences investigate his subject matter and the analytic philosopher gives him a perfect language with which to attack it Such perfection may be possible But until it is achieved, he has to do with what help he can get from his own imperfect tools, since he cannot declare a moratorium on the production of art or on its enjoyment or on his theoretical interest in it

As here defined, aesthetics is an empirical discipline. But a thoroughgoing investigation of its problems soon takes us beyond the border of the purely empirical into questions which may be called metaphysical, in the sense that they cannot be answered by anything short of a comprehensive hypothesis about the nature of being and its structure This has always been known by the majority of philosophers, and if it is necessary to state it today, the need arises from the fact that a truculent army of verbosophers seeks to legislate their limited interests into universal law. The aesthetician starts with the familiar quality of natural objects or artifacts which we usually call beautiful But the full elucidation of this quality does not merely force him to devise a complete system of aesthetics but forces him, if he is not, as Santayana said of James, "short winded in argument," to go beyond it into metaphysics.

IX

Natural Law and Social Order

WILLIAM A. BANNER, *Howard University*

THE problems of social ethics and of politics are the problems of social justice and social order. The general need for some ordering of life in society arises from the limitations and complications of private human effort In so far as individuals are not separately self-sufficient, they must live and work together in some community, whether or not the mutual promotion of common ends is any part of their intention. Whatever the mode of social arrangement which emerges out of this general need, there is in such an arrangement the root of political society. For every social pattern, as an instrument in one way or another of some human good, must determine the order of means with respect to ends and in this way set limits upon the activities of those who are embraced within the pattern.

Without such limits, social life falls away into anarchy and negates itself. Man is in this respect a political animal, requiring for his general welfare some working agreement concerning what individuals owe to each other in the preservation of society It is out of the difficulties of determining just what individuals do owe to each other and to what extent, that there arise the moral questions of social right and social responsibility. These difficulties become more pressing where men constitute a πόλις, or state, and the pluralistic activities of social life come more and more within the scope of a single authority

Social and political theory emerge in the interest of resolving the issues of social conflict and of stating what must be acknowledged to be the character of a just social order. This is not, as is erroneously thought by many, a mere *technical* problem of determining what is the pattern of social arrangement which has evolved or is evolving as an instrument of practical peace, and of indicating what features would make such an instrument more effective in its operation It is basically a *theoretical* problem, entailing a consideration of the nature of man and a determination of what, if anything, is really good and right, and for whom and in what respects. This is a moral question. The tendency in recent times to regard such questions as insoluble cannot be taken as a serious attempt to meet difficulties of the utmost gravity One must acknowledge that certain ends rather than others tend to be served by certain modes of activity in society.

It is important to know, therefore, whether the ends of social efforts are compatible with the interests and needs of those who are embraced within the social group These interests and needs can never be identified with the mode of social order through which they may seek expression and satisfaction If social order is an instrument of human good, it cannot at the same time be the norm of such good. A thing cannot be both means and end at the same time and in the same respect A social convention qua convention cannot, any more than a piece of mechanical apparatus, provide the criterion of its efficacy It is only in terms of some determinate relation between social means and human ends that social practice can be appraised as proper or improper, just or unjust The criterion of social justice must be anterior to social order as such

It is the doctrine of natural law which, in its history reaching into the classical world, has affirmed not only that justice is basically an ethical matter but also that human life has only one proper mode of well-being and that justice cannot be fundamentally one thing in one place and something else in another. This is the concept of a universal morality, both intelligible to, and binding upon, all people.[1] It is not of interest to consider here the great body of material which may be said to constitute the natural law tradition To say the least, the history of natural law ideas is a very long and complicated one, in which there is variation in the expressed content and sanction of the law of nature as well as in the philosophical context in which the notion of the law of nature rests. In this exposition of natural law ideas, what is regarded as fundamental in the doctrine for social ethics is the notion of universal moral claims or rights, which have their ground in the basic needs and tendencies common to human life in general and in the universal duties which promote the exercise of these rights

A basic tendency to satisfy a need is the foundation of a moral demand upon the individual for the realization of a natural end, and upon society inasmuch as the end cannot be achieved through solitary effort. The separate basic tendencies are chiefly the inclinations to the satisfaction of hunger and other physical appetites, the inclinations of curiosity and inventiveness, and the inclinations of sociability. These tendencies may be thought of as rooting in a central entelechy Formal determination as a basic ten-

---

[1] See Francisco Suárez, *De legibus ac Deo legislatore,* trans by Gwladys L Wilhams, Ammi Brown, and John Waldron, with revisions by Henry Davis (Oxford, Clarendon Press, 1944), Vol II, Bk II, Chap 19, 9 "   . the human race, into howsoever many different peoples and kingdoms it may be divided, always preserves a certain unity, not only in species, but also a moral and political unity [as it were], enjoined by the natural precept of mutual love and mercy, a precept which applies to all, even to strangers of every nation."

dency is a certain predisposition to utilize certain goods in the development and maintenance of life activity A basic tendency is one which embraces certain interests and activities which in their general character are essential to a complete life. The perfection of a basic tendency is always some good or end to be realized in the individual and the nature of the good or end is always indicated in the general pattern of activity followed as a mode of striving on the part of the individual.

Within a basic tendency many specific inclinations are possible, the fulfillment of which would yield varying degrees of perfection. In human striving, rational intelligence enters not merely as an aspect of perfectible activity but also as an instrument of total well-being, providing knowledge of levels of satisfaction and of the kinds of objects which are likely to yield the respective levels A basic tendency can only be considered to be fulfilled in the highest mode of perfection possible for the individual This is to say, the inclination to know can never be properly the inclination to merely partial or inadequate enlightenment, any more than the tendency to the satisfaction of hunger may be thought of as the tendency to the partial or improper satisfaction of this appetite. Perfection is properly bound up with the pursuit of any basic good.

The relation obtaining between basic need and the perfection of capacity is the foundation of moral right and moral obligation. A moral or natural right is a proper claim of the individual upon a natural end or perfection, while a moral or natural obligation is but the reflection of this claim in rationally prescribed means to the natural end A natural right is a moral quality pertaining to the individual, existing independently of any social arrangement and therefore anterior to the authority of custom or legal enactment.[2] In the context of society, natural rights are the proper demands of individuals upon the agencies of the group, and natural duties stand as the proper obligations of the individual to the maintenance of these agencies. Natural rights clearly entail natural duties, and one cannot recognize or stress the one without the other Natural rights and natural duties constitute in this way the basic framework of social order Inasmuch as they spring from the nature of man and not from social convention, these rights and duties must be regarded as no less certain and immutable than human nature itself.[3]

The notion of a common perfection which men in society may pursue together entails a basic uniformity in human life underlying human variation and diversity The emphasis on human variation has its origin, in modern times at least, in the somewhat romantic conception of nature as "a mysteri-

[2] See Hugo Grotius, *De jure belli ac pacis*, trans. by Francis W. Kelsey (Oxford, Clarendon Press, 1925), Vol II, Bk I, Chap I, iv.

[3] See *ibid*, *Prolegomena* 9, 39; Bk I, Chap. I, x, 5.

ous, all enveloping complex in which the phenomena of growth and variety are the most striking "[4] This conception was fostered by the growth in the eighteenth century of a body of concrete descriptive information which was loosely called "natural history" In Georges Buffon, for example, the great variety of nature is opposed to the idea of nature as law and invariant form. One is naturally led, he argued, to imagine order and uniformity in everything, even in the most diverse objects But this order and uniformity is less in nature than in the minds of those who investigate nature under false assumptions In this way one introduces regularity "where only variety reigns, and order in things where only confusion is perceived "[5] Buffon's conception is clearly opposed to any idea of structure in nature. "In nature there are neither classes or genera, all are mere independent individuals "[6]

This emphasis in Buffon, which is found also in Herder, continued with many theorists in the nineteenth century. The rising biological and social sciences brought into greater currency ideas of growth, development, adaptation, and variation. The evidences of human variation and diversity were seen to crowd out evidences supporting any contention concerning the essential similarity of human beings and to undermine the alleged natural basis for declarations of universal human rights It was Joseph de Maistre who declared, in words representative of a somewhat widespread opinion, "I have seen, in my time, Frenchmen, Italians, Russians, etc., . . . but as for Man, I declare I have never met him in my life, if he exists, it is without my knowledge "[7]

What is generally ignored where emphasis is placed upon human diversity is that variation in accidental features is not incompatible with uniformity in essential characteristics. In descriptive study, there is always the danger that observable diversity will be taken as basically discrete Variation, however, always entails some common form, the several manifestations of which vary in certain accidental or particular ways. The completely discrete thing, as unique, is clearly not a variation. The things which individual human beings have in common are indicated in all of the aspects in which they may be found to differ comparatively. These common features constitute the basis of the conception of human nature. Without such a conception, there can be no science of human life The real issues involved in the emphasis on variation and diversity are the general questions

[4] Laurence Stapleton, *Justice and World Society* (Chapel Hill, N. C., University of North Carolina Press, 1944), p. 50.
[5] *De la manière d'étudier et de traiter l'histoire naturelle* (Paris, De l'Imprimerie Royale, 1750), pp 9-10.
[6] *Natural History, General and Particular,* trans by William Smellie (London, A Strahan, 1885), II, 361
[7] Joseph de Maistre, *Considerations sur la France, Oeuvres* (l'édition de 1875), I, 68, quoted in Carl Becker, *The Declaration of Independence* (New York, Harcourt, Brace, 1922), p. 279

lying between realism, conceptualism, and nominalism. No attempt can be made here to consider these general issues bound up with a historic philosophic problem. It must be sufficient to state simply that the problem is basically logical and metaphysical [8] Where it is held or implied that only discrete particulars exist outside of the mind, knowledge or science as communicable apprehension is impossible. Communicable knowledge can be only of the particular qua universal.

Natural law as a scheme of social order is both descriptive and prescriptive in character. Natural law is descriptive in so far as it rests upon general modes of behavior which, however variable, are discoverable in the life of the individual and in the social processes to which individuals are committed. It is the persistence of these modes of behavior, particularly through the functions of the material, noetic, and political arts, which indicates a continuity of pattern in human need. This is not to say that every mode of persisting behavior is indicative of a proper condition of human life The prevalence of slavery in ancient cultures cannot be said to have evinced any natural right of slaveholders with respect to slaveholding But it is clear that behind even slavery there is the basic need for material goods as supplied through the productive arts, with respect to the satisfaction of which need slavery is an improper social instrument. The persistence of basic activities is independent of specific social institutions and must be viewed in relation to basic need rather than to merely contingent and, in the case of slavery, morally inadequate social forms. In its broadest features, social history exhibits a pattern of natural and universal good.[9]

Natural law is prescriptive in that it designates the perfection of life in all persons as the proper end of social order, whatever may be the actual conditions and arrangements obtaining at a time in a given society This means that the members of a society must actively choose the promotion of excellence for themselves and for the others of the group, in opposition to the indulgence of peripheral and inimical interests and in opposition to the continuance of institutional forms which tend to further such interests In any enterprise, there is a range of possibility with respect to the quality of

[8] See Morris R Cohen, "The Place of Logic in the Law," *Harvard Law Review*, XXIX, 628 "It may seem a bold and reckless statement to assert that an adequate discussion of cases like *Berry* v. *Donovan*, *Adair* v. *United States*, or *Commonwealth* v *Boston and Maine R*, involves the whole mediaeval controversy over the reality of universals And yet, the confident assertion of immutable principles of justice inhering in the very idea of free government made by the writers of these decisions, and the equally confident assertion of their critics that there are no such principles, show how impossible it is to keep out of metaphysics."

[9] This is not strictly the notion of *jus gentium* or the law of nations. Historically, *jus gentium* embraced particular practices and regulations, such as slavery, actually common to existing societies, as for example the Roman *jus gentium* grew out of the institutional relations and commercial transactions of the ancient world See Max Beer, *A History of British Socialism* (London, G. Bell and Sons, 1919-20), I, 9

the good which is sought and the number of individuals who are to have access to what is yielded For this reason, specific social arrangements are never necessary in the sense that their alteration is not conceivable Accordingly, social order as such is never normative The social norm, as the best of possible arrangements, cannot be identified with what is merely the best possible order under certain restricting conditions

The law of nature as the social norm is never represented in the regulations and practices obtaining in a given society unless these regulations and practices permit the proper access of all persons to the best things pertaining to a complete life Natural law, in prescribing the character which society should have in order to be just, brings to bear in practical matters the guidance of reason in the impartial ordering and distribution of means to ends This primacy of the theoretical in practical matters provides an objective basis for the evaluation of institutional structures having their sanction or support, if not their origin, in custom and tradition It was on this ground that Suárez in the seventeenth century rejected the view which credited *jus gentium* with intrinsic necessity, arguing that this body of common practice arose more from unconscious usage than from conscious reasoning [10]

It may be objected that the authority of a moral law lacks the sanctions necessary to make it actually binding as a rule and guide of social behavior This objection has been raised in one form or another by those, such as Jeremy Bentham, who have thought of law primarily in terms of *positive law,* that is, law commanded or ordered by a power possessing the means adequate to promote obedience. Bentham contended that right abstracted from the power or means to protect and promote it is a nonentity, a mere philosophical fiction Right must be the child of positive law.[11] To this objection it must be said that the ultimate sanction of any mode of human action is the awareness of the necessity or importance of some proper end to which the action is related as means. This is the sanction of reason following upon the sanction of nature.

Sanctions are imposed on a rational being whenever an object or end is seen to be good and its privation to entail the privation of good All of the sanctions of legal prescription ultimately depend for effectiveness on the sanction of reason in accordance with nature Where this sanction is lacking, the observance of rules and laws becomes perfunctory and empty, and

---

[10] See Suárez, *op cit*, Chap 14, 16· "Liberty rather than slavery is a precept of the natural law. Nature has made men free in a positive sense, so to speak, with an intrinsic right to liberty whereas it has not made them slaves in this positive sense, properly speaking."

[11] *Theory of Legislation* (Boston, Weeks, Jordan, 1840), pp 105 ff. Also, *Anarchical Fallacies* in *Select Extracts from the Works of Bentham,* ed by J H Burton (Edinburgh, W Tait, 1843), p 67.

enforcement is rendered difficult. The absence of the power or means to compel the acknowledgment of a right does not invalidate such a right any more than the presence of power is sufficient to establish the propriety of any given demand. The nature of authority as the rational exercise of power makes all legal sanctions merely derivative. Where legal sanctions are lacking or ineffectual, a right as *natural* exists nonetheless and enjoys for its promotion the primary sanctions of reason, upon which any and all secondary or legal sanctions must rest.

It is only in a scheme of common rights and common duties that one finds a realistic basis for social order It is patent, in spite of the diversity of individual predilection, that much of human existence revolves upon common enterprise It is highly improbable that persisting common activity is a matter merely of coincidence or of the prolonged acquiescence of some to the stronger demands and pressures of others In the economy of time and effort, it is unlikely that free men would employ their talents and labors together for ends which could not be of genuine common value The common efforts of free individuals imply a certain unanimity of purpose It is in the articulation of the intention of such common effort that the notion of the common good emerges as a social concept.

The intention of conscious common enterprise must always be some common good which is the proper end of each individual committed to its promotion. Where the ends of co-operative efforts are not genuinely common ends, social organization becomes the imposition of the wills of the clever or strong upon those less able to advance their own particular interests. Without the recognition of universal objective human good, one is left with a multiplicity of private interests and the competition among such interests, in which competition the more clever and the more powerful must be acknowledged to be the more respectable. And while this is neither an impossible nor an unheard of situation, it is unlikely that one would think of such as a just and stable order of social life In the articulation of the common enterprise of free men, one finds the indication of the nature of society as a unity of purpose based upon the common good as a final cause. This is social order based upon rights and duties which bind men in a common aspiration.

On this view, society is clearly not a loose aggregate of individuals, in an accidental unity, really independent of each other and competing fiercely with each other for the objects of their private interests. This latter view was expressed in the liberal thought of the nineteenth century and pictured the individual in his pure liberties constantly menaced by the encroachments of social authority [12] That this is a distorted account of human exist-

[12] See F J C Hearnshaw, *A Survey of Socialism* (London, Macmillan, 1928), pp. 373–80.

ence is seen upon the consideration of the limitations of individualism. If the life of the individual is not conceivable apart from the group, it is a mistake to consider individual liberties apart from social commitments and responsibilities It is erroneous, therefore, to talk of social organization in general as a menace to liberty.

It is only where social authority is misused as an instrument of oppression that human liberty is really destroyed in society Rational social order, on the other hand, is the ground of the only genuine liberty, namely, the liberty to realize the potentialities of one's nature without the hindrances of solitary effort or hostile agency. In such an order, the rights of others must be equal with one's own, and one's duties must be commensurate with his talents In a very real sense individuals as rational beings impose social duties upon themselves in accordance with what is recognized to be the common good, which is realizable only through the proper exercise of functions in society. On this moral level, there can be no real conflict between liberty and responsibility.

In being distinguished from the idea of society as an accidental unity, our theory must be distinguished also from the notion of society as a substantial unity above and beyond the individuals who comprise it. In F. H. Bradley's essay "My Station and Its Duties," society, as the moral organism, is the absolute, apart from which the individual cannot find the function which makes him himself.[13] In this realized moral ideal, one finds self-realization, duty, and happiness in one The universal substance speaks its language in the usages and laws of the people In this system, "partly by its law and institutions and still more by its spirit," there is given the life which one lives and ought to live. The individual as moral and social merely wills to particularize the moral absolute in his given station. The individual in his station has the assurance of "finding in existing reality nothing but himself." The individual, moreover, signifies his gratitude for his social being in supporting in and through his station the social system in which he finds himself. In Bradley's words, ". . . if you could be as good as your world, you would be better than most likely you are; . . . to wish to be better than the world is to be already on the threshold of immorality."[14]

Whatever may be said of the idea of duty and service in Bradley's conception of society, it is duty which is stressed, apart from corresponding right or privilege. In Bradley's scheme the individual and his good are lost through inclusion in the being of the moral absolute. What must be denied here is that society is a *substantial* thing apart from the individuals who comprise it There is no social or political good over and above all individuals to which their particular good must be permanently subordinated or

13 *Ethical Studies* (London, H. S. King, 1876), p. 147.
14 *Ibid.*, p. 180.

sacrificed Nor is the moral end aristocratic in the sense that human good cannot be hoped to be realized in and for many individuals who must nevertheless contribute to its realization in and for others Suprapersonal and aristocratic ends become a snare for the members of society at large. The end of social effort is really indicated by human nature itself It is never simply the will of society. The test of any social program is the extent to which it promotes the well-being of each member of the social group.

The basic rights of men in society fall under three categories—material, noetic, and political [15] The material rights embrace the claims to life itself and security of person and to the material means necessary for health and physical comfort. The noetic rights include the several claims to the enlargement and perfection of the rational faculties through general education, to the cultivation of intellectual pursuits and related interests through freedom of association and freedom of academic discussion, and to the freedom of contemplation in religious worship. The political rights are the several claims to participation in rational social control as a citizen. The essence of political right, negatively stated, is the claim to freedom from all restraint except that which is rationally imposed. This involves not only the right to vote but also the right to discuss freely and to be informed reliably concerning the issues which are bound up with the choices which voters must make, and the right to a "fair and public hearing" in any grievance in which the individual is involved, whether as plaintiff or defendant These natural rights entail corresponding natural duties, and these are, accordingly, duties to human material welfare, to human enlightenment and cultural expression, and to the preservation of the best political practice in the promulgation and administration of just law.

The distinction has often been made between civil and political rights, the former being the primary natural rights of the individual which are anterior to political society, and the latter the secondary rights which are determined by, and depend upon, political society. On this distinction, civil rights in society are human privileges which are inalienable by any decree and are, negatively, the liberties which set limits upon the extent of any social authority. Political rights, on the other hand, are alienable by the sovereign power acting through the established processes by which these rights were created This distinction between civil and political rights

[15] There have been many detailed formulations of human rights in recent times, not to mention the classical statements of the eighteenth century Most of these statements of rights bear a significant similarity to each other See *Universal Declaration of Human Rights,* as passed and proclaimed by the General Assembly of the United Nations on the tenth day of December 1948 (United Nations Department of Public Information, 1948). The thirty-nine rights mentioned in this world declaration readily fall into the three major categories—material, noetic, and political

rests to a large extent upon the more or less mythical notion that autonomous, prepolitical individuals enter into political agreement and in so doing alienate some part of their original prerogatives. As expressed by Rousseau: "Each man alienates by the social compact only such part of his powers, goods and liberties as it is important for the community to control, but it must be granted that the Sovereign [the majority] is the sole judge of what is important."[16]

Any such recognition of the distinction between natural and political right adds up to an abandonment of the idea of natural right in favor of mere political right It is really the sovereign power which determines which rights are inalienable and which are not. If, however, there are rights which are morally anterior to political society, they cannot be alienated under political society. Social authority may simply recognize, explicate, and foster rights the adequate exercise of which makes social authority necessary. In the words of Thomas Paine, ". . [man] did not enter into society to become worse than he was before, nor to have fewer rights than he had before, but to have these rights better served."[17]

Inasmuch as a natural right is a moral claim upon a good which is essential to a complete life, not every demand of the individual or of groups of individuals may be insisted upon as legitimate. In respecting the distinction between real and apparent good, certain interests must be rejected as in themselves inimical to the well-being of the individual and of the members of society at large The individual can reasonably demand in society only that which is proper from the point of view of what is understood concerning human good as a whole. Natural right is not, then, a felicitous designation for the immoderate interests of the individual or the partisan interests of a particular class or clique in society. Natural right designates that sort of demand which is recognizable as essential to any and every human life This is the only sort of demand with respect to which it is reasonable for men to commit their resources Only in this universality can natural right be distinguished from fictitious right. It is the danger of being ensnared by merely fictitious right which has led many political and legal theorists to oppose as unsound all doctrines of natural and inalienable rights [18]

With respect to the further question of the extent of the exercise of a natural right, it may be said that this also must be viewed under the aspect of universality The exercise of natural right by any individual or group of individuals must be compatible with the opportunity for the exercise of the same by all others. The individual cannot count for more than one. This

16 *Social Contract* (London, J M Dent and Sons, 1932), Bk II, Chap 4, p. 27.
17 *The Rights of Man* (New York, Peter Eckler, 1919), Part I, p. 44.
18 See Bentham, *Anarchical Fallacies, op cit.*, Chap. 2.

does not mean that there will not be variations in the manner and degree in which rights actually are exercised by individuals, depending upon precise capabilities and predilections What is meant is that the limits set by society upon the exercise of a right by an individual cannot be other than those imposed by the facilities which may be made available impartially to all up to the limit of capacity and use. There can be no inequalities, in the degree of the exercise of natural rights, that are established by social policy.

The scheme of natural rights and natural duties, sustaining the proper good of human life in general, constitutes the invariant pattern of all just social and political practice. This is the pattern of natural law or natural justice which, in contrast to mere conventional justice, ". . everywhere has the same force and does not exist by people's thinking this or that."[19] Natural law is the essential element, the inner invariant content of all just social policy. In all matters, therefore, where governance is possible, natural law is the foundation of right and duty, even against existing enactment and prevailing custom

It may be objected, as indeed it has been by many critics of natural law ideas, that the notion of an immutable standard of justice is absurd in the face of constantly changing conditions in society.[20] There is the question, of course, of just what must be regarded as changing in social existence. Those who would contend that basic rights and duties themselves change would seem to ignore or disallow the persisting features in human experience Such a nominalistic position would, in short, preclude any thoroughgoing account or estimate of social change itself. Change, it seems, is unintelligible apart from recognizable elements of permanence. If, on the other hand, all that is alleged is that the modes of social existence change in time and place in accordance with the introduction of artifacts and the modification of the methods of the arts, this is not incompatible with the idea of natural justice Natural law as such is not a system of positive law or positive practice General rules must embrace specifications in order to be employed as a system of law or practice in the governance of a particular group Because of the variety and diversity in social circumstances, general rules cannot be applied to all situations in the same way While principles

[19] Aristotle, *Nicomachean Ethics*, trans. by W. D Ross (Oxford, Clarendon Press, 1925), 1134b 18–20

[20] See Benedetto Croce, *The Rights of Man and the Present Historical Situation*, in *Human Rights*, ed by UNESCO (New York, Columbia University Press, 1949), p 93 "Declarations of rights (of the *natural* and *inalienable* rights of man, to quote the French Declaration of 1789) are all based upon a theory which criticism on many sides has succeeded in destroying namely, the theory of natural right, which had its own particular grounds during the Sixteenth, Seventeenth and Eighteenth Centuries, but which has become philosophically and historically quite untenable . . The rights of *man in history*   are not eternal claims but simply historical facts, manifestations of the needs of such and such an age and an attempt to satisfy these needs."

remain the same, contingent matters of detail must vary in accordance with the exigencies of time and place.[21]

Contingent matters involve contingent instrumentalities as means to ends A means is contingent when the end of which it is a means may be realized in some other way Freedom of choice in contingent matters is ultimately freedom from the bondage of stereotype in social practice. It provides the basis for rationally guided social change That which is adequate as a means to human good in one society may be inadequate as a means in another society or in the same society under changed conditions. Natural law requires a variable content in positive law and positive practice, through which the immutable is made applicable to changing conditions. This variable content, however, must always be subordinate to the invariable element and cannot contradict this element, whatever the exigencies, without losing its character as just. It is not conceivable that any institutional practice *qua* agency of human good would have one aim and function for one group and a different aim and function for another group, whatever the variations in social circumstances

Considering some aspects of social and political history, there are certain rights and duties which may appear to have chiefly a historical ground and a historical validity Thus one may think of the historical uniqueness and appropriateness, for example, of the "religious rights" of the Reformation, of the "property rights" of modern commercial and industrial enterprise, and of the new "rights of labor" to organize and bargain collectively. And it may be argued that the structure of a legal code must reflect such rights as they in turn reflect the social and political pressures of the time In an atmosphere of extensive group and class pressure, as in the contemporary world, one may also contend that rights are nothing more than the alleged propriety of particular interests and that there is no conceivable demand which may not eventually work its way onto the political scene as a natural right. The notion of right becomes, then, nothing more than a convenient social and political weapon, creating in a complex society an almost insoluble confusion of partisan interests and pressures

To this it must be said that a natural right is basically a universal moral demand and only secondarily a historic social and political phenomenon As a moral claim, a natural right is the proper ground for social and political protest, but it cannot be thought of as deriving its validity from protest and pressure. Freedom of conscience as a natural right cannot be a product

---

[21] See Suárez, *op cit*, Bk II, Chap. 12, 9 "For the natural law discerns the mutability in the subject-matter itself, and adopts its own precepts to this mutability, prescribing in regard to such subject-matter a certain sort of conduct for one condition, and another sort of conduct for another condition, so that the law itself remains at all times unchanged, although, according to our manner of speaking and by an extrinsic attribution, it would seem, after a fashion, to undergo change."

merely of struggles of the Reformation, nor can the rights demanded by
laborers, if they are genuine, represent claims peculiar to a social and economic class at a particular stage in modern social evolution It is true that it
is out of certain inequities of prevailing social practice that social conflicts
arise, bringing to the fore demands and counterdemands which are readily
identified with classes and cliques already existing within a given society.
A basic human right, however, is independent of the fortunes of social conflict and of the support or opposition of particular-interest groups. The natural rights to adequate personal property for material comfort, to education, and to religious freedom are simply the rights of the individual, whatever his historical and social predicament.

Since the early decades of the nineteenth century there has arisen, from
many sides, a vigorous reaction against the philosophy of natural right.
Many theorists have attacked the notion of natural justice as at best an
egregious fiction and at worst, as for Bentham, a defiance of reason which
renders all government impossible. The rational individualism of the
eighteenth century, with which natural law philosophy was identified in the
mind of its critics, was condemned as naive and anarchical. To the notion
of society as a deliberate order deriving its institutions from the conscious
determinations of its rational members, there was opposed the conception
of social existence as a product chiefly of irrational or unconscious forces
such as racial character, custom, and tradition More and more theorists
were disposed to regard prevailing institutions as purely historical and
cultural phenomena requiring no further validation than that contained in
their historical necessity and cultural uniqueness. The historian's and sociologist's contention that law is a cultural, rather than a moral, phenomenon
paralleled the legal scientist's view, emerging largely out of Bentham's opposition to natural law ideas, that law is a legal rather than a moral matter.
Many of these emphases and influences are recognizable, in a somewhat
different mode, in the legal formalism of more recent times.

The significant alternatives to the notion of natural justice may be
brought together under two heads—legal positivism and legal formalism.
Legal positivism is represented chiefly in the analytical and historical
schools of jurisprudence [22] Analytical jurisprudence derives philosophically
from the tradition of Hobbes, Bentham, and Austin John Austin's views on
the principles of law agree essentially with those of Hobbes and Bentham,
to both of whom he owes a great deal [23] For Austin, the matter of jurisprudence is simply and strictly positive law, which is law set by a sovereign
power to members of a political society The notion of a law of nature is an

[22] See Roscoe Pound, "The Scope and Purpose of Sociological Jurisprudence," *Harvard Law Review*, XXIV, 591–604.
[23] *The Province of Jurisprudence Determined* (London, J Murray, 1861).

isolated absurdity, resting upon the supposition of a moral instinct or a "natural or a universal and practical reason" The principle of utility is, rather, the only index to the laws of nature if such may be presumed to exist All positive rules, particular as well as general or universal, which are regarded as beneficial may also be regarded as natural.[24]

The positivism of historical jurisprudence owes its beginnings to the influences of the historical school, which had been founded upon the work of Friedrich von Savigny[25] and Sir Henry Maine[26] and upon the earlier work of Giambattista Vico [27] Historicism, as a movement in nineteenth-century thought, laid stress upon the historical or cultural situation as the only index to the validity of social practice Whatever obtains historically—customs, traditions, laws, social institutions, and so forth—is right. The only law of nature is the process of history and the social practices which emerge out of the necessity of social forces. Historicism reduces justice to discrete standards which are as autonomous as the cultural situations in which they apply

Legal positivism, in narrowing the scope of jurisprudence to prevailing positive law or custom, has the advantage of considering law as it is apart from any speculation about what law ought to be. The legal positivist is the technical legal scientist, treating of law as historical, sociological, or political fact. Legal positivism, however, provides no adequate basis for the determination of what is just law With respect to questions concerning the rightness of law or custom, the legal positivist must either ignore such questions as irrelevant to his scientific interests or simply contend that existing law is *ipso facto* just law. Neither of these alternatives is really tenable

On the one hand, law and custom as such ordain certain acts as right and forbid others as wrong Questions of value cannot be separated from these matters, in spite of all attempts to make such a separation On the other hand, it is highly improbable that members of a given society receive and accept as just whatever is ordained or forbidden by the state [28] Authority is more than the exercise of power. It is rather the justifiable exercise of power, which entails that there is a law or right which ought to be. Law orders certain behavior as means with respect to ends These ends must be plausible to those who fall within the scope of the governance of law Concrete

---

[24] The positivist doctrines of Bentham and Austin received additional formulations in the nineteenth century in the writings of the German jurists, Karl Frederick von Gerber, Paul Laband, and Georg Jellinek. In the case of Jellinek, however, ethical concepts were admitted into his "general political theory."

[25] *The History of Roman Law during the Middle Ages,* trans. by E. Cathcart (Edinburgh, A Black, 1829).

[26] *Ancient Law* (London, J. M. Dent and Sons, 1931)

[27] *La scienza nuova,* trans. into French by Jules Michelet (Brussels, A Whalen, 1835).

[28] See W. D. Ross, *The Right and the Good* (Oxford, Clarendon Press, 1930), p. 12.

matters cannot be regarded as constituting the whole content of law Law cannot be simply what is ordained or forbidden by the group, unless government is to be thought of as the systematic operation of force On such a view, however, it is clear that there can be no stable social order.

Legal formalism represents an alternative to natural law ideas which is no less unsatisfactory than legal positivism Legal formalism is the Kantian position which in recent times has been restated essentially in the work of Rudolf Stammler.[29] The error of traditional natural law philosophy, on Stammler's estimate, rests in the claim of absolute validity for material content as well as for the method by which this content is worked up.[30] For Stammler, there are no legal rules whose content is absolutely valid The only content of law is the specific material which has to do with the regulation of human life, which material is always empirical and subject to change.

While there is the need for a standard of legal regulation in order to conceive purposes from a unitary standpoint, it is a mistake, according to Stammler, to bring in the nature of man in order to determine this standard. There are no universal characteristics of human nature which can be known as such and in terms of which human good may be considered as a universal end There are accordingly no innate rights of the individual which he brings with him as a part of his history Rights are really derived from law. The limits upon the use of power must be obtained from the idea of a "legally ordered life in general." The idea or concept of law is the formal unity of purpose as the necessary condition for the organized social life of man All positive law must be regarded as an attempt to be just law. The just law is, for Stammler, the law that is consistent with the purpose of all law. It is free from all contradiction. Natural law, for Stammler, embraces purely formal concepts which are merely modes of thinking implied in all legal matters as such

It is difficult to see in what way Stammler's "natural law with a variable content" is an improvement upon the traditional philosophy of natural right The traditional doctrine is clearly the conception of a natural law with a variable content It is true that many modern representatives of natural law ideas, such as Samuel Pufendorf,[31] made the error of attempting to extract from moral principles ideal codes in which contingent matters were set up as absolutely valid and unchangeable It is also true that many writers on natural law philosophy have at times identified the law of nature with the positive law common to several nations (*jus gentium*) In

---

[29] *The Theory of Just Law*, trans by Isaac Husik (New York, Macmillan, 1925).

[30] *Ibid*, p 91

[31] *On the Law of Nature and Nations*, trans. by C H and W A Oldfather (Oxford, Clarendon Press, 1934).

his effort to correct such abuses without adopting the position of legal positivism, Stammler attempted a purely formal derivation of the concept of right The result is a greatly impoverished natural law consisting, in the purely formal elements, of universality and noncontradiction, which make a positive rule just.

In his theory of justice, Stammler is concerned with the form of law only Just law is positive law, the content of which has certain formal qualities; it is law which harmonizes in its content with its fundamental idea. Natural law is, in other words, a principle of reciprocal freedom In emphasizing the purely formal characteristics of this principle, Stammler overlooks the possibility that a standard of right may have an invariant content of its own. Purely logical or formal consistency in the structure of legislation hardly satisfies as such the requirements of a social ideal of respect for humanity. If individuals are, as Stammler holds, ends in themselves, it would seem that they are such in virtue of rights which are anterior to law and not derived from law Stammler really confuses, in his formalism, the character of law as just with the character of law as internally consistent This is a very weakened sense of justice which leaves the moral distinction between just and unjust law largely undetermined.

The revival of the discussion of natural law ideas, of which the work of Stammler was a part, was an attempt to provide an answer to legal positivism through the admission of ethical concepts into general political and legal theory [32] For the most part the older notion of natural right was ignored or rejected, with the rather general insistence that all judgments concerning human nature are of relative and comparative universality only [83] In this, these theorists have not been far removed from the positivism which they sought to correct.

There is the firm conviction in many places now that human good must be thought of in universal terms and planned for on a universal scale. Recent formulations of human rights[34] have proposed to set forth the nature of the common good and of the responsibility of organized social effort to promote this good Such statements have been set in universal terms as applying to all individuals regardless of existing physical, social, and cultural differences

The conception of universal human good cannot be reconciled with any form of nominalism or relativism. It is radically incompatible with any

[32] See Charles G Haines, *The Revival of Natural Law Concepts* (Cambridge, Mass, Harvard University Press, 1930)

[83] See Joseph Charmont, *La renaissance du droit naturel* (2nd ed, Paris, E Duchemin, L Chauny, et L Quinsac, 1927), pp. 221–22

[34] See *The Atlantic Charter*, August 1941, *The Report of the National Resources Planning Board*, March 1943, *The Universal Declaration of Human Rights*, General Assembly of the United Nations, December 1948

idealistic contention that consciousness is a productive activity. What is implied is that there are persistent structural and tendential features in human existence which are capable of being known as they are and that the recognition of these features is fundamental to any account of human nature and any consideration of human good. In the premise that human beings everywhere have a right to the same general goods of life, one has the only foundation for an alternative to that social life in which basic need is subordinated to peripheral interest and in which some individuals are required to contribute their major efforts in providing goods whose possession and use they do not share. Social order is properly an instrument of general human well-being, however else it may be conceived To the extent that this end is determinable as a common good, one has the foundation for co-operation and constraint and for genuine community and peace.

X

Reason and Practice

JOHN LADD, *Brown University*

Most discussions of the relation of reason and practice have been unsuccessful because they have been founded upon the presupposition that all reasoning is a cognitive process On this assumption practical reason is merely cognition applied to practice. I shall try to show that the reduction of all reasoning to cognition has made it impossible to explain some of the peculiar characteristics of practical reasoning, and that these characteristics require that it be considered as *sui generis* The reason involved in practice has a peculiar "logic" of its own which is not reducible to the logic which regulates "theoretical inquiry" or cognition. In other words, reasoning in ethical contexts is quite different from reasoning in cognition, and there is a "logic of practical reasoning" which is quite different from the ordinary logic of deduction and induction. If it be considered the achievement of Hume to have shown that inductive reasoning cannot be reduced to deductive reasoning, this paper will show analogously that practical reasoning can be reduced to neither deduction nor induction This is by no means a new discovery, since it was clearly recognized by Aristotle, but it is something that seems to have been forgotten in the excessive intellectualism of modern ethics.

Anti-intellectualism, or "non-cognitivism," in ethics has recently scored great successes, and many of these are justified.[1] However, this new movement, being a reaction against the approach to ethical discourse through cognition, has gone to the opposite extreme of denying that reasoning can be in any sense necessarily involved in ethical contexts The identification of reason with cognition has resulted in the identification of anticognitivism with irrationalism I shall attempt to show that if practical reasoning be recognized to be *sui generis*, it will be possible to make a place for practical reasoning and at the same time to reject ethical cognitions as its basis.

I might add incidentally that this peculiar ethical process need not be

---

[1] See C L. Stevenson, *Ethics and Language* (New Haven, Conn., Yale University Press, London, H Milford, Oxford University Press, 1944), *passim* This paper, although critical of Stevenson, owes a great deal to the stimulus of the emotivist theory.

called "reasoning" if the reader objects to this term because of a "cognitional" bias Other words would do just as well, namely, "thinking," "calculating," "deliberating," and so forth But this is the word employed since the time of the ancients in ethics as well as epistemology, and hence it seems to be the most fitting one to use.

I shall designate by the term "ethical cognitivism"[2] the view that practical reasoning is merely reasoning employed in the acquisition of ethical knowledge[3] and that this process is differentiated from other employments of reason, such as science or metaphysics, only by a difference of subject matter The ethical cognitivist assumes that there is no essential difference of method or of canons between practical and theoretical reasoning

In this paper I shall be mainly concerned with showing the inadequacies of ethical cognitivism and so will be able only to hint at some of the more positive characteristics of practical reason. I shall begin with a general discussion of ethical cognitivism and the view which I consider to be correct, which I shall label "practicalism." Then I shall discuss some more specific forms of ethical cognitivism and shall try to show that their plausibility is due to the fact that there are important analogies between practical and cognitive reasoning

To begin with, let us look at some of the important differences between cognitive reasoning and practical reasoning The first difference that strikes us is that their "outcomes" are different. Thus cognitive reasoning, for instance in the sciences, eventuates in assertion or belief, that is, something that is true or false, in Peirce's words, it aims at the "fixation of belief," and without this it may be considered to be unsuccessful Practical reasoning, on the other hand, ends in action, choice, or attitude, and if it does not produce one of these, it has failed. Moral reasoning that results only in a cognitive response is futile.[4] In the social context this has been expressed by Stevenson as the contrast of agreement in belief and agreement in attitude. To agree in principle that "x is my duty" and to feel no impulsion whatsoever to do x is absurd, whereas to agree that "x is a poison" does not imply any specific attitude toward or against x

The distinction between attitude and belief has been subjected to much criticism recently First, I might remark that I intend to use the word "attitude" for the whole array of psychological phenomena that include actions, choices, likes, feelings, interests, and so forth, and which are characterized

---

[2] I am indebted to W. K Frankena for the expressions "cognitivism" and "non-cognitivism " See his "Moral Philosophy at Mid-Century," *The Philosophical Review*, January 1951.

[3] "The direct object of Ethics is knowledge not practice " G E Moore, *Principia Ethica* (New York, Cambridge University Press, 1903), p 20

[4] See Stevenson, "The Nature of Ethical Disagreement," in Herbert Feigl and Wilfrid Sellars, *Readings in Philosophical Analysis* (New York, Century Philosophy Series, Appleton-Century-Crofts, 1949).

by being *for* or *against,* that is, "selection" and "rejection "[5] Secondly, it has frequently been suggested that belief is merely a readiness to act, and hence is itself an attitude I shall not argue with this pragmatic notion of belief, since if it be accepted, everything that I say about "practical reasoning" will hold a fortiori, that is, cognitivism in general being invalid, it will follow that ethical cognitivism must be so also However, even a pragmatist has to distinguish a cognitive belief which is a general readiness to act and which is indeterminate as to specific actions, from an ethical attitude which is a specific readiness to act (or feel) or may even be that action or feeling itself. (See note above) Thus, the belief that x is poison does not imply that the believer will either seek or avoid x—a suicide would seek it and others would avoid it The fact of belief is not sufficient to justify an inference to behavior or even to readiness to behave in any specific way. For this, additional knowledge is required On the other hand, if I think that x is good, you may infer that I will seek it if I can or at least that some sort of favoring response will follow In some such general way I believe that even a behavioristic operational formulation of the difference between belief and attitude may be possible.

If practical reasoning is characterized by its attitudinal outcome, it follows that the process of practical reasoning must be a *process of forming and transforming attitudes.* Any analysis of practical reasoning that is unable to show how this is possible is inadequate I shall try to show that cognitivist interpretations of the role of reasoning in ethics are unable to account for this feature of practical reasoning, because the difference in aim between cognition and practical reasoning involves a difference in method

For the ethical cognitivist, the process of practical reasoning is merely the cognitive process of arriving at ethical cognitions, that is, ethical truths. On this point, naturalists and intuitionists are agreed, and their disagreement is over the question of whether such cognitions are empirical or a priori I shall try to show that whether they be considered to be empirical generalizations, definitions, intuitions, or inferences—all these possible types of ethical cognition have difficulty in accounting for the attitudinal component of practical reasoning, because practical reasoning is a different kind of process from cognitive reasoning.

[5] See the article by Dewey in *Value. A Cooperative Inquiry,* ed. by R Lepley (New York, Columbia University Press, 1949), p. 65 Using "attitude" in this broad sense, I hope to avoid the current controversy over "spectator" and "agent" ethics, since practical reasoning aims at establishing approval or disapproval as well as promoting ends and actions. See Stuart Hampshire, "Fallacies in Moral Philosophy," *Mind,* LVIII (October 1949), 466–82 Moreover, the problem of whether an attitude is to be considered an *occurrent* or a *disposition* is irrelevant—actions and emotive reactions are clearly the former, general tendencies to act or react, for example, decisions and moral "principles," are clearly the latter Practical reasoning is directed at the production of both kinds of attitudes

The Bifurcation of Belief and Attitude

The ethical cognitivist maintains that ethical reasoning is aimed primarily at the establishment of an ethical belief or cognition, and only through the mediation of this belief does it establish an attitude An ethical attitude is one which is the product of an ethical belief Thus the first characteristic of ethical cognitivism is the bifurcation of ethical belief and ethical attitude.

It is important to notice that the ethical cognitivist does not limit himself to asserting that an ethical attitude is produced by some belief or other, but it is essential to his position that it be produced by a certain kind of belief which he calls "ethical" and which he differentiates from "non-ethical" beliefs.

No one could justly deny that beliefs of all sorts influence attitudes, and on this point I have no quarrel with the ethical cognitivist. What I shall deny is that there is a peculiar class of beliefs that are ethical and from which the attitude they produce derives its ethical quality. The cognitivist distinction between an ethical and a non-ethical belief may be illustrated thus: For example, the knowledge that x will cause pain will alter my attitude toward x, but the aroused attitude is not *ipso facto* ethical, for instance, this knowledge might arouse hate, and so forth, which is frowned upon in our society. The general class of beliefs that arouse or transform attitudes indiscriminately, so to speak, I shall call "factual" or "mediating beliefs," following R. B. Perry.[6] The ethical cognitivist maintains that there is a peculiar kind of "mediating beliefs" that inevitably do, or ought to, produce attitudes, and these I shall call "ethical beliefs."

Many ethical cognitivists subscribe to a rather naive psychology according to which the cognitive apparatus discovers ethical truths and then somehow commands the "will" to follow these truths. Usually the ethical beliefs are supposed to produce the attitude without any assistance from other mediating beliefs, such as extraneous considerations like hope of reward or fear of punishment. In the ideal case, the ethical belief is the *sufficient cause* of the attitude, although many admit that this may never actually happen The "ideal sufficiency" of ethical beliefs is what distinguishes them from other mediating beliefs. The good will is autonomous, that is, determined by the moral law alone Thus the second characteristic

---

[6] See *General Theory of Value: Its Meaning and Basic Principles Construed in Terms of Interest* (Cambridge, Mass., Harvard University Press, 1950), Chap 12. Perry distinguishes between two relations of cognition to interest. The one judgment which is about interests he calls a "judgment of value," and the other which is a determinant of interest he calls "mediating or interest judgment"

of ethical cognitivism is the distinction between ethical beliefs and other mediating beliefs.

We see, therefore, that ethical cognitivism makes two claims: (1) that ethical beliefs and ethical attitude are different, that is, the bifurcation of ethical belief and attitude; and (2) that mediating beliefs are to be divided into ethical beliefs and non-ethical beliefs. Most cognitivists also hold that ethical beliefs are ideally the sole and sufficient determinant of ethical attitudes (actions and feelings). Indeed, they tend to use this latter characteristic as the defining character of "ethical" beliefs

Let us ask· How does the cognitivist describe and explain the relations of ethical belief and attitude, and what is the nature of this peculiar relation of ideal sufficient determination?

Cognitivist discussions of the relation of ethical belief and attitude fall under two broad groupings, according to which aspect of the relation of ethical cognition to attitude is stressed. The first group stresses the fact that ethical cognitions are themselves founded on attitudes—that is, ethical knowledge is knowledge about attitudes The second group stresses the determining of attitude by ethical cognitions. The first interest is concerned with attitudes antecedent to cognition, the second with the cognition that is antecedent to attitude There are, therefore, two different questions about the relation of belief and attitude: (1) How are ethical cognitions to be based upon attitude? (2) How are ethical attitudes to be based upon ethical cognitions? The confusion of these two questions has given rise to much futile controversy between naturalists, who are generally answering the first, and intuitionists, who are concerned with the second. It is clear that a thoroughgoing ethical cognitivist must answer both questions, which I shall refer to as the *cognition question* and the *motivational question* respectively.

Let us consider the cognition question first It is best expressed in Perry's distinction between "judgments of value" and "mediating judgments." The first are reports of "valuings" or "interests," the second are judgments that influence the formation of interests. On Perry's view, an ethical cognition or judgment of value is based upon attitudes *that already exist* It is a judgment ex post facto All the so-called naturalistic analyses of ethical judgments are ex post facto in this sense. The main differences between the various species is a disagreement about which kind of attitude is to be taken as the referent of such ethical judgments: interests, objects of interest, hedonic qualities, and so forth. Some attitudes are regarded as more ethically relevant than others, and these give rise to a distinction between "real" and "apparent" values, for instance, "real" and "apparent" satisfactions, and so forth A real value is one that has a certain kind of permanence and objectivity and can be used to predict future attitudes Thus ethical cognitions are not merely reports of present valuings, but they use these to predict future ones [7] The attitudes that are the basis of ethical cognitions may thus be ideal in Lewis's sense of "objective " They may also be ideal as being those of some ideal person (for instance, God, the impartial spectator, and so forth).

The view that ethical cognitions are cognitions of attitudes is generally conceived as differentiating naturalists from intuitionists, but I suggest that *in effect* the ethical judgments of the intuitionists are also reports of attitudes. If the metaphysical trappings be omitted, G E Moore, W D. Ross, and others are merely voicing their own private prejudices in the language of intuitionism. This is clear when we ask for the evidence upon which the ethical statements rest. The evidence for the naturalist and the intuitionist is the same, that is, experience of feelings For example, "It is wrong not to return a borrowed book" is a belief based upon Ross's own private introspection.[8] Even if we were to allow that the attitude upon which the intuition is based is not a "natural" attitude discoverable in psychology, there is some non-natural attitude behind it.

I suggest that all "ethical beliefs" are founded upon some kind of attitude—whether this be recognized to be their basis or not My statement might be tested by an "ideal" experiment of considering a being that could only cognize and had no attitudes, feelings, prejudices, at all. Such a being would be only a thinking machine of the type considered in cybernetics It seems inconceivable that such a machine could produce ethical cognitions by itself, because it has no attitudes.

The ethical cognitivist assumes that ethical beliefs ideally give rise to the ethical attitude. If all ethical cognitions are based ex post facto upon some attitude, this implies that existing attitudes ideally would determine future attitudes The mediation of ethical beliefs merely determines which of these attitudes are to have this effect in the future For instance, the belief that "telling lies is wrong" may be verified by introspective appeal to my feelings about lying (whether reported in naturalistic or intuitionistic terms), and when this ethical belief causes me to refrain from lying in the future, it is the original feeling acting mediately through belief that is the causal determinant of my not lying

It appears, then, that ethical beliefs tend to "freeze" certain existing atti-

---

[7] "An ethical theory explains and predicts," C J Ducasse, "Nature and Function of Theory in Ethics," *Ethics*, October 1940. This is essentially what C. I Lewis does in his *An Analysis of Knowledge and Valuation* (La Salle, Ill , Open Court, 1946), although it is incorrect in his system to identify valuation with an ethical judgment

[8] That the difference is a difference of language has been clearly argued by D S. Miller, who distinguishes between objective or moral truth and the corresponding subjective or psychological truth. "Moral Truth," *Philosophical Studies*, April 1950.

tudes so that they will act in the future as well as at present. They are the bed of Procrustes that is fitted to one person (that is, one attitude) and is used thereafter as the standard to which other people (attitudes) are to be fitted They are conservators of values, and only chance allows the infiltration of a new attitude or new set of values. Ethical beliefs per se cannot give rise to totally new attitudes which are not based upon already existent attitudes The reduction of practical reasoning to the fixation of ethical beliefs and their consequent corresponding attitudes thus eliminates any novelty due to practical reasoning If practical reasoning is the forming and transforming of attitudes, ethical cognitivism accounts for neither, since it in effect makes ethical reasoning the fixation of attitudes according to an attitude that is given priority as being more "real," "rational," "stable," and so forth.

Many ethical cognitivists consider that they have answered the question about the relation of ethical belief and attitude when they show that ethical belief is belief about attitude There seems to be an implicit assumption that since these beliefs are *about* attitudes, they will ipso facto *cause* attitudes. This assumption only has to be made explicit for one to recognize its patent falsity. However, the fact still remains that most discussions of ethical beliefs end with conclusions about their subject matter, that is, the cognition question. The motivational question is never even considered. Namely, what is the relation of these ethical beliefs to future attitudes?

Many naturalistic writers are content to say that behavior based upon ethical cognitions is more "rational" or "consistent" than that based upon non-ethical cognitions The fact of being based upon a cognition is often regarded as a sufficient criterion for the rationality of the attitude It is rational because it is based upon reason (that is, cognition). This is obviously a too inclusive conception of rational action, since any kind of behavior mediated by cognition would be rational in this sense, and a thief who acted on the correct supposition that his victim had money would be acting rationally Clearly the naturalist is more exclusive—that is, he identifies rational behavior as behavior founded on ethical beliefs and not just any beliefs whatsoever. One suspects that such naturalists are resorting to what Stevenson has called a "persuasive definition," that is, they are using such words as "rational" or "consistent" in a persuasive or ethical, and not merely a descriptive, sense They wish their ethical beliefs to influence attitudes, although this is frequently not openly admitted and practically never explained

The bifurcation of ethical belief and attitude thus has the curious consequence that many ethical writers describe a subject matter—for instance, interests, satisfactions, private feelings—and fail to show the relevance of these to future attitude We may ask equally well of Perry, Bentham,

Ross, and Moore. *Why are their ethical beliefs relevant to our own future attitude?*

This leads us to the discussion of the second or motivational question that we asked the ethical cognitivists: Namely, how are ethical attitudes to be based upon ethical cognitions?

The simplest answer to this question is that ethical beliefs *ought* to be the cause of attitudes But to say this, raises a new difficulty, since the belief that "ethical beliefs ought to be the cause of attitudes" is itself merely an ethical belief and as such a demand that our attitudes conform to ethical beliefs. However we state this principle, we are unable to get out of the realm of belief to attitudes, since there is an infinite regress of ethical beliefs about ethical beliefs about ethical beliefs and attitudes It is natural to question whether the relation of ethical belief and ethical attitude can be properly described in ethical terms and thus be itself the subject matter of an ethical belief If moral obligation consists in conforming one's attitudes to ethical beliefs, why cannot it be described as conforming one's attitudes to the ethical belief that his attitudes ought to conform to ethical beliefs, or to the ethical belief in this ethical belief, and so on On strictly cognitivist grounds, moral obligation can only be a relation to which the moral judgment refers cognitively, and not the relation of the judgment (which is about it) to attitudes Otherwise the ethical belief is lifting itself up by its bootstraps, so to speak.[9]

Therefore we have to exclude an ethical description of the relevance of ethical belief to ethical attitude, that is, in terms of obligation There are only three possibilities left (1) An ethical cognition *always will* give rise to an ethical attitude, (2) An ethical cognition will give rise to the attitude *if* the proper conditions are present; (3) The connection between ethical cognition and attitude is fortuitous—sometimes it is effective and sometimes it is not (although for the ethical writer himself it may always be effective)

Many ethical cognitivists since the time of Plato have held that the cognition of good ipso facto creates an attitude. Every man acts *sub ratione boni.* I have elsewhere called this the "love of the Good" theory and have criticized it.[10] Many more modern theories distinguish between different effects of the cognition—that is, in my terminology, between different kinds of attitude caused. Thus Kant, for instance, would maintain that an ethical cognition automatically results in the attitude of respect, but not necessarily in action. For Aristotle, the internal split between "respect" and action is

[9] See my article, " 'Desirability' and 'Normativeness' in White's Article on Dewey," *The Philosophical Review,* January 1951.
[10] See my article, "Value Judgments, Emotive Meaning, and Attitudes," *The Journal of Philosophy,* March 3, 1949

characteristic of the incontinent man. Thus ethical cognitivists of this first type all agree that ethical cognitions result in some attitude, although this attitude may not be sufficiently strong to result in action. This presents the crucial problem of which both Aristotle and Kant were aware, namely, when and under what conditions will the aroused attitude eventuate in action It is usually solved by the introduction of a mysterious entity called the will.[11]

The important point is, however, that ethical cognitions inevitably arouse some kind of attitude

The second theory is actually a version of the first, since it says that an attitude will follow belief if the proper conditions are present. The inevitability of the attitude is also assumed, if in a modified form.

In both of these inevitability theories we are presented with the problem of why the ethical belief arouses the attitude How is it possible for the cognition that "x is good" or "x is wrong" to make us feel a certain way about x? Other mediating beliefs arouse attitudes (that is, desires) by telling us something about the object, for instance, that it will cause pleasure or pain. Can a belief that does not tell us anything concrete or empirical about the object arouse an attitude?

These ethical cognitivists are extremely vague on this point. They are forced to postulate a special motive in man, for instance, that man has a natural love of the good or a "sense of duty," just as he naturally loves food or sleep Harold A. Prichard, for instance, though vehemently denying that we fulfill our duties because of some interest, has to introduce the special motive of "sense of obligation" to make possible moral action as distinct from moral belief.[12] That there is such a motive that is distinct from other well-known and empirically verifiable motives is never proved, but is assumed. The "sense of obligation" is a *deus ex machina*—a "capacity" that is postulated to save the theory

Prichard's extreme intellectualism is evident in his discussion of the question "Why should I be moral?" He assumes that this question is a demand for an intellectual justification of a certain action being a duty, that is, for a premise from which it may be deduced. The question is, however, not an intellectual one but a demand for a motive. It should be stated: "What will make me (that is, motivate me) do my duty?" His answer is, of course. "The sense of duty is your motive" Prichard's misinterpretation of this question is an indication of the intuitionist's unawareness of the problem of the relation of ethical belief and motivation

There is an element of truth in Prichard's position to which I should call

[11] The conception of the "will" is analyzed in my article entitled "Free Will and Voluntary Action," *Philosophy and Phenomenological Research*, XII (March 1952)
[12] *Moral Obligation* (Oxford, Clarendon Press, 1949), p 11.

attention. The belief that so and so is my duty often does, of course, result in my doing it. Why? I suggest that it is because "duty" in these contexts has an empirical content. For instance, frequently "x is my duty" is synonymous with "The failure to do x is disapproved of by my parents (my social group, my society, my religion, my long-run self, and so forth)." Thus the belief about duty is a factual belief, which mediates my attitude in this specific instance. It is not an ethical belief, but a mediating belief, and it mediates, rather than completely determines, an attitude.

I suspect that cognitions can only be mediating beliefs if they have some empirical content. Without any empirical content those mediating beliefs which are regarded as ethical would not be able to move an individual. Thus those "ethical" statements that are couched in intuitionistic language actually implant an empirical belief in the hearer to the effect that the speaker (society, and so forth) approves or disapproves of the object, or whatever the content may be.

If it be admitted that the so-called "ethical beliefs" are mediating beliefs only inasmuch as they contain factual assertions, it is easy to understand why they can determine attitudes. They determine attitudes just as many other kinds of belief determine attitudes. There is no *peculiar* problem involved in the motivating character of ethical, as contrasted with non-ethical, beliefs. Moreover, it follows that the strict differentiation between ethical and non-ethical beliefs cannot be made in terms of subject matter or a peculiar type of motivation.

The third answer to the motivation question, namely, how can ethical beliefs determine attitudes, is the view that such determination is entirely fortuitous. Many naturalists frankly admit that there is no binding connection, actual or ideal, between ethical belief and ethical attitude.

If a naturalistic analysis of "value" in terms of, say, pleasure or interest be accepted, it is difficult to explain why a belief about such natural characteristics should per se be able to move the believer to action or feeling. Thus an entirely independent theory of motivation is necessary, which is based upon motives that actually do exist in human beings, that is, incentives and sanctions. Such is the position taken by Bentham and R. B. Perry—that value does not essentially possess a moving appeal.[18]

Nevertheless, it does seem intrinsically implausible that I can assent to an ethical belief without there being any corresponding assent in attitude. This point has been the basis of the emotivist critique of this type of naturalism. Naturalistic analyses lack the persuasive power that ethical beliefs have. If they do have some such power, it is due to the employment of "per-

[18] Perry, "Value and Its Moving Appeal," *The Philosophical Review*, XLI, No 4 (July 1932), 337–50.

suasive definitions" and "emotive expressions" The fundamental point is correct, although I should rather stress the nature of the attitudes and beliefs involved than the language used (It is conceivable that there might be a culture which had ethical beliefs and attitudes without ever using any peculiarly emotive ethical expressions)

We may always ask the Benthamite why he is interested in ethics at all. What is the purpose of the long, elaborate analyses and statements of what constitutes the greatest good? Obviously they are intended to influence behavior in a certain way. But it must be only those who are not moved by sanctions but by a "benevolent" motive for whom the ethics is written Now, why will these facts about pleasure and interest appeal to a benevolent person?

An antinaturalist might answer that implicitly the naturalist is assuming an ethical (nonnaturalistic) premise to the effect that "I ought to promote the greatest good (defined in terms of pleasure or interest) " According to such an analysis, the benevolent man is the man with the good will or the sense of duty, and he has the disposition to be moved by the ethical belief. This answer has already been discussed.

However, suppose that these factual (naturalistic) beliefs are not to operate as "ethical beliefs" but as factual considerations influencing the will, that is, as mediating beliefs As such, it is no longer believed that these considerations "ought to" determine the will but rather that they will be relevant in the deliberations of reasonable people Thus it is more reasonable to suppose that the naturalistic "judgments of value" (for instance Perry or Bentham) are not strictly ethical beliefs, nor do they uniquely determine ethical attitudes, but as mediating beliefs they are contributing components that go to make up the ethical attitudes

A more subtle form of this Benthamite position, for instance "that cognition of good would not cause us to favor it," is one recently presented by H. D Aiken [14] According to him, there are two functions of ethical discourse, the cognitive and the motivational. The cognitive function is to describe satisfactions, whereas the motivational part is to influence behavior In the case of a rational person, the former function will coincide with the latter Again, there seems to lurk in this view the hidden supposition that beliefs about satisfactions *ought to* influence behavior To say that such behavior is rational is, as Stevenson would point out, merely using this word persuasively Either cognitions about satisfactions have some special claim, or else they function as other mediating beliefs do.

I have argued that all the forms of cognitivism have made a description of practical reasoning impossible because they have so sharply separated

[14] "Evaluation and Obligation," *The Journal of Philosophy,* January 5, 1951

ethical belief and attitude. The cognitivist has made for himself an insoluble problem by insisting that ethical beliefs are somehow prior to ethical attitudes, since it is impossible to describe or explain this priority.

THE UNION OF BELIEF AND ATTITUDE: PRACTICAL REASON

The alternative to cognitivism is the recognition that in practical reason, belief and attitude are united Cognition acts on attitude, and their interaction constitutes the process of practical reasoning Thus practical reason is, as Aristotle says, "desiderative reason" or "ratiocinative desire."[15] The process of forming an "ethical belief" is the same process as that of forming an ethical attitude Strictly speaking, there is no such thing as an ethical belief which is the result of practical reasoning The result is an attitude and not a belief. Sometimes the attitude formed is a decision or selection and has been called a "judgment," for instance by Dewey However, such a decision is neither true nor false. although it may be good or bad. The decision or attitude[16] arrived at may be reflected in ethical discourse, but we should note that language is not the only means of communicating the attitude I have reached by practical reasoning. I often do this by acting rather than by talking, and when I do talk I may not always talk in sentences that are strictly true or false. Whatever the signs by which you infer my decision, such an inference produces a cognition in you, and that cognition may mediate an attitude in you Ethical language is one way of communicating the fact that the decision was arrived at by reasoning and not haphazardly. Whether the ethical statements themselves are true or false in the sense of referring to facts or non-facts seems to me a rather insignificant detail In any case, the language employed is indirect, since, for instance, to say that "x is good" does not seem on the face of it synonymous with "I like x."[17]

I shall now turn to a more detailed examination of reasoning, cognitive and practical. Since my approach has been through the consideration of the function of reasoning in practice, it will be most convenient to divide the discussion according to the three immediate ends for which it is used These are· (1) persuasion, (2) reflective appraisal of the reasoning itself, (3) discovery Thus in cognitive reasoning my purpose may be (1) to persuade you to adopt my belief, (2) to check the process by which I arrived

[15] *Nicomachaen Ethics*, 1139b 5

[16] Note that practical reasoning may result in a general attitude, that is, an attitude toward certain kinds of objects (for instance kindly acts), or it may be specific, that is, an attitude toward a specific state of affairs (for instance "peace in our time"). In the latter case it is usually indistinguishable from a decision or even an action. I have been using the word "attitude" in an all-inclusive sense.

[17] See D. S. Miller, "Moral Truth," *Philosophical Studies*, April 1950.

at my belief, or (3) to discover some new truth. Likewise, in practical reasoning my purpose may be (1) to persuade you to adopt my attitude, (2) to criticize the process leading to the attitude itself, or (3) to discover new attitudes and their corresponding values

These three uses of reason in the cognitive and practical contexts will be examined in the rest of this paper First, I shall discuss rational persuasion; secondly, reflective criticism and appraisal, finally, I shall briefly mention the process of discovery There are certain recognized rules which govern reasoning in cognition, and the question that I shall ask is whether the same rules apply to practical reasoning It will appear that there are certain important analogies which reveal something of the nature of practical reasoning.

Rational Persuasion Many ethical writers think that the primary purpose of ethical discourse is to persuade This belief may take the form of maintaining that all ethical discourse is primarily persuasive and only incidentally rational. Such a view reduces ethical discourse to propaganda It is my thesis that a distinction can be made between propaganda and rational persuasion That such a distinction exists for cognitive discourse is readily admitted A propagandist frequently uses faulty reasoning deliberately to distort the facts as well as morals. An opposite form of the emphasis on persuasion is manifested by those rationalists who confine ethical reasoning to the proving of particular ethical maxims from general ethical principles.

Both these extremes, cognitivist rationalism and the emotivist reaction to it, make the mistake of identifying reasoning with logical proof. For them both, reasoning is no different from demonstration. They therefore formulate the problem of whether practical reasoning *is possible* as the problem of *whether ethical truths can be demonstrated.* It would seem that since Hume's devastating criticism of demonstration as the basis of empirical knowledge, ethical writers would have begun to question whether it is the basis of ethics But this has hardly been done.

I shall begin by examining certain aspects of ethical inference in general. "Inference, then, may be defined as a mental process in which a thinker passes from the apprehension of something given, the datum, to something, the conclusion, related in a certain way to the datum, and accepted only because the datum has been accepted."[18] This definition is broad enough to include conclusions in the form of assertions or beliefs, and conclusions in the form of attitudes.

Ethical inference is the passage by means of thinking from certain data to an attitude (decision). I have already criticized the view that the outcome, or conclusion, is a belief, and I shall assume that it is not.

[18] Lizzie Susan Stebbing, *A Modern Introduction to Logic* (London, Methuen, 1930), p 211-12.

The data that are involved in ethical inference are of two kinds. beliefs
and attitudes When ethical inference is stated in propositional form, the
data are premises. We may distinguish therefore between ethical (attitudinal) and factual premises Now, in the broadest sense, ethical reasoning
is the forming and transforming of attitude in the light of considerations
involving other attitudes and beliefs.

Just as inferential argument involving cognitions is used to extend belief
in the premises to belief in the conclusion, so an ethical argument is aimed
at extending an attitude in the premises to an attitude in the conclusion.
Rational persuasion is thus the evoking of a new belief or attitude by an
already accepted belief or attitude through some mediating beliefs or, possibly, attitudes.

The first difficulty facing anyone using an argument from premises to a
conclusion is to find premises that are acceptable to the persuadee This is
often difficult for a cognitive argument, but it is even more difficult for an
ethical argument Since the conclusion in an ethical argument is an attitude, there must be something in the premises that corresponds to an attitude, too. Accordingly, most theories maintain that the major premise is
ethical For a cognitivist this generally means that the premise contains
ethical terms—either definable or not: Usually it is presented to us as an
intuition, a definition, or even an empirical generalization. But the cognitivist still has to explain how this ethical premise involves an attitude
Definitions and empirical generalizations are frequently cognitively acceptable although the attitude to which they are supposed to correspond
does not accompany such acceptance For instance, I might well agree to
the definition of "good" as "pleasant," since it is pointless to argue about a
verbal definition, and yet no attitude toward pleasure would be involved
Stevenson has called the use of definitions to evoke attitudes "persuasive
definitions."[19] As purely cognitive definitions, they do not persuade emotively, the emotive aspect requires some additional explanation The same
thing goes for the use of empirical generalizations as premises: Since they
do not involve an attitude, they cannot be expected to be emotively persuasive as well as cognitively persuasive.

The intuitionists are "unconsciously" aware of this difficulty, since they
reject the approach through definitions and empirical generalizations. But
they show that they fail to diagnose the problem, because by insisting that
the intuitions are purely cognitive judgments, they make it impossible to
explain the attitudinal element. The only kind of intuitionist that is able
to account for this aspect is one who recognizes the intuition to be both
a cognitive and an emotive act: for instance, Nicolai Hartmann's view that

---

[19] *Op cit.*, Chap 9.

ethical intuitions are "never purely cognitive acts, they are acts of feeling—not intellectual but emotional."[20]

One alternative is to maintain that ethical premises are not cognitive judgments at all. A. J. Ayer calls them "persuasive expressions of attitudes." John Stuart Mill implies this also when he says that the ethical premise is expressed in the "imperative mood" rather than the "indicative."[21] Aristotle denies that it is even a judgment It is, he says, an end.[22]

All three of these formulations recognize the importance of accounting for the relation of the ethical premise to attitudes. However, both Ayer and Mill merely state in so many words that attitudes are involved, but they fail to explain how they are involved. Aristotle clearly recognizes that the datum from which the conclusion is to be argued must be the attitude itself. This he calls the end, that is, object of desire The new attitude which is the conclusion follows from the old attitude and not from any emotive or imperative expressions of it The ethical premise when given in the form of a judgment is merely a recognition that the attitude (or end) exists. As such, it may be a cognition, but it is a cognition of an attitude. The act of cognizing the attitude may itself render the attitude explicit, whereas before it was implicit, that is, perhaps latent or even "unconscious."

The process of ethical persuasion is therefore one of calling the attention of the persuadee to certain attitudes of his and then leading him through the mediation of other attitudes and beliefs to the adoption of a new attitude Hence, the recognition of the attitudinal component in this process leads us to modify the traditional conception of the nature of ethical inference.

My second criticism of the traditional conception of ethical inference is directed at the assumption that ethical inference is demonstrative The assumption that demonstrative inference is the only valid type of inference has been rejected in the empirical sciences. Any empiricist now admits "problematic inferences" as the basis of empirical knowledge. But the analogous assumption about ethical reasoning has not as yet been adequately criticized by many ethical writers. Even certain emotivists maintain that one must come "to a conclusion about my action as a member of a class of acts," that is, deductively.[23]

Thus both cognitivists and emotivists assume that if reasoning were involved in practical discourse, it would be demonstrative inference. The possibility that it might be problematic inference seems to have escaped

[20] *Moral Phenomena* ("Ethics," Vol I [New York, Library of Philosophy, Macmillan, 1932]), p 177

[21] *A System of Logic* (London, Longmans, Green, 1884), Bk. VI, Chap 11, Para. 1.

[22] *De Motu Animalium*, 701a ff

[23] B Mayo, "Mr. Hampshire on Fallacies," *Mind*, July 1950, p. 386

their attention The consequence is that the denial of the applicability of
demonstration in ethics has been taken for the denial of practical reasoning

There is a natural tendency of logicians to reduce other forms of reasoning to deduction. If given the right premises, of course, any conclusion can
be validly deduced. But such a deduction must assume the premises—and
in doing this it is already begging the question, since we are interested in
how to establish the premises.

In cognitive inference, besides demonstration (for instance, deduction)
there are two types of problematic inference.[24] These are the inductive inference from a finite number of cases to a general case, and the inference
that shows one individual case to be a member of a general class The latter I shall call "subsumption." Subsumption is usually regarded as a deductive inference, but it is not for empirical instances. For instance, to prove
that Jones is subsumed under the class of murderers involves the weighing
of evidence for and against, and the subsumption can never be certain but
must remain problematic. *After* the subsumption has been established it
can be rendered in deductive logical form, but the subsumption itself cannot be established by deductive inference alone.[25] Except in mathematics
and the mathematical portion of the sciences, deduction is actually of little
use in cognitive reasoning As Aristotle says "Of accidents that are not
essential according to our definition of essential there is no demonstrative
knowledge."[26]

The apriorism that has resulted from neglecting the problematic and
empirical character of subsumption, for instance, vitiates popular as well
as professional thinking It has recently been pointed out that certain
pseudo demonstrations sound quite plausible but are actually invalid [27]
Take, for instance, the following argument. All Communists are traitors;
but Jones is a Communist. Therefore Jones is a traitor This argument
either begs the question or else it is based upon the fallacy of four terms:
In the latter case, the word "Communist" is used in two different senses,
namely (1) an ideal Communist, (2) someone who has joined the party.
The fact that Jones happened to have joined the party does not prove that
he is a traitor, since he may not be a good (that is, ideal) party member.
The reasoning attempts fallaciously to deduce from the ideal case something about the concrete unique individual I shall call this the *subsumptive
fallacy,* that is, the a priori determination of the unique case by subsump-

[24] I have borrowed the terms "demonstrative" and "problematic" inference from
W E Johnson, *Logic* (New York, Cambridge University Press, 1921), Part II I do not
pretend to be exhaustive in my account of the types of inference

[25] Logic and mathematics are the only sciences in which subsumption is strictly deductive

[26] *Analytica Posteriora,* 75a 18

[27] See Victor Lowe, "A Resurgence of 'Vicious Intellectualism,'" *The Journal of
Philosophy,* July 5, 1951.

tion under an ideal case The subsumptive fallacy is frequently employed in ethics. It should be noted that subsumption of concrete individuals *can* be rationally established although only empirically and problematically.

Most accounts of ethical demonstrations present them in a form of the "practical syllogism."[28] The usual doctrine is that the major premise is an "ethical" premise, the minor a "factual" premise, and the conclusion, of course, "ethical." Mill calls the major "rules of Art" and the minor "theorems of science "[29] Whether the ethics be teleological or deontological, the process of subsuming a particular action or object under the major ethical term is assumed to be "factual," "scientific," "descriptive," "empirical," or whatever the word chosen may be. I shall contend that this view is erroneous and that it is an ethical version of what I have called the subsumptive fallacy.

Let me give an example.

> All lying is wrong.
> Lying to prevent a murder is lying.
> Therefore I should not lie to prevent a murder.

Or:

> Peace is good
> Liquidating certain innocent people will produce peace.
> Therefore I should liquidate them.

W. D Ross recognizes that it is not possible to deduce the "actual or absolute duty to do the particular act in the particular circumstances" from general duties. The latter he calls prima-facie duties.[30] Other intuitionists also agree that the "formulation of rules does not help us to decide what is now right "[31] But since they agree that actual duties cannot be demonstrated, they infer that they cannot be decided by any process of reasoning —as opposed to direct intuition In other words, these intuitionists are cognitivists who are at the same time irrationalists!

The syllogistic reasoning that deduces the dutifulness of a particular action from the premise that it is a means to an assumed end is just as fallacious as the deontological versions. John Dewey has criticized this by

[28] Aristotle's doctrine is much more subtle than the version of the "practical syllogism" being considered here
[29] *Op cit*
[30] *The Right and the Good* (New York and London, Oxford University Press, 1930), p 28.
[31] E F Carritt, *The Theory of Morals. An Introduction to Ethical Philosophy* (New York and London, Oxford University Press, 1928), p 117 The demand for "an argument different from our original and unreflected apprehension of it .. is illegitimate." Prichard, *op cit*, p. 16.

referring to the example of the roast pig from Lamb's famous essay The burning down of a house (means) to get roast pork (end) is not justified by the end because there are other ends that are thereby jeopardized.[32] In other words, not every possible means is warranted, but only the *best* means

The type of arguments that I have presented are invalid because there is a plurality of types of duties that may conflict with each other, or else there is a plurality of ends the promotion of one of which may conflict with that of others [33] It might be thought that this difficulty would be resolved if there were only a single kind of duty or end postulated. Such monistic theories would be the only duty is to love God (or your neighbor), the categorical imperative, the greatest-happiness principle, and so forth. Such theories, however, must be rejected because they are either too vague to be applied or else too determinate to be plausible.

For instance, if the supreme absolute duty is love, the subsumption of any particular action, even given complete knowledge of its characteristics, is indeterminate. Controversy over pacificism in Christian ethics proves that it is extremely difficult to decide whether an action is due to love or not Moreover, when a particular determinate conception of love is postulated, for instance the desire not to inflict bodily injury, the view becomes implausible because it is inadequate to the subtleties and complexities of the ethical life Kant's categorical imperative produces the same dilemma. On the one hand, it is criticized for being empty, and on the other, when Kant applies it to lying, it appears too rigorous

Again, Benthamite utilitarianism is subject to the same difficulty. The problems of measurement of pleasures are notorious In any case, the decision as to whether a greater amount of pleasure over pain is involved in any particular action cannot be reached unless one specifies which pleasures are greater, and so on. In that case, however, relevant ethical considerations are excluded from our attention, for instance the claims of justice, and so forth. One suspects that for Bentham the criterion of a greater pleasure is its being a better pleasure. This is recognized in Mill's revision of utilitarianism.

We see, therefore, that for all ethical theories employing deduction, the problem of subsumption is paramount In the pluralistic theories, the problem concerns which principle the particular act should be subsumed under.

---

[32] Dewey, *Theory of Valuation* (Chicago, University of Chicago Press, 1939), pp 40 ff.

[33] See C. D Broad's distinction between monistic and pluralistic ethical theories in *Five Types of Ethical Theory* (London, K. Paul, Trench, Trubner, New York, Harcourt, Brace, 1930), p 280. By a monistic theory I mean a theory in which the major ethical premise is simply controvertible, for instance, besides "all pleasure being good," "all goods are pleasures," and so forth

In the monistic theories, we are presented with the alternatives of either an overprecise and implausible conclusion or else with a principle which can only be applied with the help of some auxiliary premise (for instance, about the nature of love, or of the "greaterness" of pleasure)

I suggest that the mistake that is made in these theories is that of assuming the minor premise to be non-ethical, that is, factual In order for any of them to be plausible, they are required to recognize the minor premise as ethical as well as the major term Thus, an action must be specified as "the most pressing duty," "the best means," "productive of the better pleasure," and so on

This was already recognized by Aristotle, the inventor of the "practical syllogism " For him, I believe, the minor premise, stating the means to the end, was also ethical. A simplified version of his syllogism would be somewhat as follows:

> Virtuous activity produces happiness (the end).
> Action x is a virtuous activity.
> Do x.

(Aristotle states the indeterminate character of the end when he says that the mean is relative to the particular circumstance and cannot be determined absolutely and a priori)[34]

I submit, therefore, that from the arguments presented, we are driven to the conclusion that ethical inference is not demonstrative Like the cognitive inferences resulting in induction and subsumption, they are problematic, that is, the conclusion does not follow necessarily from known premises deductively, but rather the premises are data upon which the conclusion is based Just as in empirical cognition the subsumption of an individual under some class is problematic and involves a careful empirical investigation of all the possible evidence, so in ethical inference the subsumption of an individual action under the class of duties or of means to the Chief Good is also problematic and demands investigation of all the alternatives The difference between empirical and ethical subsumption is due to the fact that attitudes enter into the latter. The datum which determines the ultimate decision, and which is reflected in the minor or subsuming premise, is itself an attitude. There are, of course, other non-ethical data, that is, beliefs about matters of fact, but these are not the final determinants of the ethical character of the particular action.

I hope that these considerations will rescue rational persuasion in ethics from unjust attacks leveled against it, both from the emotivists and from the intuitionists Before proceeding to the next section, however, I should

[34] *Nicomachean Ethics*, 1106a 25.

like to point out the pernicious use to which the assumption that all ethical reasoning is demonstrative has been put.

I have already mentioned the demagogic use of the subsumptive fallacy in matters of empirical belief. The similar use of this fallacy has occasioned the presumption that all ethical philosophers are propagandists To the extent to which they are deductivists this attack is justified.

I define propaganda in this context as the distortion of rational persuasion by the deliberate omission of contravening considerations and evidence This is achieved by employing a deductive argument when an investigation of all the relevant evidence is called for, for instance the labeling of Jones as a traitor because he is a Communist. Many ethical writers have used this device to advance certain causes in which they are interested. The best example of a demonstrative propagandistic ethics is that of Hobbes. Hobbes was interested in promoting obedience to an absolute sovereign That this was necessary he deduced from the major premise that peace was what all men desired (that is, the good), and the minor premise that obedience was the only means to peace. It is clear, however, that peace is only one among many goods, that is, objects of man's desire. Bentham was interested in prison reform, and he found his premise in the greatest-happiness principle. I need not mention others.[35] Logically their arguments are impeccable, but ethically the results are disastrous because they follow Procrustes's procedure of putting the ends of human nature, which are subtle and complex, into a strait jacket.

Critical Reflection upon the Reasoning. A course of cognitive reasoning can be validated, or at least invalidated, in terms of the canons of inference and evidence Although there is some dispute about the details of the logic of cognition, general agreement is possible about many of the necessary conditions of valid reasoning The canons of valid reasoning not only enable us to evaluate the reasoning itself but also indirectly through this evaluation they enable us to decide whether the assertion or belief concluded is justified or not. Thus one of the functions of the logic of inference is to give us criteria of acceptable and unacceptable belief.

The reductionist who identifies practical with cognitive reasoning will naturally prescribe the same standards of validity for both. Correct practical reasoning, like correct cognitive reasoning, would be reasoning according to the canons of inference It follows that indirectly the same criteria are used to decide whether the practical conclusion as well as the reasoning is justified. However, as I have shown, the conclusion of practical

[35] Two contemporary examples would be the deduction from the principle of natural law of the wickedness of birth control and, from the principle of human freedom, the necessity of devoting one's attention exclusively to the promotion of the proletarian revolution It is the characteristic totalitarian form of argument

reasoning is an attitude (or decision) and not a belief; hence the cognitivist is forced to apply cognitive criteria to determine the validity of an attitude. We are therefore presented with the curious anomaly that the criteria of a reasonable attitude as contrasted with an unreasonable one are given in purely logical terms Those ethical writers who speak of "rational behavior" and "rational action" and at the same time accept a cognitivist interpretation of reason could only mean by these phrases, logically validated behavior This indeed sounds ridiculous since ordinarily we assume that the principles of logic apply only to beliefs, statements, and so forth—what we may call propositions Thus the cognitivist treats attitudes as if they were propositions.

The absurdity of extending logical criteria to behavior is illustrated by Kant, who uses the principle of noncontradiction as the criterion of a reasonable maxim The difficulty in interpreting Kantian ethics created by the use of an apparently purely cognitive criterion as a criterion of maxims can only be resolved by recognizing that Kant is using "noncontradiction" in a metaphorical sense

Since practical reasoning is an attitudinal process as well as a cognitive one, we may expect the criteria of reasonableness to be attitudinal as well as cognitive Reasoning which evaluates practical reasoning must itself be practical, that is, involve *pro* or *contra* attitudes as well as beliefs This consideration has led Stevenson to point out that the phrases "good reason" and "bad reason" are themselves emotive expressions.[36] At least they involve attitudes, just as the process of practical reasoning itself involves attitudes.

The attitude according to which a certain instance of practical reasoning is determined as valid or invalid gives rise to a new value notion which is different from either duty or ends (as we have been considering them).[37] The reflective attitude toward the forming and transforming of attitude is different from direct attitudes toward actions and ends, and we may distinguish between the correlative "reflective values" and "direct values" This distinction of attitude (and value) is similar to Lovejoy's distinction between adjectival and terminal desires (or values) He writes.

The one is the desire for states-of-things which, at the moment of choice, are conceived by the chooser as *about to be* valuable, as eventually affording satisfaction to the agent or to somebody, *when realized through* the act, the other is the desire of the chooser to be able to think of himself as having or manifesting qualities *in* the act, which, *at the moment of choice*, he can regard with satisfaction, or at

[36] "Brandt's Questions about Emotive Ethics," *The Philosophical Review*, October 1950
[37] The term "end" as it has been considered hitherto is probably synonymous with Dewey's ends-in-view.

least without dissatisfaction, *as characterizing himself as agent* I shall call these two, for lack of better terms, the desire for terminal values and the desire for adjectival values.[38]

Accordingly, the validity as opposed to the invalidity of practical reasoning is determined by adjectival or reflective attitudes, and in this sense reasoning about practical reasoning is a valuation of valuations or an attitude toward attitudes.

It is relevant at this point to compare my notion of reflective practical reasoning with what is frequently called "meta-ethics" or "analytical ethics" The former is not neutral but evaluative, the second is claimed to be neutral.[39] The term "meta-ethics" is coined with the analogy of "meta-logic" of the logicians in mind However, logicians such as Quine and Carnap employ the device of giving their axioms in the "meta-language" in such a way as to prescriptively provide rules for the "formation" and "transformation" of statements in the object language [40] Hence the notion of "meta-language," being prescriptive, is more strictly analogous to my notion of "reflective practical reasoning." The so-called "meta-ethics" if it be strictly neutral, has nothing to do with ethics proper but is merely a branch of psychology or linguistics and has no more right to be called "meta-ethics" than psychology has to be called "meta-motivation" or empirical linguistics has to be called "meta-language." We must as carefully distinguish evaluative reasoning about practical reasoning from cognitive reasoning about practical reasoning (that is, the psychology of reasoning), as the corresponding prescriptive reasoning about cognitive reasoning (that is, meta-logic) from the psychological or linguistic description of the reasoning processes. The difference is that between evaluation or prescription, and cognition of the process There is thus a good analogy between reflective practical thinking and prescriptive logical thinking, and this analogy is completely ignored by the so-called "meta-ethicists."

The fact that there are certain analogies between correct practical and correct cognitive reasoning may give us some criteria of validity *by analogy* These criteria can only be briefly mentioned, but they may suggest some of the possible means for distinguishing valid from invalid practical reasoning The list is only tentative and does not pretend to be exhaustive.

I shall divide the criteria of rationality into two groups which I shall call "constitutive" and "epistemic" conditions of practical reasoning.[41]

---

[38] "Terminal and Adjectival Values," *The Journal of Philosophy*, October 12, 1950

[39] Stevenson, *Ethics and Language, op cit*, *passim*, A J. Ayer, "Analysis of Moral Judgments," *Horizon*, September 1949

[40] See W V Quine, *Mathematical Logic* (rev ed.; Cambridge, Mass , Harvard University Press, 1951), p 89. "Our initial metatheorems" reveal "an endless variety of general conditions under which statements will be theorems." See Rudolf Carnap, *Logical Syntax of Language* (London, K Paul, Trench, Trubner, 1937), *passim*.

[41] See Johnson, *op. cit*, Part I, p. 2.

The primary constitutive requirement is for some kind of order among the objects of practical reasoning. This demand may be for a system, in the logical sense, or for some other kind of *coherence* The least that is required is some recognizable difference between things that are consistent with or inconsistent with each other, and between things that are allowed and those demanded, and so on

Practical consistency is clearly a notion that needs to be clarified Logical consistency is not sufficient to make an instance of practical reasoning correct For instance, there is no logical inconsistency in willing an end and not willing any possible means to it The related conceptions of inconsistency, conflict, disagreement in attitude, and so forth, all require elucidation. Some of the possible meanings of practical consistency might be: (1) stability and security of attitudes, (2) offering a high degree of expectation for others, (3) corresponding to certain basic rather than superficial (transient) needs, (4) acting according to rules and principles, (5) being "congruent" with some general cultural pattern, and so on.

The epistemic conditions are conditions within the subject who does the reasoning The first of these is readiness to change one's mind if the data change This is the practical analogy of what Peirce calls "fallibilism." To be open-minded is perhaps more important in ethics than in the sciences, and less recognized to be so. Unfortunately, many ethical writers exalt its opposite (having a closed mind) as the essence of virtue.

A second epistemic condition is that of seeking all the relevant available information before reaching a conclusion. In ethics, as in the sciences, the chances are greater that the outcome of practical reasoning will be better if the subject is informed than if he is not. For instance, a doctor who operates without knowing about the patient's condition is likely to be less successful than one who does In practical reasoning, the data which should be available are both beliefs and attitudes An ideal practical philosopher would be one who knows the new beliefs and is also sensitive to new values.

Another condition of correct reasoning is that the data be obtained under *normal* conditions Observations are always corrected for the particular conditions of the observer, and may even be rejected because of some abnormal circumstance in the observer or his instruments Likewise, conditions must be set up for the practical reasoner—obviously he cannot be an escapee from an insane asylum, and so on These conditions have never been adequately studied.

These three epistemic conditions are conditions that must be fulfilled before practical reasoning can have any assurance of being adequate. They are necessary conditions, not sufficient conditions, and there are probably other ones not mentioned But to ask for a sufficient condition is very likely too much, for has anyone ever discovered the sufficient conditions (or criteria) of cognitive reasoning?

Discovery and Summary Many ethical writers have thought that the chief function of reason in practice is to discover new and more satisfactory objects for resolving conflicting attitudes Thus practical reason instead of being primarily persuasive or critical is rather inventive. Such is probably Dewey's view, although the other functions also play a role in his system.

Cognitive discovery depends upon breadth of imagination and wealth of experience and knowledge. Inventiveness requires putting old elements of experience together in new ways Experimentation is the key word of discovery.

The same attributes are necessary for ethical discovery Many philosophers assume that ethics has discovered all the values and duties that are possible in this world. The result has been a kind of conservatism and rejection of the novel that I have already pointed out to be the characteristic of deductive ethics. There have been great discoveries in ethics, and there probably will be many more.

Following the conclusion reached earlier, practical reasoning includes an attitudinal component, hence the process of discovery is not merely that of finding new things to believe but of finding new things to like and dislike. Practical discovery is the forming of new attitudes.

To conclude this paper, I need only summarize the argument. From the principle that the outcome of practical reasoning is an attitude, it followed that the process itself is that of forming and transforming attitudes. This is only possible if we reject the cognitivist interpretation of practical reasoning as cognitive reasoning applied to practice. Practical reasoning is *sui generis*, although it has many similarities to cognitive reasoning.

XI

The Revolt against Philosophy:
The Spell of Popper

ROBERT JORDAN, *The University of the South*

THAT the human race is in trouble again should cause no more surprise than another case of measles. But that man, the problem-solver, should still be in trouble and that his trouble should be problem-solving is, for the master of his fate and the maker of his own destiny, a paradox so frustrating that the devil alone must be responsible The explanation must be looked for in some great act of betrayal whose very existence and character have been unnoticed because of the diabolical cleverness of the deception on the one hand and our own pathetic innocence on the other That we should be delivered from the hands of our enemies, it should be sufficient to eliminate—if not the devil himself—at least the devil's disciple and his work Professor K R Popper undertakes this task of exorcism in *The Open Society and Its Enemies* [1] The devil's disciple—the great betrayer—is Plato The devil's work, of course, is rather well known in the history of Western thought. The sacred name invoked is sophistry. This catharsis may well leave the race of Platonists spiritually exhausted, but if it will save us, we should undergo the purification no matter what the pain. As balm for our wounds we are offered the soothing medication of "piecemeal social engineering"

The Prince of Darkness is receiving an inordinate amount of attention nowadays in every quarter, though the charges are not usually so sensational. For those who have read the Platonic *Dialogues* with profit as well as pleasure, it comes as no mild surprise that the friend, admirer, and disciple of Socrates is the origin and commencement of all our past, and all our present, grief Plato as Judas ought to give us pause. And this revelation,

---

[1] London, George Routledge and Sons, 1945, 2 vols. There are, of course, other devilish lieutenants, notably Hegel In this essay I am concerned only with the charges against Plato.

taken to heart, ought to cure us of any tendency to traffic with what is traditional in Western thought.

According to Popper, Plato was nothing but a racist and a fascist, and, to
put no quibbling qualification upon it, he bequeathed to posterity fascism
and racism In short, Plato is the true author of the evil we recognize today
as totalitarianism It is rather important to distinguish this charge from the
charge that there are passages in Plato which might be construed by a modern totalitarian in such a way as would enable him to call upon Plato as
authority. This charge could be borne with equanimity The real charge is
that Plato is a fascist in fact and in spirit, and that Platonism can be *identified with* totalitarianism [2] Now, to anyone who has read the eighth book of
the *Republic*, this is a sensational turning of the tables But there are other
reasons which suggest that Popper's gibe about Aristotle is possibly applicable to his own reading of Plato, namely, that it is not a sound and balanced
judgment but a reading which succeeds in "elaborately and solemnly missing the point."[3]

At least since the appearance of Crossman's *Plato Today* the debunking
of Plato has taken a form which might be called the technique of reluctant
disparagement were it not for the fact that while the disparagement becomes more and more obvious and pointed, the reluctance tends to be replaced by a certain excitement, induced, perhaps, by the thoughts of the
coming effects of disenchantment. Coupled with this technique is another
which involves the use of the open-and-shut vocabulary made popular by
Bergson Following Bergson's use of "open" and "closed" to designate both
societies and moralities, we can devise such pairs as "tribalism" and "civilization," "primitivism" and "progressivism." "arrested" and "dynamic," and
the like Popper uses both of these techniques—the first to suggest that
while he respects Plato he loves truth more, the second to suggest that the
truth he loves is something dynamic, liberating, and, in a word, "open,"
while Plato's teaching, since it cannot be characterized by any of these honorific adjectives, must be regarded as the enemy of what any enlightened
modern man would choose as worthy of his consideration, not to mention
his allegiance

The question of terms may be considered later, especially Popper's use
of "collectivism" in two senses and his attribution to Plato of "aestheticism."
The cultivation of ambiguity through the use of emotive terms might be
only a symptom of discomfort in the face of what is merely uncongenial
Presumably, there is more to Popper's charges than that. But it cannot well
be the case that "Plato hated tyranny" and was "the greatest philosopher

[2] *Ibid*, I, 4.
[3] *Ibid*, II, 1 In point of fact, Popper warns his readers that he will not give a "just
and fair" treatment of Plato. See *Ibid*, I, 28.

of all time"[4] and that, at the same time, he is a fascist and the enemy of civilization, unless some strange twists are given to these terms The latter distinctions would surely disqualify him from holding the former. That Popper apparently finds both of them irresistible does not make them any less incompatible This question is best considered in connection with what Popper proposes as a substitute for Platonism The habit of twisting vocabulary is part of the technique of deposition, but it does not prove that something serious may not lie behind it We may ask, then, if Popper's interpretation of Plato is a serious effort in understanding or whether it is distortion for the purpose of dismissal.

The first step in the process of dismissal is the effort to present Socrates as a saint and his pupil as a devil This is more than mere word-juggling, but does it make sense? The essence of this saintly Socrates is an ignorance of which he is justly proud and a distrust of reason He knows that he knows nothing, and he knows that beyond this there is no real hope of knowledge [5] Making no commitment whatsoever, beyond that of making none, he is capable of a truly remarkable modesty and self-effacement which has served ever since as a model for the scientist. This antiseptic ideal was sullied by Plato, who introduced germs of commitment which ultimately came to light as a festering sore on the body politic Plato's initial and most serious mistake was that of supposing that we can know something—really know something—about human nature and the world around us.

Now, this picture of the noncommittal Socrates is, I suggest, absurd And it requires no "Socratic-Platonic" theory or special critical apparatus to show that it is. Consider the *Apology* and the *Crito* which Popper believes to be Socratic rather than Platonic [6] Plato's early dialogues show him to be concerned with problems of practice, especially in the sphere of value And they illustrate, above all, the search for the *techne* or art of human life. The reason for this search is that upon its successful completion rests the possibility of resolving value conflicts. Socrates is presented to us as the man who questioned his fellow citizens and friends about matters of good and evil in general. It is common knowledge that the early Platonic dialogues end with these conflicts unresolved And Popper apparently believes that this negative result is essentially all there is to the Socratic method. If so, the *Apology* and particularly the *Crito* contain some inexplicable assertions.

There is no doubt that Socrates advocated what might be called method-

---

[4] *Ibid*, I, 85, 175
[5] *Ibid*, I, 112, 114, 116, 117
[6] *Ibid*, I, 258 ff.

ological skepticism, but this is not paralytic skepticism Indeed, it is unusu-
ally generous. And, in any case, it is not the only aspect of his method [7]
Consider the things that Socrates *knows* and asserts in the *Apology*[8]—that
it is disgraceful and evil to do wrong and to disobey one's superior, whether
god or man, that he must never give up the practice of philosophy, because
of its value to the state, that he will continue to point out the *truth* to anyone
he meets, that it is shameful to care for wealth and power more than for
truth and for the perfection of the soul. Indeed, he knows about good and
evil in general. Further, virtue does not come from money but money and
all good things from virtue, whether for the individual or for the state. All
this is a strong and unmistakable commitment in favor of the capacity of
human reason to apprehend the good and to act upon it when apprehended.
As a mere assertion, however, it would not be extraordinarily impressive
philosophically, since it is not self-evident And were it not for the Platonic
development of these Socratic insights, we should have nothing but a noble
statement of faith It is Plato's presentation of what both he and Socrates
were doing, and nothing else, that enables us to make any sense of Socrates's teaching at all There is, to be sure, the historical and critical problem of precisely where the two merge But there is no philosophic problem
unless we suppose that somehow the pupil *betrayed* the master. That supposition makes chaos and nonsense of the dialogues, because we are then
forced, as Popper is forced, to find pure Socratic gems of liberalism in writings by another man who was, we must suppose, illiberal and un-Socratic
That the whole matter *is* forced is confirmed by what Popper says later in
discussing more recent "enemies" of society He says that anyone who
reads the relevant letters in the case may see that Fichte perverted the teaching of Kant He then goes on to say that this "shows that my theory of
Plato's perversion of the teaching of Socrates is by no means so fantastic
as it may appear to Platonists "[9]

The *Crito* does even less to justify a "detached" Socrates It is from the
outset a defense of the capacity of human reason to *know* what is right and
wrong The sharpest possible contrast is made between the man who has
knowledge and the many whose opinions are worthless [10] It is wrong to
requite wrong with wrong, no matter what is done to us [11] How could
Popper's Socrates possibly make such a statement? Socrates further resorts
to a practical use of myth (a *Platonic* device) by having the laws speak for

---

[7] As Werner Jaeger points out, it includes exhortation as well as examination See his
Paideia The Ideals of Greek Culture (New York and London, Oxford University Press,
1939–44), II, 37 ff
[8] 29d ff
[9] Popper, *op cit*, II, 298, n 58.
[10] *Crito*, 44c, 46b–48b
[11] *Crito*, 49c–d.

themselves The common good demands that Socrates either do what the law requires or persuade the state of what is really right.[12] This is what Plato says in his seventh letter.[13]

Popper notices these assertions but does not see that, far from making the individual perfectly self-sufficient, it implies the most intimate connection between the individual and the common good What is more, it definitely shows Socrates to be committed to the possibility of a real knowledge of the good for man both as an individual and as a member of society Further, it shows that Socrates felt his mission to be of practical importance to the community In other words, the search was to *issue* in something, was to make a difference in the community.

It must be admitted, then, by anyone willing to read Plato's account of Socrates's character in the *Crito* and the *Apology* as "in the main historically correct"[14] that the account shows a perfectly clear though incomplete positive teaching. The negative Socrates is a myth. If this were not the case, Socrates would be simply a talkative old man with a certain amiable blatancy, but a negligible figure in the history of philosophy Two further points should be noticed. In the first place, in order that these positive insights would be significant and more than a pious faith, they had to be developed and expanded This was the work of Plato Hence, to suggest that there is something un-Socratic about Plato because he went beyond what we know of Socrates is to say something trivially true if the suggestion is meant simply as a statement of fact. How could it have been otherwise? It is like saying that there is something un-Newtonian about Einstein. But if, in the second place, the term "un-Socratic" is made to carry the burden of "betrayal," then we should expect to find radical differences everywhere in Plato's thought which would make the *Apology* and the *Crito* and the other Socratic dialogues incomprehensible in the light of what follows them This is simply not the case. Popper tries to show that it is the case by branding as Platonic everything he does not like in the later writings, while praising as Socratic everything that he does like. But there is no basis for these distinctions except the original decision that Plato must have betrayed his teacher.

The passages of the *Apology* and the *Crito* already referred to, indicate that there is a hierarchy of values which it is of the greatest practical importance to clarify, and that clarification was a part of Socrates's mission. We are told that this is of great political importance.[15] Therefore, it con-

12 *Crito*, 51c

13 *Ep.*, No 7, 531a–d.

14 Popper, *op cit*, I, 258, n. 56

15 *Apol*, 30a, b. See *Gorgias*, 521c–d, as against Popper, *op cit*, I, 253, n. 44 Popper omits the social aspect He believes that Socrates teaches the self-sufficiency of the individual This is half of the truth—but the other half is equally important.

cerns both individual and social ethics at the same time In short, the re-establishment of a sound social order is a moral problem It is an *individual* problem because the individual is the seat of reason—a theme, incidentally, of the *Republic*, as will be seen presently. The ordinary means of political change are not equal to this task, since civic affairs are under the influence of oratorical appeals looking not to the common good or the best interest or happiness of the individual but to what is immediately attractive, what the many want or, rather, *think* they want.[16]

All this is Socratic, and it is perfectly consonant with Plato's later writings, on the whole. But it is clear that more than this is needed if we are to have any philosophic solution of the problems which Socrates has brought to light by his questioning One of the methodological results of this inquiry was negative and served to clear the ground for Socrates's hearers so that a new start could be made. But it is mere perversity to ignore the demand for a new start This was a mistake which Plato avoided, and it is a singular criticism of him, indeed, to say that he made an alliance with the devil in doing so. The question still remains Did Plato, in extending the Socratic insights, warp them into something wholly foreign to the spirit of their discoverer?

The essence of the Socratic discovery comes to this There must be some *techne* or art of life comparable to, if not exactly the same as, the special arts of the craftsmen whom Socrates was so fond of using by way of illustration This cannot be developed in detail here But Plato's development of this basic suggestion in his early dialogues is evidence enough that, far from betraying his master, he was, in fact, extending the Socratic teaching in the way it had to be extended if Socrates's mission was to mean anything at all. It will suffice to indicate briefly how this was done. We may then look at the *Republic* and Popper's charges of totalitarianism.

As early as the *Euthyphro*[17] it becomes clear that nothing less than a general theory of value is required if conflicts of value are to be resolved. The great problem of an ethics which makes happiness a positive goal (as against an ethics which makes duty fundamental) is the problem of providing satisfaction for the demands of the human organism while at the same time achieving virtue And this is a problem because, while the demands for satisfaction are practically numberless, virtue requires that some limit be placed upon them. Nevertheless, the act of limitation is not so easy as at first sight it seems to be On the face of it, all demands are on the same footing Some principle of selection must be devised But on what basis can the selection be made? Only by determining what the nature of

---

[16] *Apol* , 36b–d, e, 38d–e
[17] 78 ff. The whole dialogue is a preface to the theory of value.

man really is—what human nature requires in order that the excellence proper to it should be realized.[18]

Now, for Plato, all of these satisfactions are provided for by some kind of art, following specific rules according to which further specific effects may be produced.[19] Thus to decide upon the satisfaction of any particular desire would suggest an appeal to the techniques of the particular art which could best accomplish the end in view, namely, the satisfaction of that desire At least this would be the most effective way of gaining the desired satisfaction. But the one question most in need of an answer is not to be answered by any of the special arts. This is the question· Should a human being satisfy the desire in question at all? Another art is required, which is capable of making a unity of the manifold of desires, capable of regarding the whole human person and his life on the whole, to answer this question. In other words, these early dialogues are concerned with specific problems which all fall under a more general problem, namely, how a man ought to live.

Plato has exhaustive interests. He resists the epitomist But if it is proper to speak of a single predominant interest in his thought, the question of living well would surely be a candidate for first place This theme receives clear and repeated emphasis. No other point of departure will lead the reader so quickly through the whole range of the *Dialogues* Thus the *Charmides* opens with a statement about the balance which is the aim of any investigation of human nature[20] and ends by suggesting that if life is to be a life of reason with an intelligible aim, there must be an art or practical knowledge of the whole dimension of life, the whole range of good and evil [21] The very same issue is presented in the *Laches* (as it is later in Book I of the *Republic*) as one of supreme importance which is related to the crisis in education to which Plato devotes so much attention.[22]

The whole matter is risky, it is not something that can be left to chance.[23] The reasons for this are finally given in the analysis of the soul in Book IV of the *Republic* But we cannot miss the continuity of the two themes—the demand for practical knowledge and the area of its application—all of the activities of living [24] The idea of a standard of value is, again, the climax of the *Lysis* [25] The life of reason and the crisis in education is the theme of the *Protagoras* The soul itself is at stake[26]—that is to say, this is the most serious

18 See *Apol*, 20b ff
19 *Alcibiades* I, 108b
20 156b–157d.
21 *Char*, 173d, 174b–c
22 *Laches*, 184d–185e, 195c–d. See 179a–d, *Protagoras*, 319d ff ; *Gorg*, 503c ff.
23 *Laches*, 185a, 187b, 200e–end.
24 *Laches*, 190d, 192e–193e, 195c–d.
25 219c.
26 *Prot.*, 313c–314c.

question we can discuss. The *Meno* reiterates the point.[27] The *Euthydemus* drives it home by showing that this rational inquiry must be taken seriously.[28]

It is not merely a question of the game of sophistry. There is a real practical purpose—knowledge with a positive content.[29] Of course, there are dangers in all this, because a complete life is an inclusive life, in keeping with the potentialities of the human person. One can live safely and cautiously, one can venture nothing and so gain nothing. But this is not Plato's notion of a life worth living. However, the enrichment of life is attended by risks which make it imperative that rational guidance be provided which will prevent the various goods of the complete life from being turned to evil uses.[30] What the sophists are called upon to do is in keeping with the Socratic quest and with their own claims: They are asked to supply the art of living which is demanded by the necessity of rational control and which they claimed as their possession.[31] They try to escape the positive commitment by word-juggling and eristic display. But genuine philosophy cannot seek this refuge and also claim to have anything significant to say. This question is considered in many passages of the dialogues,[32] but nowhere with greater emphasis than in the *Gorgias*.

The life of reason is a problem involving priority and subordination with respect to satisfactions. This is the practical issue which emerges from the various discussions of value in the early and middle dialogues. The supreme art which would resolve all of these value questions is the art that Gorgias claims to possess.[33] He has the fluid mind of a man who cannot so much as entertain the idea of failure. His business is success—prodigious success—which he achieves by means of rhetoric. But his technique of persuasion has no permanence and no rational ground. His failure to distinguish between the desires that ought to be satisfied and those that ought not to be satisfied leads Plato to reject his claim and the claim of anyone who supposes that art is irrational.[34] The technique of producing responses, even though they be invariably pleasant, is not the art of living well.[35] Thus the whole subject of the *Gorgias* is shifted by degrees from the relatively trivial question of what Gorgias thinks he is doing to the fundamental question of

[27] 91a ff
[28] 278c, 282c–283a.
[29] *Euthyd*, 281b–c.
[30] *Euthyd*, 281d–e
[31] *Euthyd*, 282d–e, see 273d
[32] For instance, *Hippias Minor*, 365, 375a ff., *Alcib*. I, 111e–112a, 114b–d, 115a–116e, 127 ff, 128b, d–e.
[33] *Gorg*, 451d, 454b See 448c.
[34] *Gorg*, 462c, 464–66, 500 ff
[35] *Gorg*, 512–13

what philosophy ought to be. And the debate about two kinds of art becomes a debate about two modes of life—and about what course of life is
the best [36] Power or success cannot even be rationally discussed until this
prior question has been answered, since power is not power at all and
success is not success, for Plato, unless it provides for the perfection of
human life [37]

The whole matter might be put in another way by saying that the parts
of virtue which Plato discusses in the *Laches* and *Charmides*, for example,
demand specific acts, but these same specific acts may be rejected by the
virtuous man in certain circumstances, and other acts substituted for them.
The ground for rejecting them and acting counter to the demand of some
part of virtue is a knowledge of wider scope than that required by the part
alone, namely, a knowledge of good and evil *in general* In short, what is
needed to resolve ethical conflicts is a knowledge which embraces the
whole dimension of value, a knowledge which has something to say about
anything whatever that bears upon the moral life, a knowledge to which
the problems connected with particular acts of virtue are subordinated
The special arts, including the fine arts, are regarded by Plato in the same
way—their use or purpose is to serve life.

Plato's discussion of the arts and conduct is one of the persistent themes
in the *Dialogues* The analysis is first applied to individual life and then to
social life. But the problem is essentially the same. The transition to social
ethics does not imply that, for Plato, the individual ceases to count for
anything, as will be shown presently. Individual and social problems are
inseparably connected for Plato, as they were for Socrates, but it is not always possible to talk about both of them at the same time There is no space
to develop this parallel here But the aim of social analysis is the same as
that of the earlier analysis of the individual predicament—to answer the
question How is a man to live? Conflicts on the social level reveal demands
too numerous to be satisfied. The analysis of social justice indicates that not
just any activity can be engaged in with safety. Critical deliberation is required The point is whether the multitude of possible activities is to be
subject to rational guidance or not—and what kind of guidance this is to be

The Platonic writings that come before the *Republic* attempt to locate
the task of practical philosophy by discovering the conditions for living the
life of reason But the analysis is limited in one way or another by the specific problem being discussed—the parts of virtue in the Socratic dialogues
or the difference between genuine and defective art in the *Gorgias* How
all of these matters fit together is a larger problem. It is taken up in the

[36] *Gorg.*, 500c. See 472c, d.
[37] *Gorg* , 466–67. See *Alcib* I, 135b, *Laws*, 711e–712a, *Rep* , 473c–d.

Republic, which is a complex of many subjects for the very good reason that the question of living well is a complex problem of individual and social ethics It is so complex that politics, education, and even fine art contribute to its final solution It is not surprising, to say the least, that the *Republic* should be an advance upon what Plato wrote previously. And two things should be remembered and will be remembered by any open-minded reader of the *Dialogues* (1) Plato would not feel called upon to repeat in the *Republic* everything he had said elsewhere and (2) we should not conclude that he has abandoned his earlier position unless there is a clear reason for doing so And there is, in the *Republic* itself, ample evidence to show that it is in general agreement with the earlier writings and is a natural extension of them.

The preceding summary will serve as a basis upon which to consider some of the fundamental points in Popper's attack It is by no means irrelevant to the charges which Popper makes against Plato For it is by selecting certain passages of the *Republic* and the *Laws* and ignoring their context, not only in these works but in Plato's writings as a whole, that Popper reaches his extreme conclusion He managed to drop out of account altogether the constant themes of perennial significance in Plato. Yet these themes are woven into the same fabric with Plato's more radical and extreme suggestions for the reform of the social order. And to attempt to interpret the *Republic* without the introductory theory of *techne* is to place oneself at a considerable disadvantage. The political art is the supreme art, representing the culmination of the Socratic and Platonic search for a *techne* of life. Therefore, it is not so much a convenience as a necessity to pay some attention to the foundation of the whole structure Plato made what everyone will agree were wrong decisions But a mistake is not a deliberate effort at a totalitarian system And Popper's charge, it should be remembered, is that Plato's system is *purely* totalitarian [38]

What is the problem of the *Republic*? It is reasonable to suggest that in the light of what precedes the *Republic* and what is the basic issue in any Platonic discussion of individual and social ethics, the problem is the familiar one of how to live In point of fact, this is what Socrates asserts in the first book "It is no ordinary matter we are discussing but the right conduct of life."[39] Popper pays no attention to this announced topic Now, the *Republic* offers, as a solution to this problem, two kinds of analysis. The one serves to establish the structure of the ideal state The other is, ultimately, far more important and is an analysis of the human soul and of psychic life. These are the main themes to which others are subordinate. If we ask why this is the case, it is necessary to refer to Plato's philosophy as practical over

[38] *Popper, op. cit*, I, 4, 75, 150.
[39] *Rep*, 352d. See 344d, e.

its whole range And this is only what we should expect from a reading of the earlier Platonic dialogues, since it has been the principal practical problem of all of them.

The point is that there is no reason to suppose that Plato would outline an "organic" theory of the state or that he would attempt to establish a social order which would be totalitarian in any sense in which we now use that word to apply to modern dictatorships. Yet Popper comes to the *Dialogues* with the full expectation of finding such a structure Of course, the words "organic" and "totalitarian" are now so highly charged with emotive significance that it is difficult to determine what meaning should be given to them But an organic state, if this phrase is to have any sinister meaning, would have to be one that has a consciousness or "life" of its own, in some sense, which it communicates to the individuals who are members of it. It would have to be a biological entity But this is not a Platonic notion. Further, it may reasonably be said that the worst evil of modern totalitarianism is the doctrine that while the individual has duties to the state, the state has no obligation whatever to consider the welfare of the individual On this view, the individual is expendable at any time, and no explanation or justification need be offered These are the doctrines that Popper attributes to Plato, his basic charge being that in Plato's commonwealth the individual is nothing [10] Even this is not strong enough, apparently, for we are told that "in the field of politics, the individual is to Plato the Evil One himself "[41] This singular view of the status of the individual, together with a fantastic conception of the Platonic conception of justice, constitutes the basic charge which Popper makes The charge cannot be sustained.

It is difficult to see how Plato's state could be construed as organic in the light of his metaphysical realism It might be held that such an interpretation could be based indirectly upon the Platonic division of labor which, if isolated and made the main point of the *Republic,* suggests that there are three special kinds of men, only one of which is really human, or human only in relation to the great Whole. This would be a mistake But, in conjunction with this initial error, the notion of justice as each doing his own work might suggest that Plato's justice must either work against or ignore the individual for the sake of, or in the interest of, something lying outside the individual, some abstract "thing" which no individual could realize or really share. That this would also be a mistake may be seen by considering what happens in Book I of the *Republic*

Here again, as in the previous summary of Plato's notion of the *techne* of

<hr />

[40] Popper, *op cit.,* I, 48, 64–68, especially 65, where it is said that Plato's state is a "super-individual'" See also pp 152–53 and II, 35

[41] *Ibid ,* I, 90 See 87 Popper makes extensive use of *Laws,* Bk. X, especially 903 ff., without pointing out that that book deals with theology, with the relation between God and the individual soul—which is not a question of politics

human life, any epitome must necessarily be inadequate Even so, two things can be discerned. Book I reminds us of problems considered in the early dialogues and, at the same time, states the major issue to be debated in the rest of the *Republic* The argument with Polemarchus introduces an important point which was discussed in the *Euthydemus*[42] where the political art was called for but seemed to have no subject matter Plato suggests, in the argument with Polemarchus, that justice cannot be a mere matter of rendering to each his due, because in every case where an action is performed it is always some special art that is best able to perform it, or able to perform it at all And the conclusion reached is the absurd one that justice, which must be universal in its scope, is good for nothing in particular [43] The art of living seems to have only this in common with the special arts, that it proceeds correctly or incorrectly But beyond this, the art of life must function on every occasion and not, like the limited arts, on certain occasions only If it did not, it would not be an art of life as a whole but of some moment of life, which is quite different. Such moments may be cultivated, of course, as some persons cultivate the aesthetic moment A certain area of life may be devoted to, say, the practice of a musical instrument and so be under the direction of a particular art. But the art of life must be relevant to all occasions and all persons, whatever this art may be [44]

Further difficulties come to light in the argument with Thrasymachus. Thrasymachus gets into trouble not so much because he conceives the good life to be one of pleasure but because, partly in agreement with Socrates, he holds that there is an art of living and one which is properly called an art in so far as it is perfected—that is, actually realized as a noetic discipline. And this leads to a consideration of what such an art involves [45] Here the art is taken as possessed in perfection because that is what Thrasymachus requires, although it is also what Socrates requires Thrasymachus also holds that the art is for the advantage of the man who practices it But Plato distinguishes between the art as practical and the art as theoretical.[46] Considered as pure theory, as art *qua* art, it is autonomous and gives rules to itself But in practice, since it cannot seek its own advantage, being perfected, it must seek the advantage of something else, namely, its object [47] Any further advantage, such as money-making, would be the consideration

[42] 291–93.

[43] *Rep*, 332d–333c.

[44] *Rep*, 334c–336b, especially 335b On the whole question of conduct in relation to the arts see H W B Joseph, *Essays in Ancient and Modern Philosophy* (New York and London, Oxford University Press, 1935), Chap. 1, especially p 10

[45] *Rep.*, 340e–342e.

[46] *Rep*, 341e, 342d. See *Statesman*, 260a, c.

[47] *Rep*, 342b, c.

of another art So it is with the ruling art which is here being discussed and which is contrasted with the art of gain.[48]

In the section on the art of gain, "usefulness" is taken in its widest possible range and is extended to honor and to such matters as the unwillingness to be ruled by inferior men The result is that while Thrasymachus agrees with Socrates on the question of the art of gain, to the extent of granting that there *is* such an art, what he *means* by gain is so far from what Socrates means that, in this respect, they are hardly on common ground at all For Socrates, gain is that which from the beginning of his mission the whole discussion of risk has been about—the whole of life, including virtue What is to be gained, ultimately, is not the whole world but one's own soul This is hardly the modern totalitarian or fascist doctrine of power and gain. It is, in fact, a repudiation of that doctrine

But the argument with Thrasymachus is unsatisfactory for the reason that Socrates mentions in bringing Book I to a close—the meaning of justice has not been made clear.[49] *Pleonexia* cannot be, Socrates holds, the principle of living the good life. It is the root of the bad conduct which must follow upon its adoption. Therefore, while Book I shows the central significance of the art of life, it does not tell us in what living well consists, and, as a result, it does not tell us what happiness is or how to achieve it There is agreement about the existence of a *techne* of human life, but Thrasymachus, if he sticks to his position, is not forced to accept Plato's notion of the *nature* of the good life He need only agree that it requires an art as the condition of achieving it. Even if it be granted that the soul's function is to rule and that it should possess the excellence proper to the fulfillment of this function,[50] we do not know precisely what is involved in living well nor whether it would result in happiness.

The *techne* is agreed upon in theory, but the practical application to various goods, particularly in connection with the question of conflict, has not been settled. The nature of justice and the nature of the soul are still difficulties that must be overcome. The contention is that the *techne* of life is what enables us to guide life in specific ways which every rational person would approve and accept. And since it has not been made clear just how this could be done, the whole question must be taken up again However, it is of the greatest importance to notice, in all of this, the clear continuity between the earlier dialogues and the first book of the *Republic*.

The continuity becomes plain again in Book IV. There is nothing sinister in the fact that the analysis of the soul is postponed until this time [51] The

---

[48] *Rep* , 342d–e, 345c–348c
[49] *Rep* , 351c – end of Bk I.
[50] *Rep* , 353d, e.
[51] See Popper, *op. cit.*, I, 77 ff.

question of justice being a vital one, the decision is made to look for it in the state first, because justice may more easily be discerned in society than in the individual [52] This requires an outline of an ideal state, because Plato would not consider any existing state capable of displaying justice clearly —which is what is desired and demanded There is no reason to regard this outline as "historicism," in Popper's sense [53] Plato would naturally think in terms of states that he knew And, in any case, the important question is not the *genesis* of the state in temporal terms Even if we suppose that Plato had this clearly in mind, we have no ground for making it the central point in his discussion, because we have been told what the central point is in Book I, and in the clearest possible way.

The problem being how to live, the construction of a state which will exhibit justice demands an analysis of society that will exhibit the elements of social structure needed to meet the basic demands of human nature. This is a timeless question. In discussing the *techne* of human life, Plato never makes it contingent upon some historical period. The whole issue is: What are the conditions for living well? And to draw attention away from the central point to some subsidiary matter is the first step in misunderstanding. The point is not that subsidiary matters should be ignored but that they should be seen *as* subsidiary and in right relation to the main issue Popper's analysis elevates a matter of minor importance to the status of a guiding principle.

Now, states can be said to live well only analogously. The problem of living applies, strictly, to the individual; it applies to states only derivatively. Individual and social life are inseparable, to be sure. But it is the problem of the individual soul that is fundamental in Plato's position.[54] Thus, having discussed a system of education in Books II and III of the *Republic*, Plato returns to the question of the soul in Book IV The activities of the state *are* the activities of the citizens carried out corporately in the light of some common purpose. There is nothing magical about the state. It has no mysterious origin. It takes its character from the characters of its citizens and from nothing else. Therefore, in order to know what the character of a state really is, whether it is just or unjust, happy or unhappy, we must investigate the character of its citizens. It is for this reason that the nature of society, the whole cultural situation, and the character of the individual are inseparably connected.[55] To consider the activities of the good

[52] *Rep* , 368d ff.

[53] Popper, *op cit* , I, 28.

[54] Popper avoids all the evidence for this by attributing all interest in individualism to Socrates alone See *op cit* , I, 91, 92, 254, n 45, where the *Gorgias* is divided into thick layers of Platonic black and thin layers of Socratic white For a discussion based upon what the *Dialogues* contain, see Jaeger, *op cit* , II, Chap 6.

[55] *Rep* , 544d–e See 435e.

life at either level is to meet the stubborn fact of conflict and, philosophically speaking, the task, indeed the necessity, of doing so The wholly perfect
individual and society would be desirable. And the Socratic *Dialogues* illustrate the fact that, initially, we tend to ask for unlimited satisfaction
and unrestrained liberty They also illustrate the fact that because of conflict and risk we do not really have this choice as rational agents And Plato
insists that no goal can safely be pursued unless there is a constitutional
government established within the soul [56]

However, the governing principle is not arbitrary It is not based upon
some whim of the ruling class It is based upon an investigation of the
psychic life—and it is Plato's purpose in discussing the soul to establish a
natural basis for government both in the individual and in the state Social
ethics is not divorced from individual ethics, because the common good is
shared by all members of the community and has no source other than
their common aims and purposes [57] Thus the attempt to dispose of Plato's
ethical theory of the individual on the ground that the state is an organism
which exists apart from the citizens and gives rise to *their* character will
not merely miss the point—it will suggest something, namely, the fascist
idea of the state, which is just the reverse of what Plato had in mind There
is more than a slight difference between saying that the individual must
make some sacrifices for the sake of the general welfare and saying that the
individual must be sacrificed for the general welfare [58]

The whole analysis of the soul is centered upon the fact of conflict In
the initial outline of the ideal state, the demands of human nature led to a
division of labor and to the establishment of special groups which would
perform specific functions This division of labor is undoubtedly too extreme, but it is not, in any event, the basic ingredient in Plato's notion of the
rational as naturally the ruling element. In one sense it is a consequence of
it The notion of specific functions in the collective sense depends upon the
analysis of the individual soul This analysis implies *some* kind of division
of labor in the community. It does not require that there be the minimum
of transfer from one group to another which Plato felt would probably be
the case. But the fact of order and priority is inescapable if there is to be
any division of function at all. The important point, in any case, is that the
division of function, for Plato, must reflect the nature of the individual
soul, because there is no other basis for it [59]

Socrates holds that there is evidence, if we really examine the nature of
psychic life, for three distinct functions—reason, appetite, and what is usu-

[56] *Rep.*, 590e–591c.
[57] *Rep.*, 435e and 544d, e.
[58] *Rep* , 419 ff.
[59] *Rep.*, 434e ff

ally called the spirited or aspirational factor in the soul.[60] A man's activity, then, is just when he is acting rationally and when the appetitive aspect of his nature is under the control of his reason Further, the individual's aspiration for goods and satisfactions must be guided, if his action is to be rational, by some apprehension of what he is really striving for and why he is striving for it. He cannot indulge himself in just any desire or an unlimited number of desires without turning his experience into chaos and making it impossible to realize any durable satisfactions at all The measure is what the individual is capable of becoming at his *best*—but this demands some *knowledge* of human nature This is the burden of Plato's entire moral philosophy Popper's assertion that anything can be defended as natural could not possibly be made on the basis of the Platonic ethics, and misses the whole point of Plato's notion of the natural order.[61]

Book IV of the *Republic* is an effort to reveal that natural order There is no further answer to the question "Why *this* order?" than simply the revelation of the order itself as the health of the soul It is revealed by examining the psychic life—its conditions and possibilities—just as one examines the physical life in order to determine the causes and conditions of physical health This examination leads Plato to conclude that by justice we must mean the natural order of the soul's functions in accordance with which control is exercised by that which ought to control, and that which ought to be governed is, in fact, governed This is the order of reason, spirit, and appetite, and injustice in the soul is a relationship among these factors which is contrary to this natural order. This is the basis of anything that can be called natural law. This is a complex question, but Plato believes that man actually has the capacity for understanding what kind of creature he is and, therefore, what he ought to do

There is a negative side to this process, because the functions of the soul do not necessarily co-operate They may conflict and so upset the natural order. It is for this reason that conflict is the origin of all our difficulties, both individual and social. And it is also for this reason that the analysis of the soul may be regarded as politically significant But there is no reason whatever to read into it some dark totalitarian purpose Plato warns against the tendency to drop the individual and concentrate on the state alone [62] There can be, Plato believes, a rebellion, within the individual, of that which is naturally subordinate against that which is by nature the directing element. When this occurs, the whole of life is turned upside down [63]

Now, the important thing to notice—and Popper ignores the significance

[60] *Rep* , 436a ff
[61] Popper, *op cit* , I, 61–62.
[62] *Rep* , 435e, 544d, e
[63] *Rep* , 442b–c See *Gorg.*, 481c.

of the passages altogether—is that Plato's conclusions are based upon an analysis of the constituent factors in human experience and do not depend upon the threefold grouping of persons within the state The analysis of the soul is a crucial part of the *Republic* if we wish to understand Plato's ideas of rule, of virtue, and of justice There is a hierarchy of functions within the individual based upon natural priority or significance The rational element in the soul, being the naturally governing element, must exercise the ruling function if life is to be other than sheer chaos. We shall hardly overlook this point when we consider Plato's account of virtue in the individual. But the same considerations hold in his social ethics, because his social ethics rests upon the same evidence

Individual virtue requires the *techne* of human life. It is an art with a broader scope than any of the special arts, and Plato's account of the soul supplies the evidence for relating the arts and conduct.[64] This is a complex problem which cannot be discussed in detail here But one of the implications of Plato's view is that justice is not merely the outward performance of social duties according to some arbitrary assignment. That would be external action without any ground or rational justification Action that is just, whether internal or external, is action that is specified by rational guidance and based upon a practical knowledge of human nature. It is justified by reference to internal characteristics and is the functioning of the individual in terms of the harmony of these internal functions Social action is the same functioning of the individual when it is translated into the social sphere of corporate action.[65] Justice in the individual is activity according to a definite structure—when the several functions of the soul perform their own tasks under the guidance of the rational factor which rules by nature [66] As R L. Nettleship puts it:

Real justice means not the mere doing of one's own business in the state, but such outward doing of one's own business as is an expression of a corresponding mode of action within the soul, if the outward action is really just, it means that the soul is just within, that like a just state the whole soul and the several parts of it perform their proper functions in relation to one another.[67]

Popper does not discuss Plato's analysis of individual justice in relation to social justice. It makes nonsense of his version of Platonic justice as that which is in the interest of a purely totalitarian state—that is, in the interest of the special ruling class.[68]

It is certainly a part of Plato's purpose to show that justice in the state is

[64] *Rep* , 443 ff.
[65] See *Alcib.* I, 114b, *Gorg.*, 471–472d.
[66] *Rep* , 441d–e, 442a.
[67] *Lectures on the Republic of Plato* (London, Macmillan, 1937), p. 160.
[68] See Popper, *op cit* , I, 77, 126.

like justice in the soul [69] But it is charged that, since Plato held an organic theory of the state, his use of the term "justice" with reference to the individual is simply a monstrous deception and that what he means, all along, is the interest of some entity which ignores, by its very nature, the character and rights of the individual. Now, Plato was interested in corporate life, that life which has in it elements shared by all the members of the group And he certainly held that this common life, this common purpose, ought really to be shared whether in sickness or in health, for better or for worse.[70] But this corporate life is not a "thing" of any kind and could not possibly be called an organism It is apprehended by reason and is immaterial [71] What is shared as the common good must be immaterial, since immaterial goods alone are capable of being shared without diminution They are the common aims and purpose to which all the individuals in a community can give their allegiance. They make up what Plato regarded as the unity of the group

Further, Plato holds that just as in the case of the individual, there is a natural order of functions enabling the individual to accomplish what he really proposes as his aim and really wants to carry out, so in the state there is a natural order of functions which enables the group to achieve what the members of the group really aspire to, in a collective capacity. There must be some kind of plan, and there must be persistence in the plan in order to sustain common activities in the face of obstacles or attacks from without. Plato would surely maintain that his doctrine of the common good cannot be repudiated without some alternative account of how people and governments order their actions We shall see presently that Popper offers no adequate alternative Plato's position is hardly overthrown by pointing out that there will be endless argument about what ought to be attempted in common and what devices may be employed in the attempt. Plato had in mind a very small state and one which was, or should be on his theory, a society of friends. As a corporate body, therefore, it might enjoy a greater measure of agreement than could conceivably be looked for in a modern nation of 150,000,000 people. There is no reason to suppose that if Plato were to be confronted with the enormous complexity of a modern state he would insist upon the details of the *Republic* or the *Laws* Yet this assumption is implicit in everything that Popper says about the identity of Platonism and modern totalitarianism

Nor is Plato's theory overthrown by pointing out the *difficulty* of deciding what should and should not be attempted. Even that decision involves

[69] *Rep* , 352a, 368d, and especially 434d ff.
[70] *Rep* , 422e–423a, 462a.
[71] *Statesman*, 286a.

a rational choice and some notion, at least, of human nature and its demands Plato tries to show in this theory of the arts why the special arts
cannot be regarded as themselves capable of settling the question of their
own relative significance At the same time he retains the expert who has
exceptional knowledge in a special field. The art of life, the political art,
has a wider range and so has something to say about all of the special arts
It also involves expert knowledge, being, for Plato, a specialty of the moral
philosopher A major theme of the *Gorgias* and the *Republic* is the significance of the philosopher as statesman and educator In this role the philosopher may call upon other experts in special fields But the knowledge of
human nature and the wisdom which is demanded for the integration of
the manifold activities of community life is the philosopher's own province
in a sense in which it is no one else's province.

Popper would have us believe that Plato draws the philosopher-states-
man out of a hat as a feat of tribal magic and that, as is the way of the
magician, he offers no explanation, first, because a trick that is explained
loses all its persuasive force and, second, because this trick involves a
betrayal of human nature itself and shows that Plato has no real evidence
for his position But the evidence is abundant In the light of the significance
which Plato gives to his discussion of the soul, not only in the *Republic*, but
in his early and middle dialogues, it is not only appropriate but necessary
to acknowledge that the ideal state is justified by a careful consideration of
the nature of human life And it is a complete inversion of Plato's position
to say that human life is explained in the light of what the state *must* be
That is why Plato's political theory is not "historicist" in Popper's sense.

Plato does, indeed, discuss origins, and he was willing to incorporate into
his own theory elements of actual societies which exemplified his principles
in some way, so long as he felt them to be consonant with his view of human
nature.[72] But he never thinks in terms of a mere "state of nature" The
important question is not what might have been the origin of the state
historically. The question is, rather· What are the conditions under which
any state at any time will really provide for the maximum development of
that human nature which it is meant to serve? There is no notion of a
return to the "tribe" for the sake of some static pattern of life which can be
sustained only by superstition and "tribal magic "[73] The ideal state is based
upon logical and psychological considerations And whatever Plato may
have thought about the origin of the state, it would in no case have a very
significant bearing upon his analysis of what the *just* state would require.
This is simply not a historical question.

[72] *Laws,* 793a ff See *Rep ,* 367e.
[73] Popper, *op. cit.,* I, 72, 151 ff , 175–77.

Popper's discussion of an alleged "law" of degeneration is also misplaced [74] Plato certainly thought that human nature, if allowed to follow
the path of least resistance, would degenerate, because the passions are
strong, and in the absence of any restraint upon appetite, the appetitive
aspect of man becomes predominant It is for this reason, and for this
reason only, that the state degenerates The process has nothing to do
with any historicist law of decline. There is no degenerate state unless there
are first degenerate men, for reasons which have already been made clear.
What, in fact, does this come to?

Plato felt that if we really look at the way men behave we shall see that
the process of becoming at once virtuous and happy is an extraordinarily
difficult one. We are not born virtuous—we are born with the capacity for
becoming so. Plato certainly thought that the virtuous man will, in the long
run be happier than the unvirtuous man and, indeed, that without virtue
man cannot really be happy at all Yet, taking man just as we happen to find
him, there is no reason to be especially optimistic about his immediate
prospects Nevertheless, we must look at him a little more closely before we
despair. If we do so, we shall find that what tends to make him degenerate
into the merely animal is only one aspect of his nature A superficial
descriptive account leads to a discouraging conclusion A more penetrating
account will upset the balance in his favor For this more cheerful view,
man's aspiration and reason must be taken into account, and when they
are, we can see that the initial pessimism need not paralyze us We can
break out of it—although *not* by doing nothing.

We must know ourselves not merely as we are at any given moment but
as we might be. Man is alone in possessing the means of seeing his life in its
whole dimension We may be optimistic in the long run—if we are willing
to trust reason—but only by being pessimistic in the short run, because
that also is what a rational approach reveals To achieve virtue we must
counter appetite with reason, and this is, initially, a painful process, as
Aristotle also pointed out If left to themselves, the capacities of man would
never develop, would never be actualized except by accident We are not,
on Plato's theory, merely animals acting by instinct We must be educated
by others, restrained and guided by those who know what we shall, in time,
also know and approve in the light of our developed reason.[75] This faith in
the ability of man to lead a life of reason is fundamental to Plato's theory
of education.

The tendency toward internal dissolution, while it is always present to
some extent, does not mean that degeneration is *inevitable* It is not a *law*
of degeneration in the sense that it enables us to assert that all human

[74] *Ibid*, I, 16 ff , 70
[75] Compare *Rep* , 443, with *Phaedrus*, 246a–257b.

behavior is predestined to follow the downward path, nor is it a biological law. The decline Plato talks about is internal, moral, psychological—not physical, although physical decline might well be a consequence of moral decline [76] Because it is not inevitable in individual life, it is not inevitable in social life either Just as we speak of the moral rehabilitation of the individual character, so Plato speaks of the moral rehabilitation not only of the individual but also the whole corporate life which is the state.

Books VIII and IX of the *Republic* could be regarded as stating a law of inevitable degeneration only if we assumed that Plato never provided a remedy and never suggested any means of reversing the process. And such an assumption would be ridiculous. The ideal or reformed state is not based upon some ancient Eden which actually existed as the original perfect state. It is a rational and immaterial conception which exemplifies the natural order of rational, spirited, and appetitive elements in human nature and which may serve as a regulative ideal because it has its foundation in that same human nature.[77] In the theoretical order it would be possible to regard social reform as permanent But not in the practical order, since Plato regards this as risky in the extreme Life can be rationally guided, but not in such a way as to eliminate all risks. We cannot get out of the human predicament altogether.

Popper charges that Plato attempts to arrest all change and return to the closed and static society of tribalism [78] Especially in these days these terms have a high voltage, emotively, and suggest at once something opposed to all progress and, in general, bad What does Plato assert? He certainly maintains that the degeneration of the individual and of the state ought to be arrested if, in fact, it is in process We should also say, presumably, that the moral disintegration of character ought to be stopped and that the decline of a society into lawlessness and chaos ought to be ended In short, any individual or group which is in the process of destroying itself through indulgence is not acting rationally and is not acting for its own good. There seems to be nothing especially diabolical in this point of view But would all activity be arrested in Plato's commonwealth?

It is difficult to see how or why it would be, since the whole purpose of community life is to make social activity a reflection of a civil human nature and so to permit and foster not merely activity (which, in itself, may be either good or bad) but rather those activities which a society of just men would approve and enjoy. To say this is not to demonstrate the truth of Plato's contention but only to state what his contention is To say that it is inadequate or that it would not work in a modern state is not to say that it

[76] See *Gorg* , 464, 520, and *Sophist*, 229.
[77] *Rep* , 592b.
[78] Popper, *op. cit.*, I, 1, 151.

is the result of a conception of political philosophy that is identical with modern totalitarianism We cannot lightly dismiss Plato's assertions unless we are willing to say that the individual is perfectly self-sufficient, that any change whatever is good simply because it is change, and that neither Plato's claim to have analyzed human nature correctly nor the empirical evidence he offers to sustain his analysis represent a significant contribution to moral philosophy.

Plato does maintain that an unstable social structure, like an unstable personality, is unable to realize and energize its capacities. And he certainly makes it plain that he considers his philosophic rule better than any other kind as a means of establishing and sustaining the rational life of man Having established this to his own satisfaction, he quite naturally regards the change to another kind of rule as a change for the worse and, therefore, to be avoided It sheds no light upon Plato or upon anything else to label his society "closed" without examining the evidence upon which that society is founded—and it is deliberately misleading to refuse to attribute to Plato those teachings which show the label to be inapplicable.

There is another error in Popper's interpretation which leads him to caricature Plato's theory of education and to distort it as he distorts the Platonic conception of human nature and natural law Popper insists that in the ideal state those who do not rule are little more than animals and are deliberately turned into human drudges in order that they may serve the appetites of the rulers for self-aggrandizement [79] The charge seems to be based mainly upon Plato's discussion of the importance of heredity Plato certainly gives it an altogether unnecessary emphasis, and it is a point on which he can be legitimately attacked But, like the strict division of labor, it is not an essential element in Plato's thought. That is to say, he could abandon his extreme position without making any significant alteration in his political or educational theory. However, if we isolate these passages[80] and regard them as having some especially symbolic significance, the impression may well be that for Plato there are some men who are not really men because they possess but one-third of the human attributes. It is a tempting solution for the hostile critic, but the text does not support it.

The idea of a special kind of man is not supported by the analysis of the soul in Book IV of the *Republic*, nor is it supported by Book I It does not occur in the early and middle dialogues, since the problem of whether or not virtue can be taught applies to men in general The same consideration holds of the myth of the *Phaedrus* where all human souls are involved [81] And it is difficult to see what could be made of the conversation between Socrates and the slave boy in the *Meno* if the attribute of ration-

[79] *Ibid* , I, 40, 137.
[80] *Rep.*, 458 ff
[81] *Phaedrus*, 246 ff., especially 247d–249c.

ality is limited to some especially gifted class [82] Nor does it fit with the *Cratylus* where the artisan is said not to copy the broken shuttle in making a new one but to keep his mind fixed upon the form—something that would be impossible for him if the artisan class possessed only an appetitive nature or soul.[83]

Further, Professor Joseph has pointed out that there is even better evidence in the *Republic* itself, one of the interesting results of which is that Plato could not defend his rigid division of classes on his own principles.[84] There are not three *kinds* of soul or three *kinds* of human nature. But neither are all individuals exactly alike in every respect The analysis of the soul in the *Republic*, Book IV, not only indicates Plato's view of their similarities but also indicates the ground of their differences While Plato could readily give up his rigid division of classes or his theory of eugenics, he could not give up his analysis of the soul. There is good reason for criticizing Plato for his extremes, but there is no excuse for inverting components of the *Republic* so as to make a subsidiary matter the key to his whole moral and political philosophy, especially when Plato corrects his own mistakes.

However, once such an inversion has been made a guiding principle of interpretation, it is no longer possible to understand Plato's view of education Every individual is a whole and remains so—the same kind of man as the philosopher. But he does not realize the rational capacity to the same degree. The multitude will never become philosophers, says Plato, but he does not rule them out by arbitrary decree or caprice on the ground that certain people must be held in subjection to do the dirty work Ultimate truth, as Cornford points out, is open to anyone on Plato's theory in the same sense in which it is now open to any man to grasp the theory of relativity.[85] Is it fascistic to suggest, as Plato does, that relatively few men will rise to the occasion? Plato's position is that while rationality is a characteristic of all men, it is not the case that all individuals are equally endowed intellectually. In short, he denies that all men are equal if "equal" means having the rational power in the same degree of development But we make so much of this today that we are interested in special schools for the gifted child on the ground that certain individual gifts ought to be allowed to develop fully The point is not whether this is justified but simply that it is hardly evidence of irrationalism on Plato's part.[86]

So far as education is concerned, one could do no better than refer briefly

---

[82] *Meno*, 81 ff.

[83] *Cratylus*, 389 ff See *Alcib.* I, 125a, and *Prot.*, 312c, d.

[84] Joseph, *op cit*, pp. 114–21 and references· *Rep* 435e–436, 591d; 441a, b; 440e–441a, 456d, 428b, 345b–347d, 343e–344c, 588b–590d, 553d, 561b, 460a, 582c, 586e; 587a, 611b–612a See also *Rep.*, 518, 441c, *Phaedo*, 64c–67d, *Timaeus*, 44d, 69e–70d.

[85] See F. M Cornford, "The Marxist View of Ancient Philosophy" (written in 1942) in *The Unwritten Philosophy and Other Essays* (New York, Cambridge University Press, 1950), p 129.

[86] Popper, *op cit*, II, 114.

to Cornford's comments on Crossman's charges of intellectual inequality and caste education in Plato.[87] These charges differ from Popper's only in being less sweeping and severe And the importance of education can hardly be overestimated since it underlies the whole functioning of the *Republic*. Plato's fundamental thesis, as Cornford indicates, is that native intellectual gifts differ in degree from person to person There are individuals who are capable of realizing the intellectual and moral capacities to the maximum degree, but they are rather rare. And, as has already been indicated, they are also prone to that inversion which Plato stressed so much as a danger. Plato also thought that the most promising solution for the problem of government was one which would insure the placement of the wisest and most ethically sensitive persons in positions of government. He also thought that, on the whole, the children of the gifted would also be equally gifted. He may have been wrong, and, in any event, he seriously overreached himself in this matter of inheritance. But his conviction does not make him an irrationalist, nor does it make him a racist in any sense which would be given to that word now. Besides, Plato realized that, in fact, these extraordinary talents might appear on *any* level of society.

In any case, the details of the Platonic scheme of education, whether we regard it as traditional or revolutionary, are philosophically less significant than is the extraordinary emphasis that Plato gives to education generally, especially moral education. For he believed that in childhood and youth the natural endowments of individuals could be brought to light in such a way as to guarantee, if development followed upon discovery, the maximum degree of self-realization It is Plato's supreme commitment about the nature of man and the life of reason. Education is basic to the ideal commonwealth, being a major topic of the *Republic* and the *Laws* If this suggests anything in the way of a modern parallel, it suggests a prophetic insight into the future significance of progressive education and psychological testing [88] Does Popper suggest that those who favor achievement and aptitude tests are reactionary and antidemocratic and really proponents of a privileged intellectual aristocracy designed to enslave the inferior?

It is hardly plausible to suggest, as Popper does,[89] that Plato distrusts reason when the Platonic commonwealth is governed by reason and maintained by the guidance of the art of education [90] But Popper charges that this education is for the few who will keep the many under subjection by sinister discrimination of the vilest sort and by the use of calculated lies,

[87] Cornford, *op. cit* , pp. 129 ff

[88] On the whole question of the modernity of Plato's theory of education see R. C. Lodge, *Plato's Theory of Education* (New York, Harcourt, Brace, 1947), Chap. 11.

[89] See Popper, *op cit* , II, Chap 24.

[90] *Rep.*, 422d, 500c, 508c, 540a, b, *Laws*, 857d, 903b ff.

which shows that Plato did not believe in truth at all.[91] Now, in the first place, education is the basic right of the Platonic commonwealth, although not everyone goes on to higher university education any more than they do in England and America today We are just beginning to explore the possibilities of educating the gifted but impecunious For Plato, this was essential, and he took greater pains than we do to match the quality of the student and the opportunity for exercising it He also insisted upon moral as well as intellectual qualities, since those who go on to higher education, in the *Republic,* must make considerable sacrifices in pleasure and secular power as part of that privilege. Popper consistently ignores the fact that, for Plato, the practice of the ruling art is a duty and not a cherished privilege.[92] Yet nothing in Plato contrasts more sharply with modern totalitarianism

In the second place, Plato makes it perfectly clear that nobility of birth does not determine the child's education or the career that the child will follow.[93] That is determined by observation and testing of a very thorough sort carried out while the child is actually exhibiting his own qualifications, and not merely by a professional psychologist but by the whole community. Plato's expectations concerning the efficacy of scientific eugenics are quite beside the point in all of this and in no way affect the principle of selection, if we are willing to read what Plato says about the matter.

However, there is the unpleasant characteristic of resorting to "falsehood"—surely a strange and unexpected characteristic to be discovered in the model of intellectual and moral virtue who is to govern the ideal state. Undoubtedly, the fascist could quote Plato here for his own purposes. It does not follow that Plato's purposes are those of the fascist. In the first place, the myth[94] which, Plato suggests, ought to be accepted by the whole community is false only in the sense that it is, in form, fictional or legendary [95] But it represents, fictionally, certain basic ideas which Plato not only accepts but even holds to be essential. First, it states that the community is a family of persons and should be cared for and defended and that all the citizens are brothers in this enterprise. It is difficult to discern any evil here, nor would Plato suggest that the assertion is not true

The second part of what is called the "lie" contains the statement that there are men composed of gold, others of silver, and still others of iron and brass, and that these correspond to rulers, auxiliaries, and artisans—which is, quite obviously, not literally true. It represents a state of affairs which

[91] Popper, *op cit*, I, 121 ff
[92] *Rep*, 517c, 520d
[93] *Rep.*, 423c, d
[94] *Rep*, 414b ff
[95] On the relative merits of the translation "spirited fiction" as against "noble lie," see Cornford, *op cit.*, pp. 132–33.

Plato discusses later in his analysis of the soul and which he tries to illustrate in the myth of the *Phaedrus* as well as in his account of the process of social and individual degeneration in the *Republic*, Books VIII and IX Any one of these three functions of the soul may predominate, and this is used in connection with the threefold division of groups in the state.

Right or wrong, the myth is based upon what Plato takes to be facts about human nature. All of which indicates that, figuratively speaking, the legend, far from being an intentional false statement—that is to say, a lie—is, in Plato's opinion, substantially true And it makes no sense whatever to regard it as a propaganda lie designed to misrepresent the facts Indeed, it presents what Plato regards as particularly significant facts in fictional form—which is characteristic of Plato's use of myth throughout his writings It requires an exceptionally literal mind to interpret this as sinister and poisonous propaganda.

In the second place, the most significant part of the "lie" is something else. It is charged that the "lie" is designed to keep the rulers and guardians in power by persuading the rest of the citizens that they ought to remain where they are—in subjection This, in itself, misrepresents Plato's conception of power which is always a moral-political concept and never a merely political concept as it is in modern usage However, the myth is a strange device for this dark purpose because it states that anyone in the iron and brass category who shows himself capable of rule or of membership in the guardian group must be promoted to that group, and that any of the upper group who show themselves to be unsatisfactory rulers must be demoted to the group made up of craftsmen and farmers Since this legend is directed at the whole community, including the upper classes, it is difficult to see how it can be called a plot against the masses by the rulers for the private gain of the ruling class Yet we are invited to read Plato in this matchless fashion The method will, assuredly, make nonsense of a great deal of philosophical writing—which suggests that the technique of distortion had better be avoided.

Popper shows an almost puritanical distaste for the literary and rhetorical side of Plato's writing, which may be responsible for one of the most curious of his interpretations—the suggestion that Plato was guilty of "aestheticism."[96] This is, of course, another depreciatory term, but Popper's charge comes to this: Plato was entranced by the notion of the autonomy of the artist, a status which allows the artist to use certain materials to embody forms solely for the sake of aesthetic contemplation and quite apart from the moral consequences that might follow. The statesman as artist, then, would be relieved of the obligation of noticing that his materials, human beings, might possibly require nonaesthetic treatment, and he

[96] Popper, *op cit*, I, 145-47

would, therefore, be able to apply himself to the creation of something aesthetically satisfying with a wholly untroubled conscience.

This is a complete inversion of Plato's theory of art Indeed, the usual estimate of Plato as an aesthetician is that he first confuses aesthetics and ethics and then subordinates the former to the latter. This is what censorship is all about in the *Republic* and the *Laws* And his censorship is another of the points on which Plato may be justly criticized. But aestheticism cannot be made compatible with Plato's theory of *techne* and his system of education through art If aestheticism means anything at all, it means an attitude in which *all* activities are regarded as final and consummative, even when some of them, at least, might more justly be regarded as essentially related to, if not dependent upon, something else—something outside them or beyond them, such as a moral action This attitude is ordinarily limited to those activities which would involve the perception of works of art, particularly works of fine art, and to the responses made to them. But the aesthete would, presumably, cultivate the aesthetic attitude in any and every context Thus, for aestheticism, the question of art and morality must be a pseudo-problem, because art is art and morality is morality, or even better, morality is just a peculiar sort of aesthetic response At any rate, art, on this view, would comprise objects and activities or responses which only accidentally, if at all, involve ethical issues Aesthetics, then, being an autonomous sphere of activity or experience, could not allow for the discussion of morals, simply because moral questions do not belong in the context of the aesthetic *qua* aesthetic

Now, the autonomy of the aesthetic experience and of the fine arts was one of the things to which Plato, rightly or wrongly, remained unalterably opposed, for reasons which have already been discussed in this essay in connection with the problem of the arts and conduct [97] Primarily, the reason was that any activity must be assessed in the light of the good life viewed on the whole There is, for Plato, no "aesthetic moment" which can be divorced from the rest of life and cultivated merely for its own sake—at least, there ought not to be. Ultimately, such moments of experience must be brought under that critical examination which determines whether or not the moment in question *ought* to have a place in a truly human life at all, and then what place it ought to have. This evaluation is not one that the fine artist or the mere aesthetician can make—any more than the physician can decide simply on the basis of the art of medicine whether it is better to live or die, although he can, of course, decide whether a man is healthy or not That is why, short of the double perfection of intellect and will which is never realized in practice even by the philosopher, aesthetic experience, for Plato, can have only a quasi-autonomy at best, and never the real and

[97] See *Rep* , 424b–e and *Laws,* 812e. See especially *Laws,* 729d–e.

complete independence which aesthetics would like to claim for itself.

Of course, this is, again, a matter having to do with *practice* and not simply with pure theory The problem of art and morality, if it is a problem, has to do with the situation of predicament and not with the formulation of a system of metaphysics. Thus when Plato is discussing the forms, particularly the Form of Beauty, as standards against which the particulars must be measured, he does not have to introduce questions of conflict [98] But that does not mean that he has abandoned everything he says elsewhere about conflict in favor of aestheticism. An aesthetic Plato is a sheer invention. Popper makes no attempt to understand Plato's theory of art which is a many-sided and complex conception And he ignores the Platonic discussion of theory and practice, especially the fact that, for Plato, the practical and the theoretical cannot be divorced without making *rational* practice impossible

The charge of aestheticism is incredible enough But the most amazing charge of all—the one that strains credulity to the breaking point—is the charge of irrationalism.[99] The evidence against Popper's interpretation on this point is so overwhelming that it would be an offense to catalogue it And the charge is best considered in connection with Popper's alternative to Platonism—piecemeal social engineering [100] It is not merely an alternative to Platonism—it is an alternative to philosophy and an alternative to reason In short, it is a species of irrationalism

It is not part of the purpose of this essay to employ the unexpected word for the sake of exhilarating surprise There are several clear indications in Popper's book that his charge of irrationalism can be justly directed not against Plato but against his own theory. Popper's characterization of Socrates as a pure paralytic methodologist, theorist, and skeptic is the first indication of his basic distrust of reason and his timidity in making any sort of commitment about the positive characteristics of a rational life. Of course, he is not consistent on this point, as will be seen presently, but that is another question. He insists that Socrates's wisdom was "simply the realization· How little do I know," whereas Plato was "no longer the modest seeker . but the proud possessor of truth," but, at the same time, he praises Socrates as "a lover of truth and wisdom."[101] But this can only mean that Socrates loves what he not only does not have but could not possibly get The Socratic method, if it is limited to a confession of ignorance, may grind away forever, but it will never issue in anything—it is ignorance in perpetuity.

[98] *Symposium*, 210 ff and *Rep* , 402c, 500d–e
[99] Popper, *op cit* , I, 142, 146–47, II, Chap 24, especially p. 232.
[100] *Ibid* , I, Chaps 9 and 10, II, Chaps 23, 24, and 25.
[101] *Ibid* , I, 112, 116

Thus, for all that Popper claims for his own view of rationality, it is, in practice, powerless and acts only as a negative force to prevent, preclude, hold up, arrest—any really rational *activity*. It is only by being inconsistent that Popper *can* praise rationality, since it turns out to have no positive function. And if he insists upon the positive function, as he does in his program of social engineering, then his charge against Plato's intellectualism loses much of its cogency. He attempts to avoid this contingency by twists in terminology, an example of which is his use of the term "collectivism." He suggests that the "good" meaning of the term must be "rational institutional planning for freedom," whereas the "bad" meaning must be that which includes the idea of working against the individual [102]

The latter was not a Platonic conception, but the former was, as Plato's theory of *techne* shows. Only, it cannot rest, Plato thought, upon invincible ignorance And if Popper wishes to embrace a positive conception of rationality, it is difficult to see how he can, in the same breath, retain his version of the method of Socrates And, since he does retain it, with exceptional emphasis, we can only wonder what collectivism in the good sense could really mean.

Popper's attitude toward pleasure and pain is consonant with this negative rationality For Plato, life was an activity, a tremendously complex activity when the whole dimension of life was taken into account Human experience is, initially, illimitable—the human soul, initially, receptive to any promise of satisfaction But, for this reason, it tends to be preoccupied with vitality and passion, and this is risky in the extreme The soul, therefore, needs education, because a sensibility that knows no limits and employs no principle of discrimination is childish. Rationality, then, ceases to be omnivorous and recognizes the limitations without which fruition is not merely postponed but made forever unattainable. However, there is no fruition without positive content The life of reason remains a full life, because satisfactions are not eliminated but controlled

Plato saw, at least, that if human life is to realize any of its vast potentialities, the riskiness has to be accepted. He shows his supreme trust in the capacity of human reason to meet this challenge and, in spite of the risks, actually to achieve something worth having. This faith, if it must be called faith, is certainly a characteristic of anything deserving the name of rationalism Yet Popper holds that Plato resolved his own inner struggle and conflict in favor of irrationalism,[103] despite the fact that Plato was willing to attempt an answer to the complex problems which Popper is content to walk away from It is a part of the Platonic analysis of the relation between art and conduct to show that we cannot walk away from life

[102] *Ibid.,* I, 221, 178
[103] *Ibid ,* I, 264, n. 59

and its risks, for the reason that, one way or another, life still goes on. Yet Popper accuses Plato of aestheticism, of playing with what Plato, over and over again, called the most serious matter we can discuss. how to live well

As a "rational" alternative, Popper offers the principle, "Minimize pain," because the search for happiness is a very dangerous business that leads to totalitarianism [104] On this view, reason becomes a convenient slave to be called upon when we get into trouble—an instrument, a tool, something which, though not very helpful, may be used to avoid utter destruction But it is never the crowning perfection of the human person which opens to the mind the possibility of a tradition of civility. Of course, Plato insisted that if happiness is to be a goal, the risk of failure or distress can never be eliminated. And if we wish to deny our own nature, we can surely be safe, dull, and, indeed, primitive We can sink into the vegetative state and attempt nothing This is not the choice that has ever displayed the misery and tragedy of the human soul—but it has never displayed its greatness either It is no dishonor to philosophy to call it a dangerous calling. There is nothing ignoble in that And philosophy has, traditionally at least, been willing to attempt what needs to be attempted if the life of reason is to have positive significance. Certainly rationality includes this aim. Popper nowhere says anything about the possible consequences of his supreme indifference to this demand

The third symptom of irrationalism shows itself in Popper's distrust of our capacity to achieve rational corporate action All we can do is set up certain safeguards against pain That these are certainly necessary no one will deny But this minimal rationality, this residue of the intellectual power, hardly deserves to be elevated to the status of rationalism at the expense of a philosophical tradition which learned from Plato that man had it in him to become akin to the divine We have been told by Norbert Wiener that man may shortly become economically valueless [105] And even allowing for a measure of exaggeration, the problem created by labor-saving machinery will certainly have to be taken more seriously than it was before. We may have enough respect for our scientific prophets to suppose that radical changes in this area of life are now possible At least we can foresee, as a real possibility, a state of affairs in which a great part of the drudgery of the world can be drastically reduced and perhaps eliminated But these are possibilities that need not be realized The means are becoming available, but what are we to do with the means? Are we to have no *positive* plan? Are we to wait in skeptical silence, congratulating ourselves on the fact that, as of the present moment, no idiot has managed

[104] *Ibid.*, II, 289, n 62
[105] *Cybernetics* (New York, John Wiley and Sons, 1949), pp. 36–39.

to destroy or enslave the world with these same instruments? Or are we to re-examine the possibilities of corporate life together as citizens of one community—of establishing a real tradition of civil living everywhere in the world If we are to act *positively*, we can hardly avoid Plato of Athens

The fourth indication of irrationalism is Popper's excessively naive optimism It is irrational because even if we overlook its incompatibility with his negative method, there is no ground for it Plato is optimistic, too. He felt that he had a right to be because he had taken the trouble to develop a theory of education, of individual and social ethics, of politics, in short, a philosophy of culture which could mitigate risks and sustain positive action. Popper is optimistic without any reason He thinks, apparently, that by doing nothing about the problems confronting us, or by poking out tentatively in projects of piecemeal social engineering, we may be sure that everything will take care of itself Even if we should suppose that this is all we can do, it is a singular characterization of it to call it rationalism It consists essentially in giving up the enterprise of trying to work out a real solution for our complex social problems

But as a symptom of irrationalism it is made even more depressing by being coupled with the traitor and scapegoat technique. The effect is to frighten us away from anything positive that has been done or suggested in the past It refuses to look at human nature closely. It supposes that man, by and large, is pretty close to the angels but that there are a few depraved individuals who, because of a certain glibness, have somehow caught the ear of the children of earth and would lead them into darkness in order to satisfy a lust for power. Popper's protest that "for those who have eaten from the tree of knowledge, paradise is lost"[106] is hardly appropriate or even possible in the light of his method, his goal of minimizing pain, and his repudiation of the tradition of philosophic rationalism We are bound to ask· "Knowledge of *what*—and for what purpose worth talking about?"

Herbert Butterfield has some rather Platonic remarks that are worth noticing in this connection He is speaking of the value of ancient studies for the contemporary world with reference to our modern tendency to think of our difficulties as scientific.

And we of the twentieth century have been particularly spoiled, for the men of the Old Testament, the ancient Greeks and all our ancestors down to the seventeenth century betray in their philosophy and their outlook a terrible awareness of the chanciness of human life, and the precarious nature of man's existence in this risky universe. These things—though they are part of the fundamental experience of mankind—have been greatly concealed from recent generations be-

[106] Popper, *op cit.*, I, 177.

cause modern science and organisation enabled us to build up so tremendous a
barrier against fire, famine, plague and violence

The modern world created so vast a system of insurance against the contin-
gencies and accidents of time, that we imagined all the risk eliminated—imagined
that it was normal to have a smooth going-on, and that the uncertainties of life in
the past had been due to mere inefficiency.[107]

The observations of the ancients are, it may be suggested, far closer to the
facts of experience than the immature optimism of Popper's social-engi-
neering program And in the light of our experience as a culture, we are
hardly in a position to speak lightly of Plato's notion of the Fall of Man,
which Popper dislikes.[108] The situation is a predicament—serious to the
point of being desperate, but still not hopeless. However, we shall need
help, and it is scarcely wisdom to brand as treasonable the efforts of those
thinkers in our tradition who have contributed most to the clarification of
our problems and even something toward their solution.

The notion that man is perfectible is intelligible and, if properly understood, the ground of rational hope But the notion that man is perfect, or
that human nature will show itself in glory with the removal of external
restraints, is absurd. Yet this is essentially Popper's position. He says: "We
may become the makers of our fate when we have ceased to pose as its
prophets."[109] And: "Man is the master of his own destiny." And further.
"In accordance with our aims, we can influence or change the history of
man just as we have changed the face of the earth."[110] Moreover "To progress is to move towards some kind of end, towards an end which exists for
us as human beings" And. "Progress rests with us, with our watchfulness,
with our efforts, with the clarity of our conception of our ends, and with
the realism of their choice "[111]

These assertions would be full of promise if the ground of our expectation had not been destroyed As it is, they can only mean that we can
master ourselves without knowing what we really are or where we are
headed We should certainly want to know what "our aims" could mean,
whether they have any positive content, whether they are good or bad, and
what makes them so And this would surely involve some definite commitment about the kind of life we should be willing to recognize as good.
Since Popper neither supplies the information nor makes the commitment,
his serene optimism is inexplicable His pretense that it represents rationalism is incredible

[107] *Christianity and History* (London, G Bell and Sons, 1950), pp. 69–70.
[108] Popper, *op cit.*, Chaps. 4 and 5, especially pp 64, 72
[109] *Ibid ,* I, 3.
[110] *Ibid ,* I, 17
[111] *Ibid.,* II, 266.

It is also dangerous. In fact, the most distressing characteristic of Popper's lack of concern is that it will, if persisted in, prepare the ground for anarchy and the use of force It was Plato who first reminded us that individuals, and therefore societies, disintegrate when the concern with fundamental moral and intellectual *value* begins to weaken—when the center of attention is shifted to the spirited and finally to the appetitive aspect of human life Then the immaterial goods, the purposes and guiding principles held in common by whole groups of persons, begin to be forgotten, and the object of life becomes a preoccupation with the calculus of pleasure and pain And Popper offers no more noble aim than this He does not suggest what will fill the vacuum created by the disappearance of positive aims and purposes Plato, allegedly the fascist, did suggest what would fill it—tyranny.[112]

If there are no guiding principles that can specify practice, then, he suggested, *rational* activity is impossible and agreement is unattainable. But conflict is a stubborn fact in the human situation, and, since conflicts will not magically disappear, force alone can resolve them. But Plato did not approve of tyranny, on Popper's own admission. Nor is it for one moment to be suggested that Popper approves of it either However, while he confidently affirms that we are responsible for our own decisions,[113] he nowhere suggests that this deliberation involves anything more significant, morally, than the minimizing of pain In any event, it is somewhat difficult to understand our obligation or responsibility in the absence of any means of even guessing just what demands are rightly to be made upon us by other human beings or what we may justly demand of them

In fact, it is not at all clear that the phrase "morally responsible for our own decisions" has any meaning at all as Popper uses it. It is, one would suppose, trivially true. Yet he seems to suggest that it implies something profoundly significant in itself. But unless the ground of obligation is clarified, there is no significance whatever in merely asserting that we are responsible. To be sure, gentle people will not trouble themselves with the question of sanctions, but the moralist's task is justification, not exhortation This task is thrust upon him by the existence of people who do not happen to be gentle The social engineer's optimism will not alter their character. And, presumably, it is the engineer who will improve society. At least, this is what Popper suggests. But the improvement of society, if the notion has any positive meaning at all, is a moral problem, not a problem of engineering.

A "just and fair" reading of Plato would reveal that he not only saw the danger of tyranny but also provided a remarkably acute analysis of its

112 *Rep* , 562a–576b
113 Popper, *op cit.,* I, 51–52.

causes Whether we accept Plato's proposals for its prevention and cure or not, we cannot afford to ignore them. To do so cuts us off from one of the most fruitful sources of information about human nature. This is the effect of *The Open Society*, because the reader will hardly get from Popper's book the idea that the author is simply criticizing Plato This is a legitimate undertaking and, indeed, an obligation. Rather, the reader will get what is far more exciting for the hysterically inclined—the conviction that the greatest philosopher of all time, to use Popper's words, was really nothing but a traitor to the human race. Therefore, he need not be read—indeed, he ought not to be read—and, in point of fact, he must not be read.

Plato made some serious mistakes. Indeed, what Popper says about the tendency to idealize Plato is partly true What we need in order to realize the value of Platonism is neither further praise of a famous man nor essays which regard Plato as a writer of merely literary or antiquarian interest, but rather systematic studies of the *Dialogues* which will exhibit the relevance of Plato's philosophy of culture for the contemporary world. This means that the *Laws* should be given the close scrutiny which the *Republic* has received—but in relation to the other dialogues and with some effort to understand Plato's real purpose. Plato shows a lack of sensitivity to the idea of subjective freedom, and he is impatient with many forms of human disquiet. No amount of special pleading will redeem the many ugly passages of the *Laws*. They can be understood and explained, but they cannot be excused [114] They are not even Platonic For it might be remembered that Plato is the best critic of his own errors

But Popper's emotional approach to the *Dialogues* and his employment of the traitor and scapegoat technique render no service to philosophy or criticism. What might have been a provocative and challenging contribution to the study of classical philosophy becomes an exercise in vituperation In the effort to see what Plato missed, there is no point in missing what he saw In a moment of charitableness Popper confesses. "It is to the credit of Plato, the disciple of Socrates, that it never occurred to him to present his enemies as the offspring of the sinister demons of darkness."[115] That was a wise course then, and it is a wise course now.

[114] For a criticism that is, at once, perceptive and severe, see V. Solovyev, *Plato* (London, Stanley Nott, 1935), pp. 77–83
[115] Popper, *op cit*, I, 267.

XII

Realism and the Philosophy of Education

HARRY S BROUDY, *State Teachers College,*
Framingham, Massachusetts

IN EDUCATIONAL PHILOSOPHY, as in general philosophy, the trick is to get off the horn of dogmatism without landing on the horn of relativism Interesting as this problem is for general philosophy, it is *crucial* for education, because education is an eminently practical enterprise wherein one generation tries to reincarnate a value schema in the lives of its progeny In education some *Weltanschauung,* implicitly or explicitly, consciously or unconsciously rooted in a metaphysical and epistemological matrix, is being acted out and not merely entertained for speculative purposes.

The philosophy of education spells out these metaphysical and epistemological presuppositions and examines critically their consequences for the solution of such educational problems as those of aims, curriculum, organization, method, and so forth. It is in this sense that this is an essay on the philosophy of education.

Our problem is set by the fact that since the turn of the century the dominant philosophy of education in America has been some form of experimentalism or instrumentalism. Some of the reasons for this success are presented in the following section Here it suffices to point out that this success has wrought changes in education which many educators and laymen deplore Some find their economic or social status threatened, some fear for their religious convictions, others find their aesthetic sensibilities offended, and still others find anything new too great a strain on their adaptive powers.

Many educators, however, reject instrumentalism as a guide to education because they do not believe that it is philosophically true. To such, this essay suggests that classical realism, purified of its accidental accretions during a long history, is a sure-footed alternative to rigid traditionalism and slippery relativism

This realism is classical only in that its three major theses have their origin in the thoughts of Plato and Aristotle and have been asserted in one form or another in every age by men who had a large part in the shaping

of Western civilization These theses (the philosophical justification of
which other essays in this book will undertake) are·

1. There is a world existing independently of my thinking or wishing [1]

2. This world has a structure and order that can, in part at least, be
known as it is by human cognition.

3. There is a natural law that describes and prescribes the relations
which obtain among the human powers, functions, and institutions as pre-
requisites for the good life in the good society.

A point of view compatible with such theses has been literally scared
out of current American educational philosophy, because the advocates of
instrumentalism have succeeded in "smearing" it with the aristocratic
predilections of its founders and the authoritarianism of a church or state
that rightly or wrongly used this view as justification It remains to be seen,
however, whether democracy, freedom, and human dignity are incompatible with the kind of realism here suggested, just as it remains to be seen
whether instrumentalism is as compatible with them as it so complacently
assumes.

I. Experimentalism as a Philosophy of Education

That experimentalism, or instrumentalism, is the dominant philosophy of
education in America today can be inferred from the prestige of its leaders
(Dewey, Kilpatrick, Bode, Counts, Raup, Axtelle, Childs, and others),
from its articulateness, and from trends in educational theory and practice.

Among the reasons for, or the results of, this dominance, very important
is the eminence of its chief protagonist, John Dewey. His equating of reflective thinking with problem-solving, and these with learning, was a
masterly stroke, because it made it possible to translate experimentalism
into a teaching method, indeed, it was quite possible for multitudes of
teachers to learn about the method without becoming conversant with the
philosophic subtleties of experimentalism. In this connection we must mention the scarcity of formal courses in philosophy in teacher-preparation
curricula This not only spares instrumentalism any widespread criticism
but it also minimizes the probability of alternative views becoming very
popular

As a result, other philosophic positions are not *explicitly* influential on
American education. Such influence as they do have is largely indirect,
that is, through their influence on psychology, sociology, and economics.
For example, dialectical materialism as sophisticated Marxism has very

---

[1] For a more precise statement of these principles, see John Wild, *Introduction to
Realistic Philosophy* (New York, Harper, 1948).

few votaries in teaching ranks, but the economic and social views of communists certainly find many sympathetic listeners among teachers who sincerely wish and work for a democratic social and economic order.

The educational import of idealism has been developed by H. H. Horne and more recently by Ulich,[2] while the fascist possibilities of absolute idealism have been candidly stated by G Gentile.[3] Yet the American teacher is an idealist only at those points where idealism makes connection with spiritual values especially as expressed in liberal Protestant Christianity I am inclined to believe that personalism as developed by E. S. Brightman, R T Flewelling, P A Bertocci[4] and others shows the greatest promise for restoring idealism as a potent systematic force in American education.

Loosely and inaccurately, all opponents to instrumentalism have been dubbed traditionalists However, the title fits only those who attempt to rationalize an educational system or practice on no other grounds than authority and tradition.

The essentialists, led by the late W C Bagley,[5] are more sophisticated about educational practice and more discerning in their opposition to instrumentalism than are the traditionalists, but the grounds on which they argue for a common culture, definite subject matter, and discipline need to be rooted more specifically in metaphysics and epistemology to avoid philosophical bankruptcy

Scholasticism as preserved in Catholic philosophy[6] and theology has an influence roughly proportional to the size of the Catholic population. Its effect on non-Catholics is limited, because its ecclesiastical superstructure is likely to be uncongenial even to those non-Catholics who are sympa-

[2] See, for example, Horne's *Philosophy of Education* (rev. ed , New York, Macmillan, 1927): his *Idealism in Education* (New York, Macmillan, 1923), also "An Idealistic Philosophy of Education" in the *Forty-first Yearbook of the National Society for the Study of Education* (Chicago, University of Chicago Press, 1942), Chap 4 See also Robert Ulich, *Fundamentals of Democratic Education* (New York, American Book, 1940).

[3] *The Reform of Education*, trans. by D Bigongari (New York, Harcourt, Brace, 1922), and M. M Thompson, *The Educational Philosophy of Giovanni Gentile* (Los Angeles, University of Southern California, 1934)

[4] E S. Brightman, "Philosophy in American Education," *The Personalist*, I (1920), 15–28, and "The Contribution of Philosophy to the Theory of Religious Education," *Boston University Bulletin*, XIII, No 25, July 15, 1924. Also P A Bertocci's review of *The Education of Free Men* by Horace Kallen, in *Harvard Educational Review*, XX, No 4 (1950), 285–302.

[5] "An Essentialist's Platform for the Advancement of American Education," *Educational Administration and Supervision*, XXIV, 241–56 Also see W W Brickman, "Essentialism Ten Years After," *School and Society*, LXVII (May 15, 1948), 1742, and I L Kandel, *The Cult of Uncertainty* (New York, Macmillan, 1943), pp 81–82

[6] A clear and succinct account of the Catholic position in educational philosophy is given by Father William McGucken in the *Forty-first Yearbook of the N. S S E*, Part I, Chap 6 See also *Philosophy and Phenomenological Research*, X, No. 2 (December 1949), 251–63, where James F. Anderson and G Watts Cunningham discuss the question Is Scholastic Philosophy Philosophical?

thetic with the Platonic-Aristotelian foundation on which it has been (arbitrarily, they would say) reared. Among the latter would have to be included many classical humanists and not a few essentialists

The other varieties of philosophic opinion frequently studied in general philosophy are not clearly represented in American education. Nominalists, empiricists, positivists, and naturalists of various colorings are likely, so far as education is concerned, to be found in the general camp of pragmatism [7] Indeed, to most classroom teachers these philosophies, together with phenomenology and existentialism, are not much more than vague technical names.

It is this philosophical innocence of the American teacher that makes it so difficult for him to bring educational issues to a philosophical level of discussion and therefore to know where he ought to be and for what he ought to fight when such issues arise.

However, there is still a more fundamental reason for the cordial reception given experimentalism in American education, namely, its success in giving the impression that it has a theoretical monopoly on two highly honorific concepts. scientific method and democracy.

A. *Scientific Method.* Traditional philosophy, Dewey tells us, precluded the possibility of experimental science because

it bequeathed the notion, which has ruled philosophy since the time of the Greeks, that the office of knowledge is to uncover the antecedently real, rather than, as is the case with our practical judgments, to gain the kind of understanding which is necessary to deal with problems as they arise.[8]

On the other hand, the ". experimental procedure is one that installs doing as the heart of knowing"[9] Further, just as physical concepts are designs for operations overtly to be performed, so mathematical ideas are "designations of possible operations . . . ," that is, "symbolic operations with respect *to one another* "[10]

It is not within the province of this essay to refute Dewey's analysis of the procedures of the experimental scientist. One can hardly fail to remark, however, that sophisticated as scientists may be about the "constructed" nature of their hypotheses and postulates, they nevertheless regard their verification as verification by a reality they did *not* construct, and not merely as evidence of their own logical or syntactical consistency The goal

[7] Theodore Brameld's reconstructionism as set forth in his *Patterns of Educational Philosophy* (New York, World Book, 1950) is an interesting variant
[8] John Dewey, *The Quest for Certainty* (New York, Minton, Balch, 1929), p. 17.
[9] *Ibid*, p 36.
[10] *Ibid*, p. 160.

of the modern scientist, it would seem, is still to disclose the nature of the antecedently real

Of more direct concern here is Dewey's brilliant transition from experimental method in physical science to the experimental method as the prototype of all reflection and thence to learning as the practice of the reflective process Says Dewey, ". . . the important thing is that thinking is the method of an educative experience. The essentials of method are therefore identical with the essentials of reflection."[11]

At a stroke, traditional theories of learning stressing the noetic apprehension of pre-existent knowledge by the learner are shown to be as old-fashioned and presumably as untenable as the Greek notions about science. Ready-made subject matter becomes as improper for education as ready-made reality is for the scientist. True learning, like true knowing, becomes the continuous solving of problems by transforming confused, obstructive, frustrating situations into clear and satisfying ones The pupil has become a little scientist.

The analogy between experimental inquiry and learning is pushed further For the learner, as for the scientist, there has to be freedom for inquiry, the results in both are tentative; in neither are tradition, cultural idiosyncrasies, or dogmatisms of any kind to predetermine the results.

It is hardly surprising that this linkage of learning and scientific method should have captured the imagination and allegiance of the educators who knew how fruitless and tiresome an exercise in the memorization of materials whose rationale had been lost in ancient cultural accidents could become Furthermore, it was clear that where learning was effective it took place pretty much as Dewey said it did, namely, by trying to overcome obstacles that intruded into the daily stream of life.

The analogy, however, cannot stand too much pushing Scientists do not select their problems as a response to felt needs but rather from the needs of the discipline in which they serve The scientist works within the rigid controls of his discipline, especially with respect to what is regarded as "knowledge" within it Actually, it takes a long apprenticeship in this pre-existent body of knowledge before fruitful experimentation is possible. The pupil, that is, the beginner in any subject, is a far cry from the scientist, he is no more a little scientist than he is a little man.

Although not all learnings are instances of problem-solving, it is true that men are highly motivated to learn whenever life confronts them with a problem in which they are genuinely concerned. The more a school approximates "life," the easier it is to motivate pupils to high endeavor. But the more the school approximates life, the less is it a school (except a school

[11] *Democracy and Education* (New York, Macmillan, 1916), p. 192.

of hard knocks) and the less reason is there for its being It is precisely because the immature (regardless of age) cannot solve problems as the ma-
ture (the learned) do, that education is needed As Rousseau insisted, the
child is not a little man.

B. *Democracy*. Democracy and scientific method are connected by the
concept of free inquiry. Says Dewey, ". . democracy means freeing intelligence for independent effectiveness—the emancipation of mind as an individual organ to do its own work "[12] But a little further he remarks: "What
does democracy mean save that the individual is to have a share in determining the conditions and the aims of his own work . . ?"[13]

Such self-determination presumably is justified by a faith in the individual's rational powers. Thus John L. Childs says· "To treat a child as an
end, means so to conduct his education that he will progressively grow in
his ability to make up his own mind about that which he shall believe   "[14]
or. "Democratic education . . holds that the nurture of human personality
involves as its very essence the nurture of mind . . ."[15]

Now such language makes one think of the Greek encomiums for mind,
intellect, and knowledge. The dignity of the human person is certainly rem-
iniscent of the first presupposition of Western religion—or of Kant's derivation of it from man's rational nature On what grounds, then, does instrumentalism justify its *monopoly* on democracy?

It might argue that all other philosophies purport to have reached absolute truth as a basis for absolute standards and consequently have *limited*
freedom of thought and action. Or it might plead that all such claims to
absolutes are spurious and that the relativistic position of instrumentalism
is the sole alternative. On either argument, democracy would have to regard instrumentalism as its only reliable defender of freedom. Both arguments have been used [16]

Now it may be true that there are no absolutes, but if so, then neither
scientific method nor democracy may be anything more than cultural idiosyncrasies. Since they are not innate ideas, nor universally held, believed,
or practiced, why they should be exalted, fought for, and so on, is a puzzle
indeed Dewey does on at least one occasion try to solve the puzzle by discussing wherein the goodness of any association lies "How numerous and
varied are the interests which are consciously shared? How full and free is
the interplay with other forms of association?"[17]

[12] *Education Today* (New York, G P Putnam's Sons, 1940), p 62
[13] *Ibid* , p 66
[14] *Education and Morals* (New York, Appleton-Century-Crofts, 1950), p 136
[15] *Ibid* , p 137.
[16] See, for example, Childs, *op cit* , Chaps 3, 4, and 5.
[17] Dewey, *Democracy and Education, op. cit.,* p 96

But the philosophical question is of course. Why are human interests valuable? Why is human life dignified? Why is truth preferable to error? Why is freedom better than servitude? Liberty, equality, and fraternity are either simple notions whose desirability is directly intuited, or this desirability (in the sense of "ought" to be desired) is derived from (1) some relation of man to a transcendent divinity who endows the human being with valid claims to liberty, equality, and fraternity, (2) the nature of man as such as a ground for such claims, or (3) the lessons of history about the general happiness of mankind when these claims were honored or not

Conceivably, liberty, equality, and fraternity might be regarded as tertiary qualities immediately "had" It is extremely doubtful, however, that "desirability" would for Dewey be a product of intuition, inasmuch as desirability is a prediction of future likings and is to be verified in due course of experience [18] With respect to *deriving* the desirability of these concepts, alternatives (1) and (2) would hardly seem congenial to instrumentalism, while (3) rarely furnishes unambiguous answers. But inasmuch as instrumentalists have not been reared *in vacuo*, they are not immune to the valuational overtones of Western religion, philosophy, and political developments Childs is very candid about the inevitability of culturally determined value preferences on the part of educators.[19] But if this is so, on what possible grounds can we oppose totalitarianism, superstition, and slavery? The truth of the matter is that instrumentalists do have their absolutes.[20]

Democracy and scientific method are for all practical purposes such absolutes. It is the instrumentalist's insistence that these are not absolutes—since there can be none—and that they emerge *somehow* from empirical inquiries into existential matters of fact that give to the whole theory the appearance of being suspended from a sky hook.

If one contends that convictions, if strong enough, make theoretical justification unnecessary, then he has removed the only barrier to justification by physical power In such circumstances arguments without power have no validity and arguments with power need none If American educators are eager to lead society to democracy, they had better look to the validation of their faith in democracy, such validation one seeks in vain except in a metaphysics and epistemology that is rational and realistic.

In other words, the rights of the individual to self-determination and his duties to determine himself in the light of the common good (which seem essential to democracy) must find their roots in the very structure of man

[18] Dewey, *The Quest for Certainty, op cit.*, pp. 260-81.
[19] *Op cit*, pp. 94 ff.
[20] See on this, John S Brubacher, "The Absolutism of Progressive and Democratic Education," *School and Society*, LIII (January 4, 1941), 1-9

and society and cannot be regarded as chance by-products of historical accidents

Man's power to envision ideationally or symbolically what is not yet embodied in material existence is the source of his claims to both freedom and dignity It frees him from the here and now and, to some extent, from what has been As some existentialists would insist, man is in a sense most truly what he can become, because through the category of possibility the future becomes a vector in the present flow of events. In virtue of this power, man can conceive an "ought" and subjects himself to laws of value; he can "create" new patterns of old elements into new possibilities of value. But possibility is a category that transcends the space-time dimension. The glibness with which problem-solving, free imaginative play, and freedom of thought are utilized by educational philosophers who also insist on being materialists is a fine example of carefree or careless thinking

II. THE PROBLEM OF AIMS IN EDUCATION

It is often charged that American education is confused In any sense that the accusation is important, it means that educators cannot envision and formulate a unified pattern of values wherewith to regulate the educative enterprise. It is particularly hard for them to do so when it is asserted that education has no aim beyond itself, because it is to be equated with life and growth[21] as intrinsic goods.

It is difficult to believe that Dewey meant the equivalence of life, growth, and education to be taken literally, albeit the insistence of many progressive-school men that the school must resemble the community indicates how literally it has been taken.

What Dewey means to emphasize is that education ought not to have as its guiding factor a vision of a remote future state of affairs, for instance that someday Johnny is to be a lawyer, a doctor, or a saint in heaven. On the contrary, if education supplies conditions ". . . which utilize adequately the present capacities of the immature, the future which grows out of the present is surely taken care of."[22] This sounds very much as if there is a predetermined design (entelechy) in which capacities will actualize themselves, for how else can Dewey be so confident that the future is "surely taken care of"? But Dewey explicitly rejects such an interpretation when he points out that by development he does not mean "   . unfolding of latent powers toward a definite goal "[23] Inasmuch as both immanent and transcendent goals are rejected, there is little left but to regard the growth

[21] Dewey, *Democracy and Education, op. cit*, pp. 59–62.
[22] *Ibid*, p. 65
[23] *Loc. cit.*

of which Dewey speaks as directionless, a charge that has been denied about as often as it has been made, but rarely, so far as I have been able to see, without inconsistency or self-contradiction. The confusion is compounded by the strategic role that problem-solving and teleology in general play in Dewey's theory of knowledge There is direction but it is to be self-direction by short-term goals that arise in the individual mind as a response to a particular problem situation. Yet without some transcendence of the existential situation, even short-term goals would be impossible

It is understandable that, beset with relativism and without the benefit of any rationally grounded hierarchy of value, educators tend to formulate general aims by listing the functions individuals perform in adult life and then converting these into aims of education by prefixing the words "good," "adequate," "worth while" to the statement of the function For example, membership in a family group is a function, worthy home membership is the educational aim. citizenship is a function, good citizenship is the educational aim. We thus get lists of educational aims for health, leisure time, vocations, aesthetic enjoyment. This device solves nothing, because first, it is precisely the *kind* of home, *kind* of leisure activity, *kind* of civic role that people disagree about, and in the second place, these functions remain co-ordinate in value.

The only remedy for the confusion is a view of human nature and of human society that enables us rationally to assert the relative priority of various human functions and to assess the claims of various human groupings. This the realist does by drawing out some of the social and ethical implications of the basic theses stated previously.

1 The concept of a natural order is intended to refer to both structure and function. What is "natural" is definitive of the normal or healthy or good Each entity has its own formal structure which in its existential history it is trying or tending to realize or complete.

2. This order as well as the formal structures of entities can be known at least to some extent as they are, that is, when we come to know their essence and their existential relations.

3 Some entities not only tend to realize perfection but can be aware of the process and its goal as well Of these latter it is proper to use the categories of "ought" and "ought not," because the very processes of awareness that make the apprehension of truth possible also make alternatives to truth equally possible. Truth and goodness are guided and defined ultimately by the nature of the object and the direction of its activity

4. Strategic for education and for the social sciences is the extension of the natural order to the structures comprising society. They, too, must have distinct functions that constitute their essence or reason for being Further, these functions are in a natural order when they together serve and achieve

the common good Otherwise, to speak of social evils and disorders is to be unintelligible.

A natural order of human life obtains when all human activities are guided by an end rationally apprehended and rationally willed Once reason discloses that man has the potentiality to live such a life, it thereby certifies that actualization of this capacity is the *only* valid end for genuinely human living.

To this end all collective and individual effort in the healthy state strives, and by this end all effort is evaluated Man as rational master of himself and of this environment, so far as it is possible, is, therefore, the goal of the good life, the good society, and of the good school

A *The Necessity and Possibility of Education* Clearly, if man were perfected automatically, no education would be needed, and if the course of this perfection were predetermined, no education would be possible The necessity for education follows from the facts that· (1) Man's action is determined by many forces of which reason is only one and rarely the strongest, (2) Perfection is not biologically transmitted We can rely on heredity only for the various grades of capacity for perfection.

As to the first fact. The physiological demands of nutrition, safety, and reproduction hold the first lien on human activity. They can in a hostile environment become the *sole* determinants of action, with reason subordinated to a mere instrument of their fulfillment The need for emotional security in the form of social approval and prestige holds the second lien and also, when starved or denied, makes reason a slave to its craving.[24]

A life characterized by self-mastery and rational self-direction presupposes first that the lower needs be satisfied but not dominant. They must be satisfied because they are the *necessary* conditions for higher modes of living, but because their satisfaction does not *guarantee* a passage to a higher level, they are not *sufficient* conditions A directive factor has to be invoked This factor is education—the deliberate effort to help the individual to self-mastery, namely, to provide some of the means for seeing his essential goal and some of the means for achieving it. This deliberate attempt to produce one mode of life rather than another is possible only because the human infant is so largely undetermined In education, as nowhere else, the category of the potential receives concrete exemplification

B. *The Aim of Education* If the aim of education is to be more specific than the "good life" (all human enterprises in the natural order have this as their aim), then it must be because education has a distinctive function.

---

[24] Suggested by A. H Maslow, "A Theory of Human Motivation," *Psychological Review*, L (1943), 370–96.

What this function is may be indicated by the following observations

1. It deals with human beings only, and only in so far as they are in one respect or another immature, unskilled, unperfected, that is, in so far as they are still potentialities.

2. Education is concerned with the *initial* phases of actualization—the patterning in the individual of modes of actualization that will continue to function after education has ceased.

3 Such modes of self-sustaining actualization are habits, and one aspect of habit—a tendency of the organism to respond in terms of previous learnings—exhibits the autodynamism of behavior at which education aims.[25]

4. Although all education when successful produces learning, education and learning are not equivalent terms Education is a deliberate attempt to produce a particular learning, whereas many learnings occur without deliberate intent on anyone's part and sometimes even contrary to the intent of the educator. I stress this distinction because one can get very foolish about aims for education if it is forgotten that a vast proportion of learning is not within the power of deliberate education to bring about or to prevent.

5. Education is not in its essence a science, but rather an art that utilizes science (knowledge) as its content and as a basis for its own method. It is not an art that transforms or transports material objects. Neither is it a political art that is responsible for the planning or execution of social action on any but a very limited scale

6 Finally, education is coextensive neither with life nor with growth, if these latter terms are to be used with any precision whatsoever.

Education, accordingly, is a distinctive enterprise with a distinctive social function. The stress on existential interdependence is a benign corrective for excessive abstraction If, however, analysis is ruled out, because *in concreto* nothing is found unrelated to anything else, then thinking itself becomes impossible In current educational thought this stress on interdependence has led to an irresponsible assumption of responsibility by the school for the improvement of man, beast, and civilization

In the field of action the key word correspondingly is "co-operation," for if all entities are interdependent, so are all tasks. Unfortunately, the strength that comes from the division of labor and the organization of diverse efforts toward a common goal is often missing, because no clear-cut division of function among social agencies is permitted. If interdependence is to be more than a muddle, if educational discussion is to be more than amiable palaver, and if co-operation is to mean more than the freedom to mind everybody else's business, then the *essential* role of each social institution has to be explicitly stated and related to the common good

[25] The dynamic aspect of habit is particularly well brought out in Dewey's *Human Nature and Conduct* (New York, Henry Holt, 1942), Part I.

Education's *own* unique aim and function is to transform the inherent capacities of the individual for rational self-determination into the habits prerequisite to the apprehension, use, and enjoyment of truth.

III PROBLEMS OF CURRICULUM

Education when successful produces reliable tendencies to apprehend, use, and enjoy truth Habits, however, draw their content from a given culture The problem of the curriculum, therefore, is the selection of proper means and materials wherewith to develop capacities into effective tendencies. The first question to be raised is What body of (1) knowledge. (2) skill, and (3) value preferences can be taught to man as man (general education)?

A. *General Education*

1. KNOWLEDGE With respect to knowledge, a distinction has to be made between the roles an individual plays by virtue of his membership in the human race and those he enacts by virtue of his specialized place in the social structure or by virtue of special endowments, talents, or disabilities. (*a*) Every man has to function as a member of the natural *sustaining* groups of family, community, state, and world [26] (*b*) He lives in a material world that needs to be transformed to maintain human activities. His own body is both an instrument in that world and a part of it (*c*) Every individual lives with himself as a particularized route to, or away from, perfection. As such he needs to apprehend his own nature and potentiality for the good and bad life.

Function (*a*) calls for knowledge about:

(i) The group structure that the attainment of a common good presupposes, its hierarchical order of ends and means, and the essential function of each group distinguished from the accidental ones;

(ii) The principles of justice governing the apportionment of rights and duties within and among the groups,

(iii) The history of their development,

(iv) Discrepancies between actual orders and the natural order.[27]

From function (*b*) follows the need of knowing the physical sciences, mathematics, and the biological sciences.

From function (*c*) follows the study of psychology, literature, philosophy, the arts, and religion.

[26] Wild, *op. cit*, Chap 10
[27] This kind of knowledge may be part of an established discipline or it may have to be supplied by the teacher or worked out by the teacher and the pupil, but it is indispensable to general education.

Does general education mean, then, the mastery of all knowledge by all men? Is it a kind of revival of Comenius's *pansophy*? Fortunately, the mastery desired here is merely that required to form *habits* rather than what would be needed to produce savants.

How much of this general education is learned and how well depends upon individual capacity. The adjustments for such individual differences will be discussed in the section on organization.

Traditionally, these requirements were held to be admirably filled by the study of the classics. But the test for materials is neither age nor respectability. It is rather what gives the desired result efficiently. As will be seen in the subsequent sections, pupils who cannot read the words of Shakespeare or Tacitus will hardly get their sense. Furthermore, the use of materials designed for another age puts a great strain on the pedagogical skill of the teacher. On the other hand, given the right pupil and teacher, some classics give more in the way of perspective and appreciation for comparable time and effort than do most contemporary materials.

2. SKILLS. Every habit has a skill component that reveals itself in an ease of performance that savors of the automatic. For general education, the skills of the curriculum need also to be general, that is, usable in a wide variety of situations (although the actual use of a skill is always in a particular existential context). Such general skills may be classified as symbolic, logical, and artistic.

(A) *Symbolic skills*. Symbolic skills refer primarily to facility in the use of linguistic and number symbols. The cultivation of such facility as an end in itself is properly deplored as verbalism, and traditional education, especially as exemplified in the Latin grammar schools, certainly was not innocent of the charge. Such verbalism is a necessary corollary of no philosophic position, save that which holds to the equivalence of symbol and thing. Experimentalism in its horror of verbalism has fled to such extremes that many a progressive teacher is somewhat uneasy if her pupils do nothing more vigorous than read a book. Yet even the progressives would agree that ability to deal with symbols is almost the equivalent of being human and rational. Symbolic skills are not ends in themselves. They are *instruments* of knowledge, but *indispensable* instruments, that is, not wholly replaceable by motion pictures, radio, television, or even direct existential involvement in existential situations.

(B) *Logical skills*. Logical skills refer to facile inference both deductive and inductive so far as this can be developed by practice. They would also include sensitivity to mistakes of inference and to similarities and differences in analogical reasonings.

These skills can be identified in many mental operations. Unfortunately, training the pupil in inference as such does not *automatically* transfer to skill of inference in legal, mathematical, or scientific materials To maintain the contrary is to maintain the doctrine of mental discipline in its least tenable form. There is, however, nothing in a realistic philosophy of education that connects it logically with this doctrine. On the contrary, if it is true that a skill achieves its generality only by being practiced on a great diversity of materials, then such a diversity is best supplied by the variety of subject matters included in the curriculum of general education

(c) *Artistic skills* Skill in the application of a principle or a piece of knowledge to the solution of a particular problem is part of what is meant by an artistic skill It connotes the involvement of the individual in an existential situation It connotes motor skill under the guidance of symbolic and logical skill. It also involves the ability to manipulate symbols, meanings, and material objects into existential patterns that have aesthetic, scientific, or technical relevance In a genuine sense, therefore, artistic skill is the goal of both knowledge and the other skills, and also serves as a test for their proper mastery.

3. PATTERNS OF PREFERENCE. If the pupil deliberates about choices, uses reliable information, and uses it skillfully, but does all this merely to secure the approval of teachers, parents, and so forth, the habit is still in an unreliable state, and education is not yet successful.[28] Only when the pupil freely chooses to practice his knowledge and skill, and derives genuine satisfaction from doing so, can we be sure that a reliable habit has been formed. Every well-developed habit contains an emotional bias favoring its own exercise.

To bring about this emotional attachment is discouragingly difficult, especially so whenever the values of the school and those of the community do not coincide—and in an imperfect state they never do. The system of punishments and rewards used by a community attaches pleasure and pain to objects and activities in a way that is not always the way of the school. Let a community value money above moral integrity or act as if it does, let it lavishly reward the titillators of animal pleasures and starve the purveyors of rational pleasures, and the school is hard put to it to form predilections in the pupil for moral integrity and rational pleasures.

This fact led Plato, in the *Republic*, to insist on the isolation of children from their natural parents and on the careful cleansing of all poetry, drama, and legends. Unless informal education can be controlled, formal education can do relatively little about the love of the good or the attitude of the pupil toward any given value It is true that formal educational systems in Russia, Japan, and Germany did seem to produce an emotional uniformity as astounding as it was dismaying, but before all the credit is given to the school, it might be well to point out that the forces controlling the schools

[28] Wild, *op. cit.*, Chap. 3.

controlled *all* other educative agencies including the radio and the press. Had not the bulk of the population adopted attitudes that were aggressive, anti-this or pro-that, the schools could not have given them to the children. That is why schools, no matter how well intentioned, cannot eliminate delinquency from children in an environment that puts a premium upon it.

This is not to say that the school can do nothing about value preferences, it cannot, however, vouch for the permanence of these preferences, because the social milieu in which an individual's adult life is lived is a more powerful vector than is the school. Let a high-school graduate with a respectable mastery of English be employed with a group to whom correct English usage is an affectation, and within five years he will have left the group, become a "regular guy," or have been reduced to silence. The same may be said with respect to tastes in literature and the other fine arts. That the college has more success in modifying tastes is due only in part to the college instruction. More important is the circumstance that college graduates are more likely to find employment and spend their adult years in groups that reinforce such tastes.

The situation is not alleviated by the fact that we cannot use religion to enforce a given pattern of value preference. We can study religion as one of several institutions, but the creedal-ritualistic components that give a religion its power over the emotions of the child cannot be taught in public schools in the United States if public peace is to be maintained.

Yet there are values, loyalty to which can be inculcated without being guilty of imposition or cultural or class bias. I refer to these dispositions that make the rational life possible, namely, devotion to truth, to the pursuit of it; a respect for man's power to see truth and to guide his life by it; a fear of smugness, complacency, and self-deception. Such values can be "indoctrinated" without fear, for they are self-correcting by their very nature and in the face of all opposition. And the better we form the skills of dealing with truth, the more pleasurable will the pupil find them to be.

B. *Special Education*

In the next section the question of adapting general education to individual differences will be considered. Here let us turn to the kind of education the individual needs in order to perform his function as a member of the instrumental groups which supply the means for realizing the common good.

It is a commonplace to point out that science and technology based thereon have made it possible for *all* men to have sufficient leisure to perfect their rational natures. What an army of slaves made possible for a few men in the time of Plato and Aristotle, technology now makes conceivable for all mankind Technology, however, has transformed the quality of work itself. The worker groups include many men who need intellectual training of one kind or another to perform their work Granted that much of this knowledge is know-how and does not presuppose the mastery of the scientific knowledge upon which it is based, there is still a wide difference between what goes on in the head of a radio technician, a navigator, a traffic engineer, and what goes on in the head of a ditchdigger or a movie ticket taker in their vocational moments. It is to the credit of Dewey that he explicated the intellectual possibilities of gainful occupations—possibilities pretty completely overlooked by Plato and Aristotle

Because the noetic habits needed for modern work cannot, in a highly complex industrialized society, be picked up informally, that is, by imitation or by simple participation, there arises a conflict between the claims of general and specific education upon the curriculum In this connection, the following observations are in order·

1. The vocationalists usually overestimate the amount of specialized training needed for the majority of jobs and tend to underestimate the training needed for membership in the sustaining groups of family, community, and state.

2. The vocationalist usually does not realize how much general education (as above outlined) does contribute to employability On the higher vocational levels this is being understood Witness the recent emphasis on general education in technical and professional schools.

3. The controversy would become less academic if the amount of specific education for given types of work were rationally determined It would also help if both parties to the debate realized that the capacity of the individual very often sets the limit for the level of both general and special education that he can reach.

On the question of curriculum then, it follows that general education is basic, vocational education supplementary, but necessary

When vocational ambition threatens to become (if indeed the threat has not been already carried out) the dominant motive in American education, it is understandable that the adherents of classical philosophy should be somewhat bitter about vocational education and somewhat heroic about the irrelevance of economic value in the justification of the liberal arts curriculum. Three points, however, might be kept in mind. First, for a subject to have economic value does not necessarily disqualify it educationally, in the second place, man in our society is a working animal, finally, the liberal arts curriculum became firmly entrenched in our culture partly because it did have a vocational value Latin, for example, was a vocational prerequisite for the statesman, the clergyman, and indeed for all the learned professions in the Middle Ages Because the lesser vocations did not at that time require formal preparation, we are too prone to argue that the training they now do require is "merely" vocational

In spite of all this, the relative position and importance of general and special education is clear, and whenever vocational training becomes dominant in an educational system, it should be regarded as a danger signal, for it means that the education of man as man is being neglected and that the needs of man as a whole are being identified with, and reduced to, his needs as a worker.

IV. IMPLICATIONS FOR ORGANIZATION

Formal education in any group raises such questions as Who shall be educated? For how long? By whom? Under what control? These are questions of organization

It would seem to follow from the principle that all men are rational that all have a natural right to the education that will allow them to perfect themselves as human beings It is unfortunately true that Plato and Aristotle proposed and sanctioned social practices that contradict this principle The principle does, nevertheless, follow from the type of realism here espoused It therefore does not commit us to a caste system of education on the one hand, nor to quantitative or qualitative equality of education on the other The individual's right to education is limited only by his capacity to learn and by the group's ability to provide opportunity to learn.

Such capacity is a function of many factors, for instance heredity, age, emotional and physical health, economic status, interparental felicity, and diet; each could be a dimension on which capacity could be gauged

In practice, the dimension most frequently used—and without doubt the least valuable—is chronological age; after that comes performance in school tasks, and finally the dimension of intelligence as determined by an intelligence test Of these, only the last is designed to gauge capacity. Pointing out correctly that in the absence of mental, physical, social, and emotional health no good learning takes place, the *avant-garde* in education and child care have drawn the dubious inference that the school has the responsibility for the various types of health maintenance and repair. It would be equally sensible to demand of a carpenter that he become a mason because a stone foundation is needed for a house he is to build

We come once more to the division of labor among the social agencies The fact that the home and other agencies have abdicated their duties in these areas does not automatically shift to the school the responsibility for them, If the school takes primary responsibility only for what it is designed to produce, namely, the habits for the apprehension, use, and enjoyment of truth, that is, intellectual development (see the previous section), then the capacity for such development is the most strategic dimension for organization This dimension I shall call the "abstraction potential" when it refers to the capacity of the pupil and the "abstraction differential" when it refers to the level of generality exemplified by a learning task.

Pupils vary with respect to the level of abstraction at which they can learn efficiently [29] Some can understand calculus, others must stop at geometry, still others cannot go beyond rote arithmetic. In history, some cannot apprehend more than the isolated historical event simply or dramatically described, others can understand sequences of cause and effect, still others can comprehend theories of causation; and a few like to discuss the theories about theories of causation.

Differences in power to deal with abstractions are evident on every level of instruction. Even in general education this differential can help determine what will be taught and on what level It can also be the rational means of determining who should go to high school, college, or university. It is an important factor in the choice of an occupation.

Because the abstraction potential can be measured, albeit not with great precision by intelligence tests, a philosophy of education need not commit itself to either a caste system of education or to a mechanical equalitarianism The individual is a *unique* pattern of value potentials This uniqueness does not mean that there is no truth that everybody ought to apprehend, it does mean that pupils vary in the level at which they can assimilate it By adhering to capacity for learning as a criterion, we can avoid the demand that everyone learn exactly the same thing in the same way and, likewise, the notion that the felt needs of children are true guides for curriculum and organization.

A Educational Control

The state in its legislative, executive, and judicial functions can, if it wishes, exercise a control over education as complete as its power permits But where the statesman rules in accordance with the concept of a natural order, he recognizes that the search for truth and its reincarnation in successive generations is not the essential function of government.

It rarely happens, however, that the material resources available for education are unlimited. It therefore becomes the duty of government to apportion the amounts of money to be spent for the several social functions.

[29] In this connection it is interesting to note that some investigators regard amnesia of color names as due to the fact that the patient is confined to the "concrete" attitude and cannot assume the "categorial" attitude Aaron Gurwitsch, "Gelb-Goldstein's Concept of 'Concrete' and 'Categorial' Attitude and the Phenomenology of Idealism," *Philosophy and Phenomenological Research*, X, No 2 (December 1949), 190 ff.

Thus, in fact, government can influence *what* is to be taught as well as furnishing the means for teaching it In an imperfect state, this fact may vitiate education and the truth itself, but the only defense against it would be the assertion that truth-seeking and truth-teaching have an autonomy that transcends all questions of power—political or otherwise In other words, we would have to assert that the authority of the philosopher, scientist, and educator is the authority of truth itself.

In natural science, scientific method and its results do exert a very powerful compulsion upon the public But in what other area is there a body of truth so compelling as to obviate wars of interpretation? Because philosophers do not agree, and because religious leaders seem a little afraid of agreement, it is the dominant group within a culture that determines what the "truth" in each debatable realm shall be

It is an old dilemma Either we commit ourselves to relativity in the field of value and surrender final authority to a power group, or we assert the objectivity of truth in these areas and immediately have twenty candidates for the Truth.

We are thus brought to the basic questions of epistemology It is not enough to assert the existence and knowability of an objective truth Philosophers have to state some of these truths and invite all rational men to examine them as means to the perfection of man and society. Provided that we do not ask men to bring to this examination what only cultural or historical accidents can supply, then the basis for freedom of thought and democracy is securely laid, not in the shifting sands of relativism nor on the stilts of dogmatism, but in the very nature of man himself That this method can have practical possibilities is witnessed by the fact that twenty-six nations, including the United States, found it possible to sign the United Nations Declaration of Rights which presupposes a concept of natural law An analogous attempt to lay bare the essentials of the education needed for the maintenance of the natural order of the good life is, therefore, not merely a speculative dream.

V. Problems of Method

The relevant question to ask about method is Does it achieve efficiently the results desired? Given the objective to achieve a certain level of mastery in reading, there is a priori no *one* method that must be judged best. In so far as results can be tested and measured, the judgment must wait upon empirical evidence. Although the quotation marks cannot be dispensed with when education is spoken of as a "science," there is hope that questions of method will in time be questions of fact

Unfortunately, the distinctions between aim, curriculum, and method in

education are not always observed in controversy. For example the doctrine of the child-centered school is at least partially false as a guide for
curriculum construction, but as a technique of instruction it is highly efficient and especially so for the lower levels of abstractive capacity Dewey's
belief in the efficacy of informal education is warranted, but the inference
that all education shall be experimental and "informal" is highly debatable.
Method is, in brief, a relatively independent variable, and it is difficult to
discern any necessary relationship between any given method and any
specific philosophic position.

The relation of the activity method to the epistemological instrumentalism of Dewey offers the least difficulty in this respect, because here thinking, purposive activity, and learning become almost indistinguishable.
While it is not particularly important to deduce any special method from
realism, what has been said suggests that the key to general method is the
same as the key to organization, namely, the matching of subject matter
and capacity in the abstraction dimension In this sense, teaching is a
translation of subject matter to an appropriate level of abstraction, that
level being determined by the abstraction potential of the pupil

VI CONCLUSION

Modern education and modern life as a whole are torn between the aggressive arrogance of totalitarian power and dogmatic tubular vision on the
one hand, and a skeptical relativistic resistance to it that is potent only in
its denials on the other. This relativism has made it impossible to think
clearly about education, because it has made it impossible and senseless to
seek the essence of anything and, therefore, of the unique function of any
social agency, not excluding education. Problems of aims, curricula, and
organization become unintelligible, because analysis allegedly does violence to their interdependence All educational problems, when carried to
the level of philosophic analysis, resolve themselves repeatedly to the same
questions: What is real? What is true? What is important? On a relativistic
basis it is useless to ask such questions, on the dogmatic basis it is useless to
answer them. The relevance of realism in this situation is to be estimated by
the degree to which it makes it possible for intelligent men of good will, by
the use of their own powers, without external coercion of any kind, to
arrive at rational conviction and agreement about answers to these questions.

XIII

A Realistic Theory of Forgiveness

J. Arthur Martin, *Wheaton College,*
Norton, Massachusetts

THE forgiveness of sins as a transaction between God and man has received rather extensive treatment at the hands of theologians. Forgiveness as a transaction between men has been almost entirely neglected by philosophers. Some philosophers would simply accept the uncritical view of common sense that forgiveness is entirely a subjective process within the mind of the offended person which results in a changed attitude on his part toward someone who has offended him. Many philosophers tend to look upon forgiveness as either supermoral or submoral. Sometimes they incline to the opinion that the man who forgives his enemy has done something which is beyond the limits of moral obligation, has gone "a second mile" as it were; at other times they look upon forgiveness with a suspicious eye, conceiving it to be a *sub rosa* tinkering with the moral order of the universe sponsored usually by theologians. At still other times philosophers have denied that there is any necessity for forgiveness, asserting that the truly "good man" is one who holds himself above offense; when confronted by the man who has wronged him, the good man will look with pity upon the wrongdoer and will even undertake to correct him, but he will not feel that there is anything to forgive.

It is my intention to analyze the basic structure of forgiveness [1] In so doing I believe it will become apparent that forgiveness is not a subjective change in the mind of one person but an alteration of the objective relationship between two persons I believe that a careful examination of forgiveness will show that forgiveness is concerned not with changing the mind of the offended person but with changing the mind of the offender, and with re-establishing between the two persons a relationship which has been destroyed Furthermore, I hope to make it apparent that forgiveness is not

---

[1] Undoubtedly, in any particular instance the practical problem of forgiveness is complicated by historical and social circumstances in which the occasion for forgiveness may arise But a satisfactory analysis of the more complicated problem presupposes an analysis of the essential structure of forgiveness. Such an analysis is what is attempted here.

a tampering with the moral law but rather is unintelligible without the moral law Forgiveness (1) presupposes the moral law as the principle which governs that relationship the destruction of which requires forgiveness, (2) presupposes the moral law as the principle which governs that relationship the re-establishment of which is the purpose of forgiveness, and (3) presupposes the moral law as the principle which governs the process which is forgiveness

Finally, I hope it will be shown that forgiveness is necessary inasmuch as the situation which calls for forgiveness is not one which can be met by the imperturbable calm of the good man The conception of forgiveness implied both by popular maxims and by the attitude of most philosophers is excessively subjective, it reduces forgiveness to a mental attitude on the part of the offended person It is the contention of this essay that forgiveness is a process aimed at re-establishing between two persons a relationship of mutual confidence and trust after such a relationship has been destroyed by the action of one of the members of that relationship

I. THE CONTEXT WITHIN WHICH FORGIVENESS IS RELEVANT

Forgiveness presupposes a relationship between two persons which has been destroyed by the action of one of the persons, and it aims at the re-establishment of the destroyed relationship This fact is sometimes obscured, because we frequently speak of forgiving what a person did. But properly speaking, the deed which is said to be forgiven is the action which has altered the relationship between the persons and which has consequently given rise to the necessity of forgiveness. Forgiveness addresses itself to the person as the doer of the deed, and it attempts to re-establish a relationship with that person which he has destroyed What kind of relationship is that, the destruction of which calls for forgiveness?

The relationship between men is frequently, some would say always, dominated by the self of one or another of the parties to the relationship Quite often such a relationship is the resultant of the forces of the selves involved, colliding and clashing with one another. In such a relationship the patterns of conduct are derived from the peculiarities of the individuals concerned Conduct is determined by, and expresses the ambitions and purposes, the interests and concerns, the often conflicting hopes and fears and hates and loves of, the particular individuals who compose the relationship, uncriticized by any appeal to any standard or norm of conduct apart from the assertiveness of the self Such a relationship is the resultant of the character of the individuals involved and of the comparative power and ingenuity of each to maintain his own intents. In such a relationship all conduct presupposes the existence of the self, and the basic purpose which

furnishes the ultimate goal of action and the supreme standard of judgment is the continuation of the self in time. Here all judgments both of
one's own conduct and that of others are based upon the uncriticized purposes of the self of the judge In this context the question "What ought I to
do?" is always a question of technique

One might call this the "selfish" relationship, although one hesitates to do
so, because selfishness has been so universally condemned by the common
consent of all civilized mankind that its existence is constantly overlooked
and its viciousness is hardly noticed unless the self assert itself in a squal-
ling, childish way What one must note is how often the self asserts itself
in a quiet, pleasant, well-mannered, deadly way It may even have a system
of morals to which it pays allegiance. But in every situation,

> . . . each in his small motion is as a lion on prowl,
> or as a python gliding to seize and devour
> some weaker Self, whereby to fortify his own.[2]

In such a relationship, forgiveness can have no more than three possible
meanings: unreasonable caprice, weakness, or dissembling craftiness. Here
an offense can only mean any action or word which is deemed by the offended party to contradict the surge of the self to express itself. Indeed, all
opposition is an offense, and by the terms of the relationship is to be re-
sisted. Acceptance of the offense is to be accounted for as unreasonable
capriciousness or as a sign of one's inability to oppose the offender successfully or as a transitory moment in a far-reaching plan of revenge.

A genuinely moral relationship between two persons is decidedly different Here conduct is governed by the mutual voluntary allegiance of both
persons to a principle which is objective, universal, and imperative, and
which defines the limits within which each person may assert himself without injuring or destroying the other. In such a relationship, each person
may exist and act with confidence and trust in respect to the other, so long
as the relationship exists, because the conduct of each, regardless of what
it is, will be within the limits defined by this principle which delimits the
rightful functioning of each in respect to the existence of the other. The
conduct of each may express the interests and ambitions of each, but so
long as that conduct remains within the limits established by this principle,
it will not destroy mutual confidence and trust. However, any action which
transgresses these limits will destroy the relationship by destroying mutual
confidence and trust. This principle is what we mean by the moral law.[3]

[2] See Robert Bridges, *The Testament of Beauty. A Poem in Four Books* (Oxford,
Clarendon Press, 1930), Book II, lines 77–79, p. 36
[3] This principle has been variously denominated I have chosen to call it the moral
law simply because that is a term in relatively common use, and it seems to me to involve fewer controversial implications than other terms which might have been used.

By saying that such a principle is *objective,* I mean that it is not dependent for its character or existence upon the historical circumstances of the character or existence of any individual, nor is it created by the mutual agreement of the persons involved in the relationship which it governs It must be discovered, not invented We cannot simply decide on what terms we will trust one another Although the principle of conduct which is to govern such a relationship must be mutually agreed upon if the relationship is to exist, nevertheless, the mere fact that both parties mutually agree to govern conduct by some common principle will not guarantee a relationship of mutual confidence and trust. Only conduct of a certain sort on the part of each person will actually elicit confidence and trust in the other from both

Being such creatures as we are, having the nature we have, what sort of conduct will induce us to trust one another? The answer to that question must be discovered by an analysis of the nature of man, of his existence and function in the universe, and of the nature of social relationships. Until such a principle be discovered and until it be understood in all its ramifications and intricacies, in all its implications and subtle applications to the multifarious complexity of human conduct, the good intentions of men will miscarry Realistic moral philosophy seeks to discover and to analyze such a principle But the objective character of such a principle is implied in the fact that we cannot *arbitrarily* define its characteristics, as we might define the rules of a game

By saying that such a principle is *universal,* I mean that it is a principle which is applicable to all men as men and to all the relationships of men at any time and in any place Its applicability is not limited to only certain historical situations. It is conceived to delimit the activity of any man at any time or place in relation to any man Regardless of what historical circumstances may arise, any action which violates this principle is an invasion of the right of another being to exist or to function, it injures or destroys his nature

The function of the moral law in human relationships is that of *the definition of the limits* within which human conduct must take place if it is not to injure or destroy another person The moral law does not give specific detailed instructions about how one is to act in every situation. The good life involves the exercise of prudential judgment and free choice of contingent means The possibility of right action in any given situation is thus not limited to one, and only one, act But whatever action is performed, it must not violate certain limits, and the definition of the limits within which conduct must be performed is the function of the moral law. This fact accounts for the tendency to express the moral law in negative terms, in the form of the "Thou shalt not———" of the Ten Commandments and of other early codes of law Furthermore, the realization of this fact would seem to obviate the complaint of the relativists that the existence of a universally applicable moral principle is inconsistent with the infinite variety of occasions for human conduct The moral law is not a recipe for the cooking up of right action, it is a principle by which are defined the limits within which right action must take place

To say that the moral law is an *imperative* is to say that the obligation which it places upon the individual to respect it and to govern conduct according to it is not derived from, nor dependent upon, the influence upon his will or imagination of any particular historical circumstances. This principle is what ought to govern the relationship between individuals whether they acknowledge that obligation or not, and regardless of what may occur in any moment of time.

This principle which we have called the moral law governs every genuinely moral relationship, but it does not generate such a relationship The establishment of the relationship and the maintenance of the relationship depend upon the activity of men The moral relationship itself comes into being as a result of the actions of men acting in accord with the moral law and out of allegiance to the moral law. Actions, not words, establish the relationship The actions must have a continuity and internal consistency if they are to establish a moral relationship, mere miscellaneous, haphazard activity will not establish such a relationship The moral law is the principle which furnishes continuity and consistency to these acts.

Furthermore, the acts must be performed out of allegiance to the moral law, a genuinely moral relationship with its accompanying character of confidence and trust between the persons concerned is not generated by an accidental congruence between conduct and the demands of the moral law. Finally, the establishment of the relationship is not exclusively in the power of one person; the action must be properly interpreted by the other member of the relationship if a relationship of mutual confidence and trust is to be established, that is, the action must be understood as action in accordance with the moral law and motivated by allegiance to that law.

The operation of the moral law in human relationships is not of the nature of mechanical compulsion It operates through the appeal which it makes to men who know and understand its nature (hence the importance of moral theory and of moral instruction) and who accept its demands and discipline their lives in accord with those demands (hence the importance of moral training).

The moral law cannot be destroyed or altered, but it can be rejected. If it be rejected, then the relationship between two persons which has been governed by mutual allegiance to this law is changed The rejection of the moral law results in the collapse of mutual confidence and trust. A relationship of mutual confidence and trust can be destroyed by an action which is a deliberate rejection of the authority of the moral law. It is to be noted that the ensuing relationship, although it is dominated by the uncriticized ambitions or purposes of the offender, is different from that primitive relationship which we called the "selfish" relationship.

In the primitive situation there was no reason to believe that the action of another person was a deliberate rejection of the authority of the moral law. In the primitive relationship there is the twofold problem of becoming aware of the moral law and of bringing conduct within the limits set by the moral law. But once a moral relationship has been established and has been destroyed, the problem is not one of establishing, but of re-establishing, a moral relationship. The problem is not one of discovering the moral law but of re-establishing its authority over the relationship. One must eliminate the suspicion which has been created by the rejection of that authority. It is one thing to establish mutual confidence and trust, it is quite another thing to re-establish these after they have been destroyed. The relationship which follows the destruction of the moral relationship I shall hereafter call the "degenerate relationship."

The deed which destroys a genuinely moral relationship is not merely a mistake. A mistake may be defined as an incongruity between the pattern of conduct intended by the agent and the pattern of conduct performed. A mistake betokens ignorance or poor judgment or a lack of skill in the performance of one's intention. Whatever be the reason for the occurrence of a mistake, a mistake does not call for forgiveness, it calls for correction. An action which is incongruous with the demands of the moral law, but which the agent did not intend to be incongruous with that law, is a moral mistake; such action also calls for correction. But an action which was intended to be incongruous with the demands of the moral law is more than a mistake. It is a transgression of that law.

A transgression calls for something more than education or instruction in what is to be done. It calls for an alteration of the intention of the agent. I believe that the purpose of punishment is the alteration of the intention of the agent. A transgression of the moral law, however, frequently involves more than the agent and the moral law; it involves another person who suffers because of the act of the agent. Such an action I would call an offense. An offense is a transgression of the moral law which injures another person. In any genuine offense, there is the pattern of conduct which is incongruous with the pattern of conduct demanded by the moral law, there is the authority of the moral law which has been rejected; and there is the offended person whose right to be in relation to the offender as defined by the moral law has been disregarded and dismissed as irrelevant. An offense calls for forgiveness.

The offense implies that the offender is not to be trusted His conduct has destroyed the relationship which has existed, and the problem is not merely that of re-establishing the authority of the moral law but also that of eliminating the suspicion and distrust which his conduct has generated. It is the fact of suspicion and distrust which hangs over the degenerate relationship which distinguishes it from the primitive relationship Forgiveness aims at re-establishing a *relationship* of mutual confidence and trust after such a relationship has been destroyed by the action of one party which can only be reasonably interpreted by the other party as a deliberate disregard of the rights of the other party as defined by the moral law.

Subjectivist theories of forgiveness misconceive both the nature of the occasion for forgiveness and also the aim of forgiveness They conceive forgiveness to be a subjective activity within the mind of the offended party. According to these subjectivist views, the problem is to alter the opinion which the offended person has of the offender so that the offended no longer holds a grudge against the offender. It is assumed that the former relationship between the persons can be re-established by the simple godlike fiat of the offended This conception of forgiveness is too abstract and too superficial both in its understanding of the occasion which calls for forgiveness and also in its analysis of the process whereby a moral relationship is re-established

Where forgiveness is demanded by the situation, the offense is not a mistaken idea in the mind of the offended person, the suspicion and distrust which exist between the two persons are not rooted in an imagined injury If the relationship has been disrupted by a mistaken idea or an imagined grievance, then the situation calls not for forgiveness but for the correction of that idea. Forgiveness presupposes the actual disruption of a certain concrete relationship. The disruption itself and the cause of the disruption are not erroneously imagined by the offended party He is right in his opinion that the relationship has been altered, fundamentally changed by the action of the offender The task of forgiveness is not that of showing a mistaken individual his mistake but of destroying the cause of the offended's justifiable distrust of the offender and of re-establishing the real relationship of mutual confidence and trust by meeting the requirements of such a relationship, which requirements are expressed by the moral law. Forgiveness is a process which involves a series of actions in the public domain of history, and not one act in the mind of the offended person The degenerate relationship can be destroyed only by action. And the relationship of mutual confidence and trust can be re-established only by action

Perhaps it should be emphasized that the relationship to be re-established calls for *mutual* confidence and trust It is not enough that the offended person regain his confidence in the offender. The offender must also

regain his confidence in the offended Since the offender has established a
relationship in which the moral law is no longer recognized as setting the
limits to the assertion of the self, he has every reason to expect vengeance
at the hands of the offended until there is some convincing evidence that the
offended has not acquiesced in the terms of the degenerate relationship
The confidence and trust of the offender in the person he has offended needs
to be re-established quite as much as the confidence and trust of the offended in the offender.

II. The Process of Forgiveness

The process of forgiveness must be initiated by the offended The offender
has lost the power to do anything which will elicit confidence and trust
from the person whom he has offended His every action is under a cloud
of suspicion In terms of the degenerate relationship which he has brought
about, it is to his advantage that the other person should trust him, and
hence any action on his part which in the moral relationship might have
strengthened the confidence of the other person in him is now subject to
the interpretation that it is designed to further and strengthen his position
in this relationship based upon the self Once mutual confidence and trust
have been destroyed, they can be re-established, if at all, only by the person who is not guilty of destroying them in the first place

The initial phase in the process of forgiveness is a twofold struggle
within the mind and soul of the offended person, it is this phase which
is usually referred to in the popular conception of forgiveness In the degenerate relationship, the limiting function of the moral law has been disregarded, and hence the relationship places a premium upon one's own
power and skill and cunning directed by oneself In terms of the degenerate
relationship, he prospers most who is least concerned for other persons.

The first moment of this initial phase in the process of forgiveness is
the struggle within the soul of the offended person to reject the terms of
the degenerate relationship, forgiveness begins with the refusal of the
offended to accept the conditions of this relationship as final Since such
acceptance by the offended person would mean that *he* would govern *his*
conduct by allegiance to his own mood and feeling without reference to the
moral law, and since in the face of the offense this allegiance to his own
self would dictate vengeance, the refusal to accept the terms of the degenerate relationship is a *refusal to seek revenge* The process of forgiveness,
then, begins with a struggle within the soul of the offended to resist the
temptation to accept the degenerate relationship, to deal with the offender
on his own terms, and to ruthlessly exploit the situation for his own ad-

vantage Without this initial self-restraint, forgiveness never gets under way

This restraining of oneself from vengeance is a necessary step in the process of forgiveness, but a more constructive issue of the struggle in the soul of the offended is also needed. Self-restraint by itself would have no moral value and might be indistinguishable from moral indifference, cowardice, or moral weakness The second struggle in the soul is that to keep oneself loyal to the moral law The offended person must be wholeheartedly devoted to the principle of conduct defined in the moral law, which is to say that he must be genuinely desirous of re-establishing the relationship of mutual confidence and trust There must be genuine *benevolence,* that is, a will which is good, which is submissive to the norm of goodness which is objective to any one self and which comprises the principle of conduct upon which is based the relationship of mutual confidence and trust. The struggle in the soul therefore is, on the one hand, a struggle to reject the impulse to vengeance, and on the other hand, a struggle to discipline desire and will by the principle of action which is above all individual selves

The outcome of this twofold struggle within the soul of the offended may be called *pardon* in the basic sense of that word, in the sense of *freely giving back,* offering once again to the offender the relationship which he has destroyed and which, in so doing, he has lost the power to re-establish This offering once again of the relationship of mutual confidence and trust cannot be won by any action of the offender, it cannot be bought from, or forced upon, the offended person It must be voluntarily given by him It derives from the will of the offended person when that will has rejected the degenerate relationship and has been firmly submitted to the demands of the principle which governs the relationship of mutual confidence and trust.

Pardon, however, should not be confused with the whole of forgiveness, it is merely the outcome of the initial phase of that process. The re-establishment of the relationship which has been destroyed must wait upon actions which really establish mutual confidence and trust between the parties to that relationship Pardon is the initial critical moment in the process of forgiveness, without it, no effort will be made to even undertake the process of forgiveness But it is only the beginning of forgiveness. Making the offer of the old relationship effective is the task which remains, and this task can be performed only by action. If the struggle described above be genuine, it must issue in action, it must appear as an event or as a series of events, and not remain a mere mental attitude The first consequence of the struggle as it emerges into the public domain of action is condemnation.

Condemnation is the *acted* refusal, beyond the privacy of the offended's mind, to accept as final and irrevocable the destruction of the moral relationship and the establishment of the degenerate relationship Without condemnation. any future dealing with the offender implies either failure to recognize or acknowledge the authority of the moral law, or indifference to moral distinctions on the part of the offended, or moral blindness and obtuseness on his part, or weakness. It may imply any of these, and any one of them would be fatal to the successful completion of the process of forgiveness Furthermore, without condemnation, the offender will not recognize his deed as an offense and therefore will not recognize that any occasion for forgiveness exists. He may readily admit that what he has done is displeasing to the other person, but he will not be disturbed by this, for he will interpret such displeasure as merely the expression of the injured self of the offended The relationship of the offense to the moral law and its character as the cause of the degenerate relationship must be made explicit Condemnation involves three phases. the condemnation by the good life, the complaint, the punishment

The good life is that life which is motivated by a voluntary allegiance to the principle of conduct which is not derived from the self but which is expressed in the moral law, and which forms the basis of all mutual confidence and trust between persons. In the situation created by the offense, the continuance of the good life by the offended person derives from the subjective moment of pardon Such a life constitutes a condemnation of the offender because the continuance of a life lived out of allegiance to this principle is an assertion in fact that the relationship which has been destroyed is right and, conversely, that the relationship which now exists is wrong and should be destroyed. The good life is a rejection of the pattern of conduct asserted by the offender and the affirmation of the rightness of the pattern of conduct rejected by him.

This condemnation of the offender by the good life of the offended is necessary for the successful expression of the complaint If the offended abandon his allegiance to the moral law, he has in effect accepted the degenerate relationship, and we shall never reach the stage of the complaint Furthermore, without this continuance in the good life, the sincerity of the complaint is compromised Without such a continuation of the good life by the offended, the only complaint possible will be an expression of his discomfiture and rage, his displeasure and anger, which complaint is devoid of power to re-establish the authority of the moral law However, this condemnation which is the good life of the offended is not sufficient in itself. Apart from the complaint, it is indistinguishable from blindness to the fact that the relationship of mutual confidence and trust no longer exists. It does not focus upon the particular cause of the destruction of the former relationship and upon the person responsible for that destruction.

The complaint is the careful, deliberate, intelligent, reasoned designation of the *cause* of the destruction of the moral relationship and of the responsibility for that destruction The complaint must indicate clearly what deed is the offense, but more than this it must demonstrate that the deed is an offense, that is, the kind of deed against which any rational, moral being has a right and a duty to protest. This demonstration must show that, given this conduct on the part of the offender, the other person can only reasonably infer that the motive for the conduct has been other than loyalty to the moral law Given this deed, it is impossible for a reasonable being to believe in the continued allegiance of the offender to that objective principle which is the basis of all mutual confidence and trust. The complaint must show that this deed derives from disregard of the moral law and from submission to some dictate of the offender's self. And finally, the complaint must attach responsibility for the deed to the person designated as the offender. It must show that *this* deed derives from the submission of *this* person to the dictates of unprincipled self-assertion.

The necessity for the complaint arises from the fact that the offender is a rational being Forgiveness is a process which involves persons, which is to say, beings who have reason and for whom, therefore, an action is not simply motion in space but an event with meaning and significance To treat an offender as though he were a *thing*, to act upon him without expressing the significance of one's action, is to nullify the whole process of forgiveness For the achievement of forgiveness it is not sufficient simply to restrain the offender from repeating the offense or to inflict such suffering upon him that even in terms of his allegiance to self a repetition of the offense is not desirable The achievement of forgiveness requires that the deed be acknowledged by the offender as an offense, that the relationship destroyed by this deed be acknowledged as good, and that the offender acknowledge his responsibility for the deed. The complaint aims at the acknowledgment of guilt on the part of the offender.

Furthermore, the complaint is necessary in order to distinguish punishment from vengeance Vengeance is derived from, and governed by, the uncriticized feeling of the offended person Punishment is derived from, and governed by, allegiance to the moral law. In the case of vengeance, if I pause at all between the action which occasions my vengeance and the deed which expresses it, I only ask "Will my action please me, express my feeling?" In the case of punishment I must ask "Will this action make the offender aware of the authority of the moral law?" The complaint aims at making this distinction clear, at pointing out that the deed of the offender is a transgression of the moral law and that the offended is right in protesting against it

The complaint is necessary, but it is not sufficient To designate the deed as wrong and the individual as responsible for the deed, and to stop with this, is to sap the moral energy of the complaint. The logical consequence of the complaint is the infliction of punishment upon the offender.

It is not within the scope of this essay to discuss extensively the philosophy of punishment. It may be sufficient to observe that punishment is the intentional infliction of suffering upon a person who has disregarded the moral law, and it is inflicted upon him *because* he has disregarded that law. The fact that punishment is always the intentional infliction of *suffering* suggests that the intention of punishment is to accomplish that which suffering can accomplish. The most obvious fact about suffering is that the person who suffers, *suffers*. He is passive, which is to say that he is the object of the action of another thing or person. Fundamentally, the experience of suffering is the experience in which one becomes aware of the reality of some other being which is not himself and which renders to him an experience which is not the fulfillment of his own intention nor the consequent of his own will. Suffering is the intense experience of myself as the *object* of the action of another, instead of myself as the *subject* of my own action.

Now if punishment is always the intentional infliction of suffering upon a wrongdoer, and if suffering as suffering can only make one aware of a reality with a being and a function of its own which is not subservient to the intention and will of the sufferer, it would appear that the purpose of punishment is to do that which suffering can do, namely, to impress upon the wrongdoer the being and the activity of a reality other than himself. Punishment is thus the sheer assertion of the objective reality of that moral order of the universe which the wrongdoer has violated. Punishment as punishment aims at this, and just this. To say that the moral justification of punishment is the reformation of the criminal's character is to assign to punishment a function which it cannot perform. To be sure, the wrongdoer needs to be reformed, but that is the task of moral education. One needs to do more than simply punish a wrongdoer.

Punishment is the assertion of the autonomous, objective, imperative character of the moral law, the reaction by a reality which claims respect when that claim has been disregarded. This reaction operates through persons who respect that moral law. *Before* a moral agent acts, the moral law claims his allegiance and respect autonomously and imperatively. The question then arises, "How is this autonomous, imperative character of the moral law to be asserted *after* the agent has acted in disregard of the law?" the answer is, "through punishment, the infliction upon the agent of that experience in which he most intensely appreciates the objective reality of some other being confronting his own reality and affecting his being without any regard for *his* private intentions and purposes." This reality asserts

itself through those persons who have become aware of it, have understood
its demand, and respect that demand.

The intention of punishment is the assertion of the objective, imperative
character of that reality which the wrongdoer by his transgression has denied It may be true that something more is demanded, that it is not enough
to simply assert the reality of something other than the wrongdoer, that
the moral law demands not only the recognition of its being but also an
understanding of its content That is to say that punishment is not a sufficient response to the transgression of the moral law Correction and instruction are also called for But no instruction will be effective unless the
wrongdoer has been made intensely aware that there is a reality there to
be understood, a reality which he cannot disregard with impunity, a reality
which does not exist for him to accept or to reject at his good pleasure but
for which he exists in the sense that this reality exists in its own right, with
its own function, and with a legitimate claim upon his obedience, which
claim he cannot declare null and void. Punishment follows after the complaint as the demonstration of the validity of the complaint and as the
assertion of the reality of the authority and power of the moral law.

The condemnation by the good life of the offended, without punishment,
is too vague and general, it fails to focus upon the particular agent who has
committed the offense. But punishment without the condemnation by the
good life is weakened in its moral integrity The fact that no man is actually
perfect always tends to weaken the moral power of punishment Practically,
it makes it more difficult to distinguish punishment from vengeance

Without the complaint, the rationale of punishment is obscure and ambiguous. In relation to punishment, the complaint is the reasoned justification of the punishment Without this careful designation of the deed as
wrong and of this individual as responsible for the deed, punishment will
be indistinguishable from vengeance. But without punishment the complaint is ineffectual.

The condemnation in its completeness is the expression of the offended
person's refusal to accept without protest or resistance the degenerate relationship. Paradoxically, while in the struggle in his own soul the offended
person's refusal to accept this degenerate relationship results in his refusal
to seek revenge, nevertheless, his objective refusal to accept this relationship results in his endeavor to punish the offender.

So far our discussion of the process of forgiveness has revolved entirely
around the activity of the offended We now must consider a change which
must be effected in the offender if the process is to continue to its completion This change is called "repentance." Repentance is a change of mind
on the part of the offender toward the situation which he has generated. It

is a change in his evaluation of the good of the deed which he has performed and of the relationship which he has established. Repentance is, in effect, the acknowledgment on the part of the offender of the need for forgiveness; it is his realization that the relationship of mutual confidence and trust must be re-established, together with the realization that this necessity has been occasioned by his action, he realizes that he is an offender.

There is both a negative and a positive aspect to repentance In its negative aspect, repentance is largely regret, merely a realization that one is not satisfied with the relationship which he has brought into existence It may mean nothing more than that one has realized that he miscalculated the satisfaction to be derived from the deed Negative repentance may be defined in terms of a negative attitude toward the deed done One wishes it undone.

Negative repentance is devoid of moral power It is not oriented around the moral relationship which has been destroyed but around the degenerate relationship which for some reason is now disapproved of. It may be simply the prelude to a new attempt to make the degenerate relationship more to one's own liking It may arise without any action on the part of the offended or it may come to be through the attempt of the offended to wreak vengeance However, if it be generated by punishment inflicted by a good man as the complement of a rational complaint, it has moral possibilities.

It may develop beyond its negative form into its positive form, into a disapproval of the deed, which disapproval is rooted in a changed evaluation of the moral relationship and a desire to re-establish that relationship The first two phases of the process of forgiveness are the key to the transformation of negative repentance into positive repentance. The continuation of the good life on the part of the offended generates shame in the offender as he contemplates his own life, and the complaint prevents the offender from misunderstanding the true cause of the present degenerate relationship and from confusing punishment with vengeance

Positive repentance is a change of mind which is oriented toward the moral relationship Whereas formerly the offender had rejected the authority of the moral law and had approved the deed which that law condemned, he now disapproves that deed and acknowledges that authority Positive repentance is a positive desire for the re-establishment of the relationship of mutual confidence and trust, and not merely a desire that what has been done were not done. Positive repentance involves the acknowledgment by the offender that the deed is wrong and that he is responsible for the deed, which is to say that it involves the acknowledgment of guilt. Positive repentance involves the acknowledgment that one's intention and purpose were wrong Even if the deed had accomplished the purpose one intended, it would be disapproved of now. One disapproves of the deed because it has been dictated by allegiance to the self without regard for the moral law, that is, without regard for the principle of conduct which governs a relationship of mutual confidence and trust—which relationship one now approves of as right.

Repentance may be said to be a prerequisite for the complete achievement of forgiveness, but not in the *quid pro quo* sense that the offended will forgive the offender *if* he repents. Without repentance, the process which has been initiated by the offended is arrested short of its completion If the offended person has acquiesced in the new relationship of self and force, repentance is not able to elicit forgiveness from him Repentance, occurring outside the framework of the process of forgiveness, appears as mere weakness to be exploited by the vengeful. Within the process of forgiveness, repentance opens the way for the process to go on to its completion. In this sense, "pardon" makes repentance morally fruitful.

The emotional concomitant of positive repentance is a complex of longing, fear, and despair. There is a longing on the part of the repentant person for the re-establishment of the moral relationship with its mutual confidence and trust. But conjoined with this, there is a fear that the offended has accepted the terms of the degenerate relationship, which fear is strengthened by the fact that every action of the offended during the first half of the process of forgiveness is so perilously close in its appearance to the action of vengeance that it may be easily confused with that And coupled with the fear is a sense of despair which arises from the realization by the offender that he is powerless to initiate the re-establishment of the moral relationship We now stand on the threshold of the next phase of the process of forgiveness, that of the positive re-establishment of a relationship of mutual confidence and trust This phase revolves around the problem of "faith."

Both the offended and the offender have rejected the degenerate relationship created by the offense, and both desire the relationship which is governed by the moral law. When the offended, both within his soul and overtly through the phases of condemnation, has rejected the degenerate relationship, when the authority and power of the moral law has been sufficiently demonstrated, and when the offender has changed his mind about the situation which he has brought about in lieu of the moral relationship, what more is required than that the two parties forget the whole incident, resume living within the limits set by the moral law, and act as if they trusted one another? The something more which is needed is an action which will remove this "as if" character from the relationship of the two There is need of an act or actions which will transform the relationship between the two from one in which both parties act as if they trusted each other to one in which they actually do trust each other. What is needed is some action which will elicit from the offender confidence and trust in the offended and, contrariwise, some action which will elicit from the offended confidence and trust in the offender.

It is the very nature of a genuine offense that it cannot be dismissed arbitrarily from the universe and be forgotten And it is essential to the complete reality and perfection of forgiveness that it not only be offered to the offender by the offended but that it be genuinely accepted, it is the elicitation of faith within the offender's soul which is the basis of his acceptance of the proffered good will of the offended And it is the acceptance by the offender of this proffered good will of the offended which completes the mutuality of confidence and trust between the two by creating in the offended a renewed confidence in the offender. Forgiveness is an objective historical process and not a mere change of attitude on the part of the offended person toward the offender If forgiveness becomes a reality, it can only mean that forgiveness has been achieved, that is, that an objective relationship of mutual confidence and trust has been actually re-established. If forgiveness is complete, it is "successful"; the offender has been brought to trust the offended, and the offended has been brought to trust the offender. The practical problem of forgiveness is. How can one rebuild confidence and trust between persons who have had reasonable ground for mutual suspicion and distrust?

The initiative is not in the power of the offender His every action is indistinguishable from a mere neglect of the offense. The attempt to live in accordance with the principles of conduct which before the offense would elicit confidence and trust is now, after the offense, in harmony with an attempt to reap the advantages of the moral relationship, as when a liar desires that all men think him honest The direct good deed of the offender will be indistinguishable from the *bribe*. A bribe is a denial of the objective authority of the moral law. It implies that a moral relationship between men may be arbitrarily *constructed* by mutual consent of the parties concerned, whereas the truth is that the principle which governs a genuine moral relationship is embedded in the very structure of man and of the universe and is there to be discovered and to be conformed to. It is not to be constructed according to man's fancy.

What is perhaps not so immediately obvious, nor so generally recognized, is the fact that the direct good deed done by the offend*ed* person to one who has offended him also lacks the power to elicit from the offender confidence and trust in the offended Against a background of mutual distrust and suspicion, the intention of every good deed is misconstrued. Having destroyed the moral relationship, the offender has no ground for believing that the good deed which the offended would do for him is anything more than a trap to ensnare the unwary. In a relationship dominated by self, in which all actions are derived from the love of self and the patterns of conduct are determined by the self, no action can be free of the suspicion of advancing the interests of the self. A deed which in the moral relationship would serve to strengthen and augment the confidence and trust of both parties in each other will serve in the degenerate relationship to increase suspicion and distrust If the direct good deed of the offender is tainted with the breath of bribery, that of the offended is under the suspicion of trickery

Against the background of the degenerate relationship, the re-establishment of mutual confidence and trust calls for an action which is manifestly a denial of the self of the agent and is at the same time in complete accord with the demands of the moral law. It must be an action which will remove all suspicion that the moral law is being used for the advancement of the purposes of the self of the agent apart from his allegiance to the moral law. On the other hand, if this action is to be anything more than an irrational suicide of the self, it must be also one which is manifestly in accord with that which the moral law demands And it must express the confidence and trust of the agent in the offender In this respect. the action has somewhat the character of a fiction It is an action whose effect can be accomplished only if it elicit from the offender confidence and trust in the offended, which confidence and trust the offender presumably does not have. Nevertheless, the action is such that it is futile and ineffective if it be not responded to with confidence in the offended by the offender The action is motivated by the desire that the relationship of mutual confidence and trust be established In short, the action must be such that its true interpretation can only be that the offended desires to re-establish the moral relationship with the offender

Action which is a denial of the self but which is contrary to the demands of the moral law is ineffective to re-establish any authority of that law; and an action which is in accordance with the demands of the moral law but which involves no denial of the self is ineffective to re-establish in the offender any confidence in the offended An action which does meet this dual requirement of denial of the self and accord with the moral law may be called a "morally effective sacrifice"

Sacrifice is a term which is derived from the field of religion, but it may be used to designate the act of the offended in the process of forgiveness, because that act has as its essential characteristics what are held to be the essential characteristics of sacrifice. These characteristics of a genuine sacrifice are two (1) costliness and (2) the intention of maintaining or of re-establishing a right relationship between the agent of the deed and the one for whom the deed is done A sacrifice is an action which costs the sacrificer something, the cost being measured in terms of loss or deprivation to himself And the sacrifice is intended to maintain or to re-establish a right relationship between two parties.

The essence of sacrifice as a factor in the process of forgiveness is the denial of the self for the sake of re-establishing a right relationship with another. It may be objected that the action designated a sacrifice is not a self-denying action because the offended willed it and wanted it It may be said, "Was not this action the expression of his most profound and persistent self, the self which has been behind this whole process of forgiveness?" The answer is, of course, "Yes" But this does not eliminate the self-denying character of the action By self-denial one means an action which could never be deduced from the premise of the assertive self. A self-denying action is one which could never be inferred from the premise of a self whose principle of conduct was the maintenance of its own self in existence as long as, and as comfortably as, possible

The act of self-denial involves two moments: (1) In the denial of the self, the self is the *object* of the action, the self in some one or many or all of its desires or ambitions is denied (2) In the denial of the self, the self is the *subject* of the action The denial of the self must be a denial of itself by itself The self is not only the patient of the act of denial but also the agent of the denial This is the difference between self-denial and frustration or defeat or compulsion This is what is meant by saying that in a sacrifice, the sacrifice must be voluntary It is not to say that the act of self-denial is unmotivated, but that the act results from the will of the agent, from his consent to, or acceptance of, the motive of the act. The extent of the self-denial involved in a sacrifice is the measure of the cost of the sacrifice

The sacrifice is a venture of confidence and trust on the part of the sacrificer in the person for whom the sacrifice is made, it is tendered with the hope that the offender will appreciate its cost and intention and will respond to the sacrifice properly A sacrifice is a manifestation of the *will* of the agent and also a manifestation of his tentative confidence and trust in the other person One may infer from the sacrifice that the agent *wills* the relationship of mutual confidence and trust He not only *wishes* it were in existence but, in so far as it is in his power to bring it about, he *wills* it to be If he did not will the re-establishment of such a relationship, he would not engage in this costly action And if he had absolutely no confidence in the other person to respond properly to this action, however much he wished the re-establishment of the moral relationship, he would not will the action.

A sacrifice is the sort of action which can elicit from the offender confidence and trust in the offended *if the sacrifice be believed in,* that is, if the sacrifice be *appreciated* by the offender as a *sacrifice* If this self-denying action be explained away as a misfortune suffered by the offended, or as a weakness, then the action will fail to elicit from the offender confidence and trust in the offended. The final step in the process of forgiveness is, then, dependent upon the interpretation which the offender puts upon the action of the offended, and upon his consequent response to that action.

The first response of the offender to the self-denying action of the offended is an evaluation of the act. Once he has become cognizant of the action, the offender must have some *belief about* the action. Even if he dismiss the event as of no significance, that is an interpretation of it, and the moral consequence of such an interpretation would be the barring of that event from further influencing his life. The beginning of any further response to the action of the offended is this initial interpretation of the significance of the action.

One's belief about the significance of an event is determined by his comprehension of what is relevant to the interpretation of that event. If the offender is to appreciate the sacrificial character of the deed of the offended, he must appreciate its cost and its intent, he must perceive that the action involved self-denial and that it was done because the offended desired to re-establish a relationship of mutual confidence and trust. If the offender believes that this event is just one more happening in a series of happenings united to each other by mechanical causation, then the action will not elicit from him any confidence and trust in the offended. If the offender believes that the action is not the action of the offended but is an event which has befallen him, that is, if the event be interpreted as not the offended's voluntary action but as an involuntary suffering, then the action will not be understood as giving any indication of the character of the will of the offended toward the offender, and consequently the event will not elicit from the offender any confidence in the offended. Regardless of how one's interpretation of the event is arrived at, the moral consequences of the event for the offender are dependent upon that interpretation, upon his belief about the event.

Where there is no recognition of the sacrificial character of the offended's action, no confidence in him is elicited from the offender; the latter remains in his state of despondent repentance. Where belief in the sacrificial character of the action does not issue in conduct governed by loyalty to the moral law, there is in effect a repudiation of the sacrificial character of the action and of the confidence of the offended in the offender. Hence, where the offender does not respond to the action of the offended with a trust which manifests itself in such action, we have a continuation of the relationship dominated by the self of the offender and calling for punishment by the offended. But where the action of the offended is believed in by the offender as evidence of the former's will that the moral relationship be re-established and as a demonstration of his confidence in the offender, the offender expresses *his* faith in the offended by acting in accordance with the moral law, that is, he governs his action by that principle which makes faith and confidence in him rational. This response of the offender to the sacrifice of the offended confirms the tentative faith of the latter in the former and hence dissolves its tentative character.

Under these circumstances the sacrificial action of the offended is successful, and the relationship which exists between the two parties is that which held before the initial offense—namely, a relationship of mutual confidence and trust in which the conduct of each person toward the other is governed by voluntary allegiance to the principle of conduct defined by the moral law, a principle indispensable to all mutual confidence and trust. Forgiveness may then be said to have been accomplished The purpose of forgiveness—the re-establishment of a relationship of mutual confidence and trust after it has been destroyed by the offense—has been achieved. Forgiveness has performed its function: the re-establishment of the moral relationship between the two persons, a relationship in which conduct keeps within the limits set by the moral law and is motivated by voluntary allegiance to that law The moral law has not been circumvented, denied, or neglected. Its authority has been sustained and re-established The moral law has not been denied, but affirmed Nor has the offense been overlooked or forgotten It has been dealt with in such a way that its destructive effect upon the relationship between the two persons has been destroyed. Forgiveness has become a reality.

XIV

Natural Law and the Problem of Asia

CHARLES MALIK, *Minister of Lebanon, Chairman of the United Nations Human Rights Commission*

ASIA has arisen, and Asia will not wait any longer. Today she is facing the rest of the world and demanding her rights There can be no delay, we must answer her definitely and soon However, Western opinion is widely divided over the policy that should be adopted toward her peoples Some say, "Give them bread", others, "Use a strong hand", others, "Convert them to your system or attach them to your realm " People say these things and think that in so saying they have solved the problem But if the present, owing to somewhat accidental and passing reasons, can suffer their error, the future is bound to explode the utter inadequacy of their view

On December 11, 1950, at the height of the Korean crisis in the United Nations, I made a statement in the Political Committee of the General Assembly at Lake Success which I entitled "The Problem of Asia " Once made, these statements are immediately mimeographed by the appropriate agencies of the United Nations and become fully available to all who wish to make use of them In a sense, they then become public property. This is why it is impossible to keep track of all the diverse uses to which such texts are put But I know that this particular study has been quoted from extensively, that the magazine *Thought* published its own condensation of it, and that the entire text has appeared in pamphlet form.

On reading this speech, Professor John Wild felt that a specially worked out adaptation of the text might appropriately fit into the present volume on realistic philosophy by "bringing out the way in which a basic concept of classical, philosophical thought is now functioning in a crucially important way in the contemporary discussion of international problems " The classical concept referred to is, of course, the notion of natural law. The present chapter is the desired adaptation which, while comprising much of the substance of the original inquiry, contains new material designed for the most part to bring out the philosophical grounds of the discussion.

I. Natural Law and Its Philosophical Presuppositions

Because our metaphysical point of departure is the doctrine of natural law, it seems necessary at the outset to state, very briefly but as exactly as possible, the fundamental metaphysical presuppositions of this doctrine and to set forth in general terms its precise contents.

The doctrine is thoroughly rooted in Aristotle and his tradition. There are many "substances," each with its own particular nature which is completely transparent to the disciplined and grounded reason. The "visible" substances, such as plants and animals, are those to which we have access by sense perception There may be innumerable "individuals" belonging to any such visible substance, but all of them are characterized by the same essential structure which reason can absolutely investigate and know Every such individual has its own "separate" existence in accordance with the immanent peculiar laws of its nature The consistency of being is the general dependability of the natural law of the species to which the individual belongs, and where there is departure from the operation of this law, there is abnormality and a perversion or distortion of nature. But it is the "rule" that explains and throws light on the "exception", never conversely.

Since substances exist separately, that is to say, exist by reason of distinct, independent, particular, natural laws, including the possibility of orderly interaction between and among them, their nature cannot be ascertained a priori. You cannot determine their character without "getting in touch" with them They must "impose" their character on you You must humbly "come to" them and learn from them what they are That is why all knowledge originates in sense perception, and that is why empiricism, if properly, naturally, and healthily understood (and not turned into its exact opposite by forcing it into artificial molds of abstract, preconceived, special, theoretic constructions), is the right epistemology.

Two fundamental traditional doctrines at once arise at this point Since one must go to the object in order to understand its nature, truth is obviously the conformation of the subject to the object. And since there does not seem to be any natural impediment preventing us from going to any object whatsoever (and if any such impediment existed, we should obviously have no notion of it at all), there is nothing in the whole wide realm of being which is, in principle, closed to our knowledge This is Aristotle's dictum that the soul is potentially all things

Things then "are" by reason of their proper nature Now man is one of the many substances that are We ask. What is his proper nature? The answer is that man is precisely that being whose nature is to apprehend or grasp or "be informed" by the nature of things, including his own In other words, there is a being who is perfectly able to conform to being, namely, to know the truth With regard to this being, "the universe" is making no joke at all Nature is not playing a trick on him, he is not "by nature" doomed to error or darkness or confusion or lostness or uncertainty. He can stand face to face with things and be perfectly sure of himself and of them. This power to grasp or apprehend the nature of things, to be informed by nature, to conform to being, to be sure of being, to know or to "be in" the truth, including one's own truth—this tremendous and most wonderful power "is" reason. Man's nature then is "to possess" reason, to "be rational," so that where there is no reason, there certainly is no man "In the nature of the case," there is free, real natural access to things through reason.

It can be shown that reason, grasping or being sure of nature, can articulate itself in the most perfect and natural manner only in the form of "S is P" in the languages where the copula is used, or in the even simpler and more natural form of "SP" where the copula is regarded as completely superfluous, as in the Semitic languages. "S" is the substance which is before one, to which one conforms, which one knows, of which one is sure, and "P" is the nature or attribute or characteristic of that substance. The thing cannot be simplified further, there must be both "S" and "P," otherwise either the independence or the knowability of substances is destroyed "S" signifies the independent existence of substance, "P" signifies that nevertheless our reason can penetrate it "S" points to things completely "outside us," with whose existence we have absolutely nothing to do, "P" affirms in the simplest possible way the natural lucidity of things to our reason. If only one term is used, then either we land in idealistic monism where all real independence is destroyed, or in some impenetrable and irrational darkness, whose forms in modern times are legion The power of reason and the independence of nature must both be equally and absolutely affirmed This is the essence of the realistic philosophy

It can also be shown (1) that the dozen or so modern errors—whether in the theoretical field, as, for instance, subjective idealism, or in the practical field, as, for instance, ethical relativism, or in the theoretico-practical field, as, for instance, Freudianism, or in the political field, as, for instance, totalitarianism, or in the economic field, as, for instance, Marxism or impersonal industrialism—spring ultimately from a fundamental sin committed against nature and reason, (2) that the realistic philosophy, properly interpreted, is the real metaphysics of freedom, and (3) that the free world, in so far as it understands the sources of its own strength and weakness, must awaken to these terrible errors that have been plaguing it for decades, if not for centuries, in order to re-establish the age-old faith in reason and trust in nature.

Whitehead's metaphysics is perhaps the most impressive explicit attempt at repudiating the substance-attribute metaphysics and the subject-predicate logic. Every substance and every quality must be dissolved in the fluency of process and in the radical interrelatedness of things. It belongs to a separate fascinating investigation to show that, in so far as this attempt was intended to apply to the real nature of things, it has failed, and in so far as it was an interesting exercise in abstract consistency, the subject-predicate formulation remains at its very heart. Whitehead's doctrines of process, perishing, past, present, and future, and God, contain real positive insight, though I believe they reduce in the last analysis to well-known truths of the positive tradition of philosophy. Nothing that he says, however, really overcomes the basic presuppositions of the Aristotelian outlook on things.

There is a certain ambiguity about the word "nature" in English that need not disturb the philosopher who sets his heart on "the nature of things." We speak of "things in a state of nature" or of "Mother nature" or of "the beauty and serenity of nature" or of the insects and birds and heaths and forests and mountains which belong to the "realm of nature" and which elicit in us certain aesthetic feelings, or simply of "Nature" with a capital "N," as certain naturalists or poets sometimes do. It belongs to another inquiry to elaborate the presuppositions of these diverse uses. Such an inquiry will reveal, I think, that in addition to the aestheticism, mysticism, and cosmologism (and much of all this is good and legitimate and "natural") entwined in this naturalistic outlook, there is the presupposition—which will sooner or later explicitly betray itself in the development of the naturalist in question—that the higher things, namely things like reason, love, joy, and forgiveness, "somehow" arise or "emerge" from a dumb or dark nature that did not contain them in the first place, or that contained them only "in germ." The explosion of this poetical myth is a task of realistic investigation. But be that as it may, this complex poetico-naturalistic sense of the term "nature" is not the authentic sense of nature in genuine realism.

The authentic sense of nature is when we speak, for instance, of 'human nature" or of "the natural or inalienable rights of man" or of "the laws of nature" or when we say "nature makes no mistakes" or "such and such a substance is *by its very nature* thus and so" or "it belongs to the nature or essence of a substance S to be P, so that if no-P, then certainly no-S." The controlling idea here is that all that there is (namely the "really real" things, to use a term of Whitehead's borrowed from Plato) is a congeries of interacting, individual substances (man, of course, included), each with a definite, specific, fully intelligible nature.

The positive sciences, with the proper realistic critique, yield real knowledge of the real. They investigate the natures of the real substances that there are, including, in the case of the visible material substances, the laws of their development Metaphysics as the science of being in general, theology as the science of the supreme being, and ethics as the science of man, in so far as the realm of values is open to his vision and in so far as he is free in the determination of his life in relation to that realm, are certainly sciences that yield knowledge of the real, although they may not be termed positive sciences in the strict sense of this phrase. As to the rights of man, they certainly must be the subject matter of anthropology properly so called, namely, the science of all those structures without any one of which man would not be himself, or would be less than himself It follows, therefore, that nowhere do we flee into a separate realm of essence away from that which substantially exists It follows, also, that the classification of the sciences and the determination of their proper hierarchy is an essential horizon of thought within which realistic investigation must be conducted.

The Universal Declaration of Human Rights which was adopted by the General Assembly of the United Nations in Paris on December 10, 1948, ought to be of some interest to the students of philosophy, and in particular to the students of realistic philosophy. Here, for the first time, the diverse effective cultures of the world, after three years of vigorous and thorough debate, agreed to proclaim a document purporting to set forth the essential rights of man

Realistic philosophical investigation can examine this declaration from the point of view (1) of its genesis, (2) of the alternative texts rejected in debate, (3) of the ideological currents which flowed into its formation, (4) of its relations to analogous documents in history, such as the Magna Carta, the Rights of Man and of the Citizen of the French Revolution, the American Bill of Rights, the revolutionary economic and social rights of the Soviet Union, (5) the discrepancy between its principles and the actual state of affairs in various countries, (6) what is ultimate and irreducible and what is derivative in its thirty articles, (7) the hierarchy of importance even among its irreducible contents, and (8) the ultimate metaphysical source of these rights, namely, the problem of natural and positive law.

No matter how effectual or ineffectual the United Nations might be from the point of view of war and peace with the present radical divisions in the world, it is difficult to understand how the one pre-eminently philosophical activity of the United Nations has not been sufficiently noticed by philosophers, let alone studied, pondered, and criticized.

II. The Problem of Asia

There is no man really living in the present who has not had the problem of Asia, in some one of its diverse facets, thrust upon his mind Here are the peoples of Asia becoming increasingly decisive in the determination of history. In their substantial existence, they raise, both to themselves and to an outside thinker who is deeply concerned about them, fundamental political and philosophical problems. This present study inquires into the great issues of Asia, not indeed in the light of some new "ism," some new illumination, a sudden new dispensation expressive of the last phase of the historical revolutionary process, but in the old light of what really and properly belongs to man. There is peace in so far as nature is not distorted and man both sees himself and is wholly himself.

The Asiatic situation will be terribly misunderstood unless one keeps in mind that the people of Asia are quite keen on the preservation of their modes of life, that they have their proper dignity and are fiercely jealous for it, that left alone they will never allow themselves to trade away their soul for material or political benefits, that they are in no particular haste to adjust themselves to Western standards; that they are not necessarily overawed by the outside world, whether it be the Soviet Union or the West, and that it cannot be taken for granted that they necessarily respect this outside world or, at least, respect it for that on account of which it respects itself. Asia may fear the Soviet Union or the West, she may even envy their technique and might. But envy and fear are one thing; respect is quite another. Today, Asia's respect cannot be taken for granted, it can only be earned.

It is also possible to get lost in a multiplicity of detail, in the endlessly conflicting claims and counterclaims, accusations and counteraccusations. A series of arresting figures, statistics, names, and dates, adding up to an imposing case, are marshaled by one side only to be countered with other statistics and listings of facts by the other side. The two arguments, taken purely by themselves and in abstraction from knowledge derived from other sources, seem on the whole, as far as the possibility of any immediate judgment is concerned, to cancel each other. As a result, one may get completely lost in utter bewilderment and confusion. Where is the truth? Or is it that there is no truth, but only the self-positing of the stronger? In such a mood, one may refuse to come to any decision, preferring to suspend judgment altogether. For how can one ascertain the truth about these matters even if there is a truth to be ascertained?

Or one may be putting such rigid blinkers around his eyes, either by sheer dint of will power or by social or political pressure from without, that he is incapable of seeing anything else except his own point of view. Contented in his own self-certainty, this blessed person knows no perplexity, no confusion. The facts before him are final and conclusive, and, therefore, there is nothing else to worry about. But such a happy person can never be

sure that the scales will not one day fall from his eyes with possible disastrous consequences to himself and others History is littered with the
corpses of those who were incapable of being profoundly perturbed and,
therefore, of stretching themselves beyond their complacency; and also, I
must add, with the corpses of their innocent victims.

Irresponsible skepticism and narrow dogmatism can lead only to chaos
and the tragedy of force It requires not only intellectual courage but also
philosophical insight to rise above these. The very existence of the United
Nations shows that it has been possible, even in this age of widespread appeal to the forces of unreason and of narrow specialization, to pass over
detail and confusion to the ultimate issues at stake During the preceding
years, United Nations' debate has clearly revealed certain basic principles
which must be involved in the establishment of any co-operative world
order. Ideas derived from many cultural traditions have contributed to this
growing body of sharable doctrine and principle So far as Western thought
is concerned, the most important contribution has been drawn from the
great stream of realistic philosophy which began in ancient Greece, and
more especially from the realistic concept of natural law.

This concept, of course, is not restricted to a single school of Western
thought, nor is it peculiar to the West But it has been most thoroughly and
exactly analyzed and studied as a principle of social, as well as of individual, action by that central tradition of realistic philosophy which began in
ancient Greece, was revived and supplemented in the Middle Ages, and
has been continuously refined and cultivated down to the present day. It is
this concept, held in common by so many schools of thought both in the
East and in the West, that lies at the root of the United Nations Universal
Declaration of Human Rights.

This fact should be a matter of deep concern to philosophers the world
over. I hope that it may be leading them to recognize the desperate need
for a further examination and clarification of this doctrine with its far-
reaching premises in both metaphysics and epistemology, and also of those
influential theories of legal positivism which overwhelmed it in the fateful
nineteenth century. But before such clarification is achieved, we must use
the soundest basic principles at our disposal in deliberating about the great
social and political problems of our time. It is only in this way that we may
hope to gain any real insight into these problems, for political insight is
grounded in philosophy Also, we may hope to gain further understanding
of our principles, for *practical* principles never become finally clear until
they are brought into a close relation with the concrete. My purpose in this
brief essay, therefore, is to apply a few basic principles of natural law to the
great, contemporary problem of Asia.

Asia, the mother continent of the human race, desires to achieve for herself an honorable place under the sun. In a crowded and contracted world, a world withal in which mighty giants are jostling each other all the time, it is not easy to find your place, occupy it, and retain it. Yet this is what is happening. Asia is emerging, Asia is carving a place for herself; Asia desires to be recognized and heard. The problem of Asia has been opening up for many a year. It is only now that it is coming to a head before our eyes in the United Nations.

Spanning the entire continent—from Japan in the extreme East to Lebanon, my own country, in the extreme West—there is a bewildering variety of ancient civilizations and cultures, each with its own coherent and time-honored outlook on God, reality, history, man, and society. These ancient civilizations flourished and deposited their meanings long before the present actors came forward onto the stage of history. In her present awakening, Asia has therefore every right to look upon the rest of the world with a certain sense of condescension, very much like the benevolent gaze of the Buddha or the inscrutable smile of the Sphinx. What, then, are we to think of the problems posed by this mighty modern awakening? What are those basic needs that are now stirring this continent to action? How can she be best understood and helped by the West to meet those needs?

According to the teaching of natural law, rational insight and judgment are the most extraordinary and distinctive endowments of human nature. Thus, the Universal Declaration of Human Rights, in its first article, states that "all human beings are born free and equal in dignity and rights. They are endowed with reason and conscience. . . ." The peculiar dignity of man lies in his possession of reason, both theoretical and practical. His most basic need, therefore, if human life is to be genuinely lived, is science and technology for the control of subhuman things, and philosophy and the sciences of man for the guidance of free persons and their culture. So in the first place (Section III), we shall look at Asia from the standpoint of this basic, natural need for science and cultural understanding.

Reason alone can grasp the complex needs of man and guide them to authentic fulfillment. What, then, are these needs? According to the United Nations Declaration, they fall into four categories of inalienable human rights—political, social, economic, and cultural. Hence, in the second place (Section IV), we shall briefly examine Asia from the standpoint of these basic human rights.

Finally, in the third place (Section V), we shall conclude with a suggestion concerning the way in which this problem of Asia might best be met by the West, not only to satisfy the need of the East, but also the desperate need of the world as a whole.

III. Science and Theory

Every age has its proper spirit, imposing rigorous demands on those who wish to live in it People may hide their face from this challenge for a year, for a decade, or even for a century, but sooner or later they must face up to this decision either to conform to this spirit—to be sure in their own creative way—or to lapse into the decadence and death of nonparticipation. History is the account of those free acts whereby diverse peoples react to and modify the insistent requirements of the spirit, and the philosophy of history is the reasoned account whereby the procession and interpenetration of ages is exhibited as to its essence and as to the inner spiritual law of its development

I believe that in so far as history has a meaning immanent to itself—that is, in so far as it yields to natural idea and reason—the freedom of the spirit is the key to its understanding Peoples write history in so far as they participate in the emancipation of man And the emphasis on community today, though twisted in certain cases into utterly revolting degradations, nevertheless springs from the same law of freedom, for only in community and in communion can man be really free—free, that is, to think, to rejoice, to develop, to suffer, and above all, to be.

The spirit of our age has, in a sense, suddenly descended upon Asia It has found the old continent somewhat unprepared for its demands For there are two deficiencies from which Asia has suffered and with which our age can never be patient. The one has to do with theory, the other with the rights of man

Asia has not sufficiently bothered to understand and control nature The forces of nature remain, for the most part, mysterious and unknown. The Asians do not feel quite at home in nature They live as though they were more or less strangers, pilgrims on this earth They do not understand or control its infinite richness. They act on the whole as though nature does not belong to them, as though they can live only on the generosity of her passive produce.

Now the mind, by the very act of piercing the structure and behavior of the material universe, places itself above that universe But when the mind, for whatever reason, abdicates in advance this its birthright, namely, the power to analyze, understand, control, and utilize all natural phenomena, then it will tend to revere nature as something above it. There is more essential fear of nature throughout Asia than there ought to be, and one major task of the present phase of history is to liberate Asia completely from this fear. This can be done only by the intensive cultivation of science, and

of that curious ancient Greek invention which we know today by the name
of "theory." It is not an accident, nor is it the pure outcome of the dark
machinations of the imperialists, that there is nowhere throughout Asia
anything comparable to the tremendous concentration of science and
theory that exists, for instance, along the Charles River in Cambridge,
Massachusetts

Asia may be immensely rich in imagination, but in theory, namely, the
detached, measured, objective, self-testing and self-expanding, rational
comprehension of the universe, Asia has been weak It is because we have
neglected the understanding of matter so much for so long that it is now
coming back on us with a vengeance Our problem throughout Asia, then,
is to strengthen ourselves in theoretical virtue, for only in this way can we
elevate ourselves, as we ought to, above nature and bend our huge natural
resources to the service of our crying human needs Asia can attain power,
dignity, and abundance only if science and theory are enthroned at the
heart of her intellectual life

The right of peoples to self-determination is consecrated in the Charter
of the United Nations. There is no doubt that the peoples of Asia can
rejoice in, and profit from, the affirmation of this political right But in this
amazingly interdependent world, where events in Tibet produce immediate reactions in antipodal San Salvador, no people can really determine
itself that is incapable of understanding and exploiting its own natural
resources.

A people's right to self-determination, therefore, remains a myth—albeit
a pleasant myth, a constructive myth, a useful myth, a truthful myth—
until that people achieves luminous mastery over nature If in the fortuitous play of the elements mother earth deposited underneath my soil certain minerals whose structure and importance neither I nor my forebears
have fathomed, and if there is an active mind elsewhere which can thoroughly penetrate and exploit this mineral wealth, I doubt whether it will
be long before that mind finds its way to my subsoil, and I doubt whether
in this interacting and unified world I have the natural right, let alone the
power, to prevent it from reaching there.

Self-determination today absolutely presupposes the capacity to determine nature, and without authentic immersion in the cumulative scientific
tradition, from Pythagoras to the present day, it is an utter illusion for any
people to suppose that it could long remain the master of its fate It is not
by words nor by the primitive reliance on the massiveness of matter and
number that freedom will be won and history made, but by the humble
acceptance of prolonged discipline in science and theory, whatever the
sacrifice entailed.

Beyond and above the din of the present stupendous conflict, raging alike before our eyes at Lake Success and on the battlefields, as well as in the hearts of men throughout Asia, stands Asia's desperate need for the skilled knowledge whereby her immeasurable resources can be turned into instruments of human welfare Asia's infinite potentialities are patient for actualization, and our age is impatient with sheer matter lying about fallow and useless Unless the peoples of Asia accept every sacrifice for the sake of participating creatively in the great movement of science and technology, Asia will always remain a problem—a problem unto herself and unto the world, for nobody, not even Tibet, is allowed these days to withdraw from the world. Only the mind lifting itself above the mists of matter and asserting its natural dominion over nature has any chance today to stand firm in the face of vigorous cultures disciplined in science and technology

Science is not merely technique, it is not just the clever utilization and exploitation of nature Science is primarily participation in a whole scientific culture, the adoption of a whole new outlook. This outlook rejoices above everything else in theory and vision for their own sake To use, you must be able to understand, and to understand, you must be able to see But to see is precisely what is meant by theory, and you must love that which you rest your sight upon if you are really to understand it It is this loving vision of nature, this ecstatic oneness with her powers, that constitutes the essence of the scientific culture To cultivate this loving vision on a wide scale entails a much greater price than Asia has been so far willing to pay Nor did the imitative externalism of Japan more than barely touch the surface of the scientific participation. These deeper things cannot be imported; they can only be appropriated, one can only be born in them anew

Science, then, is a condition at once of peace and of human happiness in Asia. Whoever supposes that we throughout Asia can really stand on our feet without science and the special mentality that goes with science is either dreaming or willfully wishing that we do not stand on our feet.

But the cultivation of science and theory on the necessary scale is going to mean radical transformations of our habits of thought. Many an outworn point of view shall be profoundly shaken, whole empires of feeling and imagination are going to collapse. There will thus occur what I might call a scientific purge of the soul of Asia But a purge of this magnitude and character, ordained by the spirit of the age, is not going to transpire without resistance, struggle, suffering, and, in some cases, even disaster The problem is not how to avoid all this, but how to mitigate it to its human minimum, to the end that, inevitable as it all is, it nevertheless takes place with the maximum possible preservation of all that is valuable and abiding in Asian life.

We face then two alternatives: either to keep on indulging our unscientific imagination—and the exigencies of the moment render the enjoyment of this pleasure increasingly difficult for us—or to open our hearts and cultures to the cleansing wind of science—and this is inevitably going to mean the fall of many an exalted idol and the dissipation of many a cherished dream. The coming great problem of Asia is how to weather as peacefully as possible the impending internal storm caused by the impact of science. There will be, I fear, many unholy alliances between forces of darkness within and forces of ill will without, aimed at the retardation of this inevitable catharsis But there will never be rest until the pregnant mind of Asia, shaking off its intellectual lethargy, steps forth in joy and in confidence into the wonderful cumulative heritage of science and theory and, welcoming in the process every laceration and every convulsion of the spirit, drives forward toward the high prize of understanding, commanding, exploiting, and feeling perfectly at home in nature.

I have so far used science in the narrower sense of the disciplined understanding and control of material nature, and indeed it is impossible to exaggerate the importance of this narrower conception for Asia and her problems But surely positive science is not exhaustive of the meaning of *scientia* There is not only nature—the soil, the minerals, the animals, the plants, the heavens, the atom—to be comprehended; there is being at large, including above all man himself and whatever higher beings man may truly communicate with Asia requires the breath of thought not only in the guise of modern science but especially in the form of philosophic reason surveying the deeper things And there is such a depth and richness of feeling and tradition in Asia that here again the spirit of the age will demand that this wealth be exposed to the light of reason and the judgment of truth

Indeed, the application of reason to the personal and holy is absolutely indispensable if Asia is really going to play an active role in the determination of things History respects only the critically self-conscious, only the man who, humble before the truth, seeks in all honesty and without any arbitrary limitations to know himself and his values For when you think of it, only that man is worthy of respect who not only liberates himself from the compulsion of the elements but also lifts himself above the mists of his own imaginings.

Asia impatiently awaits the day when her own sons will, in all tenderness, responsibility, and freedom, turn the shafts of reason to the grounded study of their own cultures, investigating their genesis, their growth, and their limitations, exhibiting their concrete structures, bringing out their supreme values, and relating them axiologically and existentially to the other great cultures of the world Only in this way can the complex unity of the spirit throughout the world be ascertained

Asia can perform a tremendous service to mankind when she responsibly takes her spiritual understanding into her own hands

Now, the tested apparatus of critical and appreciative inquiry is still exceedingly alive in the free centers of learning. Given time and effort, there is nothing in principle that prevents Asia from acquiring this apparatus Two questions alone have to be determined· whether the moral and existential price for the appropriation of this excellence is forthcoming, and the nature of the first principles from which it can proceed I say this because reason does not work automatically, nor do you just build up a tremendous institute, staff it with experts, and then sit back and expect it mechanically to grind out the truth. It all depends on the atmosphere of freedom under which you work, on the living and constant interaction which you maintain with the highest critical circles of mind in the world, and on the first principles from which you start.

Although there are natural first principles which the properly guided human mind can see and be absolutely sure of, yet in the present utter confusion of the world where nature is subverted and willful error and contradiction are frequently systematized into militant ideologies, no responsible person can be too critical of his first principles or of the way he comes by them. And in general, we can say that in her interpretation of her cultural profusion, Asia will be faced with a radical choice. either to carry out this interpretation on the simple, seductive, materialistic principle, or to evolve an autonomous principle of her own, one that is continuous both with her deepest genius and with the deepest genius of Western realism at its best.

There is nothing foreordained about the issue of this choice It depends on the free will of Asia and on the vigor with which the Western world renounces and remands its present spiritual complacency. The materialistic principle cannot be stronger throughout the world than it is today, nor more ably advocated. But there are reserves of the mind and the spirit, both in Asia and in the non-communist world, which, if properly evoked and absolutely supported, can—amidst much suffering, to be sure—compose the present upsurge of the primitive and the elemental.

IV. The Rights of Man

Whatever our deficiency throughout Asia in regard to science and reason, it is certainly our neglect of the rights of man that has most adversely affected our destiny We live in an age where people are keenly aware that whatever else they might be, they certainly are human beings with certain inalienable, natural rights—political, social, economic, and cultural They are becoming increasingly restive until they enjoy these rights. Not all the cleverness, darkness, and repression in the world can any longer cause the downtrodden and oppressed to feel that they are eternally doomed to their inferior lot. They feel that they are human beings like anyone else, and, therefore, they conclude that their low estate is not the unalterable will of divinity but an accidental and, therefore, perfectly alterable circumstance of history.

There is thus created a universal urge toward man's completion of his own humanity. How this urge attained its present momentum, how much the variegated impact of the West itself upon Asia has contributed to the kindling of this latent sense of humanity, what role the communist challenge has played and is playing in awakening men at least to their material rights—all these matters are of the essence of the understanding of the problem of Asia. But whatever the causes, the fact is that everything today conspires to make the man of Asia restless concerning himself and, therefore, increasingly dissatisfied with the objective conditions under which he has been living for ages

However momentous the consequences of this awakening might be—consequences in regard to Asia's reorganization, both internally and in relation to the outside world—it is a fine thing that a new morn is dawning in the Orient, a morn in which privilege, inequality, darkness, and rigid stratification will have to be severely modulated and man in his freedom and wholeness be rediscovered and reinstated.

I propose to delineate the general lines along which Asia will have to reconsider her conception of man if she desires to live and act in the present age.

The individual human person is an end in himself. He cannot be arbitrarily subordinated to something else, such as the clan or the class or the nation or even the government, without doing violence to his essential humanity Even where he is made to submit to limitations or controls, it must be for the sake of his larger good. Moral and social valuation must proceed from, and subserve, the dignity and integrity of the human person.

Freedom of thought, conscience, and decision is ultimate It is not enough to enjoy freedom of being, one must also have the right to freedom of becoming What I find myself to be is certainly important and worthy of all respect; but what if I want, on good grounds, to change it? Unless Asia—in theory, doctrine, and principle, and not just indulgently and sporadically here and there in practice—respects the right to change, she must remain outside the spirit of this age.

How constructively to sweep Asia into the experimental dynamism of our epoch; how, amidst all their problems, to convince her peoples, peoples who are ancient and honorable in their own traditions, that the truth is not given once and for all, that unless it is perpetually rediscovered, relived, and reinterpreted it will die with baleful consequences to man, that the good is often the enemy of the better and that it is at once our duty and our glory to seek not only the good, not only the better, but absolutely the best, a best that is concretely there to be progressively found and known and loved—this, I hold, is the deepest problem of Asia

Not feeling, not imagination, not pleasure, not words, not anecdotes, not memories, not material things, not vast expanse and impenetrable darkness, not unconscious, unquestioned, inherited belonging to a fixed group, but the living, laughing, anxious, free individual, freely appropriating all these things in a graded order, enclosed by death and summoned to wholeness of being—this, I think, is a true principle worthy of consideration by the seeking mind of the East According to this principle, man is whole and entire, he is personally free, and he is truly himself only in active participation

It must follow that everything—art, religion, literature, politics, social relationships, commerce, industry (and Asia abounds in these things)—everything should not be used as a means of covering up and reducing man, or as a device for distracting attention from him, but as so many opportunities precisely for stressing and accenting man, for promoting his humanity, for raising him to his natural stature, for liberating his powers, for constituting his integrity. Man should be more clear than he is. He should not be ashamed of his body or of his powers or of the high calling to which he is called.

Our great economic and social inequalities must be remedied. An end must be put to poverty and dispossession. While, of course, history has only unrolled so far a few thousand years of itself, yet I think it is significant that, during the whole of this short period, the masses have lived under conditions of incredible material privation. It is not really respectful of man to keep on allowing this But the continuance of this state of affairs throughout Asia is today, on the whole, neither psychologically and politically possible nor materially necessary. The masses are becoming increasingly informed about what is happening elsewhere, and, therefore, they will not stand their lot, and the possibilities of modern industry and technique, if deployed with absolute respect for man, can in most cases completely solve this particular problem of Asia. We throughout Asia will never know rest, nor participate effectively in the determination of events, until the humanity of our broad masses is fully asserted If this should mean a painful readjustment of society, so be it, let those who suffer blame only the thoughtlessness and the selfish obtuseness which have guided them for centuries.

Social and economic justice cannot mean the obliteration of structure and hierarchy nor the effacement of all distinction and all lines of authority. Such obliteration and effacement will turn justice into injustice For there is natural structure and a higher and a lower by nature. But social and economic justice does mean, and the actual Asian situation requires that it mean, that every material condition that degrades man is bad and must be eliminated, that the apportionment of the material goods of life must be based on merit and not on privilege or arbitrary power, and that man's innate insensitivity toward his neighbor must be curbed by just social legislation Asian society is impatient for a radical reformation in accordance with truth, reason, and justice. If thought and wisdom do not attack this job, revolution is certain to do it

There is not sufficient fluidity and intercourse among the diverse social classes throughout Asia Somehow this social stratification and solidification must be overcome The walls of partition separating social, racial, and religious groups from one another must be reconsidered Nothing hurts a man more deeply than to realize that, through no fault of his own, he is excluded. Communism, while erecting its own walls of partition, nevertheless makes a strong appeal to certain Asian temperaments precisely because it promises to give short shrift to certain obsolete social distinctions This is the significance of the strong sense of fellowship which communist camaraderie engenders And because Asia, owing to her age, has a profuse sedimentation of such distinctions which once perhaps had meaning and served a purpose, but today are completely out of tune with the awakened social consciousness of men everywhere, her peoples are peculiarly responsive to the lure of communism.

Asia is determined to live in the present age: hence the tremendous social fermentation that is going on, whereby a healthy, vibrant social interpenetration is more and more superseding the now blurred former class distinctions. In this way Asia must move and is moving away from the petrified depositions of the past into a phase in which the enrichment and elucidation of man is the urge and of which the satisfaction of his deep thirst for community is the outcome.

The virtue of social consciousness and responsibility is another necessity dawning upon Asia It must be humbly confessed that for too long have we throughout Asia placed private above public interest The sense of social responsibility is not sufficiently strong. Leaders in many cases are not responsibly conscious of "the people" as the matrix from which they derive themselves and their powers, to which and for which they speak, with which they interact, without which they cannot stand, to which and for which they are responsible The doctrine and habit of public service is not sufficiently visible in our practice. We are loath to sacrifice for the common good.

When I compare the privations and austerities which certain advanced nations voluntarily impose upon themselves in the interest of the whole and of greater social justice with the practice of some of us under similar trying conditions, I invariably say to myself. "They have a greater right to life and liberty than we have " And indeed, apart from questions of right, this refined sense of social responsibility will of itself grant them life and liberty and power. Thus, it is not clear to us that the other person is of infinite worth in his own right, of a worth that is certainly not inferior to ours; and that, therefore, we ought to adjust our claims and privileges to his own. But unless the category of "the other" is keenly alive in our minds and effectively operative in our institutions, we cannot speak *as a people*, nor shall our claim and clamor for justice and equality be truly heeded or respected.

The problem of Asia cannot be understood apart from another trait in which we do not particularly excel I refer to the principle of co-operation. Half of Asia's problems would be solved if only the Asians knew how to co-operate Co-operation presupposes, first, real respect and equality among those who co-operate and, second, a willing subordination of one's interests and one's point of view to some idea beyond oneself Respect for others and subordination of one's will mean that the other person in his entire integrity is perfectly clear in our mind. We suffer from a congestion of leaders and a dearth of followers Many a situation can be transformed overnight if only the people are so loved and served by their leaders that they in their turn joyously co-operate in the service of the larger good.

Law is not the expression of force or caprice, nor is it the imposition of an arbitrary will. Even where it is handed down to me by precedent and custom, it cannot be the mere fiat of the will. This is the very heart of the great conception of natural law Every law must yield to, and be illuminated by, reason. I must discern in it the expression of my highest interest. But to say "reason," is at once to say "the social principle"—not, indeed, as an unconscious, massive, hereditary element which a herd have in common, but as the active, conscious, responsible concern whereby I participate in others and they in me. Reason is the act of the social principle whereby we explain and justify ourselves and endeavor to persuade one another. Hence, the reason of law is my great teacher. A tremendous movement for the cleansing and rationalization of law is called for in Asia, a movement which will banish every dark trace of caprice and arbitrariness and, basing itself upon the notion of man as having infinite worth because he is endowed with reason and conscience, will develop a body of rules which will guarantee and promote his freedom

Time would fail me if I were to give even the briefest account of some of the other great human questions which Asia cannot but reconsider under the unrelenting challenge of the moment. I mean questions such as the dignity of labor, the place and rights of minorities, the care of the body, the place of the mother and the child, the problem of women, the life of the emotions, the supreme importance of education, the scrutiny of the contents of education, the active participation of the people in government, the boon of laughter and of joy But there is one final point on which I desire to dwell for a moment.

Consider the Asian demographic situation Would anyone believe that the population of Ceylon will be doubled in twenty-six years; that the present population of Japan, which is 83,000,000, will be doubled in thirty-three years, that the present population of Egypt, which is 20,000,000, will be doubled in twenty years, that India's population increased by about 50,000,000 during the decade 1931–41, and that, if the death rate could be lowered to the level of the United States, India would fill five earths as full as ours in a single century? These are unbelievable facts, but they are all true.

The problem of Asia, which is now so dramatically unfolding before our eyes, can never be rightly assessed in abstraction from these all-important facts Which responsible thinker, which statesman, which geopolitician, casting the eye of his concern decades ahead, can now possibly overlook these facts? Entirely apart from communism or capitalism or colonialism, and whether or not Moscow or Washington or London exist, what, I ask, is Asia going to do with this staggering outpouring of her population?

When we soberly consider this situation, when we put aside excitement and fear and narrowness of vision, and determine in all humility to fix only on the truth, we must, I think, come to the humbling conclusion that the coming years and decades, for purely demographic reasons, are going to mean tremendous problems in every sphere of human relationship and that the regulation of these problems can never come about by hatred, contradiction, suspicion, and violence, but only by that spirit of tolerance and openness of heart whereby people live and share and bear with one another The only question is. Will we have the time, will we have the opportunity to inculcate this spirit?

These, then, are the basic structures in the conception of man which Asia must reappraise if she desires to live and act in the present age. And the heartening thing is that there are genuine roots for all these values in the great Asian cultures, so that in reconstituting her conception of man, Asia need not go out of herself. But Asia must rediscover these roots, reactivate and relive them at whatever cost For when man is born, culture flourishes, and there is a strength and an endurance that will baffle the perishing of time.

Now it may be idealizing or stretching the term "democracy" too much to call the right interpretation of all these structures of man "democracy" But I hope I am not far wrong in holding that the sanctity and dignity of the human person, the ultimacy of freedom of thought and conscience, the primacy of thought and being, the disclosure of man in his wholeness, social and economic justice, the proper softening of rigidity in the social structure, social responsibility, the grace of co-operation, the rationalizing and humanizing of law, the dignity of labor, the protection of minorities, the care of children, the liberation of women, the spreading of education, the teaching of tolerance, and the principle of government as the expression of the will of the people—I hope I am right in saying that all this belongs to the essence of the democratic way of life. It must follow that just as in the realm of nature we need science, so in human affairs we need, above everything else, democracy.

Our two primary sins in Asia have been the neglect of theory and the neglect of the rights of man. That is why the present age hits us hard. Asia will always be interfered with, whether by Russia or by Europe or by America, so long as she is deficient in her regard for reason and her regard for man, which is necessarily connected with it. Prior to the very air you breathe today, the two things that strike you first, from the moment you open your eyes every morning, are science and democracy We must learn science, and we must develop democracy. For only by science and democracy can we atone for our sin against reason and our sin against man

V. The Ideological Weakness of the West

There are appalling conditions of privation and poverty throughout Asia. So long as Moscow means, truly or falsely, hope for the masses, and the Western world does not mean so with the same clarity, it is idle to speak of peaceful coexistence or of live-and-let-live. There is in this regard an unequal appeal to the suffering masses of mankind as between, for example, Moscow and Washington. Communism will then sprout from within, or at least the internal situation will be so softened as to prepare the ground for the easy march of communism from without The British Commonwealth of Nations has endeavored in the recent Colombo Conference boldly to meet this situation President Truman's Point Four is a response to the same need. I might remark in this connection that, in my opinion, the present magnitude of operations of the Point Four program must be multiplied by about one hundred times before it can begin to be adequate for the crying needs of the moment For what are five billion dollars devoted to the restoration of the balance of justice between the meaning of Moscow and the meaning of Washington in the minds of the eternally dispossessed of the world?

The balance of mind is, in a sense, the most important task. For a man, no matter how weak or poor, will be exceedingly strong and rich if only he has an idea for which he can die and, therefore, for which he can live. Communism provides such an idea. The Communists have a purpose in life beyond their immediate cares and worries The non-communist world does not have such a sense of mission. There is, therefore, an unequal intellectual struggle between it and the communist world. So long as this is the case, peaceful coexistence must remain a pious hope. For there will always be an uneasy tension in the minds of men afflicted with the widespread malady of purposelessness They will always feel they are unjustly cheated of something—the unifying and liberating sense of purpose

The source of this agonizing injustice is that the Western world no longer believes strongly enough in the importance and power of ideas In many instances Western man is too much wrapped up in himself, in his own self-pity, his own self-worry and petty little problems. He does not sufficiently rest in joy on the marvelous vision of truth—an objective and independent truth throbbing with life and meaning and salvation

The ideal of taking a college degree, getting married and settled, rearing a family, having a dependable job, making lots of money and having a comfortable and ever expanding bank account—this ideal conceived purely in these terms is not good enough It is, if I may say so, a very timid ideal. It is not dangerous enough. It does not answer man's deepest hunger for truth and community, where going out of oneself is a joy and where it is more blessed to give than to receive.

Confronted with this ideal alone, Asia is not impressed. In fact, despite all her darkness and misery, Asia can still do better And an Asian who knows something of the highest values which have characterized the Western tradition at its best can turn to the West and say, "You can do much better, also."

If the thirsty souls of honest seeking men throughout the world are going to be satisfied, a mighty, living, true faith must be discovered or created to balance the militant faith of communism. Pure nationalism will always be handicapped by reason of its particularism, whereas the need in this physically unified world is for something just as universal as communism but infinitely more profound and true He does not know the infinite, hidden riches of the non-communist world in Asia, in Europe, and in America who does not believe that such a faith can be released in it.

The present crisis is, therefore, a great opportunity It will call forth deep searchings of heart which must lead to the finding of adequate spiritual answers For too long have we buried and shelved our ultimate values, for too long have we been distracted from them by lesser things. The day of reckoning has come when we can no longer afford the luxury of living in the plains but must rise to the heights, where once again the gods can speak to men The tribulation of the days to come will bring upon men a fresh visitation of destiny, the purification of heart which comes from contact with the ultimate and awful. And in East and West alike, our spiritual and intellectual leaders will seek new dimensions, and they will find them. They will ask. Is it true that Marxism is the final dispensation that has canceled and absorbed all that we have known for thousands of years to be true and good and noble and ultimate? And they will bless the names of Marx and Lenin, not indeed for what they said and did and meant, but for having roused us from our slumber and forced us to inquire after our good and return to our God.

Appendix

ASSOCIATION FOR REALISTIC PHILOSOPHY

Platform

The Association for Realistic Philosophy is devoted to the critical clarification and defense of the following realistic theses:

FIRST, IN METAPHYSICS.

1. Being cannot be reduced to either material being or to immaterial being.
2. Empirical evidence shows that both modes of being exist in the cosmos.
3. This cosmos consists of real, substantial entities existing in themselves and ordered to one another by real, extramental relations.

SECOND, IN EPISTEMOLOGY.

These real entities and relations, together with human artifacts, can be known by the human mind as they are in themselves and can be aesthetically enjoyed

THIRD, IN PRACTICAL PHILOSOPHY

Such knowledge, especially that treating of human nature, can provide us with immutable and trustworthy principles for the guidance of individual and social action

FOURTH, IN THE HISTORY OF PHILOSOPHY:

Important truths are contained in the classical tradition of Platonic and Aristotelian philosophy.

I. METAPHYSICS

1. *Being cannot be reduced to either material being or to immaterial being.*
2. *Empirical evidence shows that both modes of being exist in the cosmos.*

I DEFINITION OF TERMS AND REFERENCE TO SUPPORTING EVIDENCE

a) The first, indefinable concept of *being*, in terms of which all other concepts are defined, is the basic concept of any realistic metaphysics. It is only by clearly focusing this concept and by constantly keeping it in the foreground of any descriptive analysis that a truly empirical attitude can be maintained and a priori reductionism be avoided *Metaphysics* abstracts from sensible quality and quantity, looking at things from the standpoint of being

b) *Material* being is quantitative, ever capable of losing its present form and of taking on another, and incommunicable (restricted to the dimensions of its matter)

c) *Noetic,* or immaterial, being is qualitative, incapable of changing into any other composite than the pure form which it is, and communicable

d) All our sensory experience provides us with evidence for the existence of material being restricted subjectively to quantitative dimensions The awareness of our own thoughts and of our ability to communicate them without alteration to others provides us with evidence for the existence of purely formal or immaterial being. Thus both modes of being exist.

II EXPLANATION AND PROGRAM

Realism is opposed to any a priori reductionism, such as: (1) that all being is "natural" or material, or, (2) that all being is mental or noetic Realism also rejects the thesis of subjectivism and holds that knowledge is relational or intentional in character.

What is primarily needed at present is a further clarification of the basic concepts of first philosophy. being, one, true, beautiful, good (general metaphysics), potency-act, essence-existence, substance-accident, and causation (finite metaphysics) We also need studies of the notion of analogy, of potency and its various modes, and especially of causation. It is only in the light of such studies that the distinction between extramental and mental existence can be made clear.

3. *This cosmos consists of real, substantial entities existing in themselves and ordered to one another by real, extramental relations*

I DEFINITION OF TERMS AND REFERENCE TO SUPPORTING EVIDENCE

a) *Accident* is that which exists only in or through something else.

b) *Substance* is that which exists in itself or through itself This does not mean that substance can exist by itself or independently. Substantial existence may be given and sustained by external causes, but as thus given and sustained it is existence-in-itself.

c) *Relation* is order or existence *to* Relations are either *logical,* like that of subject-predicate, or *extramental,* like father-of Extramental relations are either *causal capacities* in which the relation merges with the causal foundation (transcendental relations like matter), or strict relations based on a real foundation from which they are distinct, as similarity is based upon quality (*predicamental relations*) These last fall under three species *equiparant relations*, like different-from (whose converse is similar, *mutual relations*, like maker-of (whose converse is dissimilar), and *non-mutual relations*, like picture-of and knowledge-of (which have no real converse relation).

d) Things can be truly classified because they are really related by relations of similarity, and they can be truly explained because they are really related by relations of causal dependence.

e) By *cosmos* is meant not a substantial unity but many substances ordered by real relations.

II. EXPLANATION AND PROGRAM

What is usually meant by the denial of substance is either a logical atomism, which, like that of Hume, supposes that what is distinct in thought is also separable in being and thus regards everything as a substance, or an absolute monism which regards everything as one substance. Neither view can give an intelligible account of change. The former confuses it with annihilation and creation. The latter has to dismiss change as illusory

Monism also has to deny the reality of real relations because any such relation must be founded in one substance and be terminated in another. The classical realistic concept of substance is in fact a dynamic concept without which it is impossible to give any intelligible account of the facts of evolution, change, and empirical relatedness

The traditional doctrine of hylomorphic substance is essentially sound, but it involves many points requiring further clarification What is the role of matter, form, and quantity in individuation? What is an individual? What is a person? How is substance related to essence? How are relations to be exactly classified? There is a great wealth of material on these problems in the classical realistic texts. But this needs to be studied critically, purified of incidental accretions, and related to modern problems. The ancient picture of the cosmos is now, of course, outmoded. We are deeply in need of cosmological studies which will relate recent discoveries in physics and astronomy to realistic ontology The widespread notion that realism is antievolutionary is certainly false; Aristotle's *Physics* is sufficient proof of this. But the realistic theories of matter and change need to be clarified further and brought into critical relation with the modern concepts of events, evolution, and emergence.

II. EPISTEMOLOGY

These real entities and relations together with human artifacts can be known by the human mind as they are in themselves and can be aesthetically enjoyed.

I. DEFINITION OF TERMS

A form comes into physical existence when it is received subjectively by matter to form a new composite entity. A form comes into noetic existence when it is received objectively or intentionally by mind as a pure form without constituting any new composite entity Hence, a form may be physically present without being noetically present, and vice versa Knowledge is not the making or constructing of anything new It is rather the assimilation of a determinate form already in act. Hence the anti-Kantian formula The mind is existentially diverse from that which it knows but formally identical with it. Because of the existential diversity, knowing is a relation Because of the formal unity, the relation is the unique intentional relation of identity. Aesthetic enjoyment is the rest and delight of the human noetic faculties (sense and reason) in their knowledge of a given object which is peculiarly adapted to be known.

II. EXPLANATION AND PROGRAM

Natural realism of this sort is widely misunderstood at the present time and confused with other views. On the one hand it is radically opposed to what is now termed epistemological monism—the view that the species by which we know is the object which we know, that knowledge involves a sheer identity with no aspect of diversity This makes knowledge non-relational (as in Berkeleian subjectivism). On the other hand it is also radically opposed to what is now termed epistemological dualism—the view that the species by which we know is not formally identical with the object which we know, that knowledge involves a sheer diversity with no aspect of identity. This reduces knowledge to a relation of similarity (as in the so-called copy theory, representational realism, critical realism, and so forth) In contrast with these views, natural realism defends knowledge as an intentional relation terminating in the externally existent thing

Here again the tradition is more instructive with respect to the deductive elaboration of fundamental concepts than with respect to their inductive clarification Careful descriptions of the phenomena of intentionality are greatly needed along the lines of Brentano's *Psychologie.* The foundations of modern logic call for critical study. Sound textbooks of realistic logic and detailed expositions of logical concepts are urgently needed. Such treatises should devote themselves especially to these four aims (1) that of revealing the many dilutions and distortions in what now passes under the name of "Aristotelian logic"; (2) that of revealing and clarifying such key concepts as that of intentionality, first intention, second intention, real definition, supposition, and syllogism in the classical sense, (3) that of answering criticism raised against realistic logic by recent logicians, and (4) that of clarifying the fallacies and confusions underlying many so-called modern "developments"

Where the realistic tradition is weak, as on the subject of sensory cognition and on sensory illusion and perception, new work must be done Detailed studies are called for relating realistic doctrine not only to current logical discussions but also to recent studies in the field of linguistics and that of experimental psychology

III. PRACTICAL PHILOSOPHY

Such knowledge, especially that treating of human nature, can provide us with immutable and trustworthy principles for the guidance of individual and social action.

I. DEFINITION OF TERMS

Man is a finite entity requiring further accidental being, namely, action for the realization of his nature. This action must be social or co-operative The initial tendency to such action is physically inherent in every human being But this tendency cannot be adequately fulfilled unless it is directed by a rational understanding of human nature and of the universal pattern of action (both individual and social) indicated by this nature for its proper perfection. This universal pattern of action is the *law of nature* As founded on the essential nature of man as such, it is immutable But since man must act as an individual in particular circumstances, the universal natural law requires further determinations of positive law to meet the ever changing material situation.

II. EXPLANATION AND PROGRAM

This realistic view must be sharply distinguished from the following current types of ethical theory.

1 It is not Kantian because. *a*) the moral law is not laid down by an autonomous practical reason but is theoretically apprehended as in the

nature of things, *b*) it is no empty form but filled with actual content derived from the facts of human nature, and *c*) it involves no opposition of duty to interest, since the basic duty is to love, strive for what is really good.

2. It is not utilitarian because· *a*) it does not identify the good with any pleasure in *any* object, or with *any* object of *any* interest, but only with that activity which is in accord with nature; and *b*) it does not reduce virtue to the status of a mere means but regards it as an intermediate end.

3. Finally, it is not eudaemonism or self-realization, since the ultimate standard is universal human nature, not the individual self or the particular community.

Natural law ethics differs from all of these in appealing to an ultimate objective standard, nature, and in refusing to admit natural opposition between the individual good (egoism) and the common good (altruism).

Here the tradition needs both development and purification, for it has left natural law either as an almost unexpanded premise (as in Aquinas) or else it has turned it into a detailed positive code (as in Pufendorf). Much can be learned from Plato in this respect We need to clarify the basic concept and to specify its content in terms of the moral, social, and cultural problems of our time. The many attempts to use the principle of natural law in defending outworn and reactionary concepts of property rights and irresponsible individualism must be exposed and corrected. The phenomena of individual existence to which attention has been called by recent existentialism need to be recognized, carefully described, and fitted into the framework of realistic ethics and philosophical anthropology.

IV. HISTORY

Important truths are contained in the classical tradition of Platonic and Aristotelian philosophy.

The great present need is for:

1 A philosophical, as distinct from a merely philological and antiquarian, study of the classical texts, with a view to separating the living truth from dated illustrations and incidental accretions,

2. A further inductive clarification of basic concepts, less emphasis upon purely deductive elaboration, and prevention of the intrusion of dogmatic theological ideas and the resulting tendency to oppose medieval realism to that of the Greeks;

3. The preparation and publication of better translations of classic

texts and the great commentaries, classical selections for elementary courses, and systematic textbooks expressed in modern language and using modern illustrations;

4. The reinvestigation of significant historical problems, for instance, the relation of Plato and Platonism to Aristotle and the Aristotelian tradition, and the relation of St. Thomas and Thomism to Aristotle. The modern tendency to regard Plato and Aristotle as completely opposed needs critical scrutiny. Our primary aim is a truly philosophical synthesis.

NAME INDEX

A

Aiken, H. D , 245
Alexander, S , 212
Anderson, J F , 295
Aquinas, T , 35, 66. 359, 360
Aristotle, 18, 19, 58, 89, 91, 93, 94, 95,
    105, 109, 110, 116, 119, 121, 122,
    123, 152, 157, 162, 174, 177, 178,
    214, 216, 228, 235, 242, 243, 246,
    249, 250, 251, 253, 260, 278, 293,
    296, 308, 309, 334, 336, 356, 358,
    359, 360
Atomists, 9
Austin, J., 230, 231
Axtelle, G E , 294
Ayer, A. J., 249, 256

B

Bagley, W. C., 295
Barnes, E. W , 203
Baumgarten, A. G., 213
Beer, Max, 222
Bentham, J , 223, 227, 230, 231, 241,
    244, 245
Bergson, H , 58, 92–118, 260
Berkeley, G., 10, 58, 161, 357
Bertocci, P A , 295
Bigongiari, D , 295
Black, Max, 211
Boas, G., 85, 216
Bode, B H , 294
Bohr, N., 215
Bowsma, O. K , 209, 211, 212
Bradley, F. H., 95, 121, 225
Bramel, D. T., 296
Brentano, Franz, 357
Brickman, W W , 295
Bridges, R , 315
Brightman, E. S., 295
Broad, C. D., 45, 119, 252

Brooks, 203
Brubacher, J S , 299
Buffon, Georges de, 221
Butterfield, H , 289, 290

C

Carnap, R , 149, 151, 256
Carritt, E F , 251
Chandler, A , 212
Charmant, J , 233
Childs, J L , 294, 298, 299
Chisholm, R. M., 45
Churchman, C. W , 77, 79, 81
Cobitz, J L , 168
Cohen, M. R , 222
Collingwood, R. G , 212
Comenius, J A , 305
Cornford, F. M , 281, 282, 283
Cornforth, M. C , 82
Costello, H. T., 73, 75, 90
Counts, G. S., 294
Croce, B , 228
Crossman, R. H S , 260, 282
Cunningham, G. W , 295

D

Dennes, W , 70, 73, 74, 75
Descartes, R., 9, 10, 13, 40, 51, 58,
    123, 156
Dewey, J , 58, 74, 75, 76, 91, 208, 212,
    237, 246, 251, 252, 255, 294, 296–
    301, 303, 308, 312
Drake, D , 162, 163
Ducasse, C. J., 212, 240

E

Eaton, R M., 158
Edel, A., 82
Einstein, A., 197, 263

SUBJECT INDEX

A

ABSTRACTION, 168–69 its role in proposition, 50, 187, of essence by concept, 50, 187, refers to quasi-things, 144–45

ACCIDENT, *see* SUBSTANCE

AESTHETICS, 216–17 as a practical discipline, 204, 213–14, concerned with facts, 209 ff , Platonic, 284–86. theoretical and practical, 201; unpopularity of, 201–3

ANALYTIC PHILOSOPHY, 207–15

APPEARANCE, 31, 97

ARGUMENT, 188–89 as instrument for revealing *why* or *cause* of things, 194, confused with non-intentional relations, 192–95, practical, 247–54

ART, 285–86 art of life, 264–72, common elements in, 215–16

ASIA, 337 ff

ATOMISM, 42–43 its analysis of continua into discrete states, 105–9; its conception of substance and accident, 60, its view of matter and form, 61

ATTITUDE, *see* TENDENCY

AWARENESS, 47–50 always reflexive, 32, as a relation, 32, 165–66, and light, 32–33, as correlated with world, 5–6, as distinct from its object, 153–55, as formal identity with object, 27–28, 155–57, 163–66, as pervasive datum, 54, communication of, 49–50, grasps real, 29, idealistic view of, 7, immanence of, 154–55, inclusive in scope, 6–7, intentional structure of, 22–24, 153, in the world, 13, its immateriality, 157–58, 341–42, levels of, 50, not a primary object, 23, not like mirror, 5, reduced to physical, 27, subject of, 31 ff.

B

BEING, 56 as datum, 54, as bulwark of empiricism, 89, contains consciousness, 34, intelligible, 56–57, metaphysics the science of, 337, of reason, 179

BELIEF (ethical), 238–39 as united with attitude, 246 ff., in forgiveness, 331, separated from attitude, 239 ff

BIFURCATION OF BELIEF AND ATTITUDE, 238–46

BIPOLARITY OF EXPERIENCE, 22–23 each pole equally immediate, 49, in flux, 51, predominance of object in, 44–45

C

CAUSATION, 63–65 and the question *why*, 182, as known by syllogism, 188–89, physical causation and freedom, 86–87

CHANGE, 57–59 Bergson's view of, 94–100, 111–12, not a state, 104–5, 112, realistic analysis of, 58–59, 123–24; reduced to successive states, 96–98, 114, Russell's mathematical analysis of, 114, substantial, 61–62

CLASS, 137–39

COMMUNICATION, 49–50 phenomenology of neglected, 49, requires universal object, 167–68, 222

COMMUNISM, 348, 352

CONCEPT, 168–69 as relation of identity, 187, ignored by mathematical logic, 189, not isomorphic with its object, 190, of possible existent, 169, signifies essence of things, 182

CONNOTATION, 134–35, 147

CONSCIOUSNESS, *see* AWARENESS

CPSIA information can be obtained
at www.ICGtesting.com
Printed in the USA
BVHW040556290621
610612BV00005B/77